Python Programming for Arduino

Develop practical Internet of Things prototypes and applications with Arduino and Python

Pratik Desai

BIRMINGHAM - MUMBAI

Python Programming for Arduino

First published: February 2015

Production reference: 1230215

Published by Packt Publishing Ltd.
Livery Place
35 Livery Street
Birmingham B3 2PB, UK.

ISBN 978-1-78328-593-8

www.packtpub.com

Credits

Author
Pratik Desai

Reviewers
Juan Ramón González
Marco Schwartz
Josh VanderLinden

Commissioning Editor
Saleem Ahmed

Acquisition Editor
James Jones

Content Development Editor
Priyanka Shah

Technical Editor
Ankita Thakur

Copy Editors
Jasmine Nadar
Vikrant Phadke

Project Coordinator
Milton Dsouza

Proofreaders
Safis Editing
Maria Gould
Ameesha Green
Paul Hindle

Indexer
Mariammal Chettiyar

Graphics
Abhinash Sahu

Production Coordinator
Manu Joseph

Cover Work
Manu Joseph

About the Author

Pratik Desai, PhD, is the Principal Scientist and cofounder of a connected devices start-up, Imbue Labs, where he develops scalable and interoperable architecture for wearable devices and Internet of Things (IoT) platforms during the day. At night, he leads the development of an open source IoT initiative, the Semantic Repository of Things. Pratik has 8 years of research and design experience in various layers of the IoT and its predecessor technologies such as wireless sensor networks, RFID, and machine-to-machine (M2M) communication. His domains of expertise are the IoT, Semantic Web, machine learning, robotics, and artificial intelligence.

Pratik completed his MS and PhD from Wright State University, Ohio, and collaborated with the Ohio Center of Excellence in Knowledge-enabled Computing (Kno.e.sis) during his doctoral research. His doctoral research was focused on developing situation awareness frameworks for IoT devices, enabling semantic web-based reasoning and handling the uncertainty associated with sensor data.

In his personal life, Pratik is an avid DIY junkie and likes to get hands-on experience on upcoming technologies. He extensively expresses his views on technology and shares interesting developments on Twitter (`@chheplo`).

I would like to dedicate the book to my parents, who were responsible for building the foundation of what I am today. The book would not have been possible without the patience, support, and encouragement from my beloved wife, Sachi. I would also like to thank her for landing her photography skills that were used in development of some of the important images used in the book. I would also like to extend my sincere gratitude to the editors for their valuable feedbacks.

About the Reviewers

Juan Ramón González is a technical engineer of computer systems and lives in Seville (Andalusia, Spain). For the past 9 years, he has been working on free software-based projects for the regional Ministry of Education by using Python, C++, and JavaScript, among other programming languages.

He is one of the main members of the CGA project in Andalusia (Centro de Gestión Avanzado or Advanced Management Center), which manages a network with more than 4,000 servers with Debian and 500,000 client computers that run Guadalinex, a customized Ubuntu-based operating system for Andalusian schools.

As a software developer who has a passion for electronics and astronomy, he started one of the first projects to control a telescope with the Arduino microcontroller by using a computer with the Stellarium software and a driver developed with Python to communicate with the telescope. This project's sources are published on the collaborative platform GitHub. You can see the whole code and the prototype at `https://github.com/juanrmn/Arduino-Telescope-Control`.

Marco Schwartz is an electrical engineer, entrepreneur, and blogger. He has a master's degree in electrical engineering and computer science from Supélec, France, and a master's degree in micro engineering from EPFL, Switzerland.

Marco has more than 5 years of experience working in the domain of electrical engineering. His interests gravitate around electronics, home automation, the Arduino and the Raspberry Pi platforms, open source hardware projects, and 3D printing.

He runs several websites around Arduino, including the Open Home Automation website that is dedicated to building home automation systems using open source hardware.

Marco has written a book on home automation and Arduino called *Arduino Home Automation Projects, Packt Publishing*. He has also written a book on how to build Internet of Things projects with Arduino called *Internet of Things with the Arduino Yun, Packt Publishing*.

Josh VanderLinden is a lifelong technology enthusiast who has been programming since the age of 10. He enjoys learning and becoming proficient with new technologies. He has designed and built software, ranging from simple shell scripts to scalable backend server software to interactive web and desktop user interfaces. Josh has been writing software professionally using Python since 2007, and he has been building personal Arduino-based projects since 2010.

www.PacktPub.com

Support files, eBooks, discount offers, and more

For support files and downloads related to your book, please visit www.PacktPub.com.

Did you know that Packt offers eBook versions of every book published, with PDF and ePub files available? You can upgrade to the eBook version at www.PacktPub.com and as a print book customer, you are entitled to a discount on the eBook copy. Get in touch with us at service@packtpub.com for more details.

At www.PacktPub.com, you can also read a collection of free technical articles, sign up for a range of free newsletters and receive exclusive discounts and offers on Packt books and eBooks.

https://www2.packtpub.com/books/subscription/packtlib

Do you need instant solutions to your IT questions? PacktLib is Packt's online digital book library. Here, you can search, access, and read Packt's entire library of books.

Why subscribe?

- Fully searchable across every book published by Packt
- Copy and paste, print, and bookmark content
- On demand and accessible via a web browser

Free access for Packt account holders

If you have an account with Packt at www.PacktPub.com, you can use this to access PacktLib today and view 9 entirely free books. Simply use your login credentials for immediate access.

Table of Contents

Preface

In the era of the Internet of Things (IoT), it has become very important to rapidly develop and test prototypes of your hardware products while also augmenting them using software features. The Arduino movement has been the front-runner in this hardware revolution, and through its simple board designs it has made it convenient for anyone to develop DIY hardware projects. The great amount of support that is available through the open source community has made the difficulties that are associated with the development of a hardware prototype a thing of the past. On the software front, Python has been the crown jewel of the open source software community for a significant amount of time. Python is supported by a huge amount of libraries to develop various features, such as graphical user interfaces, plots, messaging, and cloud applications.

This book tries to bring you the best of both hardware and software worlds to help you develop exciting projects using Arduino and Python. The main goal of the book is to assist the reader to solve the difficult problem of interfacing Arduino hardware with Python libraries. Meanwhile, as a secondary goal, the book also provides you with exercises and projects that can be used as blueprints for your future IoT projects.

The book has been designed in such a way that every successive chapter has increasing complexity in terms of material that is covered and also more practical value. The book has three conceptual sections (getting started, implementing Python features, and network connectivity) and each section concludes with a practical project that integrates the concepts that you learned in that section.

The theoretical concepts and exercises covered in the book are meant to give you hands-on experience with Python-Arduino programming, while the projects are designed to teach you hardware prototyping methodologies for your future projects. However, you will still need extensive expertise in each domain to develop a commercial product. In the end, I hope to provide you with sufficient knowledge to jump-start your journey in this novel domain of the IoT.

What this book covers

Chapter 1, Getting Started with Python and Arduino, introduces the fundamentals of the Arduino and Python platforms. It also provides comprehensive installation and configuration steps to set up the necessary software tools.

Chapter 2, Working with the Firmata Protocol and the pySerial Library, discusses the interfacing of the Arduino hardware with the Python program by explaining the Firmata protocol and the serial interfacing library.

Chapter 3, The First Project – Motion-triggered LEDs, provides comprehensive guidelines to create your first Python-Arduino project, which controls different LEDs according to the detected motion.

Chapter 4, Diving into Python-Arduino Prototyping, takes you beyond the basic prototyping that we performed in the previous project and provides an in-depth description of prototyping methods, with appropriate examples.

Chapter 5, Working with the Python GUI, begins our two-chapter journey into developing graphical interfaces using Python. The chapter introduces the Tkinter library, which provides the graphical frontend for the Arduino hardware.

Chapter 6, Storing and Plotting Arduino Data, covers Python libraries, CSV and matplotlib that are used to store and plot the sensor data respectively.

Chapter 7, The Midterm Project – a Portable DIY Thermostat, contains a practical and deployable project that utilizes the material that we covered in previous chapters such as serial interfacing, a graphical frontend, and a plot of the sensor data.

Chapter 8, Introduction to Arduino Networking, introduces computer networking for Arduino while utilizing various protocols to establish Ethernet communication between the Python program and Arduino. This chapter also explores a messaging protocol called MQTT, with basic examples. This protocol is specifically designed for resource-constrained hardware devices such as Arduino.

Chapter 9, Arduino and the Internet of Things, discusses the domain of the IoT while providing step-by-step guidelines to develop cloud-based IoT applications.

Chapter 10, The Final Project – a Remote Home Monitoring System, teaches a design methodology for the hardware product, followed by a comprehensive project that interfaces the cloud platform with Arduino and Python.

Chapter 11, Tweet-a-PowerStrip, contains another IoT project that is based on everything that we learned in the book. The project explores a unique approach to integrate a social network, Twitter, with the Python-Arduino application.

What you need for this book

To begin with, you will just need a computer with one of the supported operating systems, Windows, Mac OS X, or Linux. The book requires various additional hardware components and software tools to implement programming exercises and projects. A list of required hardware components and locations to obtain these components are included in each chapter.

In terms of software, the book itself provides step-by-step guidelines to install and configure all the necessary software packages and dependent libraries that are utilized throughout the book. Note that the exercises and projects included in the book are designed for Python 2.7 and they have not been tested against Python 3+.

Who this book is for

If you are a student, a hobbyist, a developer, or a designer with little or no programming and hardware prototyping experience and you want to develop IoT applications, then this book is for you.

If you are a software developer and interested in gaining experience with hardware domain, this book will help you to get started. If you are a hardware engineer who wants to learn advance software features, this book can help you to begin with.

Conventions

In this book, you will find a number of text styles that distinguish between different kinds of information. Here are some examples of these styles and an explanation of their meaning.

Code words in text, database table names, folder names, filenames, file extensions, pathnames, dummy URLs, user input, and Twitter handles are shown as follows: "While assigning the value to the `weight` variable, we didn't specify the data type, but the Python interpreter assigned it as an integer type, `int`."

A block of code is set as follows:

```
/*
  Blink
  Turns on an LED on for one second, then off for one second,
repeatedly.

  This example code is in the public domain.
 */
```

```
// Pin 13 has an LED connected on most Arduino boards.
// give it a name:
int led = 13;

// the setup routine runs once when you press reset:
void setup() {
  // initialize the digital pin as an output.
  pinMode(led, OUTPUT);
}

// the loop routine runs over and over again forever:
void loop() {
  digitalWrite(led, HIGH);   // turn the LED on (HIGH is the voltage
level)
  delay(1000);               // wait for a second
  digitalWrite(led, LOW);    // turn the LED off by making the voltage
LOW
  delay(1000);               // wait for a second
}
```

Any command-line input or output is written as follows:

```
$ sudo easy_install pip
```

New terms and **important words** are shown in bold. Words that you see on the screen, for example, in menus or dialog boxes, appear in the text like this: "In the **System** window, click on the **Advanced system settings** in the left navigation bar to open a window called **System Properties**."

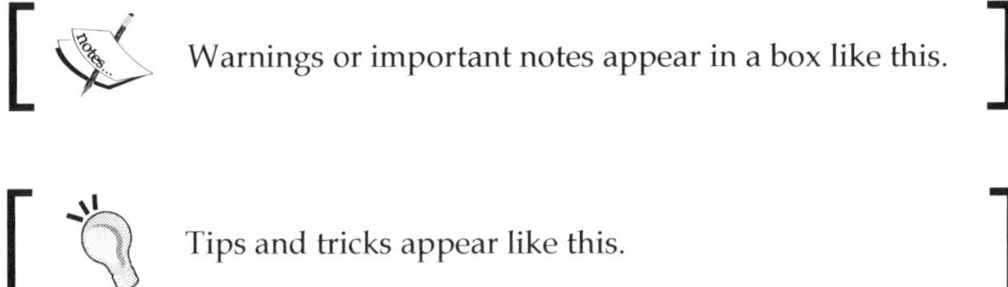

Warnings or important notes appear in a box like this.

Tips and tricks appear like this.

Reader feedback

Feedback from our readers is always welcome. Let us know what you think about this book—what you liked or disliked. Reader feedback is important for us as it helps us develop titles that you will really get the most out of.

To send us general feedback, simply e-mail feedback@packtpub.com, and mention the book's title in the subject of your message.

If there is a topic that you have expertise in and you are interested in either writing or contributing to a book, see our author guide at www.packtpub.com/authors.

Customer support

Now that you are the proud owner of a Packt book, we have a number of things to help you to get the most from your purchase.

Downloading the example code

You can download the example code files from your account at http://www.packtpub.com for all the Packt Publishing books you have purchased. If you purchased this book elsewhere, you can visit http://www.packtpub.com/support and register to have the files e-mailed directly to you.

Downloading the color images of this book

We also provide you with a PDF file that has color images of the screenshots/diagrams used in this book. The color images will help you better understand the changes in the output. You can download this file from: http://www.packtpub.com/sites/default/files/downloads/5938OS_ColoredImages.pdf.

Errata

Although we have taken every care to ensure the accuracy of our content, mistakes do happen. If you find a mistake in one of our books—maybe a mistake in the text or the code—we would be grateful if you could report this to us. By doing so, you can save other readers from frustration and help us improve subsequent versions of this book. If you find any errata, please report them by visiting http://www.packtpub.com/submit-errata, selecting your book, clicking on the **Errata Submission Form** link, and entering the details of your errata. Once your errata are verified, your submission will be accepted and the errata will be uploaded to our website or added to any list of existing errata under the Errata section of that title.

To view the previously submitted errata, go to https://www.packtpub.com/books/content/support and enter the name of the book in the search field. The required information will appear under the **Errata** section.

Piracy

Piracy of copyrighted material on the Internet is an ongoing problem across all media. At Packt, we take the protection of our copyright and licenses very seriously. If you come across any illegal copies of our works in any form on the Internet, please provide us with the location address or website name immediately so that we can pursue a remedy.

Please contact us at `copyright@packtpub.com` with a link to the suspected pirated material.

We appreciate your help in protecting our authors and our ability to bring you valuable content.

Questions

If you have a problem with any aspect of this book, you can contact us at `questions@packtpub.com`, and we will do our best to address the problem.

1
Getting Started with Python and Arduino

This chapter introduces the Python programming language and the open source electronic prototyping platform Arduino. The first section of the chapter focuses on Python and briefly describes the benefits of Python along with installation and configuration steps. The remaining part of the chapter describes Arduino and Arduino's development environment.

At the end of this chapter, you will have configured a programming environment for both Python and Arduino for your favorite operating system. If you are a beginner with either or both platforms (that is, Python and Arduino), it is advisable that you follow the given steps in this chapter, as the later chapters will assume that you have the exact configuration described here. If you have previous experience of working with these platforms, you can skip to the next chapter.

Introduction to Python

Since its introduction by Guido van Rossum in 1991, Python has grown into one of the most widely used general-purpose, high-level programming languages, and is supported by one of the largest open source developer communities. Python is an open source programming language that includes a lot of supporting libraries. These libraries are the best feature of Python, making it one of the most extensible platforms. Python is a dynamic programming language, and it uses an interpreter to execute code at runtime rather than using a compiler to compile and create executable byte codes.

The philosophy behind the development of Python was to create flexible, readable, and clear code to easily express concepts. The emphasis on using whitespace indentation in a unique way differentiates Python from other popular high-level languages. Python supports functional, imperative, and object-oriented programming with automatic memory management.

Why we use Python

Python is considered to be one of the easiest languages to learn for first-time programmers. Compared to other popular object-oriented languages such as C++ and Java, Python has the following major benefits for programmers:

- It is easy to read and understand
- It enables rapid prototyping and reduces development time
- It has a humongous amount of free library packages

Python has a huge open source community that drives forth the effort for continuous improvement of Python as a programming language. The Python community is also responsible for the development of a large amount of open library packages, which can be used to build applications that span from dynamic websites to complex data analysis applications, as well as the development of simple GUI-based applications to plot charts from complex math functions. The majority of Python library packages have systematically maintained the code that was obtained from the community with regular updates. The de facto repository that indexes the largest number of Python packages is PyPI (`http://pypi.python.org`). PyPI also provides simple ways to install various packages on your operating system, which will be covered in the upcoming section.

While working with the hardware platform, it is necessary to have some means of communication between the hardware and the computer that you are using for development. Among the common computer to hardware interfacing methods, serial- port-based communication is the most popular, and it is really simple to establish, especially for the Arduino platform. Python provides a library called `pySerial` that is really easy to use and quick to implement to interface a serial port. It is really simple to use similar libraries and Python's interactive programming abilities to rapidly test and implement your project ideas.

Nowadays, complex **Internet of Things** (**IoT**) applications not only require serial communication support, but they also need additional high-level features such as **graphical user interfaces** (**GUIs**) for operating systems, web interfaces for remote access, plots for data visualization, tools for data analysis, interfaces for data storage, and so on. Using any other programming language such as C++ or Java, the development of these features would require a large amount of programming effort due to the distributed and unorganized nature of the supporting tools. Thankfully, Python has been very successful at providing support for these types of applications for years. Python has a number of libraries to support the development of each of the features mentioned here, which are available through PyPI. These libraries are open source, easy to use, and widely supported by the community. This makes Python a language of choice for IoT applications. Additionally, Python also has support to create and ship your custom-built applications as libraries so that everyone else can also utilize them in their projects. This is a helpful feature if you are developing custom protocols, APIs, or algorithms for your own hardware products.

When do we use other languages

So, when should we not use Python for our projects? As mentioned earlier, Python is a dynamic language that reduces development time, but it also makes the execution of your code slower as compared to other static high-level languages such as C, C++, and Java. These static languages use a compiler to compile the code and create binaries that get executed during runtime, thereby increasing the runtime performance. When the performance of the code is more important than a longer development time and higher cost, you should consider these static languages. Some other drawbacks of Python include being memory heavy, not having the proper support for threading, and lacking data protection features. In short, we can say that even though Python provides quicker and easier ways for quick prototyping, we should consider other static high-level languages for development after we are done testing our prototype and we are ready to ship our product. Nowadays, this scenario is changing rapidly and companies have started utilizing Python for their industrial products.

You can obtain more Python-related information from the official website at `http://www.python.org`.

Installing Python and Setuptools

Python comes in two versions: Python v2.x and Python v3.x. (Here, x represents an appropriate version number.) While Python v2.x is a legacy branch and has better library support, Python v3.x is the future of Python. Most Linux distributions and Mac OS X operating systems are equipped with Python, and they have v2.x as their preferred and default version of Python. We will be using Python v2.7 as the default version of Python for the rest of the book due to the following reasons:

- It is the most current version of the Python v2.x branch
- It has large community support and solutions for its known issues are available through support forums
- It is supported by most of the major Python libraries

Even though the code samples, exercises, and projects provided in this book should work in any variant of Python 2.7.x, it's better to have the latest version.

Installing Python

Your fondness for an operating system is developed due to multiple factors, and you can never ignore someone's bias towards a particular OS. Thus, this book provides installation and configuration guidelines for three of the most popular operating systems: Linux, Mac OS X, and Windows. Let's begin by configuring Python for a Linux computer.

Linux

The majority of Linux distributions come with Python preinstalled. To check the latest version of the installed Python, use the following command at the terminal window:

```
$ python -V
```

Make sure that you are using an uppercase `V` as the option for the previous command. Once you execute it on the terminal, it will print the complete version number of your current Python installation. If the version is 2.7.x, you are good to go and your Linux is updated with the latest version of Python that is required for this book. However, if you have any version that is less than or equal to 2.6.x, you will need to first upgrade Python to the latest version. This process will require root privileges, as Python will be installed as a system component that will replace the previous versions.

Ubuntu

If you are using Ubuntu 11.10 or later versions, you should already have Python v2.7.x installed on your machine. You can still upgrade Python to the latest revision of v2.7.x using the following command:

```
$ sudo apt-get update && sudo apt-get --only-upgrade install python
```

If you are running an older version of Ubuntu (such as 10.04 or older), you should have 2.6 as the default version. In this case, you will need to run the following set of commands to install version 2.7:

```
$ sudo add-apt-repository ppa:fkrull/deadsnakes
$ sudo apt-get update
$ sudo apt-get install python2.7
```

The first command will add an external Ubuntu repository, which will allow you to install any version of Python. The next command will update and index the list of available packages. The last command will install the latest version of Python 2.7.

Fedora and Red Hat

Fedora and Red Hat Linux also ships with Python as an in-built package. If you want to upgrade the version of Python to the latest one, run the following command at the terminal:

```
$ sudo yum upgrade python
```

Downloading the example code

You can download the example code files from your account at `http://www.packtpub.com` for all the Packt Publishing books you have purchased. If you purchased this book elsewhere, you can visit `http://www.packtpub.com/support` and register to have the files e-mailed directly to you.

Windows

Installation and configuration of Python on Windows is not as straightforward as it is for Linux. First of all, you'll need to download a copy of Python from `http://www.python.org/getit`.

You need to be careful about the version of Python that you are downloading. From the system properties of your Windows OS, check whether the operating system is of 32 bit or 64 bit. At the time this book was being written, the latest version of Python was 2.7.6. So, download the latest available version of Python, but make sure that it is 2.7.x and not 3.x.

For many third-party Python libraries, the installation binary files for Windows are compiled for the 32-bit version. Due to this reason, we will recommend that you install the 32-bit version of Python for your Windows OS.

If you are really familiar with Python and know your way around installing libraries, you can install the 64-bit version of Python. Select and run the downloaded file to install Python. Although you can install it to any custom location, it is advisable to use the default installation location as the upcoming configuration steps use the default location. Once the installation is complete, you can find the Python command-line tool and IDLE (Python GUI) from the **Start** menu.

Although you can always open these tools from the **Start** menu for basic scripting, we will modify the Windows system parameters to make Python accessible through the Windows command prompt. To accomplish this, we will have to set up `PATH` in environment variables for the location of the Python installation directory. Let's open **System Properties** by right-clicking on **My Computer** and then selecting **Properties**. Otherwise, you can also navigate to **Start** | **Control Panel** | **System and Security** | **System**.

You will be able to see a window similar to the one that is displayed in the following screenshot. The **System** window shows you the basic information about your computer, including the type of Windows operating system that you are using (such as the 32-bit or the 64-bit version):

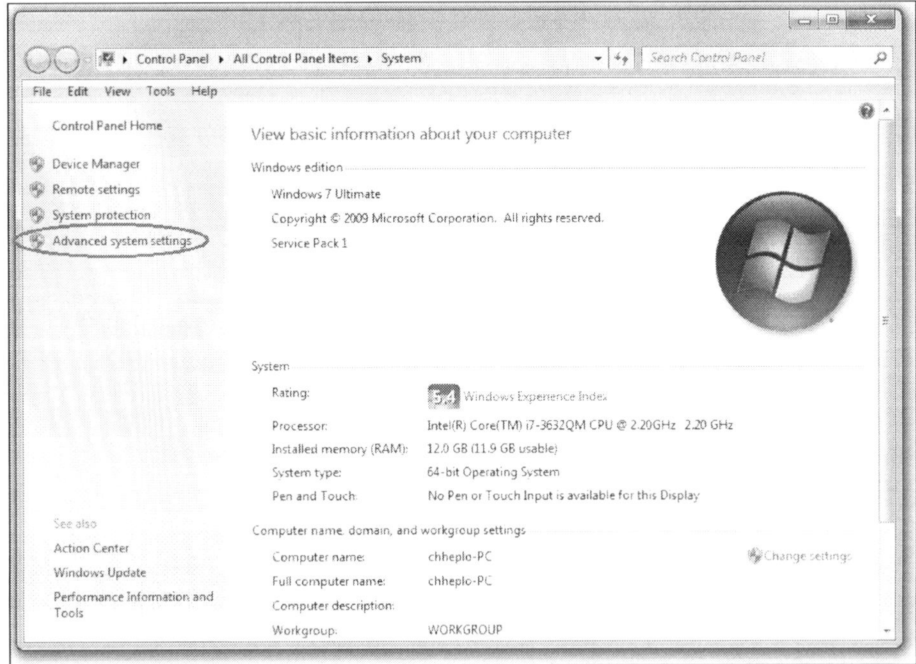

In the **System** window, click on **Advanced system settings** in the left navigation bar to open a window called **System Properties**. Click on the **Environment Variables...** button in the **System Properties** window, which is located at the bottom of the window. This will open an interface similar to the one shown in the following screenshot. In **Environment Variables**, you need to update the **PATH** system variable to add Python to the default operating system's path.

Click on the **PATH** option as displayed in the following screenshot, which will pop up an **Edit System Variable** window. Add `C:\Python27` or the full path of your custom Python installation directory at the end of your existing **PATH** variable. It is required to put a semicolon (`;`) before the Python installation path. If you already see Python's location in the **Path** variable, your system is set up for Python and you don't need to perform any changes:

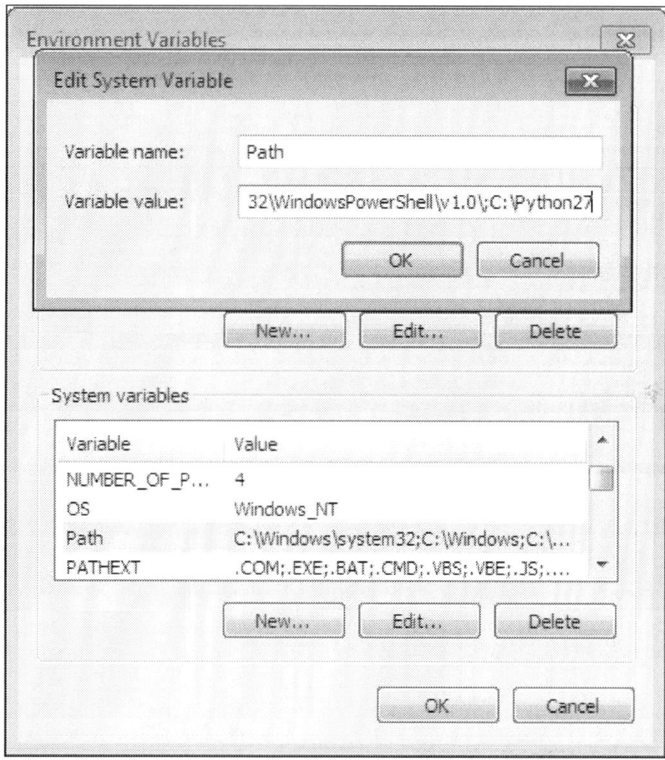

The main benefit of adding Python to the environment variables is to enable access to the Python interpreter from the command prompt. In case you don't know, the Windows command prompt can be accessed by navigating to **Start** | **Programs** | **Accessories** | **Command Prompt**.

Mac OS X

Mac OS X ships with a preinstalled copy of Python, but due to the long release cycle of the operating system, the frequency of updates for the default Python application is slow. The latest version of Mac OS X, which is 10.9 Maverick, comes equipped with Python 2.7.5, which is the latest version:

```
Tests-Mac:~ test$ python
Python 2.7.5 (default, Aug 25 2013, 00:04:04)
[GCC 4.2.1 Compatible Apple LLVM 5.0 (clang-500.0.68)] on darwin
Type "help", "copyright", "credits" or "license" for more information.
>>>
```

Previous versions such as Mac OS X 10.8 Mountain Lion and Mac OS X 10.7 Lion included Python 2.7.2 and Python 2.7.1 respectively, which are also compatible versions for this book. If you are an experienced Python user or someone who wants to work with the latest version of Python, you can download the latest version from `http://www.python.org/getit`.

Older versions of Mac OS X such as Snow Leopard and later, which came with an older version of Python, can be updated to the latest version by downloading and installing it from `http://www.python.org/getit`.

Installing Setuptools

Setuptools is a library containing a collection of utilities for building and distributing Python packages. The most important tool from this collection is called `easy_install`. It allows a user to look into PyPI, the Python package repository that we mentioned previously, and provides a simple interface to install any package by name. The `easy_install` utility automatically downloads, builds, installs, and manages packages for the user. This utility has been used in the later part of this book to install the necessary packages required for the upcoming projects of Python and Arduino. Although `easy_install` has been used as a simple way of installing Python packages, it misses out on a few useful features such as tracking actions, support for uninstallation, and support for other version control systems. In recent years, the Python community has started adopting another tool called `pip` over `easy_install` that supports these features. As both `easy_install` and `pip` utilize the same PyPI repository, going forward, you can use any of these utilities to install the required Python packages.

Just to narrow down the scope, we will be focusing on methods to install Setuptools and the default utilities that get installed with it, that is, `easy_install`. Later in this section, we will also install `pip`, just in case you want to use it too. Let's first begin by installing Setuptools for the various operating systems.

Linux

In Ubuntu, Setuptools is available in the default repository and it can be installed using the following command:

```
$ sudo apt-get install python-setuptools
```

For Fedora, it can be installed using the default software manager `yum`:

```
$ sudo yum install python-setuptools
```

For other Linux distributions, it can be downloaded and built using the following single-line script:

```
$ wget https://bitbucket.org/pypa/setuptools/raw/bootstrap/ez_setup.py -O
- | sudo python
```

Once it is installed on your Linux distribution, `easy_install` can be directly accessed from the terminal as a built-in command.

Windows

Installation of Setuptools is not that straightforward for Windows as compared to Linux. It requires the user to download the `ez_setup.py` file from the Windows section at `https://pypi.python.org/pypi/setuptools`.

Once this is downloaded, press *Shift* and right-click in the folder where you downloaded the `ez_setup.py` file. Select **Open command window here** and execute the following command:

```
> python ez_setup.py
```

This will install Setuptools in the `Scripts` folder of your default Python installation folder. Using the same method that we used when we added Python to **Environment Variables**, now include Setuptools by adding `C:\Python27\Scripts` to **PATH**, followed by the semicolon (;).

This will enable the installation of various Python packages using `easy_install` to your Python packages folder called `Libs`. Once you have added the package manager to the environment variables, you need to close and reopen the command prompt for these changes to take effect.

Mac OS X

Setuptools can be installed in Mac OS X using any of the following methods. It is advisable for beginners to use the first method, as the second method requires the external package manager Homebrew.

If you have never worked with Homebrew before, you will need to follow these steps to install Setuptools on your Mac:

1. Download `ez_setup.py` from the Unix/Mac section at `https://pypi.python.org/pypi/setuptools`.
2. Open the terminal and navigate to the directory where you downloaded this file. For most browsers, the file gets saved to the `Download` folder.
3. Run the following command in the terminal to build and set up Setuptools:

   ```
   $ sudo python ez_setup.py
   ```

If you are familiar with Homebrew-based software installation, just follow these quick steps to install Setuptools:

1. First, install `wget` from Homebrew if you don't have it already:

   ```
   $ brew install wget
   ```

2. Once you have installed `wget`, run the following command in the terminal:

   ```
   $ wget https://bitbucket.org/pypa/setuptools/raw/bootstrap/ez_
   setup.py -O - | python
   ```

More information regarding the Homebrew utility can be obtained from `http://brew.sh`.

You can install Homebrew on your Mac by running the following simple script in the terminal:

```
ruby -e "$(curl -fsSL https://raw.githubusercontent.
com/Homebrew/install/master/install)"
```

Installing pip

As you have successfully installed Setuptools, let's use it to install `pip`. For Linux or Mac OS X, you can run the following command in the terminal to install `pip`:

```
$ sudo easy_install pip
```

For Windows, open the command prompt and execute the following command:

```
> easy_install.exe pip
```

If you have already installed `pip` on your computer, please make sure that you upgrade it to the latest version to overcome the few bugs that are associated with the upgrade. You can upgrade `pip` using the following command at the terminal:

```
$ sudo easy_install --upgrade pip
```

Since you have already used `easy_install` to install a Python package, let's get ourselves more familiar with Python package management.

Installing Python packages

With the installation of `pip`, you have two different options to install any third-party Python package listed on the PyPi repository (`http://pypi.python.org`). The following are the various procedures that you need to know to work with the installation of Python packages. In the following examples, the term `PackageName` is a pseudo name that is used for a Python package that you want to work with. For your package of choice, identify the appropriate package name from the PyPi website and put its name in place of `PackageName`. In some cases, you will need root (super user) privileges to install or uninstall a package. You can use `sudo` followed by an appropriate command for these cases.

To install a Python package, execute the following command at the terminal:

```
$ easy_install PackageName
```

Otherwise, you can also execute the following command:

```
$ pip install PackageName
```

If you want to install a specific version of a package, you can use the following command:

```
$ easy_install "PackageName==version"
```

If you are not aware of the exact version number, you can also use comparison operators such as `>`, `<`, `>=`, or `<=` to specify a range for the version number. Both `easy_install` and `pip` will select the best matching version of the package from the repository and install it:

```
$ easy_install "PackageName > version"
```

Meanwhile, for `pip`, you can use the following identical commands to perform similar operations:

```
$ pip install PackageName==version
$ pip install "PackageName>=version"
```

As an example, if you want to install a version between 1.0 and 3.0, you will need to use the following command:

```
$ pip install "PackageName>=0.1,<=0.3"
```

It is really easy to upgrade a package using either `easy_install` or `pip`. The command options used by both are also very similar:

```
$ easy_install --upgrade PackageName
$ pip install --upgrade PackageName
```

Although `easy_install` doesn't support clean uninstallation of a package, you can use the following command to make sure that Python stops searching for the specified package. Later, carefully remove the package files from the installation directory:

```
$ easy_install -mxN PackageName
```

A much better way to perform a clean uninstallation of the majority of packages is to use `pip` instead of `easy_install`:

```
$ pip uninstall PackageName
```

A detailed list of the Python packages supported by Setuptools can be found at the PyPI website at `https://pypi.python.org/`.

The fundamentals of Python programming

If you have previous experience of working with any other programming language, Python is very easy to get started with. If you have never done programming before, this section will walk you through some of the basics of Python. If you have already worked with Python, you should skip this section and move on to the next one.

Assuming that the setup instructions are followed correctly, let's open the Python interpreter by executing the Python command at the terminal or the command prompt. You should get results similar to those displayed in the following screenshot. If you have installed Python by downloading the setup files from the website, you should have the Python **integrated development environment** (**IDLE**) installed as well. You can also start the Python interpreter by opening its IDLE from the location where it was installed.

As you can see, after printing some system information, the interpreter opens a prompt with three greater-than signs (>>>), which is also known as the primary prompt. The interpreter is now in the interactive mode and it is ready to execute scripts from the prompt.

```
C:\Windows\system32\cmd.exe - python
Microsoft Windows [Version 6.1.7601]
Copyright (c) 2009 Microsoft Corporation.  All rights reserved.

C:\Users\Test>python
Python 2.7.5 (default, May 15 2013, 22:43:36) [MSC v.1500 32 bit (Intel)] on win
32
Type "help", "copyright", "credits" or "license" for more information.
>>> _
```

To close the interactive mode of the Python interpreter, run the either `exit()` or `quit()`, at the primary prompt. Another method to exit from the interactive mode is to use the keyboard shortcut *Ctrl* + *D*.

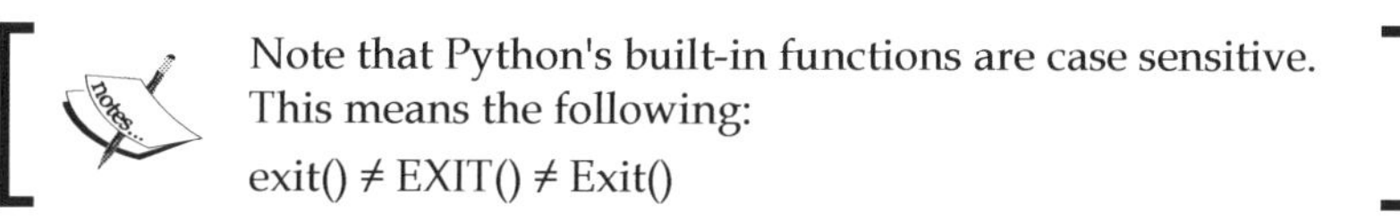

> Note that Python's built-in functions are case sensitive. This means the following:
>
> exit() ≠ EXIT() ≠ Exit()

The official Python website provides comprehensive tutorials for beginners to get started with Python programming. It is highly recommended that you visit the official Python tutorials at `https://docs.python.org/2/tutorial/index.html` if you are looking for detailed programming tutorials as compared to the upcoming brief overviews.

Python operators and built-in types

Now that you have a brief idea regarding the Python prompt, let's get you familiar with some of the basic Python commands. For these exercises, we will be using the Python IDLE, which also opens with the Python interactive prompt. You will require a method to describe the code segments, tasks, and comments when writing large and complex code. Non-executable content is called comments in any programming language, and in Python, they start with the hashtag character (#). Like comments, you will be frequently required to check the output by printing on the prompt using the print command:

```
>>> # Fundamental of Python
>>> # My first comment
```

```
 = "John" # This is my name
t name
```

Instead of IDLE, you can also access the Python interactive prompt from the terminal. When using Python from the terminal, make sure that you are taking care of the indentation properly.

Operators

Python supports the usage of basic mathematical operators such as +, -, *, and /, directly from the interpreter. Using these operators, you can perform basic calculations in the prompt, as shown in the following examples. Try these operations in your prompt in order to start using the Python interpreter as a calculator:

```
>>> 2 + 2
4
>>> (2*3) + 1
7
>>> (2*3) / 5
1
```

When working with the Python interpreter, it is recommended that you follow the Style Guide for Python Code, which is also popularly known as PEP-8 or pep8. For more information about PEP-8, visit `https://www.python.org/dev/peps/pep-0008/`.

Built-in types

Python is a dynamically typed language, which means that you don't have to explicitly declare the type of the variables when initializing them. When you assign a value to a variable, the Python interpreter automatically deduces the data type. For example, let's declare the following variables in the interactive mode of the interpreter:

```
>>> weight = height = 5
>>> weight * height
25
>>> type(weight)
<type 'int'>
```

While assigning the value to the `weight` variable, we didn't specify the data type, but the Python interpreter assigned it as an integer type, `int`. The interpreter assigned the `int` type due to the reason that the numerical value didn't contain any decimal points. Let's now declare a variable with a value containing a decimal point. The built-in function `type()` that can be used to find out the data type of a specified variable:

```
>>> length = 6.0
>>> weight * height * length
150.0
>>> type(length)
<type 'float'>
```

As you can see, the interpreter assigns the data type as `float`. The interpreter can also deduce the type of complex numbers, as shown in following examples. You can access the real and imaginary value of a complex number using the dot (`.`) operator followed by `real` and `imag`:

```
>>> val = 2.0 + 3.9j
>>> val.real
2.0
>>> val.imag
3.9
```

Just to play more with complex numbers, let's try the `abs()` and `round()` functions as displayed in the following examples. They are built-in Python functions to obtain the absolute value and the rounded number respectively:

```
>>> abs(val)
4.382921400162225
>>> round(val.imag)
4.0
```

Like numbers, the Python interpreter can also automatically identify the declaration of string data types. In Python, string values are assigned using single or double quotes around the value. When the interpreter sees any value enclosed within quotes, it considers it to be a string. Python supports the usage of the + operator to concatenate strings:

```
>>> s1 = "Hello"
>>> s2 = "World!"
>>> s1 + s2
'HelloWorld!'
>>> s1 + " " + s2
'Hello World!'
```

A character type is a string of size one and the individual characters of a string can be accessed by using index numbers. The first character of a string is indexed as 0. Play with the following scripts to understand indexing (subscripting) in Python:

```
>>> s1[0]
'H'
>>> s1[:2]
'He'
>>> s1 + s2[5:]
'Hello!'
```

Similar to the primary prompt with default notation `>>>`, the Python interactive interpreter also has a secondary prompt that uses three dots (...) when it is being used from the terminal. You won't be able to see the three dots in IDLE when you use the secondary prompt. The secondary prompt is used for a multiline construct, which requires continuous lines. Execute the following commands by manually typing them in the interpreter, and do not forget to indent the next line after the `if` statement with a tab:

```
>>> age = 14
>>> if age > 10 or age < 20:
...   print "teen"

teen
```

Data structures

Python supports four main data structures (`list`, `tuple`, `set`, and `dictionary`) and there are a number of important built-in methods around these data structures.

Lists

Lists are used to group together values of single or multiple data types. The `list` structure can be assigned by stating values in square brackets with a comma (,) as a separator:

```
>>> myList = ['a', 2, 'b', 12.0, 5, 2]
>>> myList
['a', 2, 'b', 12.0, 5, 2]
```

Like strings, values in a list can be accessed using index numbers, which starts from 0. A feature called **slicing** is used by Python to obtain a specific subset or element of the data structure using the colon operator. In a standard format, slicing can be specified using the `myList[start:end:increment]` notation. Here are a few examples to better understand the notion of slicing:

- You can access a single element in a list as follows:

  ```
  >>> myList[0]
  'a'
  ```

- You can access all the elements in the list by having empty start and end values:

  ```
  >>> myList[:]
  ['a', 2, 'b', 12.0, 5, 2]
  ```

- You can provide start and end index values to obtain a specific subset of the list:

  ```
  >>> myList[1:5]
  [2, 'b', 12.0, 5]
  ```

- Use of the minus symbol with an index number tells the interpreter to use that index number backwards. In the following example, `-1` backwards actually represents the index number `5`:

  ```
  >>> myList[1:-1]
  [2, 'b', 12.0, 5]
  ```

- You can obtain every other element of the list by providing the increment value with start and end values:

  ```
  >>> myList[0:5:2]
  ['a', 'b', 5]
  ```

- You can check the length of a list variable using the `len()` method. The usage of this method will be handy in the upcoming projects:

  ```
  >>> len(myList)
  6
  ```

- You can also perform various operations to add or delete elements in the existing list. For example, if you want to add an element at the end of the list, use the `append()` method on the list:

  ```
  >>> myList.append(10)
  >>> myList
  ['a', 2, 'b', 12.0, 5, 2, 10]
  ```

- To add an element at a specific location, you can use the `insert(i, x)` method, where `i` denotes the index value, while `x` is the actual value that you want to add to the list:

  ```
  >>> myList.insert(5,'hello')
  >>> myList
  ['a', 2, 'b', 12.0, 5, 'hello', 2, 10]
  ```

- Similarly, you can use `pop()` to remove an element from the list. A simple `pop()` function will remove the last element of the list, while an element at a specific location can be removed using `pop(i)`, where `i` is the index number:

  ```
  >>> myList.pop()
  10
  >>> myList
  ['a', 2, 'b', 12.0, 5, 'hello', 2]
  >>> myList.pop(5)
  'hello'
  >>> myList
  ['a', 2, 'b', 12.0, 5, 2]
  ```

Tuples

Tuples are immutable data structures supported by Python (different from the mutable structures of lists). An immutable data structure means that you cannot add or remove elements from the tuple data structure. Due to their immutable properties, tuples are faster to access compared to lists and are mostly used to store a constant set of values that never change.

The `tuple` data structure is declared like `list`, but by using parentheses or without any brackets:

```
>>> tupleA = 1, 2, 3
>>> tupleA
(1, 2, 3)
>>> tupleB = (1, 'a', 3)
>>> tupleB
(1, 'a', 3)
```

Just like in a `list` data structure, values in `tuple` can be accessed using index numbers:

```
>>> tupleB[1]
'a'
```

As tuples are immutable, list manipulation methods such as `append()`, `insert()`, and `pop()` don't apply for tuples.

Sets

The `set` data structure in Python is implemented to support mathematical set operations. The `set` data structure includes an unordered collection of elements without duplicates. With its mathematical use cases, this data structure is mostly used to find duplicates in lists, as conversion of a list to a set using the `set()` function removes duplicates from the list:

```
>>> listA = [1, 2, 3, 1, 5, 2]
>>> setA = set(listA)
>>> setA
set([1, 2, 3, 5])
```

Dictionaries

The `dict` data structure is used to store key-value pairs indexed by keys, which are also known in other languages as associative arrays, hashes, or hashmaps. Unlike other data structures, `dict` values can be extracted using associated keys:

```
>>> boards = {'uno':328,'mega':2560,'lily':'128'}
>>> boards['lily']
'128'
>>> boards.keys()
['lily', 'mega', 'uno']
```

You can learn more about Python data structures and associated methods at `https://docs.python.org/2/tutorial/datastructures.html`.

Controlling the flow of your program

Just like any other language, Python supports controlling the program flow using compound statements. In this section, we will briefly introduce these statements to you. You can get detailed information about them from the official Python documentation at `https://docs.python.org/2/reference/compound_stmts.html`.

The if statement

The `if` statement is the most basic and standard statement used to set up conditional flow. To better understand the `if` statement, execute the following code in the Python interpreter with different values of the `age` variable:

```
>>> age = 14
>>> if age < 18 and age > 12:
  print "Teen"
elif age < 13:
  print "Child"
else:
  print "Adult"
```

This will result in `Teen` being printed on the interpreter.

The for statement

Python's `for` statement iterates over the elements of any sequence according to the order of the elements in that sequence:

```
>>> celsius = [13, 21, 23, 8]
>>> for c in celsius:
  print " Fahrenheit: "+ str((c * 1.8) + 32)
```

This will result in the Python interpreter generating the following output that will display the calculated Fahrenheit values from the given Celsius values:

```
Fahrenheit: 55.4
Fahrenheit: 69.8
Fahrenheit: 73.4
Fahrenheit: 46.4
```

The while statement

The `while` statement is used to create a continuous loop in a Python program. A `while` loop keeps iterating over the code block until the condition is proved true:

```
>>> count = 5
>>> while (count > 0):
  print count
  count = count - 1
```

The `while` statement will keep iterating and printing the value of the variable count and also reduce its value by 1 until the condition, that is (`count > 0`), becomes true. As soon as the value of `count` is lower than or equal to 0, the `while` loop will exit the code block and stop iterating.

The other compound statements supported by Python are `try/catch` and `with`. These statements will be explained in detail in the upcoming chapters. Python also provides loop control statements such as `break`, `continue`, and `pass` that can be used while a loop is being executed using the compound statements mentioned earlier. You can learn more about these Python features from `https://docs.python.org/2/tutorial/controlflow.html`.

Built-in functions

Python supports a number of useful built-in functions that do not require any external libraries to be imported. We have described a few of these functions as a collection of a respective category, according to their functionalities.

Conversions

Conversion methods such as `int()`, `float()`, and `str()` can convert other data types into integer, float, or string data types respectively:

```
>>> a = 'a'
>>> int(a,base=16)
10
>>> i = 1
>>> str(i)
'1'
```

Similarly, `list()`, `set()`, and `tuple()` can be used to convert one data structure into another.

Math operations

Python also supports built-in mathematical functions that can find the minimum and/or maximum values from a list. Check out the following examples and play around with the different data structures to understand these methods:

```
>>> list = [1.12, 2, 2.34, 4.78]
>>> min(list)
1.12
>>> max(list)
4.78
```

The `pow(x,y)` function returns the value of `x` to the power of `y`:

```
>>> pow(3.14159, 2)
9.869587728099999
```

String operations

Python provides easy access to string manipulation through built-in functions that are optimized for performance. Let's take a look at the following examples:

- Code to replace occurrences of a string or substring with a different one:

  ```
  >>> str = "Hello World!"
  >>> str.replace("World", "Universe")
  'Hello Universe!'
  ```

- Code to split a string with a separating character where the default character is space:

  ```
  >>> str = "Hello World!"
  >>> str.split()
  ['Hello', 'World!']
  ```

- Code to split a string from a separating character for any other character:

  ```
  >>> str2 = "John, Merry, Tom"
  >>> str2.split(",")
  ['John', ' Merry', ' Tom']
  ```

- Code to convert an entire string value into uppercase or lowercase:

  ```
  >>> str = "Hello World!"
  >>> str.upper()
  'HELLO WORLD!'
  >>> str.lower()
  'hello world!'
  ```

The Python documentation on the official website covers every built-in function in detail with examples. For better understanding of Python programming, visit `https://docs.python.org/2/library/functions.html`.

Introduction to Arduino

Any electronic product that needs computation or interfacing with other computers first requires a quick prototyping of the concept using simple tools. Arduino is an open source hardware prototyping platform designed around a popular microcontroller family, and it includes a simple software development environment. Besides prototyping, you can also use Arduino for the development of your own **do-it-yourself (DIY)** projects. Arduino bridges the computational world with the physical world by letting you simply connect the sensors and actuators with a computer. Basically, you can write code to monitor and control various electronic components in your daily life by using Arduino's input/output pins and microcontroller. Examples of these components include motors, thermostats, lights, switches, and many more.

History

In 2005, Massimo Banzi, the Italian cofounder of Arduino, developed the technology for his students at **Interaction Design Institute Ivrea (IDII)**. Since then, Arduino has developed into one of the largest open source hardware platforms. All software components and schematics of the Arduino design are open source, and you can buy the hardware at a very low cost—approximately 30 dollars—or you can even make it yourself.

Why Arduino?

The major goal of the Arduino community is to continuously improve the Arduino platform with the following objectives in mind:

- The Arduino platform should be an affordable platform
- It should be easy to use and easy to code
- It should be an open source and extensible software platform
- It should be an open source and extensible hardware platform
- It should have community-supported DIY projects

These simple but powerful objectives have made Arduino a popular and widely used prototyping platform. Arduino uses Atmel's ATmega series of microcontrollers that are based on the popular hardware architecture of AVR. The huge support that is available for AVR architecture also makes Arduino a hardware platform of choice. The following image shows the basic version of the Arduino board, which is called Arduino Uno (Uno means one in Italian):

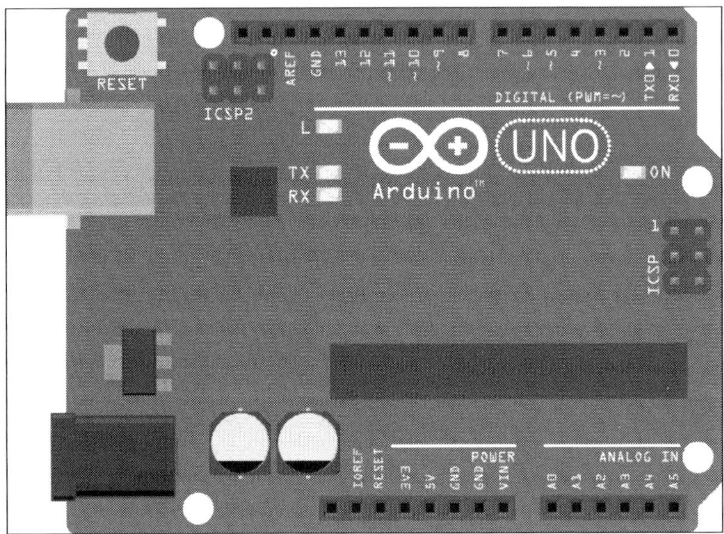

Arduino variants

Like any other project, hardware requirements are driven by project specifications. If you are developing a project that requires you to interface with a large number of external components, you need a prototyping platform that has a sufficient number of **input/output** (**I/O**) pins for interfacing. If you are working on a project that needs to perform a huge amount of complex calculations, you require a platform with more computation capability.

Fortunately, the Arduino board exists in 16 different official versions, and each version of Arduino differs from the others in terms of form factor, computational power, I/O pins, and other on-board features. Arduino Uno is the basic and most popular version, which is sufficient enough for simple DIY projects. For the majority of exercises in this book, we will be using the Arduino Uno board. You can also use another popular variant called Arduino Mega, which is a larger board with extra pins and a powerful microcontroller. The following table shows the comparison of some of the more popular and active variants of the Arduino board:

Name	Processor	Processor frequency	Digital I/O	Digital I/O with PWM	Analog I/O
Arduino Uno	ATmega328	16 MHz	14	6	6
Arduino Leonardo	ATmega32u4	16 MHz	14	6	12
Arduino Mega	ATmega2560	16 MHz	54	14	16
Arduino Nano	ATmega328	16 MHz	14	6	8
Arduino Due	AT91SAM3X8E	84 MHz	54	12	12
LilyPad Arduino	ATmega168v or ATmega328v	8 MHz	14	6	6

Any of these variants can be programmed using a common integrated development environment called **Arduino IDE**, which is described in the upcoming section. You can select any one of these Arduino boards according to your project requirements, and the Arduino IDE should be able to compile and download the program to the board.

The Arduino Uno board

As Uno is going to be the de facto board for the majority of the projects in this book, let's get ourselves familiar with the board. The latest revision of the Uno board is based on Atmel's ATmega328 microcontroller. The board extends the I/O pins of the microcontroller to the peripheral, which can then be utilized to interface components using wires. The board has a total of 20 pins to interface, out of which 14 are digital I/O pins and 6 are analog input pins. From the 14 digital I/O pins, 6 pins also support **pulse-width modulation** (**PWM**), which supports the controlled delivery of power to connected components.

The board operates on 5V. The maximum current rating of the digital I/O pins is 40 mA, which is sufficient to drive most of the DIY electronic components, excluding motors with high current requirements.

While the previous image provided an overview of the Uno board, the following diagram describes the pins on the Uno board. As you can see, the digital pins are located on one side of the board while the analog pins are on the opposite side. The board also has a couple of power pins that can be used to provide 5V and 3.3V of power to external components. The board contains ground pins on both sides of the board as well. We will be extensively using 5V of power and ground pins for our projects. Digital pins **D0** and **D1** support serial interfacing through the **Tx (transmission)** and **Rx (receiver)** interfaces respectively. The USB port on the board can be used to connect Arduino with a computer.

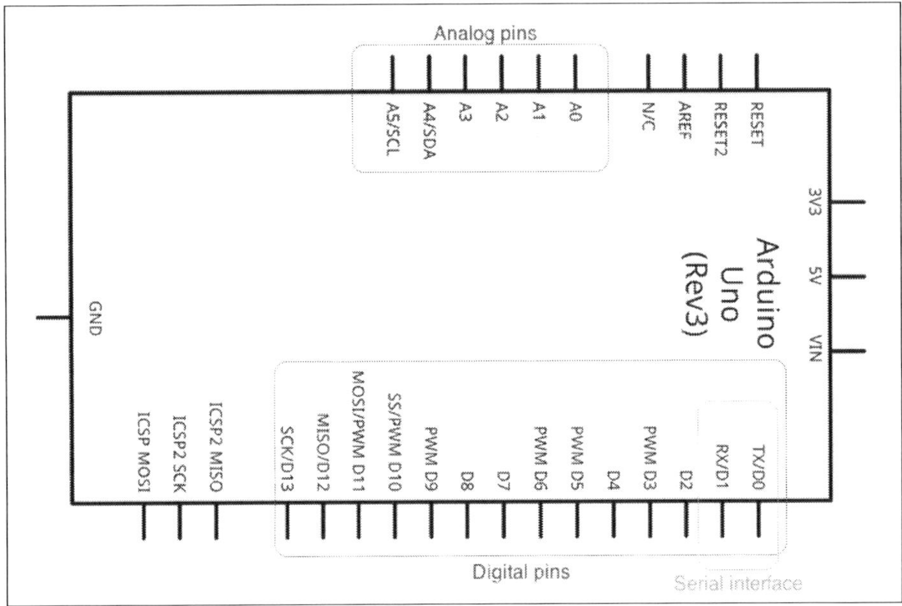

Now that we are familiar with the Arduino hardware, let's move on to programming the Arduino board.

Installing the Arduino IDE

The first step to start getting familiar with Arduino is to install the Arduino **integrated development environment (IDE)**. According to the operating system that you selected at the beginning of the Python installation section, follow the appropriate subsection to install the correct IDE.

Linux

The installation of the Arduino IDE is really simple in Ubuntu. The Ubuntu repository already includes the Arduino IDE with the required dependencies.

For Ubuntu 12.04 or a newer version, execute the following command in the terminal to install Arduino:

```
$ sudo apt-get update && sudo apt-get install arduino arduino-core
```

The latest version of the Arduino IDE in the Ubuntu repository is 1.0.3. You can obtain more information regarding other Ubuntu-related questions at `http://playground.arduino.cc/Linux/Ubuntu`.

For Fedora 17 or a newer version of Red Hat Linux, execute the following script in the terminal:

```
$ sudo yum install arduino
```

Answers to additional installation questions for Fedora can be obtained at `http://playground.arduino.cc/Linux/Fedora`.

Mac OS X

To install the Arduino IDE on Mac OS X (10.7 or newer), perform the following steps:

1. From `http://arduino.cc/en/Main/Software`, download the latest version of the Arduino IDE for Mac OS X, which was 1.0.5 when this book was being written.
2. Unzip and drag Arduino to the application folder.

The Arduino IDE is built in Java and requires that your computer is equipped with the appropriate version of Java. Open the IDE from your applications. If you don't have Java installed on your Mac, the program will prompt you with a pop-up window and ask you to install Java SE 6 runtime. Go ahead and install Java (as per the request) as the OS X will automatically install it for you.

Windows

Installation of Arduino for Windows is very simple. Download the setup file from `http://arduino.cc/en/Main/Software`. Select the most recent version of the Arduino IDE, that is, 1.0.x or a newer version.

Make sure you download the appropriate version of the Arduino IDE according to your operating system, that is, 32 bit or 64 bit. Install the IDE to the default location as specified in the installation wizard. Once installed, you can open the IDE by navigating to **Start** | **Programs**.

Getting started with the Arduino IDE

The Arduino IDE is a cross-platform application developed in Java that can be used to develop, compile, and upload programs to the Arduino board. On launching the Arduino IDE, you will find an interface similar to the one displayed in the following screenshot. The IDE contains a text editor for coding, a menu bar to access the IDE components, a toolbar to easily access the most common functions, and a text console to check the compiler outputs. A status bar at the bottom shows the selected Arduino board and the port name that it is connected to, as shown here:

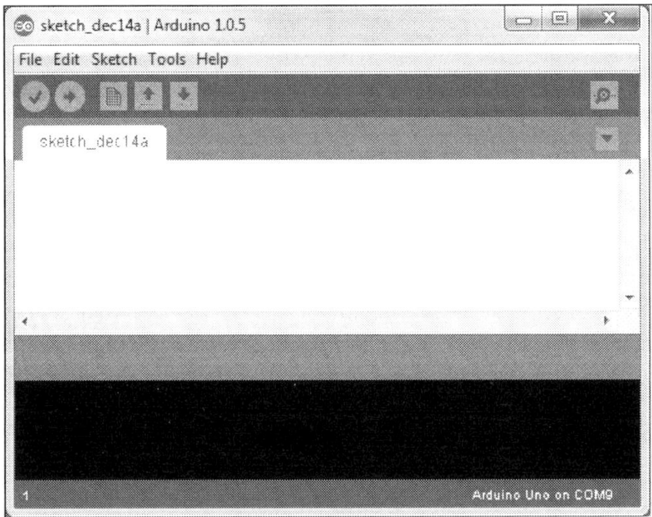

What is an Arduino sketch?

An Arduino program that is developed using the IDE is called a **sketch**. Sketches are coded in Arduino language, which is based on a custom version of C/C++. Once you are done with writing the code in the built-in text editor, you can save it using the `.ino` extension. When you save these sketch files, the IDE automatically creates a folder to store them. If you are using any other supporting files for a sketch, such as header files or library files, they are all stored at this location (which is also called a **sketchbook**).

To open a new sketchbook, open the Arduino IDE and select **New** from the **File** menu, as shown in the following screenshot:

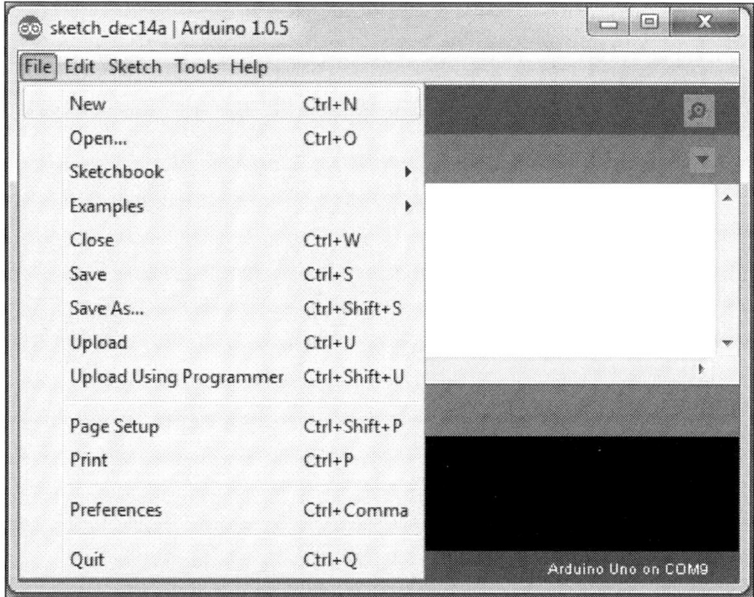

You will be prompted with an empty text editor. The text editor supports standard features (that is, copy/paste, select, find/replace, and so on). Before we go ahead with an Arduino program, let's explore the other tools provided by the IDE.

> The Arduino IDE version prior to 1.0 used the `.pde` extension to save sketchbooks. Starting from 1.0, they are saved with the `.ino` extension. You can still open files with the `.pde` extension in the latest IDE. Later, the IDE will convert it to the `.ino` extension when you save them.

Working with libraries

The Arduino IDE uses libraries to extend the functionalities of existing sketches. Libraries are a set of functions combined to perform tasks around a specific component or concept. The majority of the built-in Arduino libraries provide methods to start working with external hardware components. You can import any library by navigating to **Sketch** | **Import Library...**, as shown in the following screenshot:

You can also use a library for your sketch by just specifying the library with the `#include` statement at the beginning of the sketch, that is, `#include <Wire.h>`.

The Arduino IDE also provides the capability to add an external library that supports a specific hardware or provides additional features. In the upcoming chapters, we will be dealing with some of these external libraries, and we will go through the process of importing them at that time.

You can learn more about built-in Arduino libraries from `http://arduino.cc/en/Reference/Libraries`.

Using Arduino examples

The Arduino IDE contains a large number of built-in example sketches. These examples are designed to get the user familiar with basic Arduino concepts and built-in Arduino libraries. The examples are well maintained by the Arduino community since they have comprehensive support for each example through the Arduino website (`http://arduino.cc/en/Tutorial/HomePage`). In the Arduino IDE, you can access these examples by navigating to **File** | **Examples**, as shown in the following screenshot:

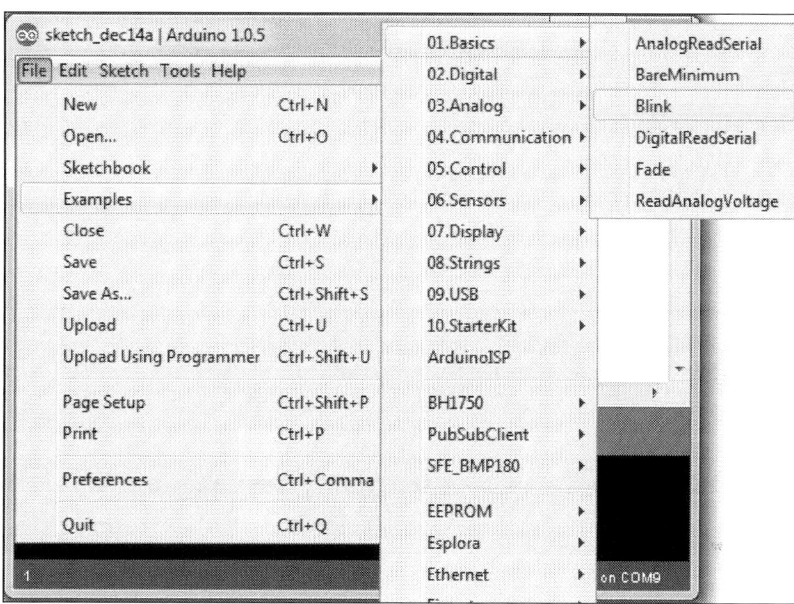

Let's start with a simple in-built example. Open the **Blink** example by navigating to **File** | **Examples** | **01.Basics** | **Blink**. The IDE will open a new window containing code that is similar to the code in the following program:

```
/*
  Blink
  Turns on an LED on for one second, then off for one second, 
repeatedly.

  This example code is in the public domain.
 */

// Pin 13 has an LED connected on most Arduino boards.
// give it a name:
```

```
int led = 13;

// the setup routine runs once when you press reset:
void setup() {
  // initialize the digital pin as an output.
  pinMode(led, OUTPUT);
}

// the loop routine runs over and over again forever:
void loop() {
  digitalWrite(led, HIGH);   // turn the LED on (HIGH is the voltage
level)
  delay(1000);               // wait for a second
  digitalWrite(led, LOW);    // turn the LED off by making the voltage
LOW
  delay(1000);               // wait for a second
}
```

This Arduino sketch is designed to blink an LED on digital pin 13. You must be wondering why we didn't discuss or ask you to bring any hardware. That's because the Arduino Uno board is equipped with an on-board LED that is connected to digital pin 13. Now, instead of diving deeper into the Arduino code, we are going to focus on the process of dealing with the Arduino board through the IDE.

Compiling and uploading sketches

Once you have your code opened in the IDE, the first thing you need to do is to select the type of Arduino board on which you are going to upload your sketch. The Arduino IDE needs to know the type of board in order to compile the program for the appropriate microcontroller, as different Arduino boards can have different Atmel microcontrollers. Therefore, you need to perform this step before you go ahead with the compiling or uploading of the program to the board.

You can select the Arduino board by navigating to **Tools** | **Board**, as displayed in the following screenshot:

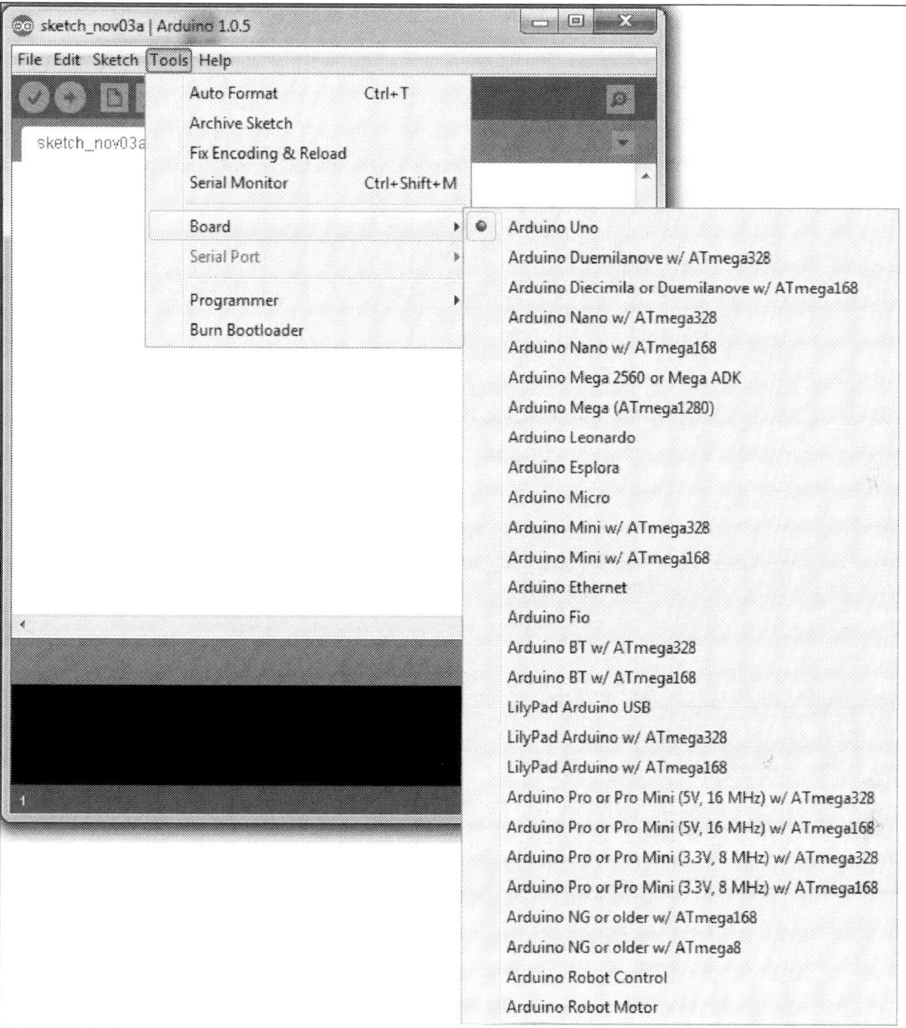

Select Arduino Uno from the list of boards, unless you are using a different Arduino board. Once you have selected the board, you can go ahead and compile the sketch. You can compile the sketch by navigating to **Sketch** | **Verify / Compile** from the menu bar or by using the keyboard shortcut *Ctrl* + *R*. If everything is set up well, you should be able to compile the code without any error.

After successfully compiling the sketch, it is time to upload the compiled code to the Arduino board. To do this, you need to make sure that your Arduino IDE is properly connected to your computer. If it is not already connected, connect your Arduino board to your computer using a USB port. Now, it is time to let your IDE know the serial port on which the board is connected. Navigate to **Tools** | **Serial Ports** and select the appropriate serial port.

In the case of some Linux distributions, you may not be able to see or upload the Arduino program to the board due to permission restriction(s) on the serial port. Running the following command on the terminal should solve that problem:

```
$ sudo usermod -a -G uucp, dialout, lock <username>
```

You can now upload the compiled sketch to your Arduino board by navigating to **File** | **Upload**. This process will use the serial connection to burn the compiled firmware in the microcontroller. Please wait for some time or until the LEDs (Tx and Rx LEDs) on the board stop flashing. Now, you have your Arduino board ready with your first sketch. You can observe the performance of the blinking LED near digital pin 13.

Using the Serial Monitor window

In the previous process, we used a **Universal Serial Bus (USB)** cable to connect your Arduino board to a USB port of your computer. The USB port is an industrial standard to provide an interface for connecting various electronic components to a computer using the serial interface. When you connect an Arduino board using USB, the computer actually interfaces it as a serial peripheral device. Throughout the book, we are going to refer to the connections made using a USB as serial connections. The **Serial Monitor** window is a built-in utility of the Arduino IDE. The **Serial Monitor** window can be accessed by navigating to **Tools** | **Serial Monitor** or by using the *Ctrl* + *Shift* + *M* keyboard shortcut. It can be configured to observe data that is being sent or received on the serial port that is used to connect the Arduino board to the computer. You can also set the baud rate for the serial communication using the drop-down menu option. This utility is going to be very useful (further on in the book) when testing your prototypes and their performances.

Introduction to Arduino programming

The Arduino platform was introduced to simplify electronic hardware prototyping for everyone. For this reason, Arduino programming was intended to be easy to learn by nonprogrammers such as designers, artists, and students. The Arduino language is implemented in C/C++, while the fundamentals of the sketch and program structures are derived from an open source programming language called **Processing** and an open source electronic prototyping language called **Wiring**.

Comments

Arduino follows a commenting format that is adopted from C and it is similar to higher-level languages; however, it is different from the Python comment format that we learned earlier in this chapter. There are various methods of commenting, which are as follows:

- **Block comment**: This is done by covering the commented text between `/*` and `*/`:

  ```
  /* This is a comment.
  *  Arduino will ignore any text till it finds until the ending
  comment syntax, which is,
  */
  ```

- **Single-line or inline comment**: This is done by using `//` before the line:

  ```
  // This syntax only applies to one line.
  // You have to use it again for each next line of comment.
  int pin = 13;     //Selected pin 13
  ```

Usually, a block comment at the beginning of the sketch is mostly used to describe the program as a whole. Single-line comments are used to describe specific functions or to-do notes, such as the following one:

```
//TODO: explain variables next.
```

Variables

Like any other high-level language, a variable is used to store data with three components: a name, a value, and a type. For example, consider the following statement:

```
int pin = 10;
```

Here, `pin` is the variable name that is defined with the type `int` and holds the value `10`. Later in the code, all occurrences of the `pin` variable will retrieve data from the declaration that we just made here. You can use any combination of alpha-numeric characters to select the variable name as long as the first character is not a number.

Constants

In the Arduino language, constants are predefined variables that are used to simplify the program:

- `HIGH, LOW`: While working with digital pins on the Arduino board, only two distinct voltage stages are possible at these pins. If a pin is being used to obtain an input, any measure above 3V is considered a `HIGH` state. If you are using a pin for output, then the `HIGH` state will set the pin voltage to 5V. The opposite voltage levels are considered as `LOW` states.
- `false, true`: These are used to represent logical true and false levels. `false` is defined as `0` and `true` is mostly defined as `1`.
- `INPUT, OUTPUT`: These constants are used to define the roles of the Arduino pins. If you set the mode of an Arduino pin as `INPUT`, the Arduino program will prepare the pin to read sensors. Similarly, the `OUTPUT` setting prepares the pins to provide a sufficient amount of current to the connected sensors.

We will utilize these constants later in the book and we will also explain them with example code.

Data types

The declaration of each custom variable requires the user to specify the data type that is associated with the variable. The Arduino language uses a standard set of data types that are used in the C language. A list of these data types and their descriptions are as follows:

- `void`: This is used in the function declaration to indicate that the function is not going to return any value:

  ```
  void setup() {
  // actions
  }
  ```

- `boolean`: Variables defined with the data type `boolean` can only hold one of two values, `true` or `false`:

  ```
  boolean ledState = false;
  ```

- `byte`: This is used to store an 8-bit unsigned number, which is basically any number from 0 to 255:

  ```
  byte b = 0xFF;
  ```

- `int`: This is short for integers. It stores 16-bit (Arduino Uno) or 32-bit (Arduino Due) numbers and it is one of the primary number storage data types for the Arduino language. Although `int` will be used to declare numbers throughout the book, the Arduino language also has `long` and `short` number data types for special cases:

  ```
  int varInt = 2147483647;
  long varLong = varInt;
  short varShort = -32768;
  ```

- `float`: This data type is used for numbers with decimal points. These are also known as floating-point numbers. `float` is one of the more widely used data types along with `int` to represent numbers in the Arduino language:

  ```
  float varFloat = 1.111;
  ```

- `char`: This data type stores a character value and occupies 1 byte of memory. When providing a value to `char` data types, character literals are declared with single quotes:

  ```
  char myCharacater = 'P';
  ```

- `array`: An `array` stores a collection of variables that is accessible by an index number. If you are familiar with arrays in C/C++, it will be easier for you to get started, as the Arduino language uses the same C/C++ arrays. The following are some of the methods to initialize an array:

  ```
  int myIntArray[] = {1, 2, 3, 4, 5};
  int tempValues[5] = { 32, 55, 72, 75};
  char msgArray[10] = "hello!";
  ```

  An array can be accessed using an index number (where the index starts from number 0):

  ```
  myIntArray[0] == 1
  msgArray[2] == 'e'
  ```

Conversions

Conversion functions are used to convert any data type value into the provided data types. The Arduino language implements the following conversion functions that can be utilized during programming:

- `char()`: This converts the value of any data type to the character data type
- `byte()`: This converts the value of any data type to the byte data type
- `int()`: This converts the value of any data type to the integer data type
- `float()`: This converts the value of any data type to the floating-point number data type

As a demonstration of using these functions, check out the following example:

```
int myInt = 10;
float myfloat = float(myInt);
```

Implementation of the preceding code will create a floating-point variable, `myFloat`, with value `10.0` using the integer value initialized by the `myInt` variable.

Functions and statements

Functions, also called **subroutines** or **procedures**, are a piece of code implemented to do specific tasks. The Arduino language has some predefined functions and the user can also write custom functions to implement certain program logic. These custom functions can then be called from any part of the sketch to perform a specific task. Functions help programmers to simplify debugging, to reduce chances for error, and to organize coding concepts:

```
void blinkLED(){
// action A;
// action B;
}
```

The Arduino language has a set of library functions to simplify the programming experience. Although not all of these library functions are required by an Arduino sketch, `setup()` and `loop()` are mandatory functions and they are required to successfully compile the sketch.

The setup() function

When Arduino runs a sketch, it first looks for the `setup()` function. The `setup()` function is used to execute important programming subroutines before the rest of the program, such as declaring constants, setting up pins, initializing serial communication, or initializing external libraries. When Arduino runs the program, it executes the `setup()` functions only once. If you check out the **Blink** sketch that we used in the previous section, you can see the initialization of the `setup()` function, as displayed in the following code snippet:

```
void setup() {
  // initialize the digital pin as an output.
  pinMode(led, OUTPUT);
}
```

As you can see in our example, we used the `pinMode()` function to assign the role of the LED pin in the `setup()` function.

The loop() function

Once Arduino has executed the `setup()` function, it starts iterating the `loop()` function continuously. While `setup()` contains the initialization parameters, `loop()` contains the logical parameters of your program:

```
void loop() {
  digitalWrite(led, HIGH);
  delay(1000);
  digitalWrite(led, LOW);
  delay(1000);
}
```

As you can see in the preceding code snippet from the **Blink** sketch, the `loop()` function executes the main code that blinks the LED and repeats the process iteratively.

The pinMode() function

The `pinMode()` function is used to set the behavior of Arduino. As we saw in the `setup()` function of the **Blink** sketch, the `pinMode()` function configures the LED pin for `OUTPUT`:

```
pinMode(led, OUTPUT)
```

Here, the `led` variable is assigned to digital pin 13, whose mode will be changed by the `pinMode()` function.

Working with pins

Once you are done configuring the pins that will be used by your program, you also need help in reading the input from these pins or for sending signals to them. Arduino provides a few specific functions to handle these scenarios:

- `digitalWrite()`: This was developed for digital I/O pins. This function sets the pin to `HIGH` (5V) or `LOW` (0V), which are already configured as `OUTPUT` using `pinMode()`. For example, the following line of code sets digital pin 13 to `HIGH`:

  ```
  digitalWrite(13, HIGH);
  ```

- `digitalRead()`: Similar to `digitalWrite()`, this function helps you to read the state of a digital pin that is configured as `INPUT`:

  ```
  value = digitalRead(13);
  ```

- `analogRead()`: This function reads the value from a specific analog pin. The value is linearly mapped between the integer value of 0 and 1023 to represent the voltage from 0V to 5V:

  ```
  value = analogRead(0);
  ```

- `analogWrite()`: This function is used to provide analog output results at a digital pin. The technique is called PWM, and this will be explained in *Chapter 4, Diving into Python-Arduino Prototyping*. It is still important to note that this function is not designed for all digital pins, but it is only for pins that are designated as PWM pins.

Statements

If you are familiar with any other object-oriented programming language, you must have used statements extensively for your programs. The Arduino language uses traditional C/C++ statements such as `if/else`, `while`, `switch/case`, and `for` to control the flow of your program. Instead of diving deep into these statements right now, they are described later in the book with practical examples.

Summary

Alright! You have successfully completed the comparatively mundane tasks of installing and configuring Python and the Arduino IDE. Your system, whether it is a Mac OS X, Linux, or Windows system, is now ready for the upcoming chapters. In this chapter, we went through the history and building blocks of Arduino. We also learned the basics of Python programming and the Arduino language. Now, you are ready to get your hands on real hardware and start exploring computer to hardware interfacing. In the next chapter, we will go through the first step of interfacing, that is, connecting Arduino to the computer using a serial interface.

2

Working with the Firmata Protocol and the pySerial Library

In the previous chapter, you learned the fundamentals of the Python programming language and the Arduino hardware platform so that you could get started. If you are reading this chapter directly without going through the previous chapter, it is assumed that you have some level of expertise or working experience with these technologies. This chapter describes two important components that are required to bridge Arduino with Python:

- The Arduino Firmata protocol
- Python's serial library called `pySerial`

Although the Firmata protocol is useful to interface Arduino with Python, it can also be used as an independent tool to develop a large variety of applications.

It is time to take your Arduino hardware out and start getting your hands dirty. During the course of this chapter, you will require an LED, a breadboard, and a 1 kilo-ohm resistor as well as the components that you already used in the previous chapter, that is, Arduino Uno and a USB cable.

> If you are using any other variant of Arduino, you can obtain further information about it from `http://arduino.cc/en/Guide/HomePage` or the community-supported Arduino forum that is located at `http://forum.arduino.cc/`.

Connecting the Arduino board

As mentioned in the previous chapter, this book supports all major operating systems, and this section will provide you with steps to connect and configure the Arduino board for these operating systems. In the previous chapter, we utilized example code to get started with the Arduino IDE. If you were unable to successfully communicate with Arduino by following the information given in the previous chapter, follow the instructions provided in this section to establish a connection between your computer and your Arduino. First, connect your Arduino board to your computer's USB port using a USB cable and follow the steps according to your operating system.

Linux

If you are using the latest version of Ubuntu Linux, once you connect the Arduino board and open the Arduino IDE, you will be asked to add your username to the dailout group, as displayed in the following screenshot. Click on the **Add** button and log out from the system. You don't need to restart the computer for the changes to take effect. Log in with the same username and open the Arduino IDE.

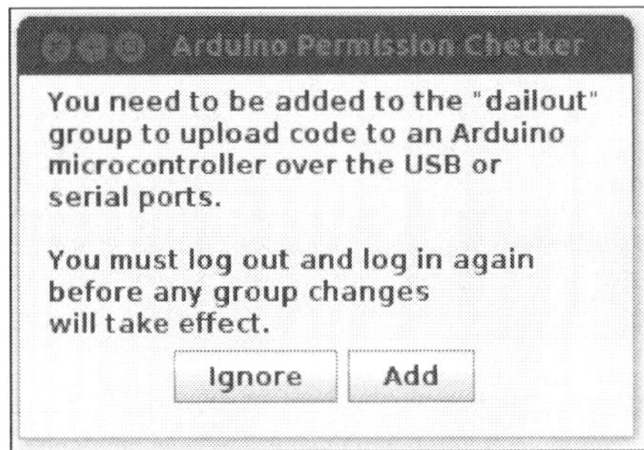

If you don't see this dialog box, check whether you can see the **Serial Port** option in the **Tools** menu of the Arduino IDE. It is possible that the installation of other programs might have added your username to the dailout group already. If you don't get the dialog box and don't have any options to select in **Serial Port**, execute the following script in the terminal, where `<username>` is your Linux username:

```
$ sudo usermod -a -G dialout <username>
```

This script will add your username to the dialout group, and it should also work for other Linux versions. In Linux, the Arduino board mostly gets connected as `/dev/ttyACMx`, where `x` is the integer value and depends on your physical port address. If you are using any other distribution of Linux other than Ubuntu, you might want to check out the proper groups associated with the Arduino serial port from the Linux installation page (`http://playground.arduino.cc/Learning/Linux`) of the Arduino website.

For the Fedora Linux distribution, add the `uucp` and `lock` groups with the `dialout` group to control the serial port:

```
$ sudo usermod -a -G uucp,dialout,lock <username>
```

Mac OS X

In Mac OS X, when you connect your Arduino through a serial port, the OS configures it as a network interface. In OS X Mavericks, once the Arduino board is connected, open **Network** from **System Preferences**. A dialog box should appear that states that a new network interface has been detected. Click on **OK** for **Thunderbolt Bridge** and then click on **Apply**. The following screenshot displays the dialog box to add a new network interface:

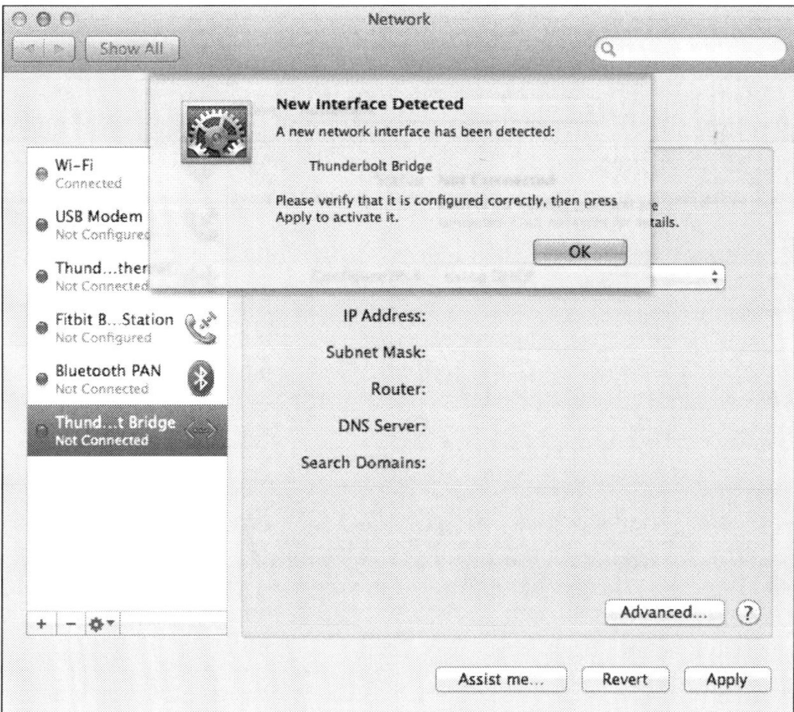

For OS X Lion or later versions, on connecting the Arduino board, a dialog box will appear that will ask you to add a new network interface. In this case, you will not have to navigate to your network preferences. If you see the network interface with the status **Not connected** and highlighted in red, don't worry about it as it should work just fine.

Open the Arduino IDE and navigate to **Serial Port** from the **Tools** menu. You should be able to see options similar to those displayed in the following screenshot. The serial port on which the Arduino board is connected might vary according to your OS X version and the physical port to which it is connected. Make sure that you select a `tty` interface for a USB modem. As displayed in the following screenshot, the Arduino board is connected to the serial port `/dev/tty.usbmodemfd121`:

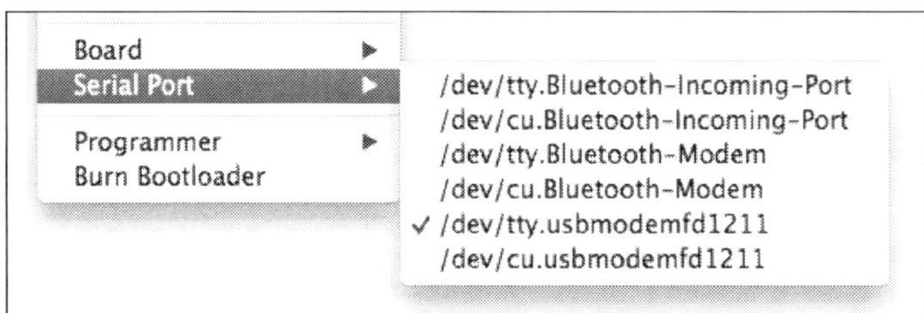

Windows

The configuration of the Arduino serial port is very straightforward if you are using Windows. When you connect your Arduino board the very first time, the operating system will automatically install the necessary drivers by itself. Once this process is complete, select an appropriate COM port from the **Serial Port** option in the menu bar. From the main menu, navigate to **Tools** | **Serial Port** and select the COM port.

Troubleshooting

Even after following the steps mentioned earlier, if you still don't see the highlighted **Serial Port** option as displayed in the following screenshot, then you have got a problem. There can be two main reasons for this: the serial port is being used by another program or the Arduino USB drivers are not installed properly.

If any program other than the Arduino IDE is using the specific serial port, terminate that program and restart the Arduino IDE. Sometimes in Linux, the `brltty` library conflicts with the Arduino serial interface. Remove this library, log out, and log back in:

```
$ sudo apt-get remove brltty
```

In Windows, reinstalling the Arduino IDE also works, as this process installs and configures the Arduino USB driver again.

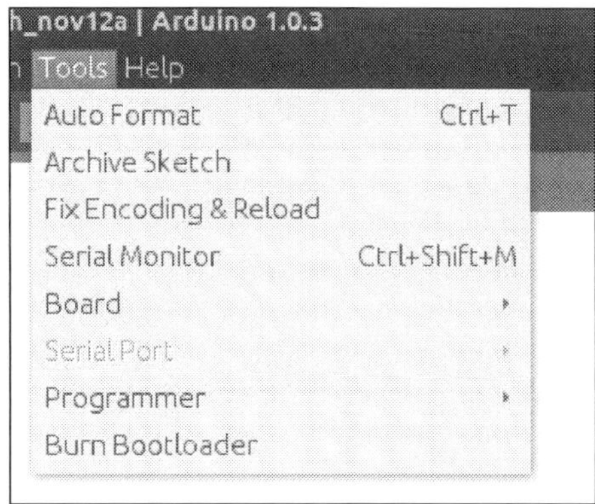

> The Arduino board can be used by only one program at a time. It is very import to make sure that any previously used program or other services are not using the serial port or Arduino when you try to use the Arduino IDE. This check will become very important when we start using multiple programs to control Arduino in the next section.

Assuming that you can now select the serial port in the Arduino IDE, we can go ahead with compiling and uploading sketches to your Arduino board. The Arduino IDE ships with preinstalled example sketches with which you can play around. However, before we go ahead and start playing with complex examples, let's go through the next section, which explains the Firmata protocol and also guides you through step-by-step instructions to compile and upload a sketch.

Introducing the Firmata protocol

Before Arduino, the domain of microcontroller-based applications was limited to hardware programmers. Arduino made it simple for developers that came from other software fields and even for the non-coding community to develop microcontroller-based hardware applications. Arduino consists of a simple hardware design with a microcontroller and I/O pins to interface external devices. If one can write an Arduino sketch that can transfer the control of the microcontroller and these pins to an external software mechanism, then it will reduce one's efforts to upload Arduino sketches for every modification. This process can be performed by developing such an Arduino program that can then be controlled using a serial port. There exists a protocol called **Firmata**, which does exactly that.

What is Firmata?

Firmata is a generic protocol that allows communication between the microcontroller and the software that is hosted on a computer. Any software from any computer host that is capable of serial communication can communicate with the microcontroller using Firmata. Firmata gives complete access of Arduino directly to the software and eliminates the processes of modifying and uploading Arduino sketches.

To utilize the Firmata protocol, a developer can upload a sketch that supports the protocol to the Arduino client as a onetime process. Afterwards, the developer can write custom software on the host computer and perform complex tasks. This software will provide commands via a serial port to the Arduino board that is equipped with Firmata. He or she can keep altering the logic on the host computer without interrupting the Arduino hardware.

The practice of writing custom Arduino sketches is still valid for standalone applications where the Arduino board has to perform a task locally. We will explore both these options in the upcoming chapters.

> You can learn more about the Firmata protocol and its latest version from the official website at `http://www.firmata.org`.

Uploading a Firmata sketch to the Arduino board

The best way to start testing the Firmata protocol is to upload a standard Firmata program to the Arduino board and use the testing software from the host. In this section, we are going to demonstrate a method to upload an Arduino sketch, which has this standard Firmata program, to the board. This is going to be the default method to upload any sketch in the future.

Implementation of the Firmata protocol requires the latest version of the Firmata firmware and you don't have to worry about writing it. The latest Arduino IDE ships with a standard version of the Firmata firmware, and we recommend that you use the latest IDE to avoid any conflict. Now, follow the following steps to upload the program to your Arduino board:

1. As shown in the following screenshot, open the **StandardFirmata** sketch by navigating to **File** | **Examples** | **Firmata** | **StandardFirmata** in the Arduino IDE:

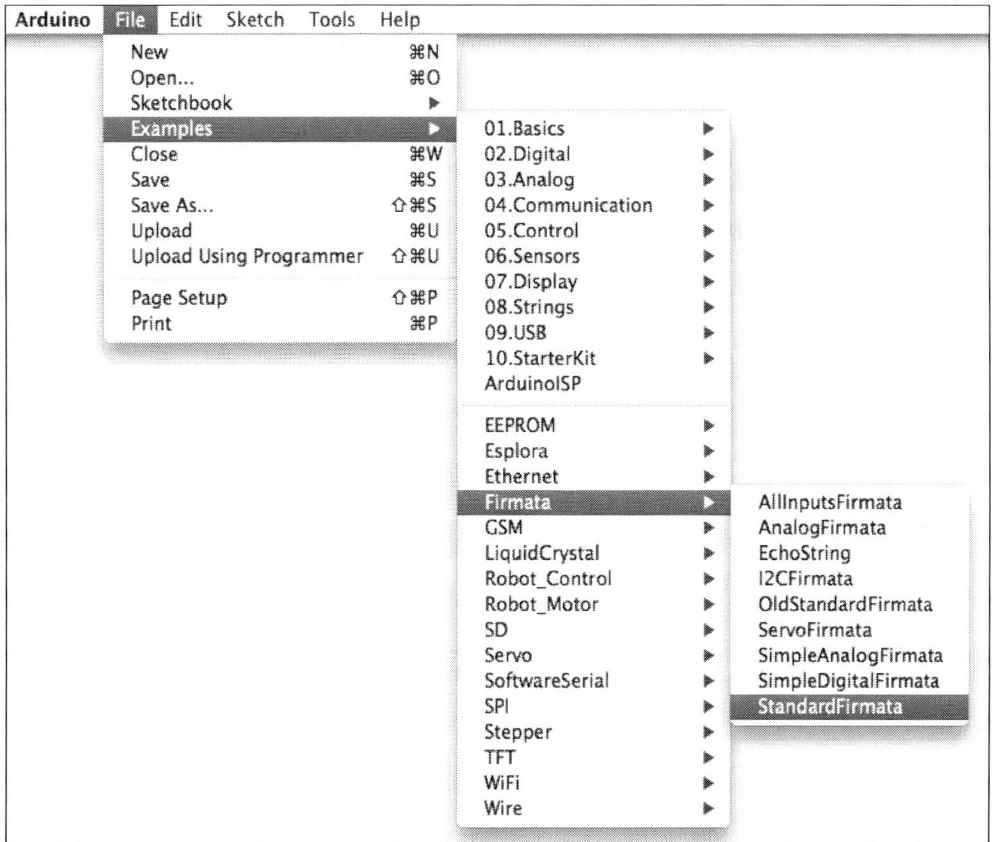

2. This action will open another sketchbook in a new window with the **StandardFirmata** sketch loaded in the editor. Do not modify anything in the sketch and go ahead with the compiling process that is described in the next step. It is important not to modify anything in the code as the test software that we are going to use complies with the latest unchanged firmware.
3. Once the **StandardFirmata** sketch is opened, the next step is to compile it for your Arduino board. In the previous section, we already connected the Arduino board to the computer and selected the proper serial port. However, if the new sketchbook has a different configuration than that, follow the steps from the previous section, that is, select the appropriate serial port and the Arduino board type.

4. To compile the current sketch, click on the **Verify** icon from the toolbar as displayed in the following screenshot. You can also compile it by navigating to **Sketch** | **Verify / Compile** or clicking on *Ctrl* + *R* (*command* + *R* if you are using Mac OS X):

   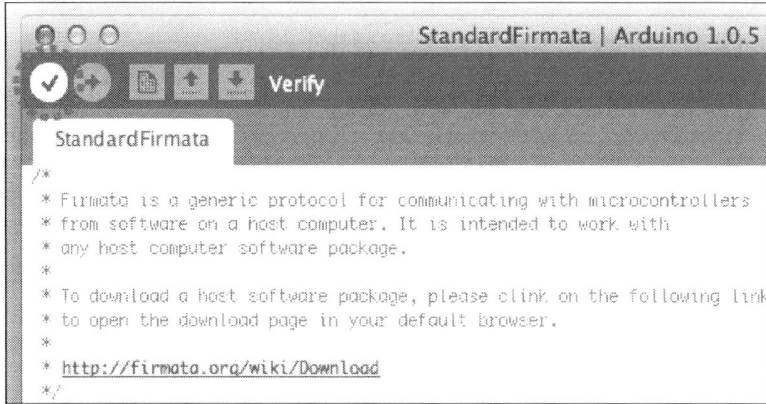

   The compilation process should complete without any errors as we are using default example code from the IDE itself. Now it's time to upload the sketch to the board. Make sure that you have connected the board.

5. Press the upload icon in the toolbar as displayed in the following screenshot. This action will upload the compiled code to your Arduino board:

   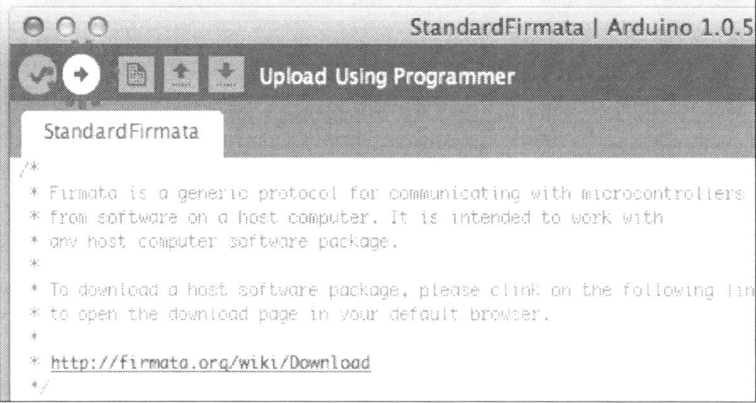

On completion, you should see the **Done uploading.** text in the IDE, as displayed in the following screenshot:

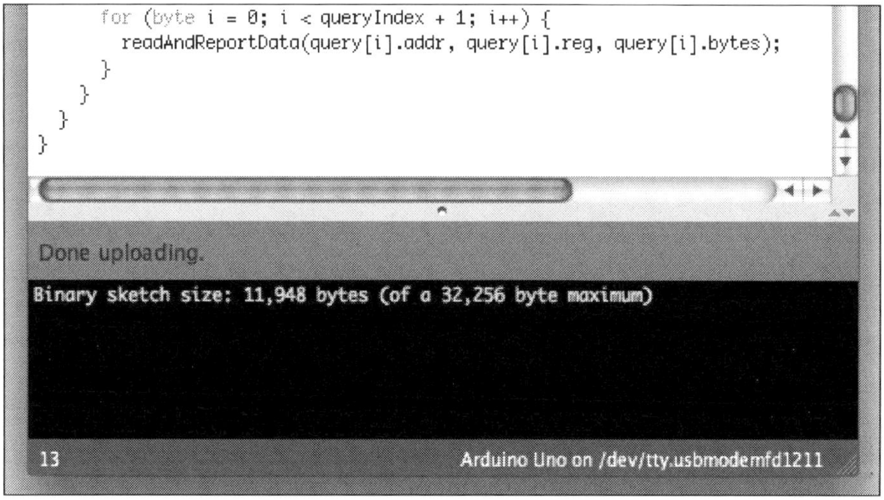

```
      for (byte i = 0; i < queryIndex + 1; i++) {
        readAndReportData(query[i].addr, query[i].reg, query[i].bytes);
      }
    }
  }
}

Done uploading.
Binary sketch size: 11,948 bytes (of a 32,256 byte maximum)

13                                Arduino Uno on /dev/tty.usbmodemfd1211
```

Your Arduino board is now ready with the latest Firmata firmware and is waiting for a request from your computer. Let's move on to the next section and start testing the Firmata protocol.

Testing the Firmata protocol

In the previous chapter, we used an on-board LED at pin 13 to test the **Blink** program. This time, we are going to use an external LED to get you started with the assembly of hardware components using your Arduino board. As all the upcoming exercises and projects will require you to interface hardware components such as sensors and actuators to your Arduino board using a breadboard, we want you to start getting hands-on experience with wiring these components.

Now is the time to use the LED that we asked you to get at the beginning of the chapter. Before we start wiring the LED, let's first understand the physics of it. The LED that you obtained should have two legs: a short one and a long one. The short leg is connected to the cathode of the LED and it needs to be connected to the ground via a resistor. As you can see in the following figure, we are using a 1 k-ohm resistor to ground the cathode of the LED. The long leg, which is connected to the anode, needs to connect to one of the digital pins of the Arduino board.

As shown in the following figure, we have connected the anode to the digital pin number 13. Look at the figure and wire the connection as displayed. Make sure that you disconnect the Arduino board from the host computer to avoid any kind of damage from static electricity.

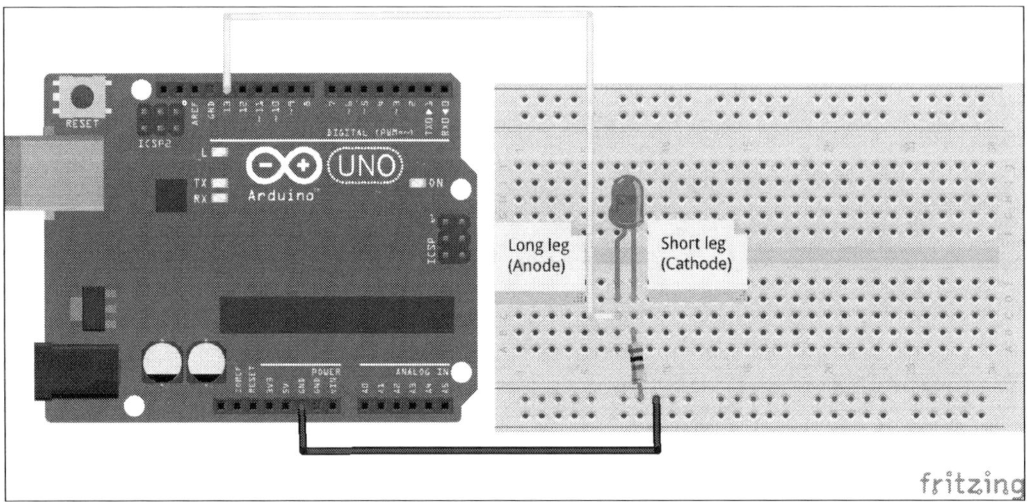

In this example, we are going to use an LED to test some basic functionalities of the Firmata protocol. We have already uploaded the Firmata code to the Arduino board and we are ready to control the LED from the host computer.

The preceding wiring figure was created using an open source tool called **Fritzing**. We are going to cover the Fritzing tool comprehensively in the next chapter, as it will be our standard software to create the wiring diagram before we perform the actual physical wiring.

There are multiple ways to communicate with the Arduino board from the host computer using Firmata, such as writing your own program in Python using the supported library or using the prebuilt testing software. Starting from the next section, we are going to write our own programs to use Firmata, but at this stage, let's use a freely available tool for testing purposes. The official Firmata website, `http://www.firmata.org`, also provides test tools that you can download from the **Firmata Test Program** section on the main page. The website includes a different variant of the tool called `firmata_test` for different operating systems. Using the following steps, you can test the implementation of the Firmata protocol:

1. Download the appropriate version of the `firmata_test` program to your computer.
2. Now, connect your Arduino board with the LED to the host computer using the USB cable and run the downloaded `firmata_test` program. You will be able to see an empty window on the successful execution of the program.
3. As displayed in the following screenshot, select the appropriate port from the drop-down menu. Make sure to select the same port that you used to upload the Arduino sketch.

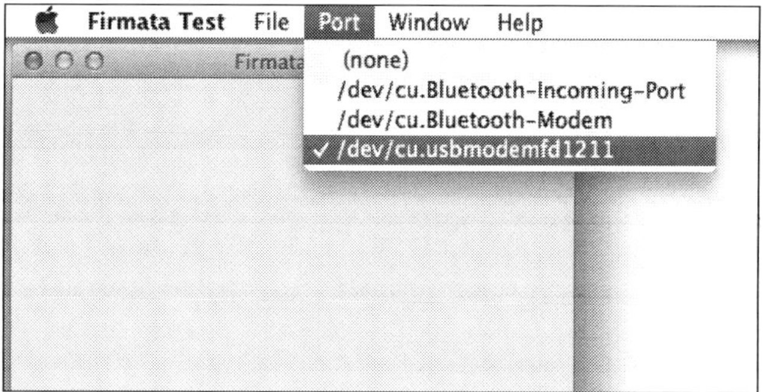

At this point, make sure that your Arduino IDE is not connected to the board using the same port number. As we mentioned earlier, the serial interface grants exclusive access to only one application at a time.

4. Once you select the Arduino serial port, the program will load multiple drop-down boxes and buttons with labels that contain the pin number. You can see in the following screenshot that the program is loaded with 12 digital pins (from pin 2 to pin 13) and six analog pins (from pin 14 to pin 19). As we are using the Arduino Uno board for our applications, the test program only loads pins that are part of Arduino Uno. If you are using Arduino Mega or any other board, the number of pins displayed in the program will be according to the pins supported by that particular variant of the Arduino board.

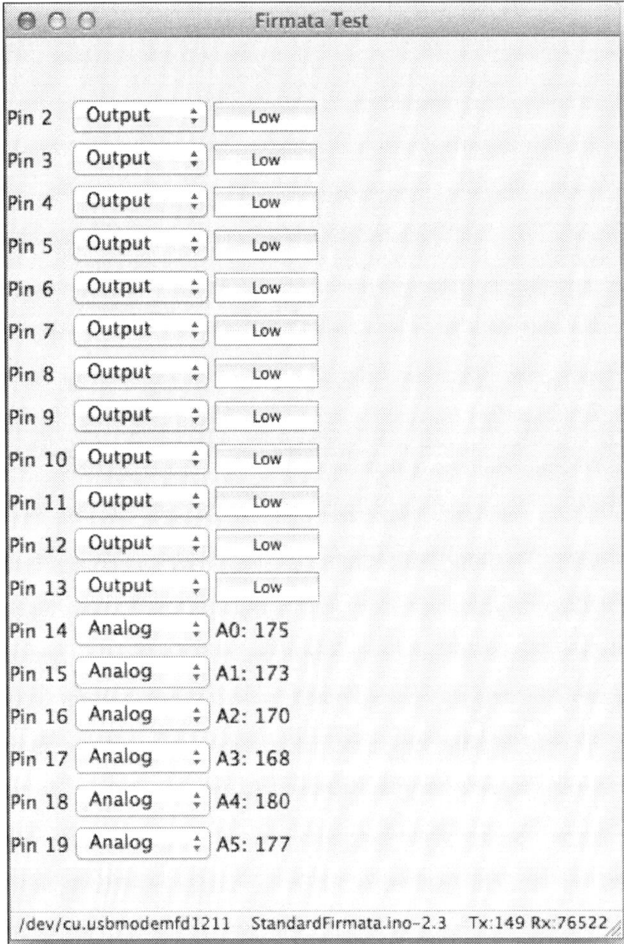

Working with the firmata_test program on Linux

On a Linux platform, you might have to modify the property of the downloaded file and make it executable. From the same directory, run the following command in the terminal to make it executable:

```
$ chmod +x firmata_test
```

Once you have changed the permissions, use the following command to run the program from the terminal:

```
$ ./firmata_test
```

5. As you can see in the program window, you have two other columns as well as the column containing the labels. The second column in the program lets you select the role for the appropriate pins. You can specify the role of digital pins (in the case of Arduino Uno, from 2 to 13) as input or output. As displayed in the following screenshot, you will see **Low** in the third column as soon as you select the role of pins 2 and 3 as input pins. This is correct, as we don't have any input connected to these pins. You can play with the program by changing the roles and values of multiple pins.

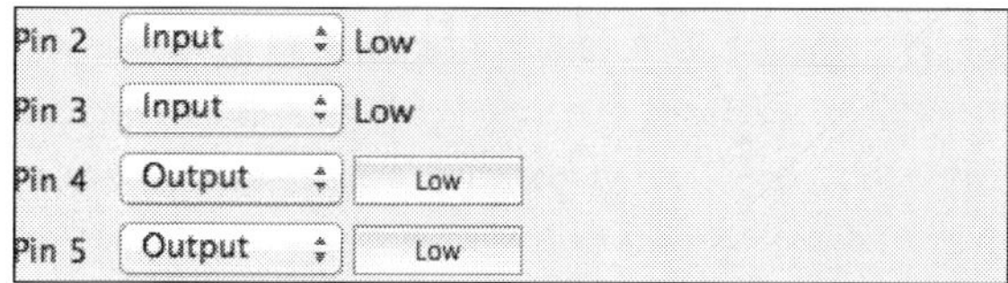

As we have connected the LED to digital pin 13, we are not expecting any physical changes on the board while you are playing around with the other pins.

6. Now, select pin 13 as an output pin and press the **Low** button. This will change the button's label to **High** and you will see that the LED is turned on. By performing this action, we have changed the logic of the digital pin 13 to 1, that is, **High**, which translates to +5 volts at the pin. This potential will be sufficient to light the LED. You can change the level of pin 13 back to 0 by clicking on the button again and turning it to **Low**. This will change the potential back to 0 volts.

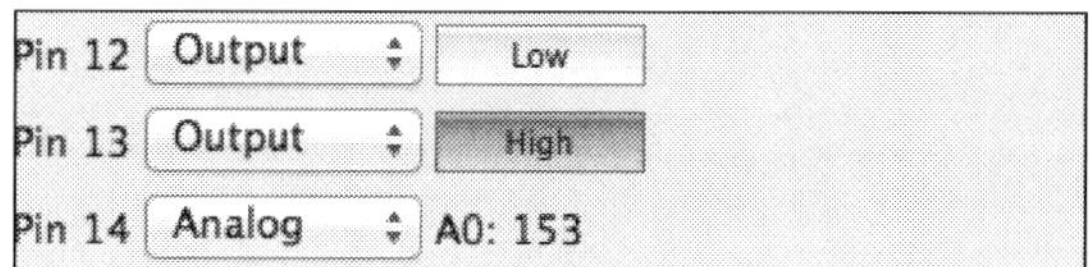

The program that we used here is perfect to test the fundamentals, but it cannot be used to write complex applications using the Firmata protocol. In real-world applications, we really need to execute the Firmata methods using custom code, which in addition to switching the LED status also includes the implementation of smart logic and algorithms, interfacing other components, and so on. We are going to use Python for these applications, starting from the next section.

Getting started with pySerial

You learned about the Firmata protocol in the previous section. This is an easy and quick way to start working with Arduino. Although the Firmata protocol helps you to develop complex applications from your computer without modifying the Arduino sketch, we are not ready to start coding these applications.

The first step towards writing these complex applications is to provide an interface between your programming environment and the Arduino via a serial port. In this book, you will be required to establish a connection between the Python interpreter and Arduino for every project that we develop.

Writing your own library, which includes implementation of functions and specifications to enable communication on a serial protocol, is an inconvenient and time consuming process. We are going to avoid that by using an open source, well maintained Python library called `pySerial`.

The `pySerial` library enables communication with Arduino by encapsulating the access for the serial port. This module provides access to the serial port settings through Python properties and allows you to configure the serial port directly through the interpreter. `pySerial` will be the bridge for any future communication between the Python and Arduino. Let's start by installing `pySerial`.

Installing pySerial

We installed the package manager Setuptools in *Chapter 1, Getting Started with Python and Arduino*. If you have skipped that chapter and are not sure about it, then please go through that section. If you already know how to install and configure Python library packages, skip these installation steps.

From this stage, we are going to use only pip-based installation commands due to their obvious advantages that were described in *Chapter 1, Getting Started with Python and Arduino*:

1. Open a terminal or command prompt and execute the following command:

   ```
   > pip install pyserial
   ```

   The Windows operating system does not require administrator-level user access to execute the command, but you should have root privileges to install Python packages in Unix-based operating systems, as follows:

   ```
   $ sudo pip install pyserial
   ```

   If you want to install the `pySerial` library from source, download the archive from `http://pypi.python.org/pypi/pyserial`, unpack it, and from the `pySerial` directory, run the following command:

   ```
   $ sudo python setup.py install
   ```

2. If Python and Setuptools are installed properly, you should see the following output at the command line after the installation is complete:

   ```
   .
   .
   Processing dependencies for pyserial
   Finished processing dependencies for pyserial
   ```

   This means that you have successfully installed the `pySerial` library and you are good to go to the next section.

3. Now, to check whether or not `pySerial` is successfully installed, start your Python interpreter and import the `pySerial` library using the following command:

   ```
   >>> import serial
   ```

Playing with a pySerial example

Your Arduino board has the Firmata sketch **StandardFirmata** from the previous example. To play with `pySerial`, we are not going to use the Firmata protocol anymore. Instead, we are going to use another simple Arduino sketch that implements serial communication that can be captured on the Python interpreter.

Sticking with the promise of not performing any coding for the Arduino sketch, let's select an example sketch from the Arduino IDE:

1. As displayed in the following screenshot, navigate to **File** | **Examples** | **01. Basics** | **DigitalReadSerial**.

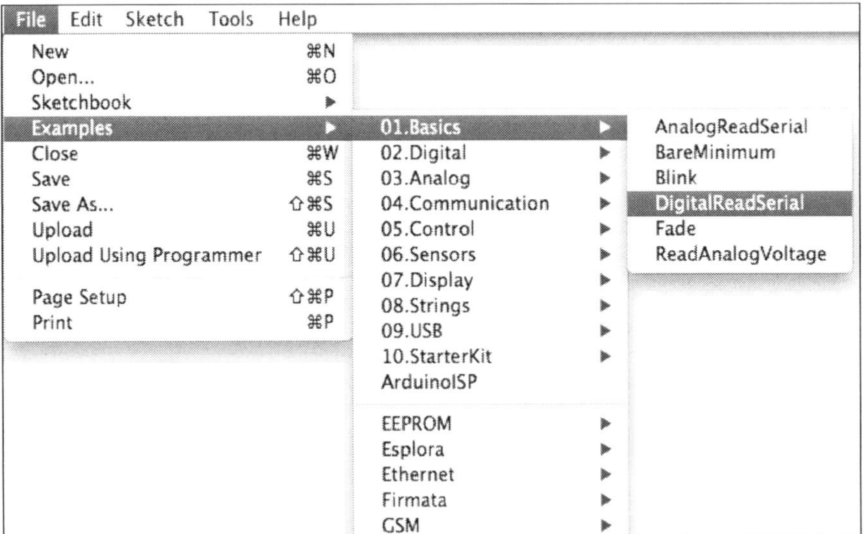

2. Compile and upload the program to the Arduino board using the same method that was described earlier. Select the appropriate serial port on which your Arduino is connected and make a note of it. As you can see in the sketch, this simple Arduino code transmits the status of digital pin 2 that is on the serial port with a baud rate of 9600 bps.
3. Without disconnecting the Arduino board from your computer, open the Python interpreter. Then, execute the following commands on the Python interpreter. Make sure that you replace `/dev/ttyACM0` with the port name that you noted down earlier:

```
>>> import serial
>>> s = serial.Serial('/dev/ttyACM0',9600)
>>> while True:
    print s.readline()
```

4. On execution, you should get repeated `0` values in the Python interpreter. Press *Ctrl* + *C* to terminate this code. As you can see, the Arduino code will keep sending messages due to the loop function that was used in the sketch. We don't have anything connected to pin 2, and because of this, we are getting the status `0`, that is, `Low`.

5. If you know what you are doing, you can connect any digital sensor to pin 2 and run the script again to see the changed status.

In the preceding Python script, the `serial.Serial` method interfaces and opens the specified serial port, while the `readline()` method reads each line from this interface, terminated with `\n`, that is, the newline character.

The newline character is a special character that signifies the end of a line of text. It is also known as **End of Line** (**EOL**) or **Line feed + Carriage Return** (**LF + CR**). Learn more about the newline character at `http://en.wikipedia.org/wiki/Newline`.

Bridging pySerial and Firmata

In the Firmata section, we already learned how useful it is to use the Firmata protocol instead of constantly modifying the Arduino sketch and uploading it for simple programs. `pySerial` is a simple library that provides a bridge between Arduino and Python via a serial port, but it lacks any support for the Firmata protocol. As mentioned earlier, the biggest benefit of Python can be described in one sentence, "There is a library for that." So, there exists a Python library called `pyFirmata` that is built on `pySerial` to support the Firmata protocol. There are a few other Python libraries that also support Firmata, but we will only be focusing on `pyFirmata` in this chapter. We will be extensively using this library for various upcoming projects as well:

1. Let's start by installing `pyFirmata` just like any other Python package by using Setuptools:

   ```
   $ sudo pin install pyfirmata
   ```

   In the previous section, while testing `pySerial`, we uploaded the `DigitalSerialRead` sketch to the Arduino board.

2. To communicate using the Firmata protocol, you need to upload the **StandardFirmata** sketch again, just as we did in the *Uploading a Firmata sketch to the Arduino board* section.

3. Once you have uploaded this sketch, open the Python interpreter and execute the following script. This script imports the `pyfirmata` library to the interpreter. It also defines the pin number and the port.

   ```
   >>> import pyfirmata
   >>> pin= 13
   >>> port = '/dev/ttyACM0'
   ```

4. After this, we need to associate the port with the microcontroller board type:

```
>>> board = pyfirmata.Arduino(port)
```

   While executing the previous script, two LEDs on the Arduino will flicker as the communication link between the Python interpreter and the board gets established. In the *Testing the Firmata protocol* section, we used a prebuilt program to turn an LED on and off. Once the Arduino board is associated to the Python interpreter, these functions can be performed directly from the prompt.

5. You can now start playing with Arduino pins. Turn on the LED by executing the following command:

```
>>> board.digital[pin].write(1)
```

6. You can turn off the LED by executing the following command. Here, in both commands, we set the state of digital pin 13 by passing values `1` (**High**) or `0` (**Low**):

```
>>> board.digital[pin].write(0)
```

7. Similarly, you can also read the status of a pin from the prompt:

```
>>> board.digital[pin].read()
```

If we combined this script in an executable file with a `.py` extension, we can have a Python program that can be run directly to control the LED rather than running these individual scripts on a terminal. Later, this program can be extended to perform complex functions without writing or changing the Arduino sketch.

Although we are running individual scripts at the Python prompt, we will be going through the process of creating Python executable files in the next chapter.

Summary

By introducing the Firmata library, we avoided writing any custom Arduino sketches in this chapter. We will continue this practice during the remaining part of this book and will only use or make custom sketches when required. In this chapter, you interacted with the Arduino board by making the LED blink, which is the easiest way to get started on a hardware project. Now it's time for your first project, where we are also going to make some more LEDs blink. One might ask the question that if we have already done it, then why do we need another project to make LEDs blink? Let's find out.

3
The First Project – Motion-triggered LEDs

In the preceding chapter, you learned the basics of Python-Arduino interfacing. We went through some exercises to provide hands-on experience with a useful Arduino protocol, Firmata, and the Python library. Now, it's time for your first 'Python + Arduino' project.

We will start this chapter by discussing the project goals and the required components to design the software flow and the hardware layout for the project. Just like any other microcontroller-based hardware project, you can use code and implement the entire logic of your project on Arduino itself. However, the goal of this book is to help you to utilize Python in such a way that you can simplify and extend your hardware projects. Although we will be using a hybrid approach with a Python program assisted by an Arduino sketch in the upcoming chapters, we would like you to get familiar with both ways of programming. As this is your first experience of building a hardware project, the chapter provides you with two different programming methods for the project: just using an Arduino sketch and using a Python program with the Firmata protocol on Arduino. The method with the Arduino sketch is included so that you get the complete experience with the Arduino components such as I/O pins and serial communication.

Motion-triggered LEDs – the project description

When you start learning any programming language, in most cases, you will be writing code to print 'Hello World!'. Meanwhile, in hardware projects, the majority of tutorials begin by helping a user to write the code to blink an LED. These exercises or projects are useful for developers to get started with the language, but mostly, they do not carry any importance towards real-world applications. However, we don't want to overwhelm you with a complex and sophisticated project that might require you to have a good amount of domain knowledge.

While working with the Firmata protocol in the previous chapter, we already blinked an LED on the Arduino board. To keep the tradition alive (of having a blinking LED as a first major project) and also build excitement towards the project, let's put a twist in the blinking LED project. In this project, we will blink two different LEDs, but instead of performing these actions in a random manner, we will do it for events that are measured using a motion sensor. Although the difficultly level of the project is simple since it is your first project, it carries real-world application value and can be used as a simple application in your day-to-day life.

The project goal

The project goal can be described in one sentence as follows: "Generate an alert using a red LED for any detected motion and display the normal condition using a green LED." In comprehensive list of goals, you will have to perform the following tasks to satisfy the mentioned project goal:

- Detect any motion in the environment as an event using a **passive infrared** (**PIR**) sensor
- Perform a blink action using a red LED for this event
- Otherwise, perform a blink action using a green LED
- Keep the system in loop after the action has been performed and wait for the next event

The project can be implemented as a DIY application or as part of other projects with minor modifications. The following are some examples where the concepts from this project can be utilized:

- As a DIY security system, to monitor movement in a room (`http://www.instructables.com/id/PIR-Sensor-Security/`)

- In smart home applications, it can be used to automatically turn off lights if no one is present (`http://www.instructables.com/id/Arduino-Home-Monitor-System/`)
- It can be used in automatic garage door opener applications with the support of additional hardware components and appropriate code
- In DIY wildlife recording projects, it can be used to trigger a camera instead of an LED when any motion is detected (`http://www.instructables.com/id/Motion-triggered-camera/`)

The list of components

In the previous chapter, we only used an LED for programming using Arduino, an Arduino USB cable, and a computer. The major hardware component required for this project is a PIR motion sensor. You will also need an additional LED. We recommend that you have a different colored LED than the one that you already have. The description of the necessary components is as follows:

- **PIR sensors**: These are widely used as motion detection sensors for DIY projects. They are small, inexpensive, consume less power, and are compatible with hardware platforms such as Arduino. A PIR sensor uses a pair of pyroelectric sensors that detect infrared radiation. If there is no motion, the output of these sensors cancels each other out. Any movement in the environment will produce different levels of infrared radiation by these pyroelectric sensors and the difference will trigger an output that is `HIGH` (+5 volts). We will be using the PIR sensor that is sold by SparkFun, and you can obtain it from `https://www.sparkfun.com/products/8630`. The PIR sensor comes equipped with the required printed circuit board (PCB). It has range of up to 20 feet (6 meters), which is sufficient for the project. The following image displays the PIR sensor available on the SparkFun website:

Image courtesy: Sparkfun Inc.

Source: Sparkfun Inc.

- **LEDs**: We recommend that you use green and red LEDs for the project. If they are unavailable, you can use any two LEDs with different colors.
- **Wires, resistors, and the breadboard**: You will require a bunch of wires and a breadboard to complete the connections. As a best practice, have at least three different colors of wire connectors to represent power, ground, and signal. You will also need two 220 ohm and one 10 kilo-ohm pull resistors.
- **The Arduino board**: The Arduino Uno board is sufficient for the project requirements. You can also use Arduino Mega or any other Arduino board for this project. The project requires only three I/O pins and any available Arduino board is equipped with more than three I/O pins.
- **A USB cable**: You will need a USB cable to upload the Arduino code and perform serial communication with the Arduino board.
- **A computer**: We have already configured a computer with Python and the Arduino IDE for your favorite operating system in the previous chapters. You will need this computer for the project. Make sure that you have all the software components that we installed and configured in the previous chapters.

The software flow design

The first step, before jumping to work on any hardware system, is to design the project flow using logic. We recommend that you have your project sketched as a flowchart to better understand the layout of the components and the flow of the code. The following diagram shows the flow of the project where you can see that the project runs in loops once motion is detected and the appropriate LED actions are performed:

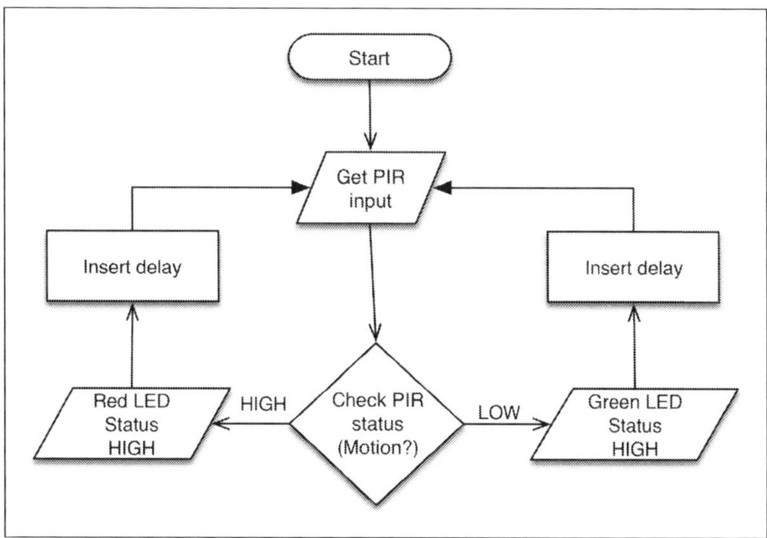

As you can see, the program logic starts by detecting the state of the PIR sensor and performs the appropriate actions accordingly. With a single Arduino instruction, you can only turn the LED on or off. To perform the blinking operation, we will need to repeatedly perform the turning-on and turning-off actions with a time delay between the actions. We will also insert a delay between the execution of each successive loop so that the PIR sensor output can settle down. Note that we will use the same flow when writing the code for both the programming methods.

The hardware system design

Designing a diagram for your software flow helps you to write the program and also assists you in identifying actions and events for the project. The process of hardware system design includes circuit connections, schematic design, simulation, verification, and testing. This design process provides a detailed understanding of the project and the hardware components. It also helps in preliminary verification and testing of the project architecture. Before we jump to the hardware design process of this project, let's get ourselves familiar with the helpful tools.

Introducing Fritzing – a hardware prototyping software

You are not required to design the hardware system for this project. By and large, in this book, the hardware system designs will be provided, as the primary focus of the book is on programming rather than hardware design.

If you are interested in system design or rapid prototyping of the hardware components, the open source software tool used for this purpose is called **Fritzing**. The schematics for your projects can be designed using Fritzing and it can be obtained from `http://fritzing.org/download/`.

Fritzing is a community-supported electronic design automation software initiative for designers, artists, and hobbyists. It lets you convert your hardware sketch from paper to software as a circuit diagram. Fritzing also provides you with a tool to create PCB layouts from your designs. Fritzing extensively supports Arduino and other popular open source DIY hardware platforms. You can explore Fritzing via built-in example projects.

Install and run Fritzing. The following screenshot shows one of the default projects that are displayed after opening Fritzing:

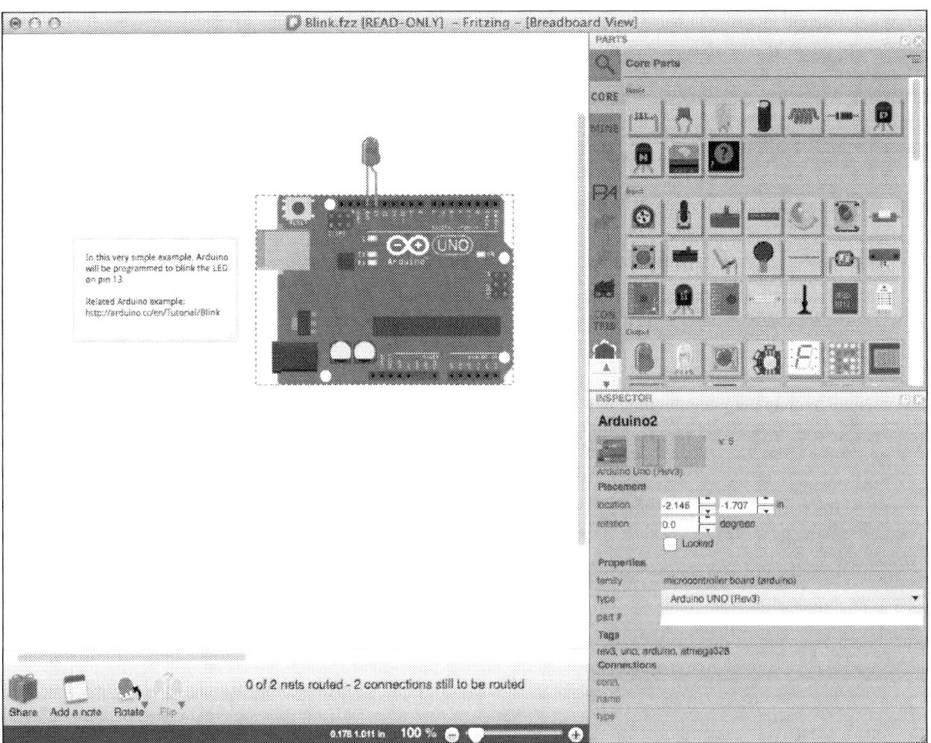

As you can see, a toolbox containing virtual hardware components is located to the right of the opened window. The main editing space, located in the center, lets the user drag and drop components from the toolbox and also allows the user to complete connections between these components. You can learn more about the features provided by Fritzing and go through some hands-on tutorials at `http://fritzing.org/learning/`.

Working with the breadboard

Once you are familiar with Fritzing, you have the flexibility to create your own circuits, or you can always use the Fritzing files provided with the book. However, there is another challenge, that is, porting your virtual circuit to a physical one. One of the fundamental components used by electronics projects that let you implement connections and build the physical circuit is the **breadboard**.

The breadboard contains intelligently organized metal rows hidden under an assembly containing plastic holes. This assembly helps the user to connect wires without going through any soldering work. It is really easy to insert and remove wires or electronics components through the holes. The following figure shows a small breadboard with a couple of components and a few wire connections:

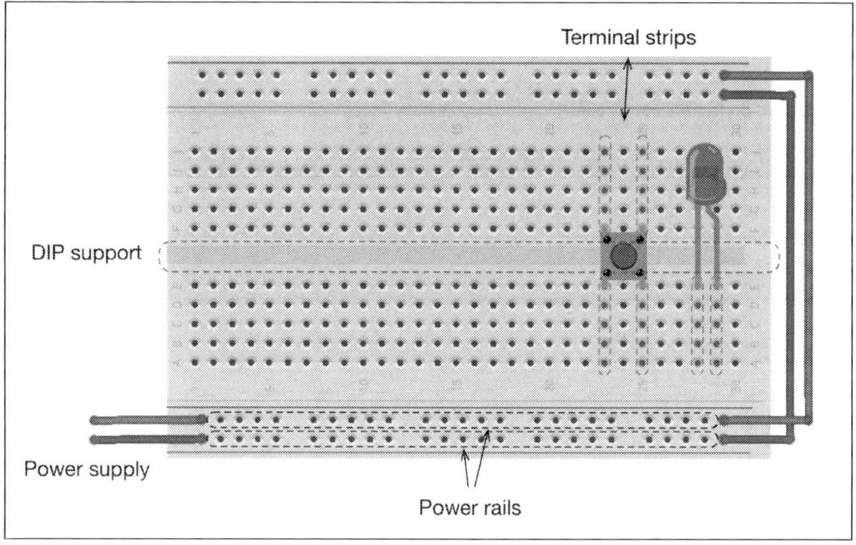

Find out more about breadboards and the tutorials to use them at `http://learn.sparkfun.com/tutorials/how-to-use-a-breadboard`.

A breadboard mostly has two types of connection strips: terminal strips and power rails. As displayed in the preceding figure, terminal strips are vertical columns with electrically shorted holes. In simple words, once you connect any component to one of the terminal strips, the component will be electrically connected to each hole in the column. The columns of terminal strips are separated by the **Dual in-line Package (DIP)** support gap. (DIP is a common housing for electronics components.) In the same column, terminal strips above and below the DIP support gap are electrically independent. Meanwhile, the power rails are shorted horizontally throughout the entire row of the breadboard. The power rails are mostly used to connect positive and ground connections from the power supply, so it can be distributed easily to all components.

History of breadboards

In the early years of electronics, people used actual breadboards (that were used to cut bread) to connect their large components with just nails and wires. Once electronics components started getting smaller, the board to assemble circuits also became better. The term stuck through this evolution, and we still call the modern boards breadboards. If you are interested, you can check out `http://www.instructables.com/id/Use-a-real-Bread-Board-for-prototyping-your-circui/`, which provides instructions to assemble a circuit using the original breadboards.

Designing the hardware prototype

It's time to collect the hardware components mentioned earlier and start building the system. The next figure shows the circuit for the project that has been developed using Fritzing. If you have prior experience of working with circuit assembly, go ahead and connect the components as displayed in the figure:

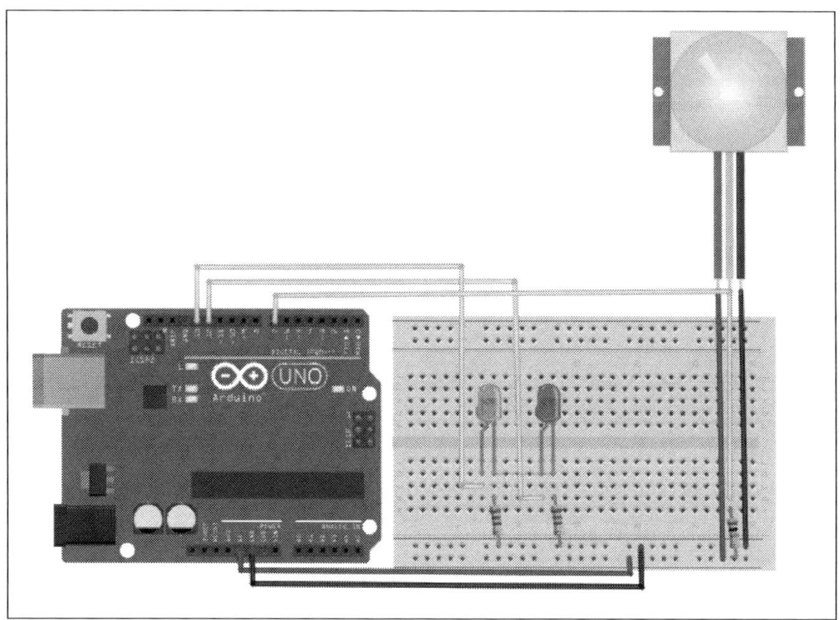

If this is your first experience of working with sensors and the breadboard, use the following steps to complete the circuit assembly:

1. Connect VCC (+5V) and ground from the Arduino to the breadboard.
2. Connect the anode (long lead) of the red LED to digital pin 12 of the Arduino board. Connect the cathode (short lead) of the red LED to ground with 220 ohm resistors.
3. Connect the anode (long lead) of the green LED to digital pin 13 of the Arduino board. Connect the cathode (short lead) of the green LED to ground with 220 ohm resistors.
4. Connect VDD of the PIR sensor to VCC on the breadboard. Use the same wire color to represent the same category of connections. This will greatly help in troubleshooting the circuit.
5. Connect the signal (middle pin) of the PIR sensor to Arduino digital pin 7 with a 10 kilo-ohm pull-up resistor.

The majority of experts prefer a schematic diagram instead of the prototype diagram that we used previously. Schematic diagrams are useful when you are using compatible components instead of the exact components from the prototype diagram. The following is a schematic diagram of the electronics circuit that we designed earlier. This diagram is also obtained using Fritzing:

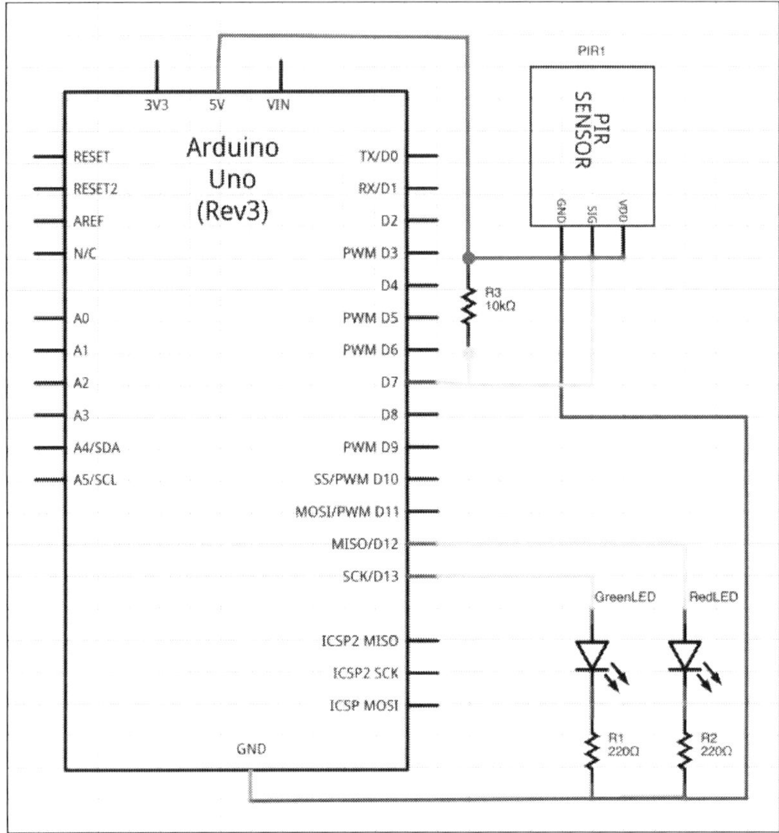

Your system is now ready to run the Arduino program. As we will be using the same hardware for both the programming methods, you are almost done working with electronics unless you encounter a problem. Just to make sure that everything is connected perfectly, let's check out these connections in the next section.

Note that pull-up resistors are used to make sure that the output signal from a PIR sensor settles at the expected logic level.

Testing hardware connections

Once the circuit connections are complete, you can go directly to the programming sections. As a best practice, we recommend that you verify the circuit connections and check the sensor's status. We are assuming that your Arduino board is already equipped with the **StandardFirmata** sketch that we discussed in the previous chapter. Otherwise, refer to the previous chapter and upload the **StandardFirmata** sketch to your Arduino board.

The best way to verify our circuit implementation is to use the Firmata test program that we used in the previous chapter. According to the project setup, the PIR sensor provides event inputs to Arduino pin 7. In the test program, change the type of pin 7 to **Input** and wave your hand over the sensor, and you should be able to see the status of the pin as **High**, as displayed in the following screenshot:

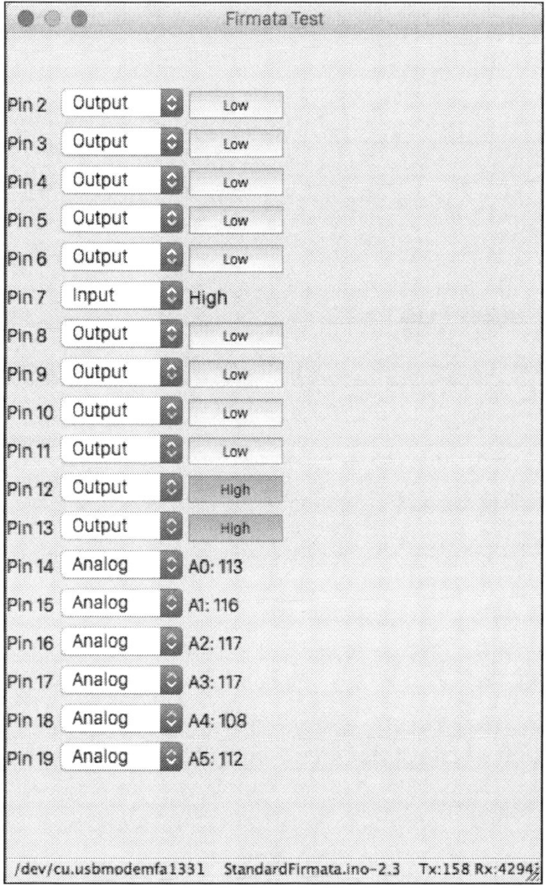

Check the LED connections by setting up pins 12 and 13 as output pins and toggling the buttons to set the status of the pins. If you see the LEDs blinking while you are toggling the button, then your connections are working perfectly.

If you cannot successfully perform these checks, verify and repeat the design steps.

Method 1 – using a standalone Arduino sketch

As we discussed in the previous chapters, a project can be implemented by creating project-specific native Arduino code or by using a Python-Arduino hybrid approach.

The native Arduino sketches are useful in applications where negligible or no communication with a computer system is required. Although this type of standalone project enables continuous operation in the absence of serial connectivity, it is difficult to keep updating and uploading an Arduino sketch for minor modifications.

If you look at the various applications of this project, you will notice that only a few of them require the project to be implemented as a standalone system that just detects motion and blinks LEDs. This type of system can be easily implemented by a simple Arduino sketch.

The project setup

Before we go ahead with the project, make sure that you have the following things in place:

- The hardware components are set up and are functioning correctly
- Your Arduino is connected to the computer using a USB cable
- Your computer has the Arduino IDE and you can access the connected Arduino board through the IDE

The Arduino sketch

This section describes the Arduino code for the project. Before we get into a step-by-step description of the code, let's first follow these steps to run the project:

1. Open the Arduino IDE.
2. From the **File** menu, open a new sketchbook.

3. Copy the following Arduino code to the sketch and save it:

```
int pirPin = 7; //Pin number for PIR sensor
int redLedPin = 12; //Pin number for Red LED
int greenLedPin = 13; //Pin number for Green LED

void setup(){
 Serial.begin(9600);
 pinMode(pirPin, INPUT);
 pinMode(redLedPin, OUTPUT);
 pinMode(greenLedPin, OUTPUT);
}
void loop(){
  int pirVal = digitalRead(pirPin);
  if(pirVal == LOW){ //was motion detected
    blinkLED(greenLedPin, "No motion detected.");
  } else {
    blinkLED(redLedPin, "Motion detected.");
  }
}
// Function which blinks LED at specified pin number
void blinkLED(int pin, String message){
  digitalWrite(pin,HIGH);
  Serial.println(message);
  delay(1000);
  digitalWrite(pin,LOW);
  delay(2000);
}
```

4. Compile and upload the sketch to the Arduino board.

Now, you have completed your project with the first programming method and successfully deployed it to your hardware. It should be running the designed algorithm to detect motion events and perform the blink action.

As your project is functioning properly, it's time to understand the code. Like any other Arduino program, the code has two mandatory functions: `setup()` and `loop()`. It also has a custom function, `blinkLED()`, for a specific action that will be explained later.

The setup() function

As you can see in the preceding code snippet, we assigned variables to the Arduino pin at the beginning of the program. In the `setup()` function, we configured these variables to be defined as input or output pins:

```
pinMode(pirPin, INPUT);
pinMode(redLedPin, OUTPUT);
pinMode(greenLedPin, OUTPUT);
```

Here, `pirPin`, `redLedPin`, and `greenLedPin` are digital pins 7, 12, and 13 respectively. In the same function, we also configured the Arduino board to provide serial connectively at the baud rate of 9600 bps:

```
Serial.begin(9600);
```

The loop() function

In the `loop()` function, we are repeatedly monitoring the input from the `pirPin` digital pin to detect motion. The output of this pin is `HIGH` when motion is detected and `LOW` otherwise. This logic is implemented using a simple `if-else` statement. When this condition is satisfied, the function calls a user-defined function, `blinkLED()`, to perform the appropriate action on the LEDs.

User-defined functions are a very important aspect of any programming language. Let's spend some time learning how you can create your own Arduino functions to perform various actions.

Working with custom Arduino functions

Functions are used when a segment of code is repeatedly executed to perform the same action. A user can create a custom function to organize the code or perform reoccurring actions. To successfully utilize a custom function, a user needs to call them from mandatory Arduino functions such as `loop()`, `setup()`, or any other function that leads to these mandatory functions:

```
return-type function_name (parameters){
  # Action to be performed
  Action_1;
  Action_2;
  Return expression;
}
```

In the preceding Arduino function framework, `return-type` can be any Arduino data type such as `int`, `float`, `string`, and so on, or `void` if the code is not returning anything. The following is the custom function that we used in our project code:

```
void blinkLED(int pin, String message){
  digitalWrite(pin,HIGH);
  Serial.println(message);
  delay(1000);
  digitalWrite(pin,LOW);
  delay(2000);
}
```

In our project, the `blinkLED()` function is not retuning any value when it is called from the `loop()` function. Hence, `return-type` is `void`. When calling the function, we pass the pin number and a message as parameters:

```
blinkLED(greenLedPin, "No motion detected.");
```

These parameters are then utilized in the performed action (writing a message on a serial port and setting up the LED status) by the `blinkLED()` function. This function also introduces a delay to perform the blink action by using the `delay()` function.

Testing

We verified the designed system in the *Testing hardware connection* section using manual inputs via the Firmata test program. As we have now implemented the software design, we need to verify that the project is performing objective tasks autonomously and repeatedly.

With the USB port connected to the computer, open the serial monitoring tool from the Arduino IDE by navigating to **Tools** | **Serial Monitor** or by pressing *Ctrl* + *Shift* + *M*. You should start seeing a message similar to the one displayed in the following screenshot on the **Serial Monitor** window:

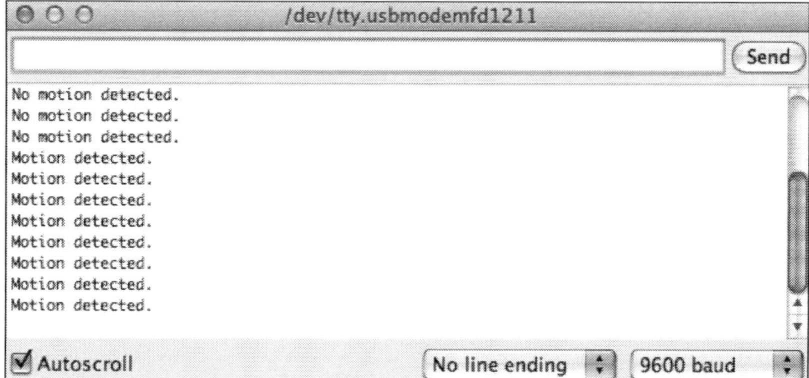

While writing the `blinkLED()` function to perform actions, we included an action to write a string via a serial port. Move your hand over the PIR sensor in such a way that the PIR sensor can detect motion. This event should trigger the system to blink the red LED and display a string, `Motion detected`, on the serial monitor. Once you stay steady and avoid any motion for a while, you will be able to see the green LED blinking until the next movement gets detected via the PIR sensor.

Troubleshooting

Troubleshooting is an important process if anything goes awry. These are a few example problems and the troubleshooting steps for them:

- Serial output is correct, but there are no blinking LEDs:
  - Check the LED connections on the breadboard
- The LED blinks, but there is no serial output:
  - Check the port on which the serial monitor is configured
  - Check whether the baud rate in the serial monitor is correct (9600 bps)
- There is no serial output and no blinking LEDs:
  - Check the PIR sensor connection and make sure that you are getting signal from the PIR sensor
  - Check your Arduino code
  - Check power and ground connections

Method 2 – using Python and Firmata

In the previous chapter, we discussed the benefits of using Python programming that is assisted by Firmata over using native Arduino sketches. The Python-based programming approach provides tangible experience when performing any algorithmic or parametric changes. In this section, we are going to explore these benefits and also learn important Python programming paradigms.

The project setup

Let's make sure that you have done the following before we go ahead with Python programming:

- Made sure that the hardware components are set up, as described in the system design

- Connected the Arduino to your computer using a USB cable
- Uploaded the **StandardFirmata** sketch back to Arduino
- Made sure that you have Python and the Python packages (`pySerial` and `pyFirmata`) installed on your computer
- Obtained a text editor to write Python codes

Working with Python executable files

In the previous chapters, we explored Python programming using the interactive Python interpreter. However, when working with large projects, it is very difficult to keep using the Python interactive interpreter for repetitive tasks. Like other programming languages, the preferred method is to create Python executable files and run them from the terminal.

Python executable files carry the `.py` extension and are formatted as plain text. Any text editor can be used to create these files. The popular editors used to create and edit Python files are Notepad++, nano, vi, and so on. This list also includes the default editor that is shipped with the Python setup files called IDLE. You can use the editor of your choice, but make sure that you save the files with the `.py` extension. Let's copy the following lines of code in a new file and save it as `test.py`:

```
#!/usr/bin/python
a = "Python"
b = "Programming"
print a + " "+ b
```

To run this file, execute the following command on the terminal where the `test.py` file is saved:

```
$ python test.py
```

You should be able to see the text `Python Programming` printed on the terminal. As you can see, the file starts with `#!/usr/bin/python`, which is the default Python installation location. By adding this line in your Python code, you can directly execute a Python file from the terminal. In Unix-based operating systems, you need to make the `test.py` file executable through the following command:

```
$ chmod +x test.py
```

Now, as your file is executable, you can directly run the file using the following command:

```
$./test.py
```

For Unix-based operating systems, an alternative way to provide the Python interpreter location is to use the following line of code instead of the one that we used:

```
#!/usr/bin/env python
```

In Windows operating systems, Python files automatically become executable because of the `.py` extension. You can just run the program files by double-clicking and opening them.

The Python code

As you now know how to create and run Python code, let's create a new Python file with the following code snippet and run it. Make sure to change the value of the `port` variable according to your operating system, as described in the previous chapter:

```
#!/usr/bin/python

# Import required libraries
import pyfirmata
from time import sleep

# Define custom function to perform Blink action
def blinkLED(pin, message):
    print message
    board.digital[pin].write(1)
    sleep(1)
    board.digital[pin].write(0)
    sleep(1)

# Associate port and board with pyFirmata
port = '/dev/ttyACM0'
board = pyfirmata.Arduino(port)

# Use iterator thread to avoid buffer overflow
it = pyfirmata.util.Iterator(board)
it.start()

# Define pins
pirPin = board.get_pin('d:7:i')
redPin = 12
greenPin = 13
```

```
# Check for PIR sensor input
while True:
    # Ignore case when receiving None value from pin
    value = pirPin.read()
    while value is None:
        pass

    if value is True:
        # Perform Blink using custom function
        blinkLED(redPin, "Motion Detected")

    else:
        # Perform Blink using custom function
        blinkLED(greenPin, "No motion Detected")

# Release the board
board.exit()
```

You have successfully created and executed your first Arduino project using Python. There are two main programming components in this code: `pyFirmata` methods and the Python function to perform the blinking action. The program repeatedly detects the motion events and performs the blinking action. In the previous section, this problem was solved by using the default Arduino function `loop()`. In this method, we have implemented the `while` statement to keep the program in loop until the code is manually terminated by the user. You can terminate the code using the keyboard combination *Ctrl* + *C*.

Working with pyFirmata methods

As part of working with the Arduino board and the Firmata protocol, you have to start by initializing the Arduino board as a variable. The `pyFirmata` method that lets a user assign the board to a Python variable is as follows:

```
board = pyfirmata.Arduino(port)
```

Once the value of the variable is assigned, you can perform various actions such as reading a pin or sending a signal to the pin using that variable. To assign a role to a pin, the `get_pin()` method is used. In the following line of code, `d` represents the digital pin, `7` is the pin number, and `i` represents that the type of pin is an input pin:

```
pirPin = board.get_pin('d:7:i')
```

Once a pin and its role are assigned to a variable, that variable can be used to read or write values on the pin:

```
Value = pirPin.read()
```

One can directly write data to a specific pin, as described in following code:

```
board.digital[pin].write(1)
```

Here, the `write(1)` method sends a `HIGH` signal to the pin. We will be learning additional `pyFirmata` methods in the upcoming chapters.

Working with Python functions

A Python function begins with the `def` keyword followed by the function name and the input parameters or arguments. The function definition ends with a colon (`:`) and it is indented afterwards. The `return` statement terminates the function. It also passes the expression to the place where the function is called. If the `return` statement is kept without an expression, it is considered to pass the return value `None`:

```
def function_name(parameters):
  action_1
  action_2
  return [expression]
```

The preceding framework can be used to create custom functions to perform recurring tasks. In our project, we have the `blinkLED(pin, message)` function to perform the blinking LED action. This function sends `1` (`HIGH`) and `0` (`LOW`) value to the specified digital pin while also printing `message` on the terminal. It also introduces delay to simulate the blinking action:

```
def blinkLED(pin, message):
    print message
    board.digital[pin].write(1)
    sleep(1)
    board.digital[pin].write(0)
    sleep(1)
```

Testing

You can start testing the project as soon as you run the Python code on the terminal. If everything goes according to design, you should be able to see the following output in the terminal:

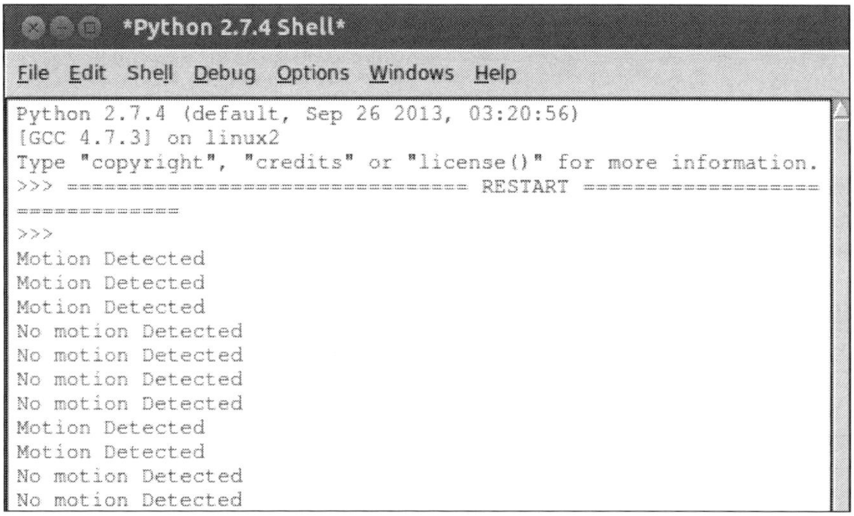

```
*Python 2.7.4 Shell*
File Edit Shell Debug Options Windows Help
Python 2.7.4 (default, Sep 26 2013, 03:20:56)
[GCC 4.7.3] on linux2
Type "copyright", "credits" or "license()" for more information.
>>> ================================ RESTART ==================
=============
>>>
Motion Detected
Motion Detected
Motion Detected
No motion Detected
No motion Detected
No motion Detected
No motion Detected
Motion Detected
Motion Detected
No motion Detected
No motion Detected
```

You should be able to see the `Motion Detected` string on the terminal when any motion is detected by the PIR sensor. If you find any abnormal behavior in the output, then please check the Python code.

A benefit of using Python is that minor modifications such as changing the blinking speed or swapping roles of the LEDs can be performed by just changing the Python code, without dealing with the Arduino or the electrical circuit.

Troubleshooting

When you run the project, you might require troubleshooting for the following probable problems:

- Serial output is correct, but there are no blinking LEDs:
    - Check the LED connections on the breadboard
- The LED blinks, but there is no serial output:
    - Check whether you have successfully installed the standard Firmata sketch to the board

- There is no serial output and no blinking LEDs:
    - Check whether any program other than Python is using the serial port. Close any program that might be using that serial port, including the Arduino IDE.
    - Verify all the circuit connections.
    - Make sure that the port name specified in the Python code is correct.

Summary

Between the two programming methods that you learned in this chapter, the method that uses just an Arduino sketch represents the traditional paradigm of programming a microcontroller. While this method is simple to implement, it lacks the extensiveness that is achieved by Python-Arduino interfacing. Although we will use extensive Arduino coding in all the projects beginning from now, exercises and projects will have Python-Arduino interfacing as the primary way of programming.

Starting from the next chapter, we are going to explore the additional aspects of Python programming that can extend the usability of an Arduino-based hardware project while keeping the programming difficulty levels to a minimum. We will begin with Python-Arduino prototyping and then create graphical interfaces for user interaction, before stopping for the second project that utilizes these concepts.

4
Diving into Python-Arduino Prototyping

On the completion of the first project, you successfully started Python-Arduino interfacing. We also interfaced multiple hardware components, that is, motion sensor and LEDs with Arduino via digital pins. During the project, you learned more about the Firmata protocol while utilizing simple Python methods that helped you to establish a connection between your Arduino board and the Python program. When you are working on complex projects, you need more than basic methods to implement the different features that are required by the projects and their associated electronics components. This chapter is designed to give you a comprehensive experience of interfacing so that you can start working on hard problems from the next chapter onwards. We have described various interfacing protocols at the Python-Arduino and Arduino-to-components levels. This chapter also includes practical examples for these protocols with appropriate code and circuit diagrams. In this chapter, we are going to cover the following main topics:

- Introduction to Prototyping
- Detailed description of various `pyFirmata` methods to port Arduino functionalities into Python
- Python-Arduino interfacing examples using Firmata for basic electronic components such as the potentiometer, the buzzer, the DC motor, and the servomotor
- Introduction to the **inter-integrated circuit** (**I2C**) protocol and prototyping examples for the I2C components such as the temperature sensor (TMP102) and the light sensor (BH1750)

Prototyping

Just for a moment, let's step back and look at the project that we built in the previous chapter. The project had a very simple goal and we were able to develop it quite comfortably. However, the project is certainly not ready to be a consumer product since it doesn't have significant functionalities and most importantly, it is not a robust product that can be repeatedly produced as it is. What you can tell about your current project is that it is a DIY project for personal use or just a model that can be developed further to be a great product.

Now, if you are looking to develop a commercial product or just a DIY project that is really robust and scalable, you must consider starting it by making a model first. At this stage, you need to envision the product with the required features that need to be developed and the number of components that are required to deploy these features. Prototyping is basically a rapid way to create a working model of your envisioned idea before developing it into a fully functional project or product. The proof of concept prototype that is developed during this prototyping process lets you to identify the feasibility of your idea, and in some cases, it helps you to explore the potential of your project. The prototyping or functional model-making process is essential for any industry and not just for electronics.

In the electronics domain, prototyping can be used at the very first stage of interfacing components to a computer, instead of directly spending a significant amount of resources for the schematic design, PCB manufacturing, and developing the complete code base. This stage helps you to identify major flaws in your circuit design and check the mutual compatibility of the selected components.

Fortunately, Arduino and the existing software support around Arduino have really simplified electronics' prototyping. In the upcoming sections, we will go through various helper functions and interfacing exercises to help you proceed with your own projects. These examples or templates are designed in such a fashion that they can be used as a blueprint for larger projects.

Before diving into these prototyping examples, let's understand two different abstractions of interfacing that we are going to explore in this chapter:

- **Interfacing Arduino with Python**: We have learned the easiest method of Python-Arduino interfacing using the Firmata protocol. On the Arduino board, the Firmata protocol is implemented using the **StandardFirmata** firmware, while on the Python end, we used the Firmata libraries, `pyFirmata` or `pyMata`, for Python. Another Python-Arduino interfacing method includes the use of simple but nonstandard serial commands using the custom Arduino sketch and the `pySerial` library in the Python program. It is also possible to use a computer network to establish communication between Python and Arduino, which is covered later in the book.

- **Interfacing electronic components with Arduino**: The second interfacing abstraction is associated with Arduino and the physical components. As we already did, various electronics components can be simply interfaced with the Arduino board using digital or analog pins. These components deal with either digital or analog signals. A few digital pins on the Arduino board support PWM communication for specific hardware devices. The other alternative interfacing methods include I2C and **serial peripheral interface (SPI)** communication. The I2C method is comprehensively explained in the final section of this chapter.

Working with pyFirmata methods

The `pyFirmata` package provides useful methods to bridge the gap between Python and Arduino's Firmata protocol. Although these methods are described with specific examples, you can use them in various different ways. This section also provides a detailed description of a few additional methods that were not used in the previous project and lists the missing features.

Setting up the Arduino board

To set up your Arduino board in a Python program using `pyFirmata`, you need to specifically follow the steps that we have covered. We have distributed the entire code that is required for the setup process into small code snippets in each step. While writing your code, you will have to carefully use the code snippets that are appropriate for your application. You can always refer to the example Python files containing the complete code. Before we go ahead, let's first make sure that your Arduino board is equipped with the latest version of the **StandardFirmata** program and is connected to your computer:

1. Depending upon the Arduino board that is being utilized, start by importing the appropriate `pyFirmata` classes to the Python code. Currently, the inbuilt `pyFirmata` classes only support the Arduino Uno and Arduino Mega boards:

   ```
   from pyfirmata import Arduino
   ```

   In the case of Arduino Mega, use the following line of code:

   ```
   from pyfirmata import ArduinoMega
   ```

2. Before we start executing any methods that are associated with handling pins, you need to properly set up the Arduino board. To perform this task, we have to first identify the USB port to which the Arduino board is connected and assign this location to a variable in the form of a string object. For Mac OS X, the port string should approximately look like this:

   ```
   port = '/dev/cu.usbmodemfa1331'
   ```

   For Windows, use the following string structure:

   ```
   port = 'COM3'
   ```

   In the case of the Linux operating system, use the following line of code:

   ```
   port = '/dev/ttyACM0'
   ```

   The port's location might be different according to your computer configuration. You can identify the correct location of your Arduino USB port by using the Arduino IDE, as described in *Chapter 2, Working with the Firmata Protocol and the pySerial Library*.

3. Once you have imported the Arduino class and assigned the port to a variable object, it's time to engage Arduino with `pyFirmata` and associate this relationship to another variable:

   ```
   board = Arduino(port)
   ```

   Similarly, for Arduino Mega, use this:

   ```
   board = ArduinoMega(port)
   ```

4. The synchronization between the Arduino board and `pyFirmata` requires some time. Adding sleep time between the preceding assignment and the next set of instructions can help to avoid any issues that are related to serial port buffering. The easiest way to add sleep time is to use the inbuilt Python method, `sleep(time)`:

   ```
   from time import sleep
   sleep(1)
   ```

   The `sleep()` method takes seconds as the parameter and a floating-point number can be used to provide the specific sleep time. For example, for 200 milliseconds, it will be `sleep(0.2)`.

At this point, you have successfully synchronized your Arduino Uno or Arduino Mega board to the computer using `pyFirmata`. What if you want to use a different variant (other than Arduino Uno or ArduinoMega) of the Arduino board?

- Any board layout in `pyFirmata` is defined as a dictionary object. The following is a sample of the dictionary object for the Arduino board:

```
arduino = {
    'digital' : tuple(x for x in range(14)),
    'analog' : tuple(x for x in range(6)),
    'pwm' : (3, 5, 6, 9, 10, 11),
    'use_ports' : True,
    'disabled' : (0, 1) # Rx, Tx, Crystal
}
```

- For your variant of the Arduino board, you have to first create a custom dictionary object. To create this object, you need to know the hardware layout of your board. For example, an Arduino Nano board has a layout similar to a regular Arduino board, but it has eight instead of six analog ports. Therefore, the preceding dictionary object can be customized as follows:

```
nano = {
    'digital' : tuple(x for x in range(14)),
    'analog' : tuple(x for x in range(8)),
    'pwm' : (3, 5, 6, 9, 10, 11),
    'use_ports' : True,
    'disabled' : (0, 1) # Rx, Tx, Crystal
}
```

- As you have already synchronized the Arduino board earlier, modify the layout of the board using the `setup_layout(layout)` method:

```
board.setup_layout(nano)
```

  This command will modify the default layout of the synchronized Arduino board to the Arduino Nano layout or any other variant for which you have customized the dictionary object.

Configuring Arduino pins

Once your Arduino board is synchronized, it is time to configure the digital and analog pins that are going to be used as part of your program. Arduino board has digital I/O pins and analog input pins that can be utilized to perform various operations. As we already know, some of these digital pins are also capable of PWM.

The direct method

Now before we start writing or reading any data to these pins, we have to first assign modes to these pins. In the Arduino sketch-based approach that we used in the previous chapter, we used the `pinMode` function, that is, `pinMode(11, INPUT)` for this operation. Similarly, in `pyFirmata`, this assignment operation is performed using the `mode` method on the board object as shown in the following code snippet:

```
from pyfirmata import Arduino
from pyfirmata import INPUT, OUTPUT, PWM

# Setting up Arduino board
port = '/dev/cu.usbmodemfa1331'
board = Arduino(port)

# Assigning modes to digital pins
board.digital[13].mode = OUTPUT
board.analog[0].mode = INPUT
```

The `pyFirmata` library includes classes for the `INPUT` and `OUTPUT` modes, which are required to be imported before you utilized them. The preceding example shows the delegation of digital pin 13 as an output and the analog pin 0 as an input. The mode method is performed on the variable assigned to the configured Arduino board using the `digital[]` and `analog[]` array index assignment.

The `pyFirmata` library also supports additional modes such as `PWM` and `SERVO`. The `PWM` mode is used to get analog results from digital pins, while the `SERVO` mode helps a digital pin to set the angle of the shaft between 0 to 180 degrees. The `PWM` and `SERVO` modes are explained with detailed examples later in this chapter. If you are using any of these modes, import their appropriate classes from the `pyFirmata` library. Once these classes are imported from the `pyFirmata` package, the modes for the appropriate pins can be assigned using the following lines of code:

```
board.digital[3].mode = PWM
board.digital[10].mode = SERVO
```

In electronics, PWM is a signal modulation technique that is greatly used to provide controlled amount of power to components. While dealing with digital signals, the PWM technique is used to obtain analog results by utilizing square waves and controlling the width of the signal.

As we already know, the digital pins of the Arduino board can only have two states, 5V (HIGH) and 0V (LOW). One can generate square pulses by controlling the switching pattern between HIGH and LOW and thus generate the pulse. By changing the width of these pulses, you can simulate any voltage between 0V and 5V. As you can see in the following diagram, we have a square wave with 25 percent width of the duty cycle. It means that we are simulating 0.25 * 5V = 1.25V for the period of that duty cycle:

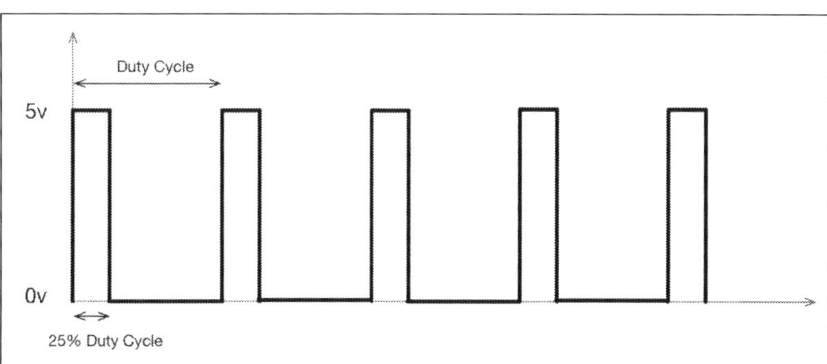

The Arduino language supports PWM using the `analogWrite()` function, where the voltage range between 0V and 5V is linearly scaled for values between 0 and 255. For example, 50 percent duty cycle (simulation of 2.5V) translates to a value of 127, which can be coded in Arduino as `analogWrite(13,127)`. Here, the number `13` represents the digital pin that supports PWM on the Arduino Uno board. Similarly, a 20 percent duty cycle (1V) translates to `analogWrite(13,64)`.

Assigning pin modes

The direct method of configuring pins is mostly used for a single line of execution calls. In a project containing a large code and complex logic, it is convenient to assign a pin with its role to a variable object. With an assignment like this, you can later utilize the assigned variable throughout the program for various actions, instead of calling the direct method every time you need to use that pin. In `pyFirmata`, this assignment can be performed using the `get_pin(pin_def)` method:

```
from pyfirmata import Arduino
port = '/dev/cu.usbmodemfa1311'
```

```
board = Arduino(port)

# pin mode assignment
ledPin = board.get_pin('d:13:o')
```

The `get_pin()` method lets you assign pin modes using the `pin_def` string parameter, `'d:13:o'`. The three components of `pin_def` are pin type, pin number, and pin mode separated by a colon (`:`) operator. The pin types (analog and digital) are denoted with `a` and `d` respectively. The `get_pin()` method supports three modes, `i` for input, `o` for output, and `p` for PWM. In the previous code sample, `'d:13:o'` specifies the digital pin 13 as an output. In another example, if you want to set up the analog pin 1 as an input, the parameter string will be `'a:1:i'`.

Working with pins

Now you have configured your Arduino pins, it's time to start performing actions using them. Two different types of methods are supported while working with pins: reporting methods and I/O operation methods.

Reporting data

When pins get configured in a program as analog input pins, they start sending input values to the serial port. If the program does not utilize this incoming data, the data starts getting buffered at the serial port and quickly overflows. The `pyFirmata` library provides the reporting and iterator methods to deal with this phenomenon.

The `enable_reporting()` method is used to set the input pin to start reporting. This method needs to be utilized before performing a reading operation on the pin:

```
board.analog[3].enable_reporting()
```

Once the reading operation is complete, the pin can be set to disable reporting:

```
board.analog[3].disable_reporting()
```

In the preceding example, we assumed that you had already set up the Arduino board and configured the mode of the analog pin 3 as `INPUT`.

The `pyFirmata` library also provides the `Iterator()` class to read and handle data over the serial port. While working with analog pins, we recommend that you start an iterator thread in the main loop to update the pin value to the latest one. If the iterator method is not used, the buffered data might overflow your serial port. This class is defined in the `util` module of the `pyFirmata` package and needs to be imported before it is utilized in the code:

```
from pyfirmata import Arduino, util
# Setting up the Arduino board
port = 'COM3'
board = Arduino(port)
sleep(5)

# Start Iterator to avoid serial overflow
it = util.Iterator(board)
it.start()
```

Manual operations

As we have configured the Arduino pins to suitable modes and their reporting characteristic, we can start monitoring them. The `pyFirmata` library provides the `write()` and `read()` methods for the configured pins.

The write() method

The `write()` method is used to write a value to the pin. If the pin's mode is set to `OUTPUT`, the value parameter is a Boolean, that is, `0` or `1`:

```
board.digital[pin].mode = OUTPUT
board.digital[pin].write(1)
```

If you have used an alternative method of assigning the pin's mode, you can use the `write()` method as follows:

```
ledPin = board.get_pin('d:13:o')
ledPin.write(1)
```

In the case of the PWM signal, the Arduino accepts a value between 0 and 255 that represents the length of the duty cycle between 0 and 100 percent. The `pyFirmata` library provides a simplified method to deal with the PWM values as instead of values between 0 and 255, you can just provide a float value between 0 and 1.0. For example, if you want a 50 percent duty cycle (2.5V analog value), you can specify `0.5` with the `write()` method. The `pyFirmata` library will take care of the translation and send the appropriate value, that is, `127`, to the Arduino board via the Firmata protocol:

```
board.digital[pin].mode = PWM
board.digital[pin].write(0.5)
```

Similarly, for the indirect method of assignment, you can use some code similar to the following snippet:

```
pwmPin = board.get_pin('d:13:p')
pwmPin.write(0.5)
```

If you are using the SERVO mode, you need to provide the value in degrees between 0 and 180. Unfortunately, the SERVO mode is only applicable for direct assignment of the pins and will be available in future for indirect assignments:

```
board.digital[pin].mode = SERVO
board.digital[pin].write(90)
```

The read() method

The read() method provides an output value at the specified Arduino pin. When the Iterator() class is being used, the value received using this method is the latest updated value at the serial port. When you read a digital pin, you can get only one of the two inputs, HIGH or LOW, which will translate to 1 or 0 in Python:

```
board.digital[pin].read()
```

The analog pins of Arduino linearly translate the input voltages between 0 and +5V to 0 and 1023. However, in pyFirmata, the values between 0 and +5V are linearly translated into the float values of 0 and 1.0. For example, if the voltage at the analog pin is 1V, an Arduino program will measure a value somewhere around 204, but you will receive the float value as 0.2 while using pyFirmata's read() method in Python.

Additional functions

Besides the method that has already been described, the pyFirmata library also provides some utility functions for additional customization, which are as follows:

- servo_config(pin,min_pulse=544,max_pulse=2400,angle=0): This method helps to set up the SERVO mode with further customization such as the minimum pulse value, maximum pulse value, and starting angle. One can set the initial angle of the servomotor using the angle parameter.
- pass_time(seconds): This method provides a functionality similar to that found in the default Python's default method sleep() that is provided by the time module. However, the pass_time function provides a non-blocking timeout in seconds.
- get_firmata_version(): This function returns a tuple that contains the version of the Firmata protocol from the Arduino board:

  ```
  board.get_firmata_version()
  ```

- exit(): We recommend that you disconnect the Arduino board from pyFirmata once you have completed running your code. This will free the serial port, which can be then utilized by other programs:

  ```
  board.exit()
  ```

Upcoming functions

The `pyFirmata` library is currently under development and it continuously receives updates to add and improve various methods. Although most of the native Arduino methods are available in the `pyFirmata` library via the Firmata protocol, there are few functions that are still missing or under development and they are as follows:

- `pulseIn`/`pulseOut`: These native Arduino functions wait for the Arduino pin to achieve the specified value. The waiting period is returned in microseconds. This method is widely used by Ping (ultrasonic distance measurement) sensors. Implementation of this method using `pyFirmata` requires major changes to the standard Firmata protocol.
- `shiftIn`/`shiftOut`: These functions shift a byte of data in or out, one bit at a time. The `pyFirmata` library lacks supports for these functions and can be implemented using the various Python programming tricks.

Prototyping templates using Firmata

The goal of this section is to provide prototyping templates while also explaining various Python methods and programming techniques. It tries to cover some of the most popular sensors with coding examples that are used by DIY Arduino projects. This section is designed to utilize the Firmata protocol to implement these Python programs. It also includes various Python programming paradigms such as working with indefinite loops, creating custom functions, working with random numbers, acquiring manual inputs from prompt, and so on. These prototyping templates are designed in such a way that they can be easily included in large projects or they can be blueprints for a larger project that can be developed around them. You learned about the `pyFirmata` package comprehensively in the previous section and we will only utilize those `pyFirmata` functions in the upcoming examples. An alternative Python library that supports the Firmata protocol is covered later in the chapter.

Potentiometer – continuous observation from an analog input

A potentiometer is a variable resistor that can be controlled using a knob. It has three terminals out of which two of them are Vref and ground, while the third one provides a variable output. The output of the potentiometer varies between the supplied voltages, according to the position of the knob. In Arduino, you can connect the potentiometer with +5V and the ground pins of the board to provide the supply voltage. When the variable terminal is interfaced with the Arduino analog input, this voltage values translates between 0 and 1023 respectively. In the case of `pyFirmata`, the value of the analog observation translates between 0 and 1.

This coding template containing the potentiometer can be applied to projects in which external manual control to a system is required. The potentiometer output that translates to the analog input of Arduino can be used to control an actuator such as a motor or an LED. In some cases, the input can also be used to control the flow of the program by applying its values to a variable.

Connections

Connect the output of the potentiometer to analog pin A0 as shown in the following diagram. Complete the circuit by connecting Vref and the ground terminals of the potentiometers to +5V and the ground of the Arduino board respectively:

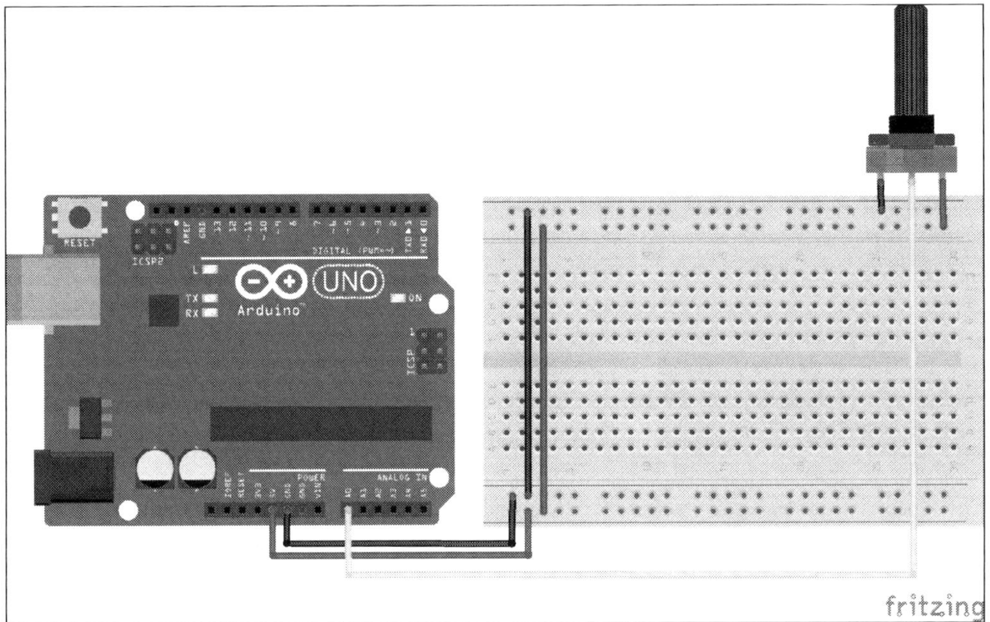

The Python code

Assuming that you already have the **StandardFirmata** firmware uploaded to the Arduino board, you are required to run a Python code on your computer to complete its interfacing with the potentiometer. A Python code template with the name `potentiometer.py` to help you get started with this example is located in the code bundle of this book, which can be downloaded from `https://www.packtpub.com/books/content/support/1961`. Let's open this file to understand the program. As you can see, we are using the `pyFirmata` library with other Python modules such as `time` and `os`:

```
from pyfirmata import Arduino, util
from time import sleep
import os
```

In the second step of the program, we are initializing the Arduino board and starting the `Iterator()` function over it:

```
port = 'COM3'
board = Arduino(port)
sleep(5)
it = util.Iterator(board)
it.start()
```

Once the board has been initialized, we need to assign a role to the analog pin, `0`, as it is going to be used as an input pin. We are using the `get_pin()` method to assign a role to the analog pin, `0`:

```
a0 = board.get_pin('a:0:i')
```

Now, as part of the main program, we need to continuously monitor the output of the potentiometer at the pin, `a0`, that we just defined. We are using the `while` statement to create an indefinite loop for the script that will read and print the analog input. The problem with this indefinite `while` loop is that the program will not close properly when it is interrupted and it will not release the board by executing the `board.exit()` method. To avoid this, we will use another control statement from the Python programming paradigm, called `try/except`:

```
try:
  while True:
    p = a0.read()
    print p
except KeyboardInterrupt:
  board.exit()
  os._exit()
```

Using this statement, the program will keep running the `while` loop until the keyboard interruption occurs, which is *Ctrl* + *C*, and the program will execute the script under the `except` statement. This includes releasing the board using `board.exit()` and existing the program using the `os._exit()` method. In summary, the program will keep printing the output of the potentiometer until someone presses *Ctrl* + *C* to interrupt the program.

The `try/except` statement provides a very efficient way to capture exceptions in Python. It is advisable to utilize this statement throughout the development process to cleverly debug your programs. You can learn about Python errors and exceptions from the following links:

- `https://docs.python.org/2/reference/compound_stmts.html#try`
- `https://docs.python.org/2/tutorial/errors.html`

Buzzer – generating sound alarm pattern

Digital buzzer sensors are used in various applications that require alarm notifications. These sensors produce sound when they are supplied with a digital `HIGH` value (that is, +5V), which can be provided by using Arduino digital pins. Similar to the LED example in the previous chapter, they are very easy to interface with Arduino. However, rather than performing a simple digital output, we are implementing Python programming tricks to generate different sound patterns and produce various sound effects. The same code template can be also used to produce different LED blink patterns.

An analog digital buzzer can be found at `http://www.amazon.com/Arduino-Compatible-Speaker-arduino-sensors/dp/B0090X0634`.

Connections

As displayed in the following circuit diagram, connect the VCC and the ground of the sensor board to 5V and the ground pin of the Arduino board respectively. Connect the signal pin of the sensor to the digital pin 2 via the 220-ohm resistor. You can use any digital pin to connect the buzzer. Just make sure that you update the Python code to reflect the pin that you have selected.

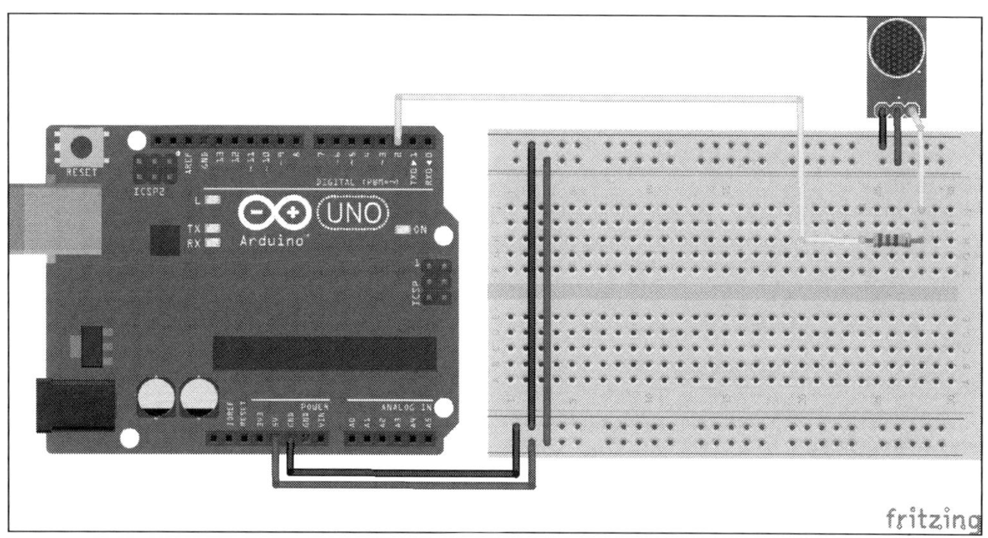

The Python code

In the code example, two different sound patterns are generated using arrays of time delays. To perform these actions, we are going to implement a custom Python function that will take the pin number, the recurrence time, and the pattern number as input. Before we jump to explain the code, let's open the program file, `buzzerPattern.py`, from the code folder. In the beginning of the code, you can find the Python function, `buzzerPattern()` that will be called from the main program with appropriate options. As this function is the core of the entire program, let's try to understand it. The function contains two hardcoded pattern arrays, `pattern1` and `pattern2`. Each contains the on and off time for the buzzer for a second, which is the duty cycle of the pattern. For example, in `pattern1`, `0.8` represents the time the buzzer needs to be on and `0.2` represents the opposite. The function will repeat this buzzer pattern for `recurrence` times that is specified by the function argument. Once the `for` loop with the value of `recurrence` is started, the function will check for the pattern number from the function argument and execute the pattern. We are using the `flag` variable to alternatively use elements of the `pattern` array to control the buzzer. Once the entire recurrence loop is complete, we will turn off the buzzer completely again, if it is on, and safely disengage the board using the `exit()` method:

```
def buzzerPattern(pin, recurrence, pattern):
  pattern1 = [0.8, 0.2]
  pattern2 = [0.2, 0.8]
  flag = True
```

```
    for i in range(recurrence):
      if pattern == 1:
        p = pattern1
      elif pattern == 2:
        p = pattern2
      else:
        print "Please enter valid pattern. 1 or 2."
        exit
      for delay in p:
        if flag is True:
          board.digital[pin].write(1)
          flag = False
          sleep(delay)
        else:
          board.digital[pin].write(0)
          flag = True
          sleep(delay)
    board.digital[pin].write(0)
    board.exit()
```

If you want to change the time delays or implement a totally different pattern, you can play around with the `pattern` arrays.

The remaining part of the program is relatively simple as it contains code for importing libraries and initializing the Arduino board. Once the board is initialized, we will execute the `buzzerPattern()` function with the input argument, `(2, 10, 1)`. This argument will ask the function to play `pattern1` 10 times on the pin number 2:

```
from pyfirmata import Arduino
from time import sleep

port = '/dev/cu.usbmodemfa1331'
board = Arduino(port)
sleep(5)

buzzerPattern(2, 10, 1)
```

DC motor – controlling motor speed using PWM

DC motors are widely used in robotics applications. They are available in a wide range of voltage specifications, depending upon the application. In this example, we are utilizing a 5V DC motor because we want to supply the power using the Arduino board itself. As the Arduino digital pin can only have two states, that is, `HIGH` (+5V) or `LOW` (0V), it is impossible to control the speed of the motor using just the `OUTPUT` mode. As a solution, we are going to implement the `PWM` mode via digital pins that are capable of supporting PWM. While using `pyFirmata`, pins configured with the `PWM` mode take any float input values between 0 and 1.0, which represent 0V and 5V respectively.

Connections

Depending upon the load, DC motors can sometimes draw large amounts of current and harm the Arduino board. To avoid any damage to the Arduino board due to any large accidental current draw, we will use a transistor as a switch, which only uses a small amount of current to control the large amount of current in the DC motor. To complete the circuit connection as displayed in the following diagram, you will need an NPN transistor (TIP120, N2222, or a similar one), one diode (1N4001 or similar one) and a 220-ohm resistor with your DC motor. Connect the base of the transistor to the digital pin 3 that also supports the PWM mode. Connect the remaining components as displayed in the diagram:

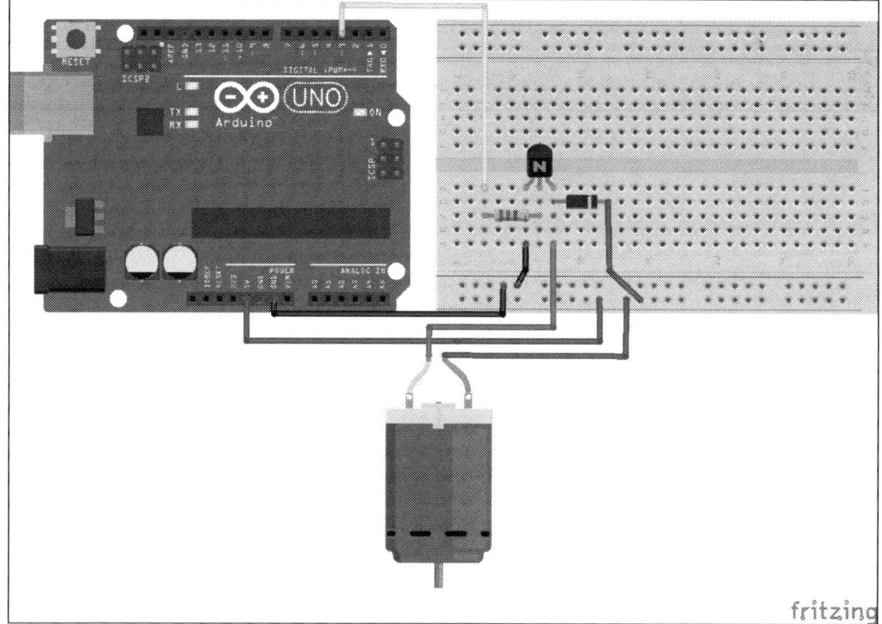

To find out more about transistor terminals (collector, emitter, and base) and to associate transistor pins with their respective terminals, you can refer to their datasheets or the following websites:

- `http://en.wikipedia.org/wiki/Transistor`
- `http://www.onsemi.com/pub/Collateral/TIP120-D.PDF`
- `http://www.mouser.com/ds/2/68/PN2221-2222A-11964.pdf`

The Python code

The Python recipe with the name `dcMotorPWM.py` for a DC motor is located in the code bundle of this book, which can be downloaded from `https://www.packtpub.com/books/content/support/1961`. Open the Python file to further understand the usage of PWM to control the speed of the DC motor. The custom function, `dcMotorControl()`, takes motor speed and time duration as input parameters as described in the following code snippet:

```
def dcMotorControl(r, deltaT):
  pwmPin.write(r/100.00)
  sleep(deltaT)
  pwmPin.write(0)
```

Just like the previous examples, we are using a similar code to import the necessary library and initialize the Arduino board. After initialization, we are assigning the mode of the digital pin 3 as `PWM`, which can be seen from the utilization of the `get_pin('d:3:p')` method. This code reflects the indirect mode of pin mode assignment that we learned in the previous section:

```
# Set mode of pin 3 as PWM
pwmPin = board.get_pin('d:3:p')
```

As part of collecting manual inputs from the user, we are running a combination of the `try/except` statement (to release the board on exit) and the `while` statement (to obtain continuous inputs from the user). The code template introduces the `input()` method to obtain custom values (motor speed and duration to run the motor) from Python's interactive terminal. Once these values are obtained from the user, the program calls the `dcMotorControl()` function to perform the motor action:

```
try:
  while True:
    r = input("Enter value to set motor speed: ")
    if (r > 100) or (r <= 0):
      print "Enter appropriate value."
      board.exit()
```

```
        break
      t = input("How long? (seconds)")
      dcMotorControl(r, t)
  except KeyboardInterrupt:
    board.exit()
    os._exit
```

LED – controlling LED brightness using PWM

In the previous template, we controlled the speed of DC motor using PWM. One can also control the brightness of the LED using the same method. Instead of asking the user to input brightness, we are going to use the Python module `random` in this template. We will use this module to generate a random number between 1 and 100, which will be later used to write that value on the pin and randomly change the brightness of the LED. This `randint()` function is a really useful feature provided by the `random` module and it is widely used in testing prototypes by rapidly sending random signals.

> The `randint()` function takes the `randint(startValue, endValue)` syntax and returns the random integer between the range established by `startValue` and `endValue`.

Connections

Like we used in the previous chapter's project, we will need a pull-up resistor to connect the LED with the Arduino pin. As displayed in the following diagram, simply connect the anode of the LED (longer leg) to the digital pin 11 via one 220-ohm resistor and connect the cathode (shorter leg) to the ground:

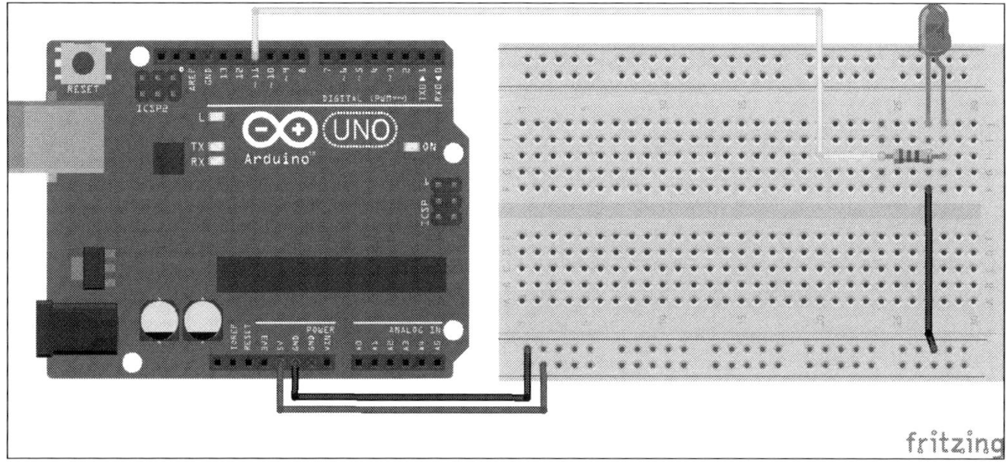

It is important to note that the digital pin 11 on Arduino Uno is also capable of performing PWM along with digital pins 3, 5, 6, 9, and 10.

The Python code

The Python code with the title `ledBrightnessPWM.py` for this exercise is located in the code bundle of this book, which can be downloaded from `https://www.packtpub.com/books/content/support/1961`. Open the file to explore the code. As you can see in this code template, a float value between 0 and 1.0 is randomly selected before passing it to the PWM pin. This method generates random LED brightness for a given amount of time. This practice can be used to generate random input samples for various other testing projects.

As you can see, the first few lines of the code import the necessary libraries and initialize the board. Although the board variable, `/dev/cu.usbmodemfa1311`, is selected for Mac OS X, you can use your operating system's specific variable name in the following code snippet. You can obtain more information about choosing this variable name from the *Setting up the Arduino board* section at the beginning of this chapter.

```
from pyfirmata import Arduino, INPUT, PWM
from time import sleep
import random

port = '/dev/cu.usbmodemfa1311'
board = Arduino(port)
sleep(5)
```

In this example, we are utilizing the direct method of pin mode assignment. As you can see in the following code snippet, the digital pin 11 is being assigned to the `PWM` mode:

```
pin = 11
board.digital[pin].mode = PWM
```

Once the pin mode is assigned, the program will run a loop using the `for` statement while randomly generating an integer number between 0 and 100, and then send the appropriate PWM value to the pin according to the generated number. With the execution of this, you will be able to see the LED randomly changing its brightness for approximately 10 seconds:

```
for i in range(0, 99):
  r = random.randint(1, 100)
  board.digital[pin].write(r / 100.00)
  sleep(0.1)
```

Once you are done with the loop, you need to safely disengage the Arduino board after turning off the LED one last time. It is a good practice to turn off the LED or any connected sensor at the end of the program before exiting the board, to prevent any sensor from running accidentally:

```
board.digital[pin].write(0)
board.exit()
```

If you want to homogenously glow the LED instead of randomly changing its brightness, replace the code in the `for` loop with the following code snippet. Here, we are changing the PWM input to the incrementing variable, `i`, instead of the random variable, `r`:

```
for i in range(0, 99):
  board.digital[pin].write(i / 100.00)
  sleep(0.1)
```

Servomotor – moving the motor to a certain angle

Servomotors are widely used electronic components in applications such as pan-tilt camera control, robotic arms, mobile robot movements, and so on where precise movement of the motor shaft is required. This precise control of the motor shaft is possible because of the position sensing decoder, which is an integral part of the servomotor assembly. A standard servomotor allows the angle of the shaft to be set between 0 and 180 degrees. The `pyFirmata` library provides the `SERVO` mode that can be implemented on every digital pin. This prototyping exercise provides a template and guidelines to interface a servomotor with Python.

Connections

Typically, a servomotor has wires that are color-coded red, black, and yellow respectively to connect with the power, ground, and signal of the Arduino board. Connect the power and the ground of the servomotor to 5V and the ground of the Arduino board. As displayed in the following diagram, connect the yellow signal wire to the digital pin 13:

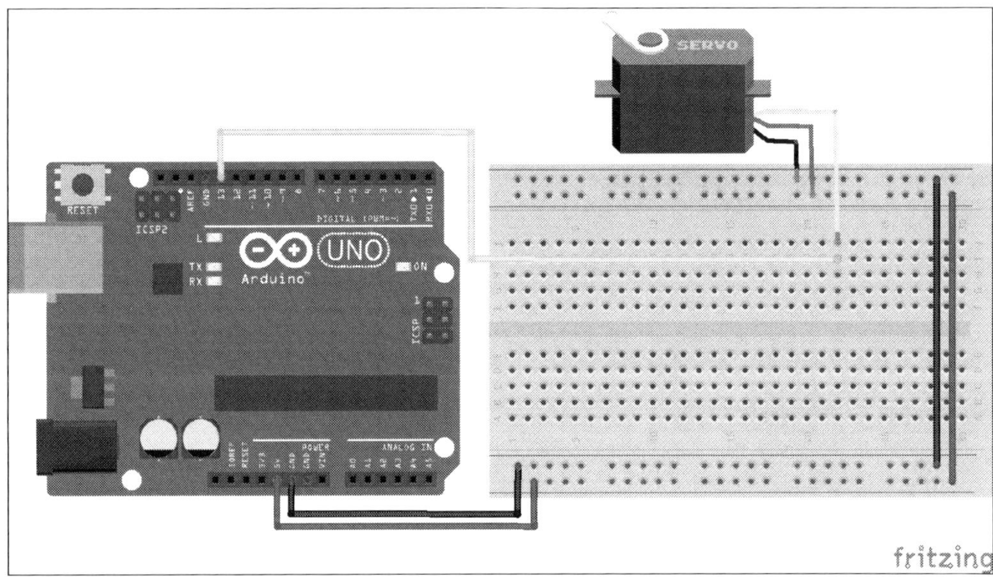

If you want to use any other digital pin, make sure that you change the pin number in the Python program in the next section. Once you have made the appropriate connections, let's move on to the Python program.

The Python code

The Python file consisting of this code is named `servoCustomAngle.py` and is located in the code bundle of this book, which can be downloaded from `https://www.packtpub.com/books/content/support/19610`. Open this file in your Python editor. Like other examples, the starting section of the program contains the code to import the libraries and set up the Arduino board:

```
from pyfirmata import Arduino, SERVO
from time import sleep

# Setting up the Arduino board
port = 'COM5'
board = Arduino(port)
```

```
# Need to give some time to pyFirmata and Arduino to synchronize
sleep(5)
```

Now that you have Python ready to communicate with the Arduino board, let's configure the digital pin that is going to be used to connect the servomotor to the Arduino board. We will complete this task by setting the `mode` of pin 13 to `SERVO`:

```
# Set mode of the pin 13 as SERVO
pin = 13
board.digital[pin].mode = SERVO
```

The `setServoAngle(pin,angle)` custom function takes the pins on which the servomotor is connected and the custom angle as input parameters. This function can be used as a part of various large projects that involve servos:

```
# Custom angle to set Servo motor angle
def setServoAngle(pin, angle):
  board.digital[pin].write(angle)
  sleep(0.015)
```

In the main logic of this template, we want to incrementally move the motor shaft in one direction until it achieves the maximum achievable angle (180 degrees) and then move it back to the original position with the same incremental speed. In the `while` loop, we will ask the user to provide input to continue this routine, which will be captured using the `raw_input()` function. The user can enter the character `y` to continue this routine or enter any other character to abort the loop:

```
# Testing the function by rotating motor in both direction
while True:
  for i in range(0, 180):
    setServoAngle(pin, i)
  for i in range(180, 1, -1):
    setServoAngle(pin, i)

  # Continue or break the testing process
  i = raw_input("Enter 'y' to continue or Enter to quit): ")
  if i == 'y':
    pass
  else:
    board.exit()
    break
```

While working with all these prototyping examples, we used the direct communication method by using digital and analog pins to connect the sensors with Arduino. Now, let's get familiar with another widely used communication method between Arduino and the sensors, which is called I2C communication.

Prototyping with the I2C protocol

In the previous section, sensors or actuators were directly communicating with Arduino via digital, analog, or PWM pins. These methods are utilized by a large number of basic, low-level sensors and you will be widely using them in your future Arduino projects. Beside these methods, there is a wide variety of popular sensors that are based on **integrated circuit** (**IC**), which require different ways of communication. These IC-based advanced sensors utilize I2C- or SPI bus-based methods to communicate with the microcontroller. As we are going to use I2C-based sensors in the upcoming projects, the section will only cover the I2C protocol and practical example to understand the protocol in a better way. Once you understand the fundamentals of the I2C protocol, you can learn the SPI protocol very quickly.

You can learn more about SPI protocol and the supported Arduino SPI library from the following links:

- `http://arduino.cc/en/Reference/SPI`
- `http://www.instructables.com/id/Using-an-Arduino-to-Control-or-Test-an-SPI-electro/`

In 1982, the Philips company needed to find out a simple and efficient way to establish communication between a microcontroller and the peripheral chips on TV sets, which led to the development of the I2C communication protocol. The I2C protocol connects the microcontroller or the CPU to a large number of low-speed peripheral devices using just two wires. Examples of such peripheral devices or sensors include I/O devices, A/D converters, D/A converters, EEPROM, and many similar devices. I2C uses the concept of master-slave devices, where the microcontroller is the master and the peripherals are the slave devices.
The following diagram shows an example of the I2C communication bus:

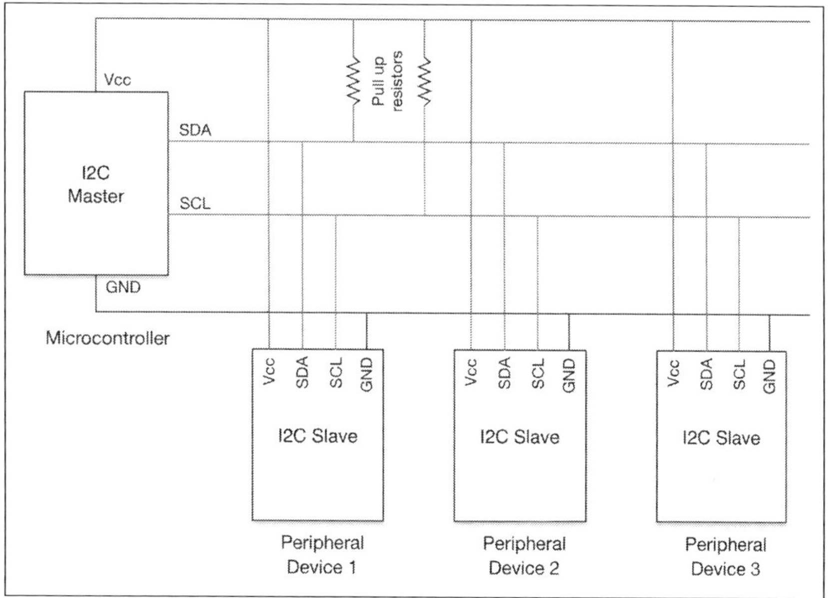

As displayed in the preceding diagram, the master device contains two bidirectional lines: **Serial Data Line** (**SDA**) and **Serial Clock Line** (**SCL**). In the case of Arduino Uno, the analog pins 4 and 5 provide interfaces for SDA and SCL. It is important to note that these pin configurations will change with different variants of the Arduino board. The peripheral sensors that are working as slaves connect to these lines, which are also supported by the pull resistors. The master device is responsible for generating the clock signal on the SCL and initializing communication with the slaves. The slave devices receive the clock and respond to the commands sent by the master device.

The order of the slave devices is not important as the master device communicates with the slaves using their part address. To initialize the communication, the master sends one of the following types of message on the bus with the specific part address:

- A single message in which data is written on the slave
- A single message in which data is read from the slave
- Multiple messages in which first data is requested from the slave and then the received data is read

To support I2C protocol in Arduino programming, the Arduino IDE comes equipped with a default library called `Wire`. This library can be imported to your Arduino sketch by adding the following line of code at the beginning of your program:

```
#include <Wire.h>
```

To initialize I2C communication, the `Wire` library uses a combination of the following functions to write data on the slave device:

```
Wire.beginTransmission(0x48);
Wire.write(0);
Wire.endTransmission();
```

These slave devices are differentiated using unique part addresses. As you can see in the preceding example, `0x48` is the part address of a connected slave device.

The `Wire` library also provides the `Wire.read()` and `Wire.requestFrom()` functions to read and request data from the slave devices. These functions are explained in detail in the next section.

You can learn more about the I2C protocol and the `Wire` library from the following links:

- `http://www.instructables.com/id/I2C-between-Arduinos/`
- `http://arduino.cc/en/reference/wire`

Arduino examples for I2C interfacing

In order to practice prototyping exercises for the I2C protocol, let's utilize two popular I2C sensors that detect temperature and ambient light in the environment. As the first step towards understanding I2C messaging, we will work with Arduino sketches for I2C interfacing, and later, we will develop similar functionalities using Python.

Arduino coding for the TMP102 temperature sensor

TMP102 is one of the widely used digital sensors to measure ambient temperature. TMP102 provides better resolution and accuracy compared to traditional analog temperature sensors such as LM35 or TMP36. The following is an image of TMP102:

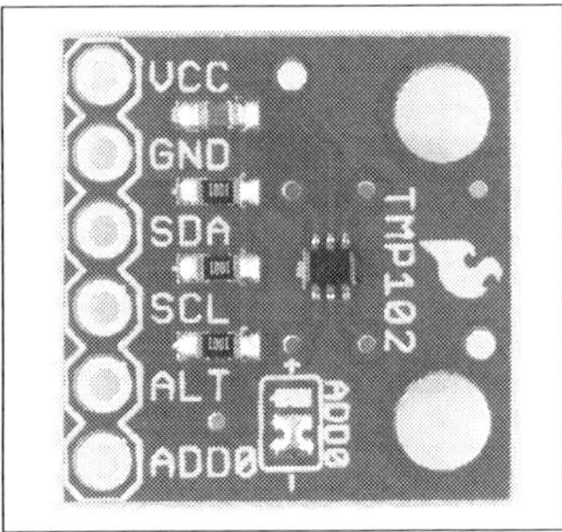

The previous image shows a breakout board with the available pins for the TMP102 sensor. Please keep in mind that the TMP102 sensor that you obtain might have a different pin layout compared to the one displayed in the image. It is always advisable to check the datasheet of your sensor breakout board before making any connections. As you can see in the image, the TMP102 sensor supports the I2C protocol and is equipped with SDA and SCL pins. Connect analog pins 4 and 5 of your Arduino Uno board to the SDA and SCL pins of the TMP102 sensor. Also, connect +5V and the ground as displayed in the following diagram. In this example, we are using the Arduino Uno board as the master and TMP102 as the slave peripheral, where the part address of TMP102 is `0x48` in hex:

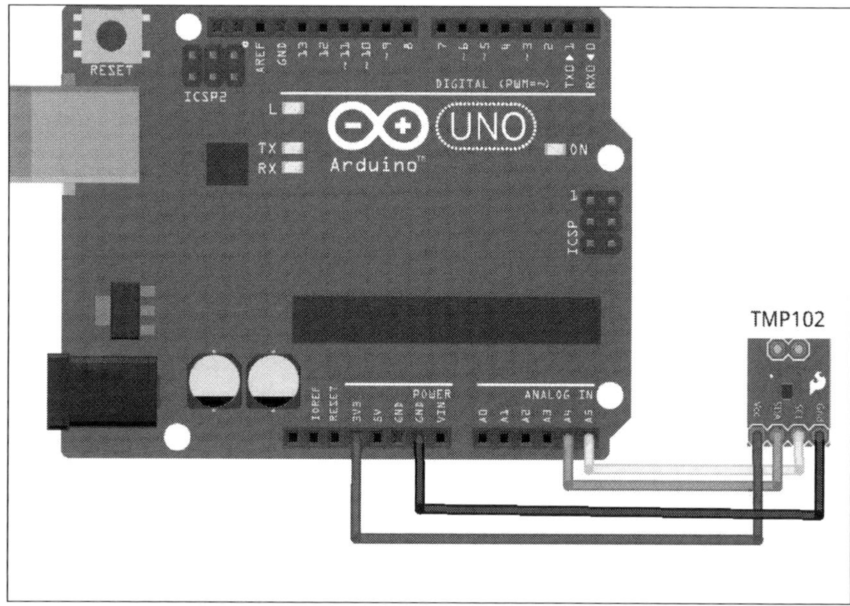

You can obtain the TMP102 sensor breakout board from SparkFun Electronics at `https://www.sparkfun.com/products/11931`.

The datasheet of this board can be obtained at `https://www.sparkfun.com/datasheets/Sensors/Temperature/tmp102.pdf`.

Now, connect your Arduino board to your computer using a USB cable and create a new sketch in the Arduino IDE using the following code snippet. Once you have selected the appropriate serial port and type of board in the Arduino IDE, upload and run the code. If all the steps are performed as described, on execution, you will be able to see the temperature reading in **Celsius** and **Fahrenheit** in the **Serial Monitor** window:

```
#include <Wire.h>
int partAddress = 0x48;

void setup(){
  Serial.begin(9600);
  Wire.begin();
}

void loop(){

  Wire.requestFrom(partAddress,2);
  byte MSB = Wire.read();
  byte LSB = Wire.read();

  int TemperatureData = ((MSB << 8) | LSB) >> 4;

  float celsius = TemperatureData*0.0625;
  Serial.print("Celsius: ");
  Serial.println(celsius);

  float fahrenheit = (1.8 * celsius) + 32;
  Serial.print("Fahrenheit: ");
  Serial.println(fahrenheit);

  delay(500);
}
```

In the preceding code snippet, the `Wire.requestFrom(partAddress,2)` function requests two bytes from the slave TMP102. The slave sends data bytes to the master, which get captured by the `Wire.read()` function and are stored as two different bits: **most significant bit (MSB)** and **least significant bit (LSB)**. These bytes are converted into an integer value, which is then converted into the actual Celsius reading by multiplying the incremental fraction of the TMP102 sensor that is obtained from the datasheet. TMP102 is one of the easiest I2C sensors to interface with Arduino as the sensor values can be obtained via a simple I2C request method.

Arduino coding for the BH1750 light sensor

BH1750 is a digital light sensor that measures the amount of visible light in a given area. Although various DIY projects utilize simple photocells as a cheap alternative, the BH1750 sensor is known for higher resolution and accuracy in a wide range of applications. The ambient light, also called luminous flux or lux, is measured in unit lumen. The BH1750 sensor supports I2C communication with part address `0x23`, with `0x5C` as the secondary address if you are using multiple BH1750 sensors. The following is an image of a typical breakout board consisting of BH1750:

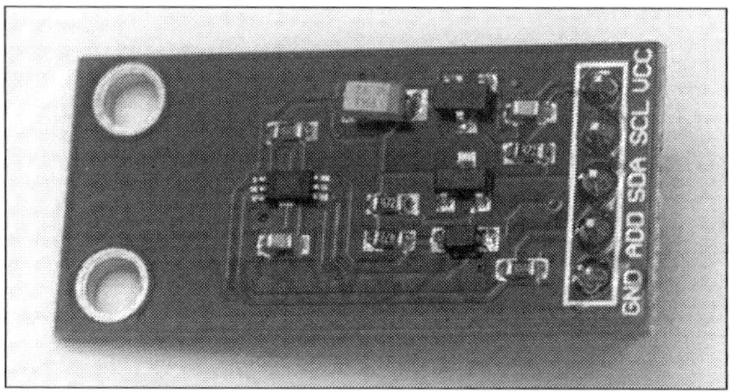

Connect the SDA and SCL pins of the BH1750 breakout board to analog pins 4 and 5 of the Arduino Uno board, as displayed in the following circuit diagram. Also, complete the +5V and ground connections as displayed in the following diagram:

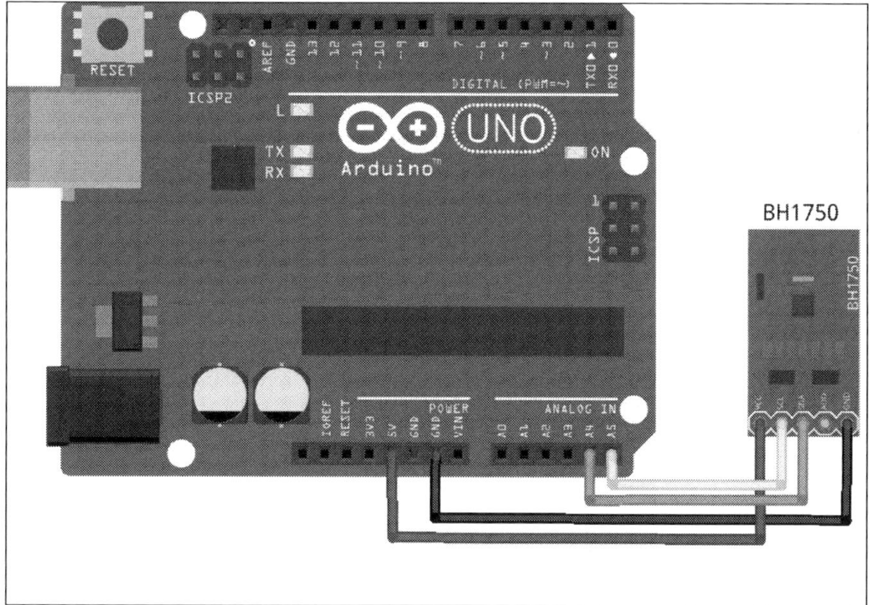

In the previous example, we used functions from the `Wire` library to complete the I2C communication. Although `BH1750` is a simple and convenient I2C sensor, in the case of a sensor with multiple measurement capabilities, it is not convenient to code directly using the `Wire` library. In this situation, you can use sensor-specific Arduino libraries that are developed by the manufacturer or the open source community. For `BH1750`, we will demonstrate the use of such a library to assist the I2C coding. Before we can use this library, we will have to import it to the Arduino IDE. It is really important to know the process of importing libraries to your Arduino IDE as you will be repeating this process to install other libraries in future. Execute the following steps to import the `BH1750` library to your Arduino IDE:

1. Download and extract *Chapter 7, The Midterm Project – a Portable DIY Thermostat*, code examples in a folder.
2. Open the Arduino IDE and navigate to **Sketch | Import Library... | Add Library...**.
3. When you are asked for a directory, go to the `BH1750` folder in the downloaded file and click on **Select**.
4. To check if your library is installed, navigate to **Sketch | Import Library...** and look for **BH1750** in the drop-down list.
5. Finally, restart the Arduino IDE.

If you are using an Arduino IDE with version 1.0.4 or an older version, you might not be able to find the **Import Library...** option from the menu. In this case, you need to follow the tutorial at `http://arduino.cc/en/Guide/Libraries`.

The `BH1750` library has a method to directly obtain ambient light values. Let's test this library using a built-in code example.

After restarting your Arduino IDE, navigate to **File | Examples | BH1750** and open the **BH1750test** Arduino sketch. This should open the following code snippet in the Arduino IDE. Set up an appropriate serial port and upload the code to your Arduino board. Once the code is executed, you will be able to check the luminous flux (`lux`) values using the serial monitor of the Arduino IDE. Make sure that the serial monitor is configured to 9600 baud:

```
#include <Wire.h>
#include <BH1750.h>

BH1750 lightMeter;

void setup(){
```

```
  Serial.begin(9600);
  lightMeter.begin();
  Serial.println("Running...");
}

void loop() {
  uint16_t lux = lightMeter.readLightLevel();
  Serial.print("Light: ");
  Serial.print(lux);
  Serial.println(" lx");
  delay(1000);
}
```

As you can see from the preceding code snippet, we have imported the `BH1750` library by including `BH1750.h` file with `Wire.h`. This library provides the `readLightLevel()` function, which will fetch the ambient light value from the sensor and provide it as an integer. As the Arduino code runs in a loop with a delay of 1000 milliseconds, the `lux` values will be fetched from the sensor and sent to the serial port every second. You can observe these values in the **Serial Monitor** window.

PyMata for quick I2C prototyping

We have been using `pyFirmata` as our default Python library to interface the Firmata protocol. The `pyFirmata` library is a very useful Python library to get started with the Firmata protocol, as it provides many simple and effective methods to define the Firmata ports and their roles. Due to these reasons, we extensively used `pyFirmata` for rapid prototyping in the previous section. Although `pyFirmata` supports analog, digital, PWM, and SERVO modes with easy-to-use methods, it provides limited support to the I2C protocol.

In this section, we are going to use a different Python Firmata library called `PyMata` to get familiar with Python-based prototyping of I2C sensors. The `PyMata` library supports regular Firmata methods and also provides full support for the I2C messaging protocol.

`PyMata` can be easily installed using Setuptools, which we used in the previous chapters to install other Python libraries. We are assuming that you already have Setuptools and `pip` on your computer. Let's start performing the following steps:

1. To install `PyMata` on a Windows computer, execute the following command in the command prompt:

   ```
   C:\> easy_install.exe pymata
   ```

2. If you are using Linux or Mac OS X, use the following command in the terminal to install the `PyMata` library:

   ```
   $ sudo pip install pymata
   ```

3. If everything is set up properly, this process will complete without any error. You can confirm `PyMata` by opening Python's interactive prompt and importing `PyMata`:

   ```
   >>> import PyMata
   ```

4. If the execution of the preceding command fails, you need to check the installation process for any error. Resolve the error and repeat the installation process.

Interfacing TMP102 using PyMata

In order to utilize `PyMata` functionalities, you will need your Arduino board to be equipped with the standard firmata firmware just like the `pyFirmata` library. Before we proceed to explain the `PyMata` functions, let's first run the following code snippet. Connect your TMP102 temperature sensor as explained in the previous section. Using the Arduino IDE, navigate to **File** | **Examples** | **Firmata** and upload the standard Firmata sketch from there to your Arduino board. Now, create a Python executable file using the following code snippet. Change the value of port (`COM5`), if needed, to an appropriate port name as required by your operating system. Finally, run the program:

```
import time
from PyMata.pymata import PyMata

#Initialize Arduino using port name
port = PyMata("COM5")

#Configure I2C pin
port.i2c_config(0, port.ANALOG, 4, 5)

# One shot read asking peripheral to send 2 bytes
port.i2c_read(0x48, 0, 2, port.I2C_READ)
# Wait for peripheral to send the data
time.sleep(3)

# Read from the peripheral
data = port.i2c_get_read_data(0x48)

# Obtain temperature from received data
TemperatureSum = (data[1] << 8 | data[2]) >> 4

celsius = TemperatureSum * 0.0625
```

```
print celsius

fahrenheit = (1.8 * celsius) + 32
print fahrenheit

firmata.close()
```

On the execution of the preceding code snippet, you will be able to see the temperature reading in Fahrenheit and Celsius. As you can see from the inline comments in the code, the first step to utilize Arduino using `PyMata` is to initialize the port using the `PyMata` constructor. `PyMata` supports the configuration of I2C pins via the `i2c_config()` function. `PyMata` also supports simultaneous reading and writing operations via the `i2c_read()` and `i2c_write()` functions.

Interfacing BH1750 using PyMata

In the case of BH1750, the previous `PyMata` code snippet can be utilized with minor modifications to obtain ambient light sensor data. As the first change, you want to replace the part address of TMP102 (`0x48`) with the one of BH1750 (`0x23`) in the following code snippet. You will also have to convert the raw values received from the sensor into the `lux` value using the given formula. After these modifications, run the following program from the terminal:

```
import time
from PyMata.pymata import PyMata

port = PyMata("COM5")
port.i2c_config(0, port.ANALOG, 4, 5)

# Request BH1750 to send 2 bytes
port.i2c_read(0x23, 0, 2, port.I2C_READ)
# Wait for BH1750 to send the data
time.sleep(3)

# Read data from BH1750
data = port.i2c_get_read_data(0x23)

# Obtain lux values from received data
LuxSum = (data[1] << 8 | data[2]) >> 4

lux = LuxSum/1.2
print str(lux) + ' lux'

firmata.close()
```

On running the preceding code snippet, you will be able to see the ambient light sensor reading in `lux` at the terminal. This process can be used in a large number of I2C devices to read the registered information. In complex I2C devices, you will have to follow their datasheet or examples to organize the read and write commands of the I2C.

Useful pySerial commands

The standard Firmata protocol and Python's Firmata libraries are very useful for testing or quick prototyping of the I2C sensors. Although they have many advantages, Firmata-based projects face the following disadvantages:

- **Delay in real-time execution**: Firmata-based approaches require a series of serial communication messages to receive and send data, which adds additional delay and reduces the speed of execution.
- **Unwanted space**: The Firmata protocol contains a large amount of additional code to support various other Arduino functions. In a well-defined project, you don't really need the complete set of functions.
- **Limited support**: Although a version of Firmata includes I2C support, it is quite difficult to implement complex I2C functions without adding delay.

In summary, you can always use Firmata-based approaches to quickly prototype your projects, but when you are working on production-level or advanced projects, you can use alternative methods. In these scenarios, you can use custom Arduino code that is supported by Python's serial library, `pySerial`, to enable communication for very specific functionalities. In this section, we are going to cover a few helpful `pySerial` methods that you can use if you have to utilize the library directly.

Connecting with the serial port

Once you have connected your Arduino to a USB port of your computer, you can open the port in your Python code using the `Serial` class as displayed in the following code example:

```
import serial
port = serial.Serial('COM5',9600, timeout=1)
```

In addition to port name and baud rate, you can also specify a number of serial port parameters such as `timeout`, `bytesize`, `parity`, `stopbits`, and so on using `Serial()`. It is necessary to initialize the serial port before executing any other command from the `pySerial` library.

Reading a line from the port

Once the serial port is opened, you can start reading the port using `readline()`. The `readline()` function requires the timeout to be specified while initializing the port, otherwise the code can terminate with an exception:

```
line = port.readline()
```

The `readline()` function will process each line from the port that is terminated with the end line character `\n`.

Flushing the port to avoid buffer overflow

While working with `pySerial`, it is necessary to flush the input buffer to avoid buffer overflow and maintain real-time operations:

```
port.flushInput()
```

If the port's baud rate is high and the processing of the input data is slow, buffer overflow may occur, reducing the speed of execution and making the experience sluggish.

Closing the port

It is a good coding practice to close the serial port once the process is complete. This practice can eliminate the port-blocking problem once the Python code is terminated:

```
port.close()
```

Summary

In this chapter, you learned important methods that are required to successfully interface the Arduino board with Python. You were also introduced to various prototyping code templates with practical applications. These prototyping templates helped us to learn new Python programing paradigms and Firmata methods. Later in the chapter, we dived further into prototyping by learning more about the different ways of establishing communication between sensors and the Arduino board. Although we covered a vast amount of programming concepts with these prototyping examples, the goal of the chapter was to make you familiar with the interfacing problems and provide quick recipes for your projects.

We are assuming that by now you are comfortable testing your sensors or project prototypes using Python and Arduino. It's time to start working towards creating your applications that have complex Python features such as user controls, charts, and plots. In the next chapter, we are going to develop custom graphical user interfaces (GUIs) for your Python-Arduino projects.

5
Working with the Python GUI

In the first four chapters, we used the Python interactive prompt or Arduino serial monitor to observe the results. The method of using text-based output on prompt may be useful for basic and quick prototyping, but when it comes to an advanced level of prototyping and demonstrating your prototype or final product, you need to have a nice looking and user-friendly interface. GUI helps users to understand various components of your hardware project and easily interact with it. It can also help you to validate the results from your project.

Python has a number of widely used GUI frameworks such as `Tkinter`, `wxPython`, `PyQt`, `PySide`, and `PyGTK`. Each of these frameworks possesses an almost complete set of features that are required to create professional applications. Due to the complexity involved, these frameworks have different levels of learning curves for first-time Python programmers. Now, as this book is dedicated to Python programming for Arduino-based projects, we can't spend a large amount of time learning the nitty-gritty of a specific framework. Instead, we will choose our interface library based on the following criteria:

- Ease to install and get started
- Ease to implement with negligible learning efforts
- Use of minimum computational resources

The framework that satisfies all these requirements is `Tkinter` (`https://wiki.python.org/moin/TkInter`). `Tkinter` is also the default standard GUI library deployed with all Python installations.

Although `Tkinter` is the de-facto GUI package for Python, you can learn more about other GUI frameworks that were mentioned earlier from their official websites, which are as follows:

- **wxPython**: `http://www.wxpython.org/`
- **PyGTK**: `http://www.pygtk.org/`
- **PySide**: `http://qt-project.org/wiki/PySide`
- **PyQt**: `http://sourceforge.net/projects/pyqt/`

Learning Tkinter for GUI design

`Tkinter`, short for `Tk` interface, is a cross-platform Python interface for the `Tk` GUI toolkit. `Tkinter` provides a thin layer on Python while `Tk` provides the graphical widgets. `Tkinter` is a cross-platform library and gets deployed as part of Python installation packages for major operating systems. For Mac OS X 10.9, `Tkinter` is installed with the default Python framework. For Windows, when you install Python from the installation file, `Tkinter` gets installed with it.

`Tkinter` is designed to take minimal programming efforts for developing graphical applications, while also being powerful enough to provide support for the majority of GUI application features. If required, `Tkinter` can also be extended with plugins. `Tkinter` via `Tk` offers an operating system's natural look and feel after the release of `Tk` Version 8.0.

To test your current version of the `Tk` toolkit, use the following commands on the Python prompt:

```
>>> import Tkinter
>>> Tkinter._test()
```

You will be prompted with an image similar to that displayed in the following screenshot that contains information about your `Tk` version:

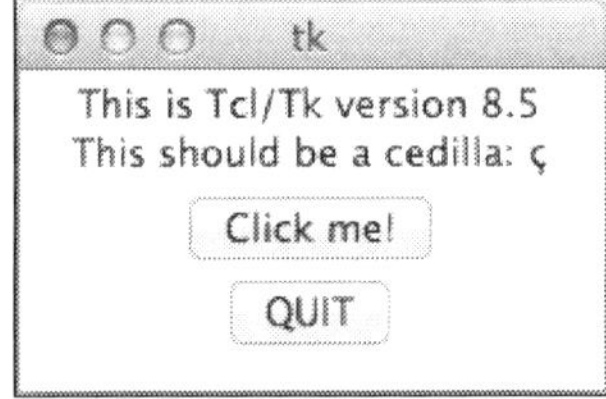

If you face any problem in getting this window, check your Python installation and reinstall it, as you won't be able to move further ahead in this chapter without the `Tkinter` library and the `Tk` toolkit.

The `Tkinter` interface supports various widgets to develop GUIs. The following table describes a few of the important widgets that we will be using in this chapter:

Widget	Description
`Tk()`	This is the root widget that is required by each program
`Label()`	This shows a text or an image
`Button()`	This is a simple button that can be used to execute actions
`Entry()`	This is a text field to provide inputs to the program
`Scale()`	This provides a numeric value by dragging the slider
`Checkbox()`	This enables you to toggle between two values by checking the box

A detailed description of the `Tkinter` functions and methods to implement the majority of functionalities provided by the `Tk` toolkit can be obtained from `https://docs.python.org/2/library/tk.html`.

Your first Python GUI program

As we discussed in an earlier chapter, the first program while learning any programming language includes printing `Hello World!`. Now, as we are starting Python programming for GUI, let's start by printing the same string in a GUI window instead of a prompt.

Just to start with GUI programming, we are going to execute a Python program and then jump into explaining the structure and the details of the code. Let's create a Python executable file using the following lines of code, name it `helloGUI.py`, and then run it. The execution process should complete without any dependency errors:

```
import Tkinter

# Initialize main windows with title and size
top = Tkinter.Tk()
top.title("Hello GUI")
top.minsize(200,30)

# Label widget
helloLabel = Tkinter.Label(top, text = "Hello World!")
```

```
helloLabel.pack()

# Start and open the window
top.mainloop()
```

You should be prompted with the following window on the successful execution of the preceding code snippet. As you can see, the `Hello World!` string has been printed inside the window and has **Hello GUI** as the title of the window:

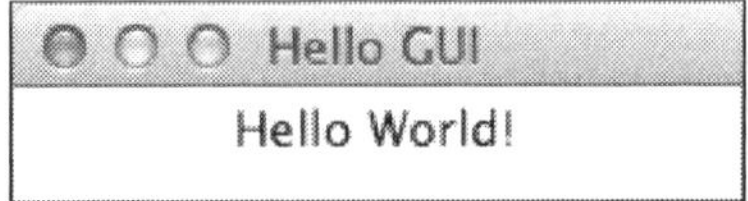

So, what exactly happened? As you can see from the code snippet, we instantiated various `Tkinter` widgets one by one to obtain this result. These widgets are the building blocks for any Python GUI application that is developed using `Tkinter`. Let's start with the first and the most important widget, `Tk()`.

The root widget Tk() and the top-level methods

The `Tk()` widget initializes a main empty window with a title bar. This is a root widget and it is required by each program only once. The main window gets its decoration and styles from the operating system's environment. Therefore, when you run the same `Tkinter` code on different operating systems, you will get the same window and title bar but in a different style.

Once you create a root widget, you can perform some top-level methods to decorate, describe, or resize this window. In code, we are using the `title()` method to set the title of the main window. This `title()` method takes a string as an input argument:

```
Top = Tkinter.Tk()
top.title("Hello GUI")
```

Next, we call the `minsize()` method on the main window to set the minimum size of the window with the argument `(width, height)`:

```
top.minsize(200,30)
```

Similarly, you can also use the `maxsize()` method to specify the maximum size that the main window should have. In the `minsize()` and `maxsize()` methods, the values of `width` and `height` are provided in the number of pixels.

Once the entire program has been instantiated, the `mainloop()` function is required to start the event loop:

```
top.mainloop()
```

You won't be able to see any other widgets, including the main window, if the code does not enter in the main event loop. The event loop will be alive until the window is manually closed or the quit method is called.

You might have various questions about updating the window, programmatically closing it, arranging widgets in the grid, and so on. There are definitely a lot more top-level methods than the ones specified earlier.

The Label() widget

The other widget used in the code beside `Tk()` is `Label()`. The `Tkinter` widgets are part of the widget hierarchy, where `Label()` is the child of the root widget, `Tk()`. This widget cannot be called without specifying the root widget or the main window on which the label needs to be displayed. The major use of this widget is to display text or image in the main window. In the following line of code, we use it to display the `Hello World!` string:

```
helloLabel = Tkinter.Label(top, text = "Hello World!")
```

Here, we created and initialized a label object called `helloLabel`, which has two input parameters: the `top` variable that specifies the root widget and a `text` string. The `Label()` widget is highly customizable and accepts various configuration parameters for adjusting the width, border, background, and justification as options. Examples involving these customizations are covered in the upcoming sections. You can learn more about the supported input arguments at `http://effbot.org/tkinterbook/label.htm`.

The Pack geometry manager

The Pack geometry manager organizes widgets in rows and columns. To use this, `Tkinter` requires the `pack()` method to be called for each widget to make the widget visible on the main window:

```
helloLabel.pack()
```

The Pack geometry manager can be used by all `Tkinter` widgets, except root, to organize the widget in the root window. In the case of multiple widgets, if the positions for the widgets are not specified, the Pack manager arranges them in the same root window. The Pack manager is simple to implement, but it has a limitation in terms of its degree of customization. An alternative geometry manager that is helpful to create a complex layout is called **Grid**, which is explained in the upcoming sections.

We will cover additional widgets and their associated methods in the upcoming coding exercises. In these exercises, we will explain each individual widget with practical applications to give you a better understanding of the use cases.

The Button() widget – interfacing GUI with Arduino and LEDs

Now that you have had your first hands-on experience in creating a Python graphical interface, let's integrate Arduino with it. Python makes it easy to interface various heterogeneous packages within each other and that is what you are going to do. In the next coding exercise, we will use `Tkinter` and `pyFirmata` to make the GUI work with Arduino. In this exercise, we are going to use the `Button()` widget to control the LEDs interfaced with the Arduino board.

Before we jump to the exercises, let's build the circuit that we will need for all upcoming programs. The following is a Fritzing diagram of the circuit where we use two different colored LEDs with pull up resistors. Connect these LEDs to digital pins 10 and 11 on your Arduino Uno board, as displayed in the following diagram:

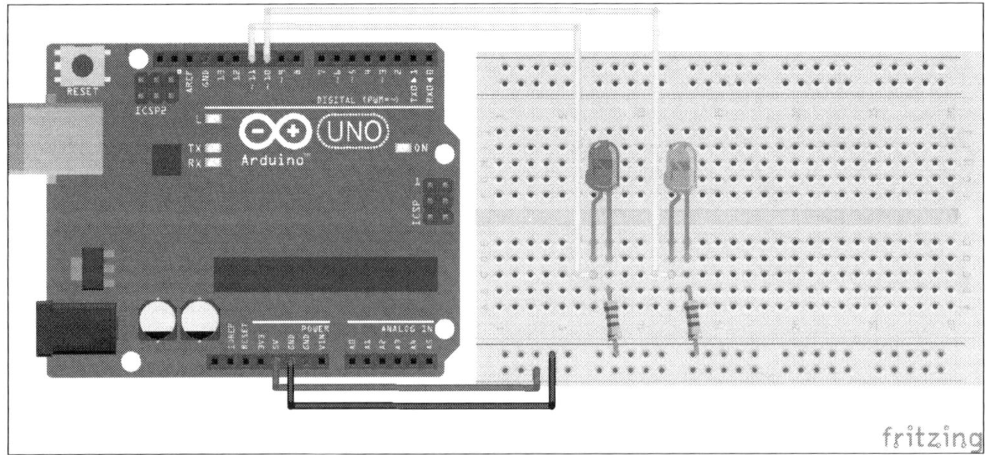

[While working with the programs provided in this and upcoming sections, you will have to replace the Arduino port that is used to define the board variable according to your operating system. To find out which port your Arduino board is connected to, follow the detailed instructions provided in *Chapter 2, Working with the Firmata Protocol and the pySerial Library*. Also, make sure that you provide the correct pin number in the code if you are planning to use any pins other than 10 and 11. For some exercises, you will have to use the PWM pins, so make sure that you have correct pins.]

In the previous exercise, we asked you to use the entire code snippet as a Python file and run it. This might not be possible in the upcoming exercises due to the length of the program and the complexity involved. Therefore, we have assembled these exercises in the program files that can be accessed from the code folder of *Chapter 4, Diving into Python-Arduino Prototyping*, which can be downloaded from `https://www.packtpub.com/books/content/support/1961`. For the `Button()` widget exercise, open the `exampleButton.py` file from the code folder of *Chapter 4, Diving into Python-Arduino Prototyping*. The code contains three main components:

- The `pyFirmata` library and Arduino configurations
- The `Tkinter` widget definitions for a button
- The LED blink function that gets executed when you press the button

As you can see in the following code snippet, we have first imported libraries and initialized the Arduino board using `pyFirmata` methods. For this exercise, we are only going to work with one LED and we have initialized only the `ledPin` variable for it:

```
import Tkinter
import pyfirmata
from time import sleep
port = '/dev/cu.usbmodemfa1331'
board = pyfirmata.Arduino(port)
sleep(5)
ledPin = board.get_pin('d:11:o')
```

[As we are using the `pyFirmata` library for all the exercises in this chapter, make sure that you have uploaded the latest version of the standard Firmata sketch on your Arduino board.]

In the second part of the code, we have initialized the root `Tkinter` widget as `top` and provided a title string. We have also fixed the size of this window using the `minsize()` method. In order to get more familiar with the root widget, you can play around with the minimum and maximum size of the window:

```
top = Tkinter.Tk()
top.title("Blink LED using button")
top.minsize(300,30)
```

The `Button()` widget is a standard `Tkinter` widget that is mostly used to obtain the manual, external input stimulus from the user. Like the `Label()` widget, the `Button()` widget can be used to display text or images. Unlike the `Label()` widget, it can be associated with actions or methods when it is pressed. When the button is pressed, `Tkinter` executes the methods or commands specified by the `command` option:

```
startButton = Tkinter.Button(top,
                             text="Start",
                             command=onStartButtonPress)
startButton.pack()
```

In this initialization, the function associated with the button is `onStartButtonPress` and the `"Start"` string is displayed as the title of the button. Similarly, the `top` object specifies the parent or the root widget. Once the button is instantiated, you will need to use the `pack()` method to make it available in the main window.

In the preceding lines of code, the `onStartButonPress()` function includes the scripts that are required to blink the LEDs and change the state of the button. A button state can have the state as `NORMAL`, `ACTIVE`, or `DISABLED`. If it is not specified, the default state of any button is `NORMAL`. The `ACTIVE` and `DISABLED` states are useful in applications when repeated pressing of the button needs to be avoided. After turning the LED on using the `write(1)` method, we will add a time delay of 5 seconds using the `sleep(5)` function before turning it off with the `write(0)` method:

```
def onStartButtonPress():
  startButton.config(state=Tkinter.DISABLED)
  ledPin.write(1)
  # LED is on for fix amount of time specified below
  sleep(5)
  ledPin.write(0)
  startButton.config(state=Tkinter.ACTIVE)
```

At the end of the program, we will execute the `mainloop()` method to initiate the `Tkinter` loop. Until this function is executed, the main window won't appear.

To run the code, make appropriate changes to the Arduino `board` variable and execute the program. The following screenshot with a button and title bar will appear as the output of the program. Clicking on the **Start** button will turn on the LED on the Arduino board for the specified time delay. Meanwhile, when the LED is on, you will not be able to click on the **Start** button again. Now, in this particular program, we haven't provided sufficient code to safely disengage the Arduino board and it will be covered in upcoming exercises.

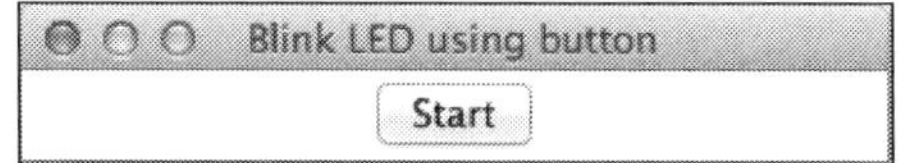

The Entry() widget – providing manual user inputs

In the previous exercise, you used a button to blink the LED on the Arduino board for a fixed amount of time. Let's say that you want to change this fixed time delay and specify a value according to your application's requirement. To perform this operation, you will need a widget that accepts custom values that can then be converted into the delay. Just like any other GUI framework, `Tkinter` provides the interface for a similar widget called `Entry()` and we will utilize this in the next exercise.

Keep the same Arduino and LED configurations that you used for the previous exercise and open the `exampleEntry.py` file. In the beginning of the code, you will find the same configuration for the Arduino board and the LED pin that we used in the previous exercise. Moving on to the next stage, you will be able to see the following code snippet that defines the root widget. In this code snippet, we have changed the title of the main window to reflect the premise of the exercise. The use of unique strings for the title of the window will help you to differentiate these windows according to their properties, when you are dealing with multiple windows in one application:

```
top = Tkinter.Tk()
top.title("Specify time using Entry")
```

Although the `Entry()` widget can be easily initialized by specifying the parent widget as the only parameter, it also supports a large number of parameters to customize the widget. For example, in our exercise, we are using the `bd` parameter to specify the width of the widget border and `width` to provide the expected width of the widget. You can learn more about the available options at `http://effbot.org/tkinterbook/entry.htm`:

```
timePeriodEntry = Tkinter.Entry(top,
                                bd=5,
```

```
                                          width=25)
timePeriodEntry.pack()
timePeriodEntry.focus_set()
startButton = Tkinter.Button(top,
                             text="Start",
                             command=onStartButtonPress)
startButton.pack()
```

In the preceding lines of code, we have initialized two widget objects in our main window: `timePeriodEntry` for the `Entry()` widget and `startButton` that we used in the previous exercise for the `Button()` widget. The Pack geometry manager always sets the graphical pointer to the last widget that has been added to the main window. We can manually shift the focus of the graphical pointer to the `timePeriodEntry` widget using the `focus_set()` method.

Contrary to the `onStartButtonPress()` function in the previous exercise, this function doesn't use the time delay fix. It, instead, obtains the value from the `timePeriodEntry` object. You can use the `get()` method to obtain the entered value from the `timePeriodEntry` object and convert it into a floating value using the `float()` function. As you can see in the following code snippet, we use this float value as the time delay between switching the LED off from the on state:

```
def onStartButtonPress():
  # Value for delay is obtained from the Entry widget input
  timePeriod = timePeriodEntry.get()
  timePeriod = float(timePeriod)
  startButton.config(state=Tkinter.DISABLED)
  ledPin.write(1)
  sleep(timePeriod)
  ledPin.write(0)
  startButton.config(state=Tkinter.ACTIVE)
```

Once you have understood the process of initializing the `Entry()` widget and the method to obtain a custom value from it, let's execute the code.

When you run this exercise, you should be able to see a window similar to the one displayed in the following screenshot. Enter a time delay value in seconds and click on **Start** to see the results on the LED. Basically, when the button is pressed, the program will call the `onStartButtonPress()` function and it will utilize this value to produce the time delay.

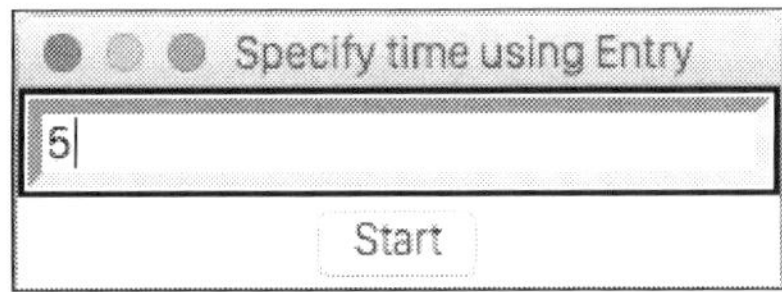

The Scale() widget – adjusting the brightness of an LED

In this section, we will develop some code to change an LED's brightness using the Python GUI. Previously, we learned that you can use a digital pin of Arduino to produce an analog output using PWM. Although you can use the `Entry()` widget to provide one time value for the PWM signal, it will be useful to have a widget that can dynamically provide this value. As brightness can be fluctuated between 0 and 100 percent, it makes sense to use a slider that varies between 0 and 100. The `Tkinter` library provides this kind of sliding interface using the `Scale()` widget.

As we are working to change the brightness of the LED and supply analog input, we will be using a digital pin with the PWM support. In the previous exercise, we used digital pin 11, which already supports PWM. If you are using a custom version of the circuit different to the one provided earlier, we recommend that you change it to a pin that supports PWM. Now it is time to open the program file, `exampleScale.py`, for this exercise.

The first stage of the program that involves importing the necessary libraries and initializing the Arduino board using `pyFirmata` is almost the same as in the previous exercise. Change the string that is used to specify the appropriate value for the port variable according to the operating system and the port that you are using. We will also instantiate the root window with the unique title for this exercise, as we did in the previous exercises. This part of the program will often reoccur for a large number of exercises and you can refer to the previous exercise for more information.

In the next stage, we will continue building the code that we developed earlier to provide a manual time delay for the LED. We will also use the same `Entry()` widget to obtain the time interval as an input:

```
timePeriodEntry = Tkinter.Entry(top,
                                bd=5,
                                width=25)
timePeriodEntry.pack()
timePeriodEntry.focus_set()
```

The `Scale()` widget offers a slider knob that can be moved over a fixed scale to provide a numeric value as an output. The starting and the ending values for this scale are provided using the `from_` and `to` options. The orientation of this slider can also be configured using the `orient` option, where the acceptable values for the orientation are `HORIZONTAL` and `VERTICAL`. However, you will have to import `HORIZONTAL` and `VERTICAL` constants from the `Tkinter` library before utilizing them here.

If no options are provided, the default widget uses the scale from 0 to 100 and the vertical orientation. In our program, we have used the horizontal orientation as a demonstration of the `orient` option. Once you have defined the widget object, `brightnessScale`, you will have to add it to the Pack geometry manager using `pack()`:

```
brightnessScale = Tkinter.Scale(top,
                                from_=0, to=100,
                                orient=Tkinter.HORIZONTAL)
brightnessScale.pack()
```

In order to start the process and reuse the previous code, we have kept the instantiation of the `startButton` widget and the `onStartButtonPress` function as it is. However, the property of the function is changed to accommodate the `Scale()` widget:

```
startButton = Tkinter.Button(top,
                             text="Start",
                             command=onStartButtonPress)
startButton.pack()
```

In this version of the `onStartButtonPress()` function, we will obtain the `ledBrightness` value by using the `get()` method on the `brightnessScale` widget object, where the `get()` method will return the value of the current location of the slider. As the PWM input requires values between 0 and 1, and the obtained slider value is between 0 and 100, we will convert the slider value into the appropriate PWM input by dividing it with 100. This new value will then be used with the `write()` method and this will ultimately turn on the LED with the applied brightness for the time period that is provided by the `timePeriodEntry` value:

```
def onStartButtonPress():
  timePeriod = timePeriodEntry.get()
  timePeriod = float(timePeriod)
  ledBrightness = brightnessScale.get()
  ledBrightness = float(ledBrightness)
  startButton.config(state=Tkinter.DISABLED)
  ledPin.write(ledBrightness/100.0)
  sleep(timePeriod)
  ledPin.write(0)
  startButton.config(state=Tkinter.ACTIVE)
```

For information about the `Scale()` widget, you can refer to `http://effbot.org/tkinterbook/scale.htm`. Now, run the `exampleScale.py` file. You will be able to see the following screenshot with the `Entry()` and `Scale()` widgets. Enter the time delay, drag the slider to the brightness that you want, and then click on the **Start** button:

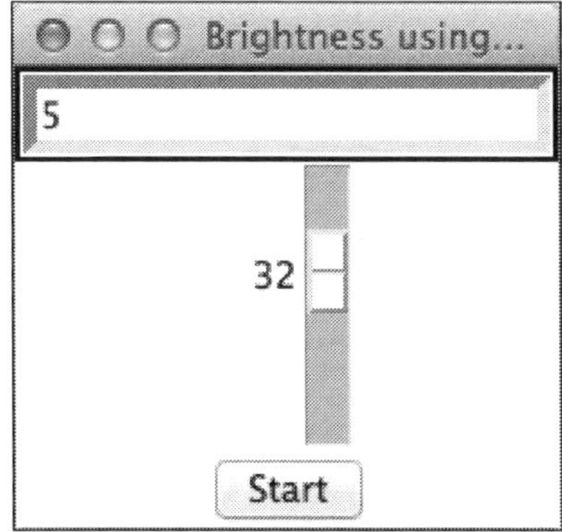

You will be able to see the LED light up with the brightness set by the `Scale()` widget. Once the LED is turned off after the given time delay, you can reset the slider to another position to dynamically vary the value for the brightness.

The Grid geometry manager

In the previous exercise, we added three different widgets to the root window using the **Pack** geometry manager and the `pack()` method. We didn't actively organize these widgets but the Pack manager automatically arranged them in the vertical position. While designing a meaningful interface, you need to arrange these widgets in the appropriate order. If you look at the previous output window, it is really difficult to identify the function of each widget or their association with others. In order to design an intuitive GUI, you also need to describe these widgets using the appropriate labels. As a solution, `Tkinter` provides an alternative way to organize your widgets that is called **Grid geometry manager**.

The Grid geometry manager provides a **two-dimensional** (**2D**) table interface to arrange widgets. Every cell that results from the row and column of the 2D table can be used as a place for the widgets. You will learn the various options that are provided by the `grid()` class to organize widgets in the next programming exercise. Open the `exampleGridManager.py` file from the code folder of this chapter. In terms of functionalities, this file contains the same program that we built in the previous exercise. However, we have added more `Label()` widgets and organized them using the Grid geometry manager to simplify the GUI and make it more useful.

As you can observe in the code, the `timePeriodEntry` object (an `Entry()` widget) now uses the `grid()` method instead of the `pack()` method. The `grid()` method is initialized with the column and row options. The values supplied for these options determine the position of the cell where the `timePeriodEntry` object will be placed.

On the other hand, we have also created a label object using the `Label()` widget and placed it beside the `Entry()` widget in the same row. The label contains a description string that is specified using the `text` option. After placing it in a cell using the `grid()` method, widgets are arranged in the center in that cell. To change this alignment, you can use the `sticky` option with one or more values from `N`, `E`, `S`, and `W`, that is, north, east, south, and west:

```
timePeriodEntry = Tkinter.Entry(top, bd=5)
timePeriodEntry.grid(column=1, row=1)
timePeriodEntry.focus_set()
Tkinter.Label(top, text="Time (seconds)").grid(column=2, row=1)
```

We have repeated this practice of placing the widget in a cell and describing it using a `Label()` widget for the objects of the `Scale()` and `Button()` widgets as well:

```
brightnessScale = Tkinter.Scale(top, from_=0, to=100, orient=Tkinter.
HORIZONTAL)
brightnessScale.grid(column=1, row=2)
Tkinter.Label(top, text="Brightness (%)").grid(column=2, row=2)

startButton = Tkinter.Button(top, text="Start",
command=onStartButtonPress)
startButton.grid(column=1, row=3)
```

As you can see in the preceding code snippet, we are using different row values for the widgets while having similar column values. As a result, our widgets will be organized in the same column and they will have their description labels in the next column of the same row. You can skip to the output window if you want to check this organization pattern.

So far, we were relying on the user to manually close the main window. However, you can create another `Button()` widget and through that, call the method to close this window. In this coding exercise, we have an additional button compared to the previous exercise that is called `exitButton`. The `command` parameter associated with this button is `quit`, which ends the loop started by the `Tkinter` method `top.mainloop()` and closes the GUI:

```
exitButton = Tkinter.Button(top,
                            text="Exit",
                            command=top.quit)
exitButton.grid(column=2, row=3)
```

In this code sample, the `quit` method is initialized as a `command` option and it can be also be called as a method:

```
top.quit()
```

Before we go ahead to the next step, perform the appropriate changes in the code and run the program. You will be prompted with a window similar to the one displayed in the following screenshot:

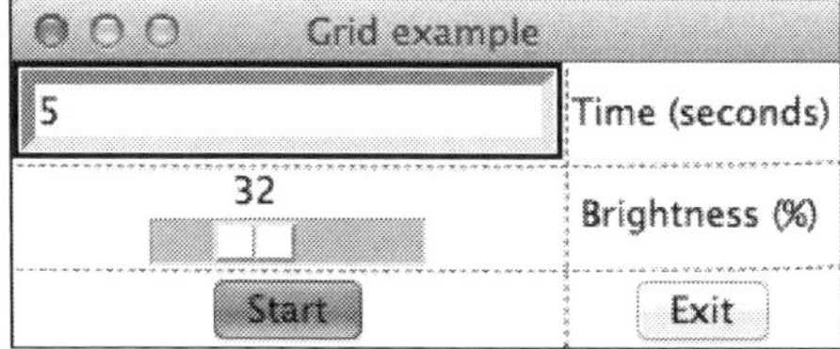

The red dotted lines are inserted later to help you identify the grid and they won't appear in the window that is opened by running the program. You can now clearly identify the role of each widget due to the presence of the description label beside them. In the opened window, play around with the time and brightness values while using the **Start** and **Exit** buttons to perform the associated actions. From the next exercise, we will start using the `grid()` method regularly to arrange the widgets.

The Checkbutton() widget – selecting LEDs

While developing complex projects, you will encounter scenarios where you have to depend on the user to select single or multiple options from a given set of values. For example, when you have multiple numbers of LEDs interfaced with the Arduino board and you want the user to select an LED or LEDs that need to be turned on. This level of customization makes your interface more interactive and useful. The `Tkinter` library provides an interface for a standard widget called `Checkbutton()` that enables the manual selection process from the given options.

In this exercise, we are going to work with both the LEDs, green and red, that you connected to the Arduino board at the beginning. The entire Python program for this exercise is located in the code folder with the name `exampleCheckbutton.py`. Open the file with the same editor that you have been using all along. This program implements the `Checkbutton()` widget for users to select the red and/or green LED when the **Start** button is clicked.

To understand the entire program logic, let's start from the initialization and importing of the libraries. As you can see, now we have two pin assignments for digital pins 10 and 11 as `redPin` and `greenPin` respectively. The code for the initialization of the Arduino board is unchanged:

```
port = '/dev/cu.usbmodemfa1331'
board = pyfirmata.Arduino(port)
```

```
sleep(5)
redPin = board.get_pin('d:10:o')
greenPin = board.get_pin('d:11:o')
```

In our utilization of the `Checkbutton()` widget, we are using a very useful `Tkinter` variable class that is called `IntVar()`.The `Tkinter` variable can tell the system when the value of the variable is changed. To better understand the `Tkinter` variable class and its specific utilization in our exercise, take a look at the following code snippet from the program:

```
redVar = Tkinter.IntVar()
redCheckBox = Tkinter.Checkbutton(top,
                                  text="Red LED",
                                  variable=redVar)
redCheckBox.grid(column=1, row=1)
```

The `Checkbutton()` widget lets a user select between two different values. These values are usually `1` (on) or `0` (off), making the `Checkbutton()` widget a switch. To capture this selection, the `variable` option is required in the widget definition. A variable can be initialized using one of the `Tkinter` variable class, `IntVar()`.

As you can see, the `redVar` variable object that is instantiated using the `IntVar()` class is used for the `variable` option while defining the `Checkbutton()` widget, `redCheckButton`. Therefore, any operation on the `redCheckButton` object will be translated to the `redVar` variable object. As `IntVar()` is a `Tkinter` class, it automatically takes care of any changes in the variable values through the `Checkbutton()` widget. Therefore, it is advisable to use the `Tkinter` variable class for the `Checkbutton()` widget instead of the default Python variables. After defining the `Checkbutton()` widget for the red LED, we have repeated this process for the green LED, as shown in the following code snippet:

```
greenVar = Tkinter.IntVar()
greenCheckBox = Tkinter.Checkbutton(top,
                                    text="Green LED",
                                    variable=greenVar)
greenCheckBox.grid(column=2, row=1)
```

This program also contains the **Start** and **Exit** buttons and their respective association with the `onStartButtonPress` and `top.quit()` functions, similar to how we used them in the previous exercise. When called, the `onStartButtonPress` function will obtain the values of the `IntVar()` variables, `redVar` and `greenVar`, using the `get()` method. In this case, the variable value of the `Checkbutton()` widget will be `1` when it is checked and `0` otherwise. This will enable the program to send the value `1` or `0` to the Arduino pin using the `write()` method by checking or unchecking the widget and ultimately, turn the LED on or off:

```
def onStartButtonPress():
  redPin.write(redVar.get())
  greenPin.write(greenVar.get())
```

As you can see, the code also implements an additional **Stop** button to turn off the LEDs that were turned on using the **Start** button:

```
stopButton = Tkinter.Button(top,
                            text="Stop",
                            command=onStopButtonPress)
stopButton.grid(column=2, row=2)
```

The `onStopButtonPrerss()` function associated with this button turns off both the LEDs by using `write(0)` on both the pins:

```
def onStopButtonPress():
  redPin.write(0)
  greenPin.write(0)
```

Since you have now learned about the `Tkinter` variables and the `Checkbutton()` widget, let's run the Python program, `exampleCheckbutton.py`. As you can see in the next screenshot, the GUI has two `Checkbutton()` widgets each for the red and green LEDs. As there is a separate initialization of the `Checkbutton()` widgets, a user can check both the red and green LEDs. `Tkinter` also provides similar widgets such as `Radiobutton()` and `Listbox()` for cases where you want to select only a single value from the given options.

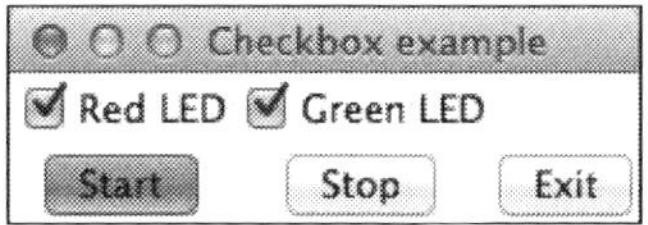

You can learn more about the `Radiobutton()` and `Listbox()` widgets from the following web pages:

- `http://effbot.org/tkinterbook/radiobutton.htm`
- `http://effbot.org/tkinterbook/listbox.htm`

The Label() widget – monitoring I/O pins

Arduino projects often deal with real-time systems and are required to continuously monitor input values from digital and analog pins. Therefore, if these values are being displayed on a graphical interface, they need to be updated periodically or when the state of a pin changes.

If you observe the previous GUI exercises, you will notice that we initialized the root window using `mainloop()` at the end of the code, which started the `Tkinter` loop and initialized all the widgets with the updated values. Once the `mainloop()` was initialized, we did not use any other `Tkinter` class or method to periodically update the widgets with the latest values.

In this exercise, we will use a potentiometer to provide variable input to the analog pin 0, which will be reflected by Tkinter's `Label()` widget. To update the label and display the values of the analog input, we are going to implement a few Python and `Tkinter` tricks. As we are using a potentiometer to provide input, you will need to change the circuit as displayed in the following diagram, before jumping to the Python program:

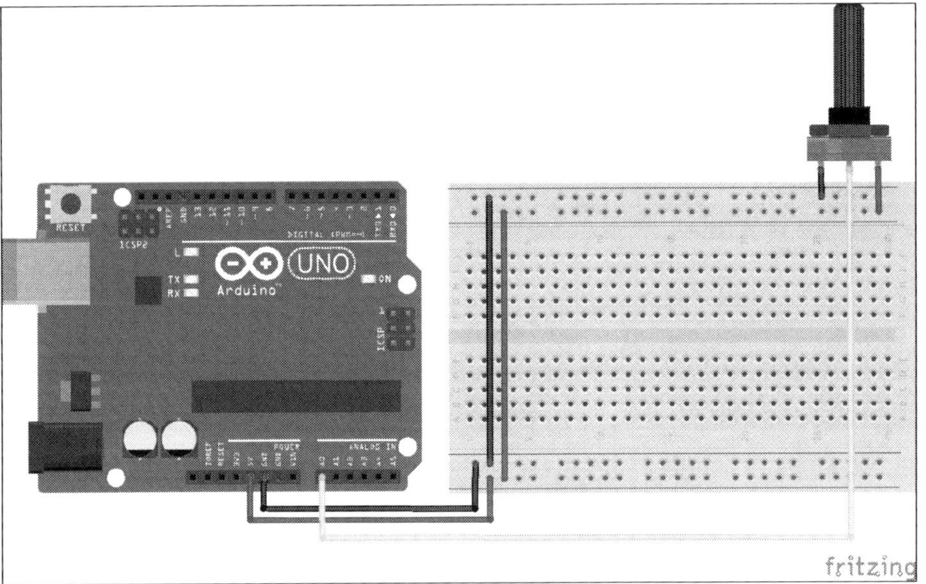

The Python file for this exercise is located in the code folder as the `workingWithLabels.py` file. For this exercise, let's run the code first to understand the premise of the exercise. Make sure that you have the appropriate string for the Arduino board when you define the `port` variable. On successful execution, the program will display the following screenshot and you can click on the **Start** button to initiate the continuous update of the potentiometer's input value:

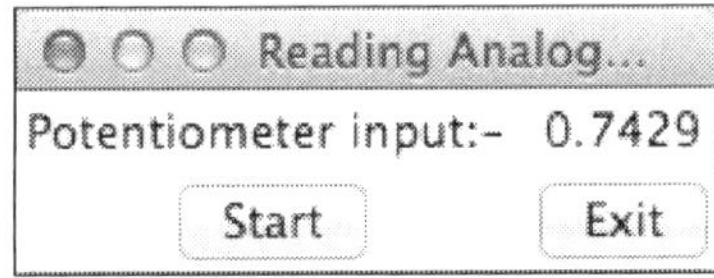

So, how did we do this? This code contains complex logic and a different program flow compared to what we have done so far. As you can see from the code, we are using a variable called `flag` to track the state of the **Exit** button while continuously running the `while` loop that monitors and updates the value. To understand the program properly, let's first get familiar with the following new `Tkinter` classes and methods:

- `BooleanVar()`: Just like the `IntVar()` variable class that we used to track the integer values, `BooleanVar()` is a `Tkinter` variable class that tracks changes in Boolean:

  ```
  flag = Tkinter.BooleanVar(top)
  flag.set(True)
  ```

  In the preceding code snippet, we have created a variable object, `flag`, using the `BooleanVar()` class and set the value of the object as `True`. Being a Boolean object, `flag` can only have two values, `True` or `False`. `Tkinter` also provides classes for string and double type with the `StringVar()` and `DoubleVar()` classes respectively.

  Due to this, when the **Start** button is clicked, the system starts updating the analog read value. The **Exit** button sets the `flag` variable to `false`, breaks the `while` loop, and stops the monitoring process.

- `update_idletasks`: While using the `Tkinter` library in Python, you can link a Python code to any changes that happen in a `Tk()` widget. This linked Python code is called a **callback**. The `update_idletasks` method calls all idle tasks without processing any callbacks. This method also redraws the geometry widgets, if required:

  ```
  AnalogReadLabel.update_idletasks()
  ```

  In our exercise, this method can be used to continuously update the label with the latest potentiometer value.

- `update`: This top-level method processes all the pending events and callbacks and also redraws any widget, if it is necessary:

  ```
  top.update()
  ```

  We are using this method with the root window so that it can perform the callback for the **Start** button.

Now let's go back to the opened Python program. As you can see, besides assigning an analog pin through the `get_pin()` method and initializing the `Iterator()` class over the Arduino board, the code contains similar programming patterns that we used in the exercises for the other `Tkinter` widgets. In this code, we are performing the read operation for the analog pin inside the `onStartButtonPress()` function This function checks the status of the `flag` variable while performing the `read()` operation on the pin and subsequently updates the value of the `analogReadLabel()` widget if the value of the `flag` variable is `True`. If the value of the `flag` variable is found to be `False`, the function will exit after disengaging the Arduino board and closing the root window. Due to the use of the `while` statement, this process will continuously check the `flag` value until it is broken by the `onExitButtonPress()` function by changing the `flag` value to `False`:

```
def onStartButtonPress():
  while True:
    if flag.get():
      analogReadLabel.config(text=str(a0.read()))
      analogReadLabel.update_idletasks()
      top.update()
    else:
      break
  board.exit()
  top.destroy()
```

The `onExitButtonPress()` function is called from the **Exit** button and it simply resets the `flag` variable to `False` using the `set()` method:

```
def onExitButtonPress():
  flag.set(False)
```

Remaking your first Python-Arduino project with a GUI

Just to refresh your memory, I would like to remind you that we created a motion detection system that generated alerts by blinking the red LED when a motion was detected. While working with the project, we were printing the state of the proximity sensor onto the Python prompt. In this exercise, we are going to use the concepts that you learned in the previous exercises and we will create an interface for our project.

As part of this exercise, you have to connect the same circuit that we used in *Chapter 3, The First Project – Motion-triggered LEDs*. Make sure you have the exact same circuit with the PIR sensor and the LEDs before you move ahead. Once you are ready with your hardware, open the `firstProjectWithGUI.py` file from the code folder of this chapter. In the code, change the appropriate port values and run the GUI for the project.

As you can see in the pin assignments, we now have three digital pins—two of them as outputs and one as an input. The output pins are assigned to the red and green LEDs while the input pin is assigned to the PIR motion sensor. If the PIR sensor is in idle mode, we will perform a onetime `read()` operation to wake up the sensor:

```
pirPin = board.get_pin('d:8:i')
redPin = board.get_pin('d:10:o')
greenPin = board.get_pin('d:11:o')
pirPin.read()
```

One of the important functions that is implemented by the code is `blinkLED()`. This function updates the `Label()` widget that is assigned to describe the status of the motion sensor. It also blinks the physical LEDs using the `write()` method and the inserted time delay. As input parameters, the `blinkLED()` function accepts the pin object and a message string from the function call, where the pin objects, that is, `redPin` or `greenPin`, should be one of the pin assignment for the LEDs:

```
def blinkLED(pin, message):
  MotionLabel.config(text=message)
  MotionLabel.update_idletasks()
  top.update()
  pin.write(1)
  sleep(1)
  pin.write(0)
  sleep(1)
```

The other two `Tkinter` related functions, `onStartButtonPress()` and `onExitButtonPress()`, are basically derived from the previous exercise. In this version of `onStartButtonPress()`, we call the `blinkLED()` function if the `flag` variable is `True` and the motion is detected using `pinPir.read()`:

```
def onStartButtonPress():
  while True:
    if flag.get():
      if pirPin.read() is True:
```

```
            blinkLED(redPin, "Motion Detected")
          else:
            blinkLED(greenPin, "No motion Detected")
        else:
          break
      board.exit()
      top.destroy()
```

The program also instantiates two buttons, **Start** and **Exit**, and one label using the methods similar to those we used in the previous exercises.

As you can observe from the code, the logic behind the motion detection system is still the same. We are only adding a layer of graphical interface to display the state of the detected motion continuously using a `Label()` widget. We have also added the **Start** and **Exit** buttons to control the project execution cycle. Once you run the code, you will be able to see a window similar to the one displayed in the following screenshot. Click on the **Start** button and wave in front of the motion sensor. If the sensor detects the motion, the label will change from **No motion detected** to **Motion detected**.

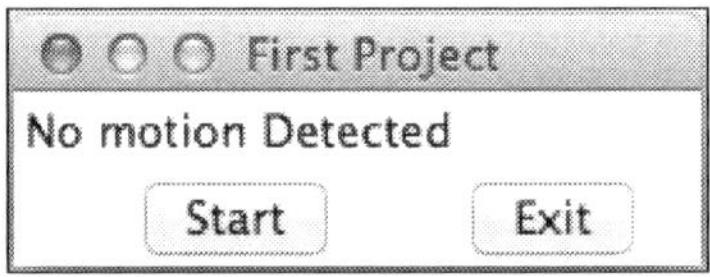

Summary

Now you have hands-on experience of building a basic GUI to handle Arduino projects. With minor modifications to the included exercises, you can use them to create a GUI for a large variety of Arduino prototyping projects. In the previous two exercises, we displayed the sensor outputs as strings in label widgets. It will be more meaningful if these numerical values are plotted as a graph and stored for further analysis. This is what you are going to perform in the next chapter.

6
Storing and Plotting Arduino Data

Sensors that are connected to Arduino produce lots of analog and digital data. Analog sensors produce data points as numerical information while digital sensors produce Boolean values, that is, 1 (on) or 0 (off). Until now, we printed this data as a string on the command prompt or displayed it in a GUI. The data was being printed in real time and it was not being saved for any further analysis. Instead of using the string format, if the data is printed as a plot or graph, it will provide useful information for us to rapidly understand it and derive conclusions. Plots are even more useful for real-time applications as they can provide information regarding the system's behavior for better understanding of the data.

This chapter is organized around two major sections: storing the Arduino sensor data and plotting this data. We will start by creating and manipulating files using Python. After that, we will work with methods for storing Arduino data in the CSV file format. In the second section, you will be introduced to the Python plotting library, `matplotlib`. Then, we will work with examples that deal with plotting data from a saved file and also from real-time sensor readings. In the end, we will try to integrate the `matplotlib` plots with the `Tkinter` window that we created in the previous chapter.

In terms of hardware components, we will be working with familiar sensors such as a potentiometer and the PIR motion sensor, which we used in the previous chapters, so, you will not have to learn or buy any additional sensors for this chapter.

Working with files in Python

Python provides built-in methods to create and modify files. File-related Python operations are useful in a large number of programming exercises. These methods are provided by standard Python modules and do not require installation of additional packages.

The open() method

The `open()` method is a default method that is available in Python and it is one of the most widely used functions to manipulate files. Now, the first step of dealing with a file is to open it:

```
>>> f = open('test.txt', 'w')
```

This command will create a `test.txt` file in the same folder in which you started the Python interpreter or the location from where the code is being executed. The preceding command uses the `w` mode that opens a file for writing or creates a new one if it doesn't exist. The other modes that can be used with the `open()` function are displayed in the following table:

Mode	Description
`w`	This opens or creates a file for writing only. It overwrites an existing file.
`w+`	This opens or creates a file for writing and reading. It overwrites an existing file.
`r`	This opens a file for reading only.
`r+`	This opens a file for reading and writing.
`a`	This opens a file for appending. It starts appending from the end of the document.
`a+`	This opens a file for appending and reading. It starts appending from the end of the document.

Make sure that you have the proper read and write permissions for the files if you are utilizing these modes in a Unix or Linux environment.

The write() method

Once the file is open in one of the writing or appending modes, you can start writing to the file object using this method. The `write()` method only takes a string as an input argument. Any other data format needs to be converted into a string before it is written:

```
>>> f.write("Hello World!\n")
```

In this example, we are writing the `Hello World!` string that ends with a new line character, `\n`. This new line character has been explained in the previous chapter and you can obtain more information about it at `http://en.wikipedia.org/wiki/Newline`.

You can also use the `writelines()` method if you want to write a sequence of strings to the file:

```
>>> sq = ["Python programming for Arduino\n", "Bye\n"]
>>> f.writelines(sq)
```

The close() method

The `close()` method closes the file and free system resources that are occupied by the file. Once they are closed, you can't use the file object as it has been flushed already. It is a good practice to close the file once you are done working with a file:

```
>>> f.close()
```

The read() method

This `read()` method reads the content of an opened file from the beginning to the end. To use this method, you need to open the file with one of the reading compatible modes such as `w+`, `r`, `r+`, or `a+`:

```
>>> f = open('test.txt', 'r')
>>> f.read()
'Hello World!\nPython programming for Arduino\nBye\n'
>>> f.close()
```

As the `read()` method grabs the entire contents of the file into memory, you can use it with the optional size parameter to avoid any memory congestion while working with large files. As an alternative method, you can use the `readlines()` method to read the content of an opened file line by line:

```
>>> f = open('test.txt', 'r')
>>> l = f.readlines()
>>> print l
['Hello World!\n', 'Python programming for Arduino\n', 'Bye\n']
>>> f.close()
```

As you can see in the preceding example, each string is printed as an element of a list that you can access individually. You can play around with these methods to get familiar with creating and modifying files. These exercises will be handy for the upcoming coding exercises.

The with statement – Python context manager

Although the `with` statement can be used to cover the execution of a code block that is defined by a context manager, it is widely used in Python to deal with files. Execute the following command on the Python interactive prompt, assuming that you have already executed the previous commands and have the `test.txt` file with some data:

```
>>> with open('test.txt', 'r') as f:
  lines = f.readlines()
  for l in lines:
    print l
```

On execution, you will be able to see each line of the file printed on the command prompt. The `with` statement while used with the `open()` method creates a context manager, which executes the wrapped code while automatically taking care of closing the file. This is the recommended method to work with files in Python and we will be utilizing it in all of our exercises. You can learn more about the Python context manager on the following websites:

- `https://docs.python.org/2/reference/compound_stmts.html#with`
- `http://preshing.com/20110920/the-python-with-statement-by-example/`

Using CSV files to store data

Now you know methods to open, manipulate, and close files using Python. In the previous examples, we used the Python interpreter and string data to get familiar with these methods. But when it comes to saving a large number of numerical values from sensor data, the **comma separated values** (**CSV**) file format is one of the most widely used file formats other than text. As the name states, values are separated and stored using commas or other delimiters such as a space or tab. Python has a built-in module to deal with CSV files.

To begin with, use the following code snippet to create a Python file and run your first CSV program:

```
import csv
data = [[1, 2, 3], ['a', 'b', 'c'], ['Python', 'Arduino',
'Programming']]

with open('example.csv', 'w') as f:
  w = csv.writer(f)
  for row in data:
    w.writerow(row)
```

You can also open the `csvWriter.py` file from this chapter's code folder, which contains the same code. After executing the code, you will be able to find a file named `example.csv` in the same location as this file, which will contain the data separated with commas.

As you can see in the code, the CSV module offers the `writer()` function on the opened file that initializes a `writer` object. The `writer` object takes a sequence or array of data (integer, float, string, and so on) as input and joins the values of this array using the delimiter character:

```
w = csv.writer(f)
```

In the preceding example, since we are not using a delimiter option, the program will take the default character comma as the delimiter. If you want to use space as the delimiter character, you can use the following `writer()` option:

```
w = csv.writer(f, delimiter=' ')
```

To write each element of a list to a new line of this `writer` object, we use the `writerow()` method.

Similarly, Python CSV module also provides the `reader()` function to read a CSV file. Check out the following example to learn more about this function, or you can open the `csvReader.py` file from the next chapter's code folder:

```
import csv
with open('example.csv', 'r') as file:
    r = csv.reader(file)
    for row in r:
        print row
```

The `reader()` function creates a `reader` object to iterate over lines in the opened CSV file. The reader object retrieves each element of a row by splitting it using the delimiter. You can access each line of the file by iterating over the object using the `for` loop as displayed in the preceding code snippet, or use the `next()` method every time you want to access the next line. On execution of the previous code, you will be able to see three separate array lists that are printed with three individual elements.

To open the CSV files externally, you can use a spreadsheet program such as Microsoft Excel, OpenOffice Calc, or Apple Numbers.

Storing Arduino data in a CSV file

In the previous two sections, you learned methods to store values in a CSV file. Although the data required for the file was already initialized in the code, the same code could be modified to store Arduino input data.

To begin with storing Arduino data, let's create a circuit that produces these values for us. We used a motion sensor in the project of *Chapter 3, The First Project – Motion-triggered LEDs*, and a potentiometer in the exercise of *Chapter 4, Diving into Python-Arduino Prototyping*. We will be using these two sensors to provide us with digital and analog input values respectively. To develop the circuit required for this exercise, connect the potentiometer to the analog pin 0 and the PIR motion sensor to digital pin 11, as displayed in the following diagram:

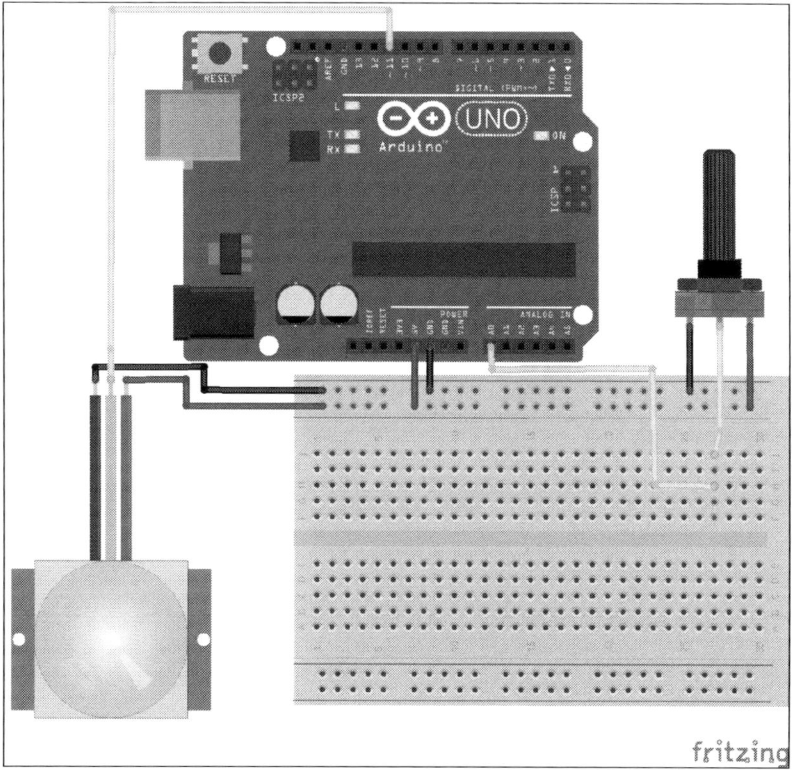

Connect other Arduino pins such as 5V and the ground, as shown in the preceding Fritzing diagram. As we are going to use `pyFirmata` to interface Python with the Arduino board, you will have to upload the **StandardFirmata** sketch to the Arduino board using the method described in *Chapter 3, The First Project – Motion-triggered LEDs*.

When you are working with prototyping, you really don't need large, powerful, and computation-intensive databases to deal with information. The easiest and quickest way to work with sensor data in this phase is by using CSV files.

Once you have your Arduino board ready with the appropriate connections, use the following code snippet to create a Python file and run it. You can also open the `csvArduinoStore.py` file from this chapter's code folder:

```
import csv
import pyfirmata
from time import sleep
```

```
port = '/dev/cu.usbmodemfa1331'
board = pyfirmata.Arduino(port)

it = pyfirmata.util.Iterator(board)
it.start()

pirPin = board.get_pin('d:11:i')
a0 = board.get_pin('a:0:i')

with open('SensorDataStore.csv', 'w') as f:
    w = csv.writer(f)
    w.writerow(["Number", "Potentiometer", "Motion sensor"])
    i = 0
    pirData = pirPin.read()
    potData = a0.read()
    while i < 25:
        sleep(1)
        if pirData is not None:
            i += 1
            row = [i, potData, pirData]
            w.writerow(row)
    print "Done. CSV file is ready!"

board.exit()
```

While the code is running, rotate the knob of the potentiometer and wave your hand in front of the motion sensors. This action will help you to generate and measure distinct values from these sensors. Meanwhile, the program will log this data in the `SensorDataStore.csv` file. When complete, open the `SensorDataStore.csv` file using any text viewer or spreadsheet program and you will be able to see these sensor values stored in the file. Now, let's try to understand the program.

As you can observe from the code, we are not utilizing a new module to interface the Arduino board or store sensor values to the file. Instead, we have utilized the same methods that we used in the previous exercises. The code has two distinct components: Python-Arduino interfacing and storing data to a CSV file. By skipping the explanation of `pyFirmata` methods to interface the Arduino board, let's focus on the code that is associated with storing the sensor data. The first line that we will write to the CSV file using `writerow()` is the header line that explains the content of the columns:

```
w.writerow(["Number", "Potentiometer", "Motion sensor"])
```

Later, we will obtain the readings from the sensors and write them to the CSV file, as shown in the following code snippet. We will repeat this process 25 times as defined by the variable, `i`. You can change the value of `i` according to your requirements.

```
while i < 25:
    sleep(1)
    if pirData is not None:
        i += 1
        row = [i, potData, pirData]
        w.writerow(row)
```

The next question is how can you utilize this coding exercise in your custom projects? The program has three main sections that can be customized to accomplish your project requirements, which are as follows:

- **Arduino pins**: You can change the Arduino pin numbers and the number of pins to be utilized. You can do this by adding additional sensor values to the row object.
- **The CSV file**: The name of the file and its location can be changed from `SensorDataStore.csv` to the one that is specific to your application.
- **The number of data points**: We have collected 25 different pairs of data points while running the `while` loop for 25 iterations. You can change this value. You can also change the time delay between each successive point from one second, as used in the program, to the value that you need.

Getting started with matplotlib

The `matplotlib` library is one of the most popular and widely supported Python plotting libraries. Although `matplotlib` is inspired by MATLAB, it is independent of MATLAB. Similar to other Python libraries that we have been using, it is an open source Python library. The `matplotlib` library assists in creating 2D plots from simple lines of code from easy to use built-in functions and methods. The `matplotlib` library is extensively used in Python-based applications for data visualization and analysis. It utilizes `NumPy` (the short form of numerical Python) and `SciPy` (short form of scientific Python) packages for mathematical calculations for the analysis. These packages are major dependencies for `matplotlib` including `freetype` and `pyparsing`. Make sure that you have these packages preinstalled on your system if you are using any other installation methods besides the ones mentioned in the next section. You can obtain more information about the `matplotlib` library from its official website (`http://matplotlib.org/`).

Configuring matplotlib on Windows

Before we install `matplotlib` on Windows, make sure that you have your Windows operating system with the latest version of Python 2.x distribution. In *Chapter 1, Getting Started with Python and Arduino*, we installed Setuptools to download and install additional Python packages. Make sure that you have Setuptools installed and configured properly. Before we advance further, we will have to install dependencies for `matplotlib`. Open the command prompt and use the following command to install the `dateutil` and `pyparsing` packages:

```
> easy_install.exe python_dateutil
> easy_install.exe pyparsing
```

Once you have successfully installed these packages, download and install the precompiled `NumPy` package from `http://sourceforge.net/projects/numpy/`. Make sure that you choose the appropriate installation files for Python 2.7 and the type of your Windows operating system.

Now, your computer should have satisfied all the prerequisites for `matplotlib`. Download and install the precompiled `matplotlib` package from `http://matplotlib.org/downloads.html`.

In this installation process, we have avoided the usage of Setuptools for `NumPy` and `matplotlib` because of some known issues related to `matplotlib` in the Windows operating system. If you can figure out ways to install these packages using Setuptools, then you can skip the preceding manual steps.

Configuring matplotlib on Mac OS X

Installation of `matplotlib` on Mac OS X can be difficult depending upon the version of Mac OS X and the availability of dependencies. Make sure that you have Setuptools installed as described in *Chapter 1, Getting Started with Python and Arduino*. Assuming that you already have Setuptools and `pip`, run the following command on the terminal:

```
$ sudo pip install matplotlib
```

Executing this command will lead to one of the following three possibilities:

- Successful installation of the latest `matplotlib` version
- Notification that the requirements are already satisfied but the installed version is older than the current version, which is 1.3 at the moment
- Error while installing the `matplotlib` package

If you encounter the first possibility, then you can advance to the next section; otherwise follow the troubleshooting instructions. You can check your `matplotlib` version using the following commands on the Python interactive prompt:

```
>>> import matplotlib
>>> matplotlib.__version__
```

Upgrading matplotlib

If you encounter the second possibility, which states that the existing version of the `matplotlib` is older than the current version, use the following command to upgrade the `matplotlib` package:

```
$ sudo pip install --upgrade matplotlib
```

Go through the next section in case you end up with errors during this upgrade.

Troubleshooting installation errors

If you encounter any errors during the `matplotlib` installation via `pip`, it is most likely that you are missing some dependency packages. Follow these steps one by one to troubleshoot the errors.

> After every step, use one of the following commands to check whether the error is resolved:
>
> ```
> $ sudo pip install matplotlib
> $ sudo pip install --upgrade matplotlib
> ```

1. Install Xcode from Apple's App Store. Open Xcode and navigate to the **Download** tab in **Preferences....** Download and install **Command Line Tools** from **Preferences....** This step should solve any compilation-related errors.
2. Install `homebrew` using the following command in the terminal:

   ```
   $ ruby -e "$("$(curl -fsSL https://raw.github.com/Homebrew/
   homebrew/go/install)")"
   ```

3. Install the following packages using `homebrew`:

   ```
   $ brew install freetype
   $ brew install pkg-config
   ```

If you still receive an error with the `freetype` package, try to create a link for `freetype` using the following command:

```
$ brew link freetype
$ ln -s /usr/local/opt/freetype/include/freetype2 /usr/local/include/freetype
```

If you receive any further errors after performing the preceding steps, go to the `matplotlib` forums at `http://matplotlib.1069221.n5.nabble.com/` for those specific errors.

> If you use `matplotlib` in Mac OS X, you need to set up the appropriate drawing backend as shown in the following code snippet:
>
> ```
> import matplotlib
> matplotlib.use('TkAgg''')
> ```
>
> You can learn more about drawing backends for `matplotlib` at `http://matplotlib.org/faq/usage_faq.html#what-is-a-backend`.

Setting up matplotlib on Ubuntu

The installation of `matplotlib` and the required dependencies is a very straightforward process on Ubuntu. We can perform this operation without using Setuptools and with the help of the Ubuntu package manager. The following simple command should do the trick for you:

```
$ sudo apt-get install python-matplotlib
```

When prompted to select dependencies, click on **Yes** to install them all. You should be able to find the `matplotlib` package in other popular Linux distributions too.

Plotting random numbers using matplotlib

The `matplotlib` library provides a collection of basic plotting-related functions and methods via the `pyplot` framework. The `pyplot` framework contains functions for creating figures, drawing plots, setting up titles, setting up axes, and many additional plotting methods. One of the import functions provided by `pyplot` is `figure()`. This initializes an empty figure canvas that can be selected for your plot or a set of plots:

```
fig1 = pyplot.figure(1)
```

You can similarly create multiple figures by specifying a number as the parameter, that is, `figure(2)`. If a figure with this number already exists, the method activates the existing figure that can then be further used for plotting.

The `matplotlib` library provides the `plot()` method to create line charts. The `plot()` method takes a list or an array data structure that is made up of integer or floating point numbers as input. If two arrays are used as inputs, `plot()` utilizes them as values for the *x* axis and the *y* axis. If only one list or array is provided, `plot()` assumes it to be the sequence values for the *y* axis and uses auto-generated incremental values for the *x* axis:

```
pyplot.plot(x, y)
```

The third optional parameter that is supported by the `plot()` method is for the format string. These parameters help users to change the style of line and markers with different colors. In our example, we are using the solid line style. So, the `plot()` function for our plot looks like this:

```
pyplot.plot(x, y, '-')
```

The `plot()` function provides a selection from a large collection of styles and colors. To find more information about these parameters, use Python's `help()` function on the `plot()` function of `matplotlib`:

```
>>> import matplotlib
>>> help(matplotlib.pyplot.plot)
```

This `help()` function will provide the necessary information to create plotting styles with different markers, line styles, and colors. You can exit this help menu by typing `q` at the prompt.

Now, as we have explored plotting sufficiently, let's create your first Python plot using the following code snippet. The program containing this code is also located in this chapter's code folder with the name `plotBasic.py`:

```
from matplotlib import pyplot
import random

x = range(0,25)
y = [random.randint(0,100) for r in range(0,25)]

fig1 = pyplot.figure()
pyplot.plot(x, y, '-')
pyplot.title('First Plot - Random integers')
pyplot.xlabel('X Axis')
pyplot.ylabel('Y Axis')

pyplot.show()
```

In the previous exercise, we randomly generated a dataset for the *y* axis using the `randint()` method. You can see a plot depicting this data with the solid line style in an opened window after running the program. As you can see in the code snippet, we used the additional `pyplot` methods such as `title()`, `xlabel()`, `ylabel()`, and `plot()`. These methods are self-explanatory and they are largely used to make your plots more informative and meaningful.

At end of the example, we used one of the most important `pyplot` methods called `show()`. The `show()` method displays the generated plots in a figure. This method is not mandatory to display figures when running from Python's interactive prompt. The following screenshot illustrates the plot of randomly generated values using `matplotlib`:

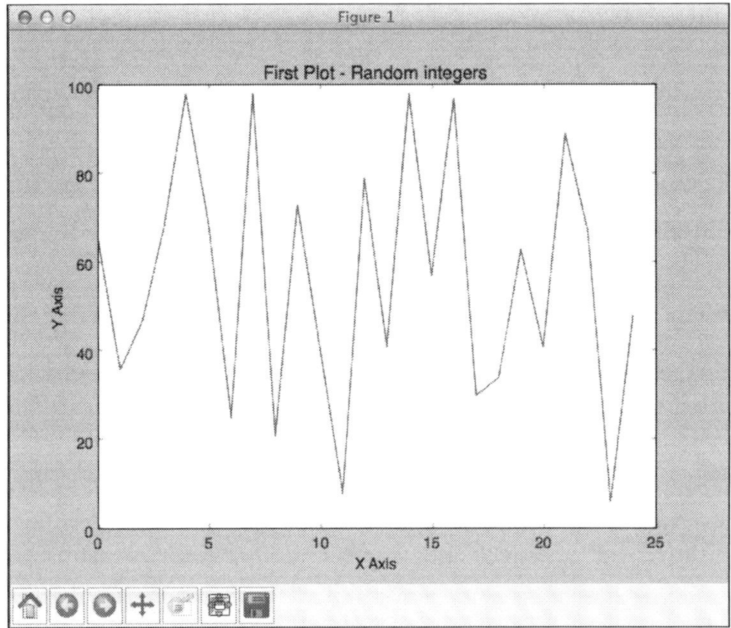

Plotting data from a CSV file

At the beginning of the chapter, we created a CSV file from Arduino data. We will be using that `SensorDataStore.csv` file for this section. If you recall, we used two different sensors to log the data. Hence, we have two arrays of values, one from a digital sensor and another from the analog one. Now, in the previous example, we just plotted one set of values for the *y* axis. So, how are we going to plot two arrays separately and in a meaningful way?

Let's start by creating a new Python program using the following lines of code or by opening the `plotCSV.py` file from this chapter's code folder:

```
import csv
from matplotlib import pyplot

i = []
mValues = []
pValues = []

with open('SensorDataStore.csv', 'r') as f:
    reader = csv.reader(f)
    header = next(reader, None)
    for row in reader:
        i.append(int(row[0]))
        pValues.append(float(row[1]))
        if row[2] == 'True':
            mValues.append(1)
        else:
            mValues.append(0)

pyplot.subplot(2, 1, 1)
pyplot.plot(i, pValues, '-')
pyplot.title('Line plot - ' + header[1])
pyplot.xlim([1, 25])
pyplot.xlabel('X Axis')
pyplot.ylabel('Y Axis')

pyplot.subplot(2, 1, 2)
pyplot.bar(i, mValues)
pyplot.title('Bar chart - ' + header[2])
pyplot.xlim([1, 25])
pyplot.xlabel('X Axis')
pyplot.ylabel('Y Axis')

pyplot.tight_layout()

pyplot.show()
```

In this program, we have created two arrays of sensor values—`pValues` and `mValues`—by reading the `SensorDataStore.csv` file row by row. Here, `pValues` and `mValues` represent the sensor data for the potentiometer and the motion sensor respectively. Once we had these two lists, we plotted them using the `matplotlib` methods.

The `matplotlib` library provides various ways to plot different arrays of values. You can individually plot them in two different figures using `figure()`, that is, `figure(1)` and `figure(2)`, or plot both in a single plot in which they overlay each other. The `pyplot` method also offers a third meaningful alternative by allowing multiple plots in a single figure via the `subplot()` method:

```
pyplot.subplot(2,1,1)
```

This method is structured as `subplot(nrows, ncols, plot_number)`, which creates grids on the figure canvas using row and column numbers, that is, `nrows` and `ncols` respectively. This method places the plot on the specific cell that is provided by the `plot_number` parameter. For example, through `subplot(2, 1, 1)`, we created a table of two rows and one column and placed the first subplot in the first cell of the table. Similarly, the next set of values was used for the second subplot and was placed in the second cell, that is, row 2 and column 1:

```
pyplot.subplot(2, 1, 2)
```

In the first subplot, we have used the `plot()` method to create a plot using the analog value from the potentiometer, that is, `pValues`. While in the second subplot, we created a bar chart instead of a line chart to display the digital values from the motion sensor. The bar chart functionality was provided by the `bar()` method.

As you can see in the code snippet, we have utilized an additional `pyplot()` method called `xlim()`. The `xlim([x_minimum, x_maximum])` or `ylim([y_minimum, y_maximum])` methods are used to confine the plot between the given maximum and minimum values of the particular axes.

Before we displayed these subplots in the figure using the `show()` method, we used the `tight_layout()` function to organize the title and label texts in the figure. The `tight_layout()` function is a very important `matplotlib` module that nicely fit the subplot parameters in one figure. You can check the effects of this module by commenting that line and running the code again. The following screenshot shows these subplots with labels and a title in one figure object:

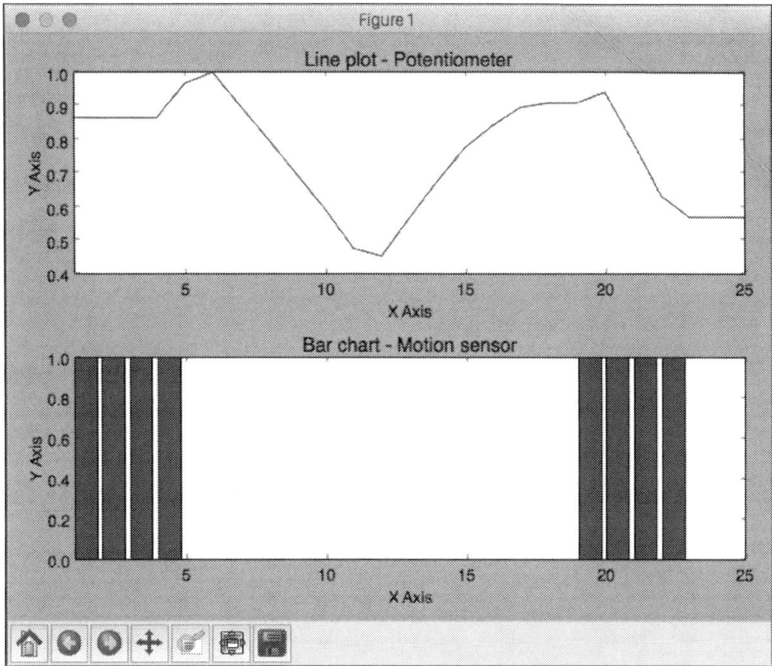

Plotting real-time Arduino data

In the previous chapter, while dealing with GUI and Arduino data, you must have noticed that the code was updating the interface with every new value that was obtained from the Arduino sensors. Similarly, in this exercise, we will be redrawing the plot every time we receive new values from Arduino. Basically, we will be plotting and updating a real-time chart instead of plotting the entire set of sensor values as we did in the previous exercise.

We will be using the same Arduino circuit that you built in the previous exercises. Here, we will utilize only the potentiometer section of the circuit to obtain the analog sensor values. Now, before we explain the new methods used in this exercise, let's first open the program file for this exercise. You can find the program file from this chapter's folder; it is named `plotLive.py`. In the code, change the appropriate parameters for the Arduino board and execute the code. While the code is running, rotate the knob of the potentiometer to observe the real-time changes in the plot.

On running the program, you will get a screen similar to the following screenshot that shows a plot from real-time Arduino data.

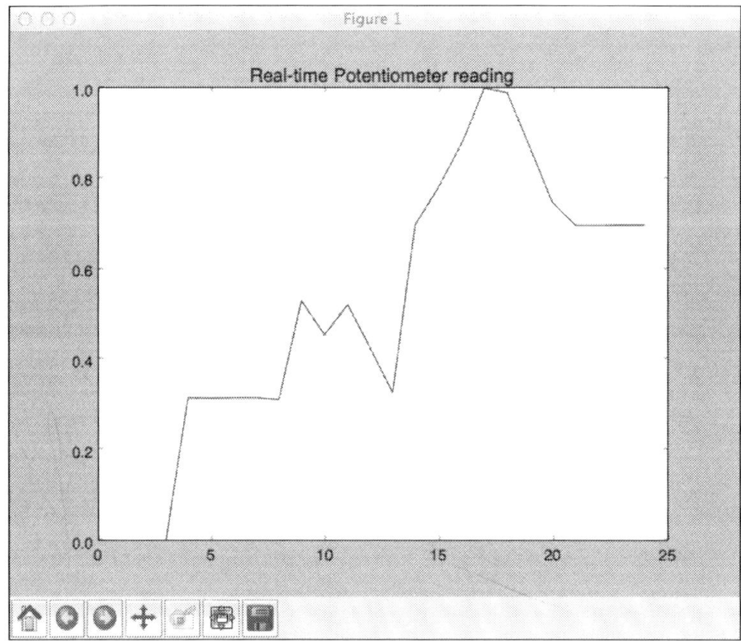

One can make various conclusions about the potentiometer's knob rotation or some other sensor behavior by just looking at the plot. These types of plots are widely used in the graphical dashboard for real-time monitoring applications. Now, let's try to understand the methods that are used in the following code snippet to make this possible.

```
import sys, csv
from matplotlib import pyplot
import pyfirmata
from time import sleep
import numpy as np

# Associate port and board with pyFirmata
port = '/dev/cu.usbmodemfa1321''
board = pyfirmata.Arduino(port)

# Using iterator thread to avoid buffer overflow
it = pyfirmata.util.Iterator(board)
it.start()
```

```
# Assign a role and variable to analog pin 0
a0 = board.get_pin(''a:0:i'')

# Initialize interactive mode
pyplot.ion()

pData = [0] * 25
fig = pyplot.figure()
pyplot.title(''Real-time Potentiometer reading'')
ax1 = pyplot.axes()
l1, = pyplot.plot(pData)
pyplot.ylim([0,1])

# real-time plotting loop
while True:
    try:
        sleep(1)
        pData.append(float(a0.read()))
        pyplot.ylim([0, 1])
        del pData[0]
        l1.set_xdata([i for i in xrange(25)])
        l1.set_ydata(pData)  # update the data
        pyplot.draw()  # update the plot
    except KeyboardInterrupt:
        board.exit()
        break
```

The real-time plotting in this exercise is achieved by using a combination of the `pyplot` functions `ion()`, `draw()`, `set_xdata()`, and `set_data()`. The `ion()` method initializes the interactive mode of `pyplot`. The interactive mode helps to dynamically change the *x* and *y* values of the plots in the figure:

```
pyplot.ion()
```

Once the interactive mode is set to `True`, the plot will only be drawn when the `draw()` method is called.

Just like the previous Arduino interfacing exercises, at the beginning of the code, we initialized the Arduino board using `pyFirmata` and the setup pins to obtain the sensor values. As you can see in the following line of code, after setting up the Arduino board and `pyplot` interactive mode, we initialized the plot with a set of blank data, `0` in our case:

```
pData = [0] * 25
```

This array for *y* values, `pData`, is then used to append values from the sensor in the `while` loop. The `while` loop keeps appending the newest values to this data array and redraws the plot with these updated arrays for the *x* and *y* values. In this example, we are appending new sensor values at the end of the array while simultaneously removing the first element of the array to limit the size of the array:

```
pData.append(float(a0.read()))
del pData[0]
```

The `set_xdata()` and `set_ydata()` methods are used to update the *x* and *y* axes data from these arrays. These updated values are plotted using the `draw()` method on each iteration of the `while` loop:

```
l1.set_xdata([i for i in xrange(25)])
l1.set_ydata(pData)  # update the data
pyplot.draw()  # update the plot
```

You will also notice that we are utilizing an `xrange()` function to generate a range of values according to the provided length, which is `25` in our case. The code snippet, `[i for i in xrange(25)]`, will generate a list of 25 integer numbers that start incrementally at 0 and end at 24.

Integrating plots in the Tkinter window

Due to the powerful integration capabilities of Python, it is very convenient to interface the plots generated by the `matplotlib` library with the `Tkinter` graphical interface. In the last exercise of the previous chapter, we integrated `Tkinter` with `pyFirmata` to implement the project of *Chapter 3, The First Project – Motion-triggered LEDs*, with the GUI. In this exercise, we will extend this integration further by utilizing `matplotlib`. We will perform this action by utilizing the same Arduino circuit that we have been using in this chapter and expand the code that we used in the previous exercise. Meanwhile, we are not introducing any new methods in this exercise; instead we will be utilizing what you learned until now. Open the `plotTkinter.py` file from this chapter's code folder.

As mentioned earlier, the program utilizes three major Python libraries and interfaces them with each other to develop an excellent Python-Arduino application. The first interfacing point is between `Tkinter` and `matplotlib`. As you can see in the following lines of code, we have initialized three button objects, `startButton`, `pauseButton`, and `exitButton`, for the **Start**, **Pause**, and **Exit** buttons respectively:

```
startButton = Tkinter.Button(top,
                             text="Start",
                             command=onStartButtonPress)
```

```
startButton.grid(column=1, row=2)
pauseButton = Tkinter.Button(top,
                             text="Pause",
                             command=onPauseButtonPress)
pauseButton.grid(column=2, row=2)
exitButton = Tkinter.Button(top,
                            text="Exit",
                            command=onExitButtonPress)
exitButton.grid(column=3, row=2)
```

The **Start** and **Exit** buttons provide control points for `matplotlib` operations such as updating the plot and closing the plot through their respective `onStartButtonPress()` and `onExitButtonPress()` functions. The `onStartButtonPress()` function also consists of the interfacing point between the `matplotlib` and `pyFirmata` libraries. As you can observe from the following code snippet, we will start updating the plot using the `draw()` method and the `Tkinter` window using the `update()` method for each observation from the analog pin a0, which is obtained using the `read()` method:

```
def onStartButtonPress():
    while True:
        if flag.get():
            sleep(1)
            pData.append(float(a0.read()))
            pyplot.ylim([0, 1])
            del pData[0]
            l1.set_xdata([i for i in xrange(25)])
            l1.set_ydata(pData)  # update the data
            pyplot.draw()  # update the plot
            top.update()
        else:
            flag.set(True)
            break
```

The `onExitButtonPress()` function implements the `exit` function as described by the name itself. It closes the `pyplot` figure and the `Tkinter` window before disengaging the Arduino board from the serial port.

Now, execute the program after making the appropriate changes to the Arduino port parameter. You should be able to see a window on your screen that is similar to the one displayed in the following screenshot. With this code, you can now control your real-time plots using the **Start** and **Pause** buttons. Click on the **Start** button and start rotating the potentiometer knob. When you click on the **Pause** button, you can observe that the program has stopped plotting new values. While **Pause** is pressed, even rotating the knob will not result in any updates to the plot.

As soon as you click on the **Start** button again, you will again see the plot get updated with real-time values, discarding the values generated while paused. Click on the **Exit** button to safely close the program:

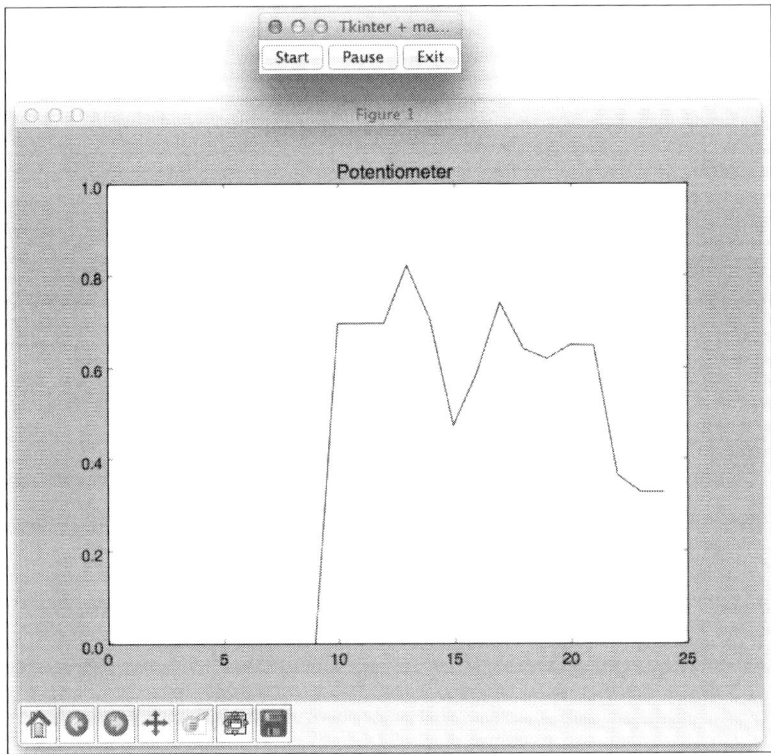

Summary

In this chapter, we introduced two major Python programming paradigms: creating, reading, and writing files using Python while also storing data into these files and plotting sensor values and updating plots in real time. We also explored methods to store and plot real-time Arduino sensor data. Besides helping you in your Arduino projects, these methods can also be used in your everyday Python projects. Throughout the chapter, using simple exercises, we interfaced the newly learned CSV and `matplotlib` modules with the `Tkinter` and `pyFirmata` modules that we learned in the previous chapters. In the next chapter, you will be introduced to your second project—a portable unit that measures and displays environmental data such as temperature, humidity, and ambient light. We will be utilizing the concepts that we have learned so far to build this project.

7

The Midterm Project – a Portable DIY Thermostat

After the first Python-Arduino project, you learned the process of prototyping various sensors, developing user interfaces, and plotting sensor data. The concepts that you learned in the previous chapters can be utilized to create a wide variety of Arduino-based hardware projects. The inception of a good application concept always begins with a real-world necessity and ends up as a practical project if it is executed properly. In this chapter, we will demonstrate this project-building process with an example of a portable sensor unit. As you can estimate from the chapter title, we will be building a simple and portable DIY thermostat that can be deployed without a desktop computer or a laptop.

To begin with, we will describe the proposed thermostat with specific goals and processes to achieve them. Once the strategy to achieve these goals has been laid down, you will be introduced to the two successive programming stages to develop the deployable and portable unit. In the first stage, we will utilize a traditional computer to successfully develop the program to interface Arduino with Python. In the second stage, we will replace this computer with a Raspberry Pi to make it portable and deployable.

Thermostat – the project description

From the multiple projects that we can build using the things that you learned, a project that helps you to monitor your surrounding environment really stands out as an important real-world application. From the various environment-monitoring projects such as weather station, thermostat, and plant monitoring system, we will be developing the thermostat as it focuses on indoor environment and can be part of your daily routine.

The thermostat is one of the most important components of any remote home monitoring system and home automation system. A popular commercial example of a connected thermostat is the Nest Thermostat (`https://www.nest.com`), which provides intelligent remote monitoring and scheduling features for your existing home's heating and cooling system. Before we think about a full-stack product such as Nest, we need first need to build a DIY thermostat with the basic set of features. Later, we can build upon this project by adding features to improve the DIY thermostat experience. Let's first outline the features that we are planning to implement in this version of the thermostat project.

Project background

Temperature, humidity, and ambient light are the three main physical characteristics that we want to monitor using the thermostat. In terms of user experience, we want to have an elegant user interface to display the measured sensor data. The user experience can be more resourceful if any of this sensor data is plotted as a line graph. In the case of a thermostat, the visual representation of the sensor data provides a more meaningful comprehension of the environment than just displaying plain numerical values.

One of the major objectives of the project is to make the thermostat portable and deployable so that it can be used in your day-to-day life. To satisfy this requirement, the thermostat display needs to be changed from a regular monitor to something small and more portable. To ensure its real-world and meaningful application, the thermostat should demonstrate real-time operation.

It is important to note that the thermostat will not be interfacing with any actuators such as home cooling and heating systems. As the interfacing of these systems with the thermostat project requires high-level understanding and experience of working with heating and cooling systems, it will deviate the flow of the chapter from its original goal of teaching you Arduino and Python programming.

Project goals and stages

In order to describe the features that we want to have in the thermostat, let's first identify the goals and milestones to achieve these objectives. The major goals for the project can be determined as follows:

- Identify the necessary sensors and hardware components for the project
- Design and assemble the circuit for the thermostat using these sensors and the Arduino board

- Design an effective user experience and develop software to accommodate the user experience
- Develop and implement code to interface the designed hardware with the software components

The code development process of the thermostat project is divided into two major stages. The objectives of the first stage include sensor interfacing, the development of the Arduino sketch, and the development of the Python code on your regular computer that you have been using all along. The coding milestone for the first stage can be further distributed as follows:

- Develop the Arduino sketch to interface sensors and buttons while providing output of the sensor data to the Python program via the serial port
- Develop the Python code to obtain sensor data from the serial port using the `pySerial` library and display the data using GUI that is designed in `Tkinter`
- Create a plot to demonstrate the real-time humidity readings using the `matplotlib` library

In the second stage, we will attach the Arduino hardware to a single-board computer and a miniature display to make it mobile and deployable. The milestone to achieve objective of the second stage are as follows:

- Install and configure a single-board computer, Raspberry Pi, to run the Python code from the first stage
- Interface and configure the miniature screen with the Raspberry Pi
- Optimize the GUI and plot window to adjust to this small screen's resolution

In the following subsection of this section, you will be notified about the list of required components for both the stages, followed by the hardware circuit design and the software flow design. The programming exercises for these stages are explained in the next two sections of the chapter.

The list of required components

Instead of going through the process of identifying the required components, we have already selected the components for this project based on their utilization in the previous exercises, ease of use, and availability. You can replace these components according to their availability at the time you are building this project or your familiarity with other sensors. Just make sure that you take care of modifications in the circuit connections and code, if these new components are not compatible with the ones that we are using.

In the first stage of prototyping, we will need components to develop the electronic circuit for the thermostat unit. As we mentioned earlier, we are going to measure temperature, humidity, and ambient light through our unit. We already learned about the temperature sensor TMP102 and the ambient light sensor BH1750 in *Chapter 4, Diving into Python-Arduino Prototyping*. We will be using these sensors for this project with the humidity sensor HIH-4030. The project will utilize the same Arduino Uno board that you have been using throughout the previous chapters with the necessary cables. We will also need two push buttons to provide manual inputs to the unit. The summary of the required components for the first stage is provided in the following table:

Component (first stage)	**Quantity**	**Website**
Arduino Uno	1	`https://www.sparkfun.com/products/11021`
USB cable for Arduino	1	`https://www.sparkfun.com/products/512`
Breadboard	1	`https://www.sparkfun.com/products/9567`
TMP102 temperature sensor	1	`https://www.sparkfun.com/products/11931`
HIH-4030 humidity sensor	1	`https://www.sparkfun.com/products/9569`
BH1750 ambient light sensor	1	`http://www.robotshop.com/en/dfrobot-light-sensor-bh1750.html`
Push button switch	2	`https://www.sparkfun.com/products/97`
1 kilo-ohm resistor	2	
10 kilo-ohm resistor	2	
Connection wires	As required	

Although the table provides links for few specific website, you can obtain these components from your preferred providers. The two major components HIH-4030 humidity sensor and push button switch that we haven't used previously are described as follows:

- **HIH-4030 humidity sensor**: This measures and provides relative humidity results as an analog output. The output of the sensor can be directly connected to any analog pin of Arduino. The following image shows the breakout board with the HIH-4030 sensor that is sold by SparkFun Electronics. You can learn more about the HIH-4030 sensor from its datasheet, which can be obtained from `https://www.sparkfun.com/datasheets/Sensors/Weather/SEN-09569-HIH-4030-datasheet.pdf`:

- **Push button switch**: Push button switches are small switches that can be used on a breadboard. When pressed, the switch output changes its status to **HIGH**, which is **LOW** otherwise.

In the second stage, we are going to make the sensor unit mobile by replacing your computer with a Raspberry Pi. For that, you will need the following components to get started:

Component (second stage)	Quantity	Image
Raspberry Pi	1	`https://www.sparkfun.com/products/11546`
Micro USB cable with a power adapter	1	`http://www.amazon.com/CanaKit-Raspberry-Supply-Adapter-Charger/dp/B00GF9T3I0/`
8 GB SD card	1	`https://www.sparkfun.com/products/12998`
TFT LCD screen	1	`http://www.amazon.com/gp/product/B00GASHVDU/`
A USB hub	Optional	

Further explanations of these components are provided later in the chapter.

Hardware design

The entire hardware architecture of the thermostat can be divided into two units, a physical world interfacing unit and a computation unit. The physical world interfacing unit, as its name indicates, monitors phenomenon of the physical world such as temperature, humidity, and ambient light using sensors connected to the Arduino board. The physical world interfacing unit is interchangeably mentioned as the thermostat sensor unit throughout the chapter. The computational unit is responsible for displaying the sensor information via the GUI and plots.

The following diagram shows the hardware components for the first stage where the thermostat sensor unit is connected to a computer using the USB port. In the thermostat sensor unit, various sensor components are connected to the Arduino board using I2C, analog, and digital pins:

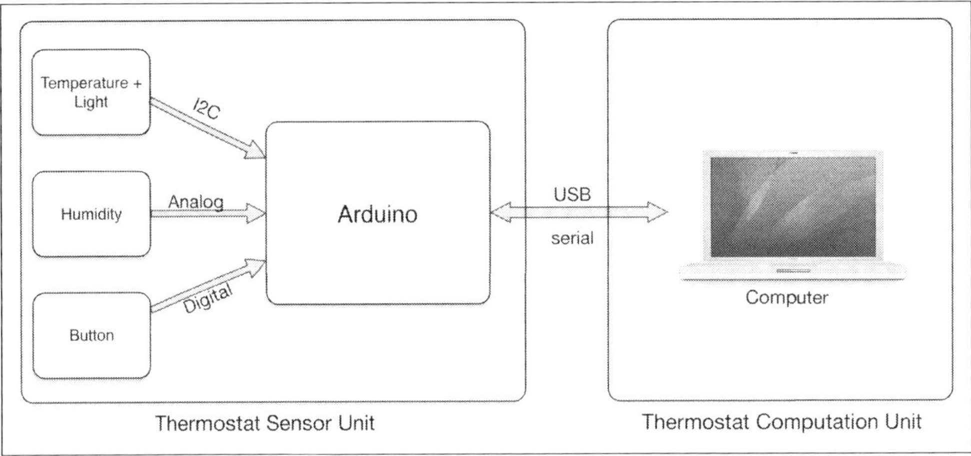

In the second programming stage where we are going make our thermostat into a mobile and deployable unit, you will be using a single-board computer, Raspberry Pi, as the computational device. In this stage, we will use a miniature **thin-film transistor liquid-crystal display** (**TFT LCD**) screen that is connected to a Raspberry Pi via **general-purpose input/output** (**GPIO**) pins and is used as a display unit to replace the traditional monitor or laptop screen. The following diagram shows this new thermostat computational unit, which truly reduces the overall size of the thermostat and makes it portable and mobile. Circuit connections for the Arduino board are unchanged for this stage and we will use the same hardware without any major modifications.

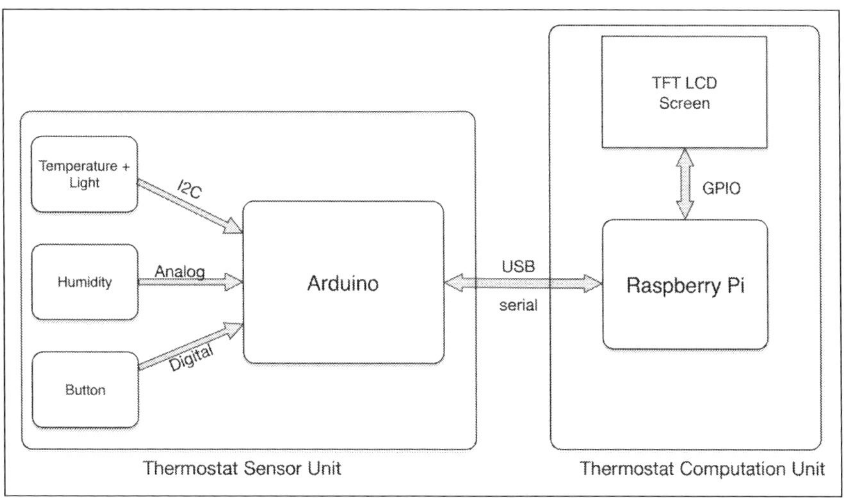

As the common unit for both stages of the project, the Arduino-centric thermostat sensor unit requires slightly more complex circuit connections compared to other exercises that you have been through. In this section, we are going to interface the necessary sensors and push buttons to their respective pins on the Arduino board and you will need a breadboard to make these connections. If you are familiar with PCB prototyping, you can create your own PCB board by soldering these components and avoid the breadboard. PCB boards are more robust compared to breadboards and less prone to loose connections. Use the following instructions and the Fritzing diagram to complete the circuit connections:

1. As you can see in the following diagram, connect the SDA and SCL pins of TMP102 and BH1750 to analog pins 4 and 5 of the Arduino board and create an I2C bus. To make these connections, you can use multiple color-coded wires to simplify the debugging process.
2. Use two 10 kilo-ohm pull-up resistors with the SDA and SCL lines.
3. Contrary to these I2C sensors, the HIH-4030 humidity sensor is a simple analog sensor and can be directly connected to the analog pin. Connect the HIH-4030 to the analog pin A0.
4. Connect VCC and the ground of TMP102, BH1750, and HIH-4030 to +5V and the ground of the Arduino board using power strips of the breadboard, as displayed in the diagram. We recommend that you use red and black wires to represent the +5V and ground lines respectively.
5. The push button provides the output as **HIGH** or **LOW** state and interfaced using digital pins. As displayed in the circuit, connect these push buttons to digital pins 2 and 3 using two 1 kilo-ohm resistors.

6. Complete the remaining connections as displayed in the following diagram. Make sure that you have firmly connected all the wires before powering up the Arduino board:

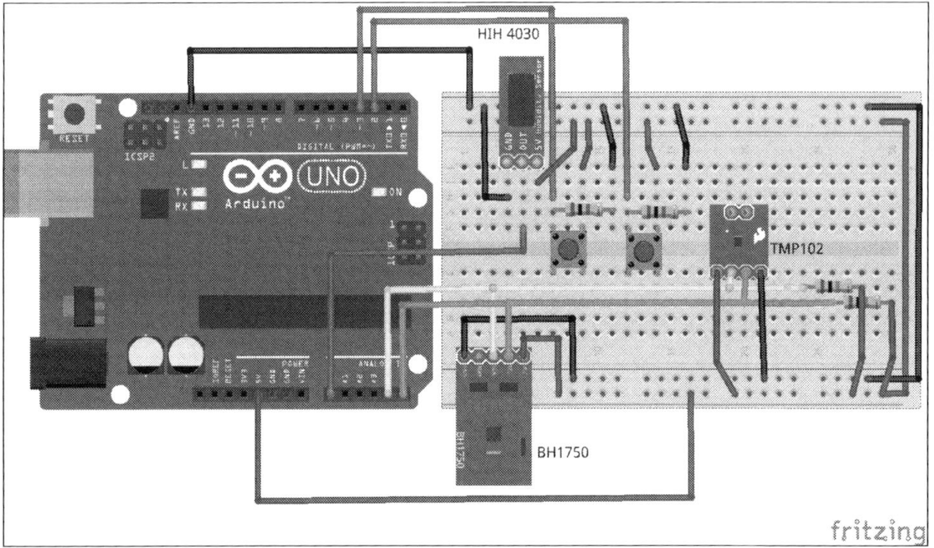

Make sure that you always disconnect your Arduino board from the power source or a USB port before making any connections. This will prevent any damage to the board due to short circuiting.

Complete all the connections for the thermostat sensor unit before heading to the next section. As this unit is being used in both the programming stages, you won't be performing any further changes to the thermostat sensor unit.

Software flow for user experience design

One of the critical components of any project is its usability or accessibility. When you are working on making your project prototype into a product, it is necessary to have an intuitive and resourceful user interface so that the user can easily interact with your product. Hence, it is necessary to define the user experience and software flow of a project before you start coding. The software flow includes the flow chart and the logical components of the program that are derived from the project requirements. According to the goals that we have defined for the thermostat project, the software flow can be demonstrated in the following diagram:

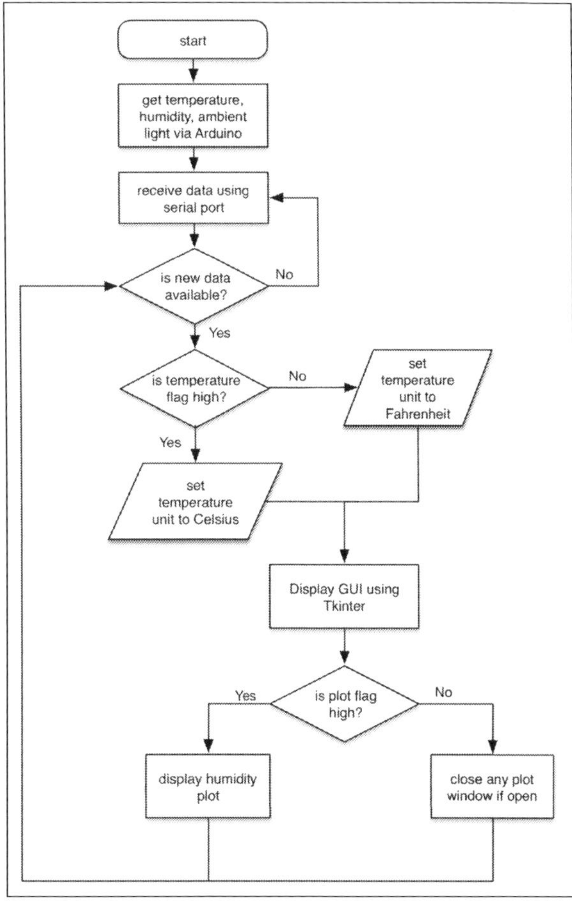

In the implementation, the software flow of the project begins by measuring the temperature, humidity, and ambient light from Arduino and printing them on a serial port line by line. The Python program obtains the sensor data from Arduino via the serial port before presenting the data on the screen. Meanwhile, the Python program keeps looking for a new line of data.

A user can interact with the thermostat using a push button, which will let the user change the unit for the temperature data. Once the button is pressed, the flag gets changed to **HIGH** and the temperature unit is changed to **Celsius** from its default unit, **Fahrenheit**. If the button is pressed again, the opposite process will happen and the unit will be changed back to its default value. Similarly, another user interaction point is the second push button that allows a user to open a plot for real-time humidity values. The second push button also utilizes a similar method of using flags to capture the input and opens a new plot window. If the same button is pushed sequentially, the program will close the plot window.

Stage 1 – prototyping the thermostat

In this prototyping stage, we will develop the Arduino and Python code for our thermostat, which will be later used in the second stage with minor changes. Before you start the coding exercise, make sure that you have the thermostat sensor unit ready with the Arduino board and the connected sensors, as described in the previous section. For this stage, you will be using your regular computer which is equipped with the Arduino IDE and the Python programming environment. The prototyping stage requires two levels of programming, the Arduino sketch for the thermostat sensor unit and the Python code for the computational unit. Let's get started with coding for our thermostat.

The Arduino sketch for the thermostat

The goal of this Arduino program is to interface sensors, get measurements from the sensors, and print them on the serial port. As we discussed earlier, rather than using the standard Firmata sketch that we used in the previous project, we are going to develop a custom Arduino sketch in this project. To get started, open the `Thermostat_Arduino.ino` sketch from this chapter's code folder, which is part of the source code that you received for the book.

Connect the USB port of the Arduino board, which is now part of the thermostat sensor unit, to your computer. Select the appropriate board and port names in the Arduino IDE and verify the code. Upload the code to your Arduino board and open the **Serial Monitor** window once the code is successfully uploaded. You should be able to see text similar to that displayed in the following screenshot:

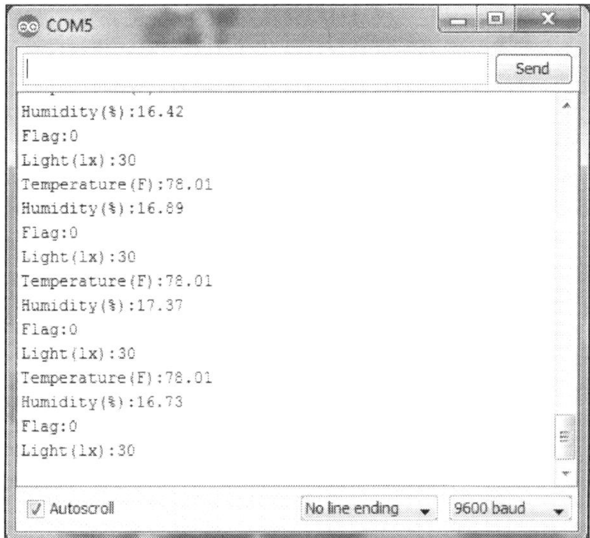

The Arduino code structure and basic declarations are already explained in various sections throughout the book. Instead of explaining the entire code line by line, we will focus here on the main components of the software flow that we described earlier.

Interfacing the temperature sensor

In the Arduino sketch, the temperature data is obtained from the TMP102 sensor using the `getTemperature()` function. The function implements the `Wire` library on the I2C address of TMP102 to read the sensor data. This is then converted into proper temperature values:

```
float getTemperature(){
  Wire.requestFrom(tmp102Address, 2);

  byte MSB = Wire.read();
  byte LSB = Wire.read();

  //it's a 12bit int, using two's compliment for negative
  int TemperatureSum = ((MSB << 8) | LSB) >> 4;

  float celsius = TemperatureSum*0.0625;
  return celsius;
}
```

The `getTemperature()` function returns the temperature values in Celsius, which is then sent to the serial port.

Interfacing the humidity sensor

Although the humidity sensor provides the analog output, it is not straightforward to obtain relative humidity since it also depends upon the temperature. The `getHumidity()` function calculates the relative humidity from the analog output provided by the HIH-4030 sensor. The formulas to calculate the relative humidity are obtained from the datasheet and reference examples of the sensor. If you are using a different humidity sensor, please make sure that you change the formulas accordingly, as they may change the results significantly:

```
float getHumidity(float degreesCelsius){
//caculate relative humidity
float supplyVolt = 5.0;

// Get the sensor value:
int HIH4030_Value = analogRead(HIH4030_Pin);
// convert to voltage value
float voltage = HIH4030_Value/1023. * supplyVolt;
```

```
    // convert the voltage to a relative humidity
    float sensorRH = 161.0 * voltage / supplyVolt - 25.8;
    float trueRH = sensorRH / (1.0546 - 0.0026 * degreesCelsius);

    return trueRH;
}
```

As we are calculating relative humidity, the returned humidity values are sent to the serial port with percentage as the unit.

Interfacing the light sensor

To interface the BH1750 light sensor, we will use the BH1750 Arduino library, which we used earlier. Using this library, the ambient light value can be directly obtained using the following line of code:

```
uint16_t lux = lightMeter.readLightLevel();
```

This line provides the luminance values in the unit of `lux`. These values are also sent to the serial port so the Python program can utilize it further.

Using Arduino interrupts

Until now you used the Arduino program to read the physical state of an I/O pin using the `DigitalRead()` or `AnalogRead()` functions. How would you automatically obtain the state change instead of periodically reading the pins and waiting for the state to change? Arduino interrupts provide a very convenient way of capturing signals for the Arduino board. Interrupts are a very powerful way of automatically controlling various things in Arduino. Arduino supports interrupts using the `attachInterrupt()` method. In terms of the physical pins, Arduino Uno provides two interrupts: interrupt 0 (on digital pin 2) and interrupt 1 (on digital pin 3). Various Arduino boards have different specifications for interrupt pins. If you are using any board other than Uno, please refer to Arduino's website to find out about the interrupt pin for your board.

The `attachInterrupt()` function takes three input arguments (`pin`, `ISR`, and `mode`). In these input arguments, `pin` refers to the number of the interrupt pin, `ISR` (which stands for Interrupt Service Routine) refers to the function that gets called when the interrupt occurs, and `mode` defines the condition when the interrupt should be triggered. We have utilized this function in our Arduino program, as described in the following code snippet:

```
attachInterrupt(0, button1Press, RISING);
attachInterrupt(1, button2Press, RISING);
```

The supported `mode` for `attachInterrupt()` are `LOW`, `CHANGE`, `RISING`, and `FALLING`. In our case, the interrupts are triggered when the mode is `RISING`, that is, the pin goes from low to high. For interrupts declared at 0 and 1, we call the `button1Press` and `button2Press` functions that will change `flagTemperature` and `flagPlot` respectively. When `flagTemperature` is set to `HIGH`, Arduino sends the temperature in Celsius, otherwise it sends the temperature in Fahrenheit. When `flagPlot` is `HIGH`, Arduino will print the flag on the serial port, which will be used by the Python program later to open the plot window. You can learn more about Arduino interrupts from the tutorial at `http://arduino.cc/en/Reference/attachInterrupt`.

Designing the GUI and plot in Python

Once your thermostat sensor unit starts sending sensor data to the serial port, it is time to execute the second part of this stage, the Python code for the GUI and the plot. From this chapter's code folder, open the Python file called `Thermostat_Stage1.py`. In the file, go to the line that contains the `Serial()` function where the serial port is declared. Change the serial port name from `COM5` to the appropriate one. You can find this information from the Arduino IDE. Save the change and exit the editor. From the same folder, run the following command on the terminal:

```
$ python Thermostat_Stage1.py
```

This will execute the Python code and you will be able to see the GUI window on the screen.

Using pySerial to stream sensor data in your Python program

As described in the software flow, the program receives the sensor data from the Arduino using the `pySerial` library. The code that declares the serial port in the Python code is as follows:

```
Import serial
port = serial.Serial('COM5',9600, timeout=1)
```

It is very important to specify the `timeout` parameter while using the `pySerial` library, as the code may have an error if `timeout` is not specified.

Designing the GUI using Tkinter

The GUI for this project is designed using the `Tkinter` library that we used earlier. As a GUI-building exercise, three columns of labels (labels to display the sensor type, the observation values, and observation units) are programmed as shown in the following code snippet:

```
# Labels for sensor name
Tkinter.Label(top, text = "Temperature").grid(column = 1, row = 1)
Tkinter.Label(top, text = "Humidity").grid(column = 1, row = 2)
Tkinter.Label(top, text = "Light").grid(column = 1, row = 3)

# Labels for observation values
TempLabel = Tkinter.Label(top, text = " ")
TempLabel.grid(column = 2, row = 1)
HumdLabel = Tkinter.Label(top, text = " ")
HumdLabel.grid(column = 2, row = 2)
LighLabel = Tkinter.Label(top, text = " ")
LighLabel.grid(column = 2, row = 3)

# Labels for observation unit
TempUnitLabel = Tkinter.Label(top, text = " ")
TempUnitLabel.grid(column = 3, row = 1)
HumdUnitLabel = Tkinter.Label(top, text = "%")
HumdUnitLabel.grid(column = 3, row = 2)
LighUnitLabel = Tkinter.Label(top, text = "lx")
LighUnitLabel.grid(column = 3, row = 3)
```

Once you initialize the code and before you click on the **Start** button, you will be able to see the following window. The observation labels are populated without any values at this stage:

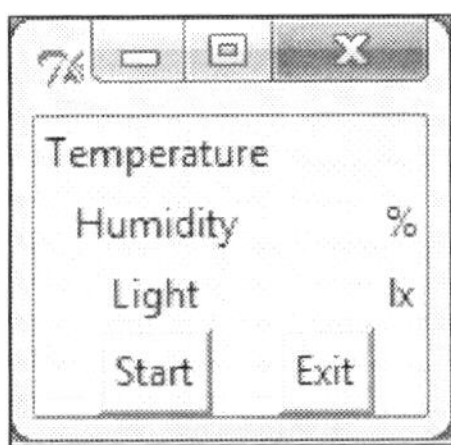

Once the **Start** button is clicked, the program will engage the thermostat sensor unit and start reading the sensor values from the serial port. Using the lines that are obtained from the serial port, the program will populate the observation labels with the obtained values. The following code snippet updates the temperature values in the observation label and also updates the temperature unit:

```
TempLabel.config(text = cleanText(reading[1]))
TempUnitLabel.config(text = "C")
TempUnitLabel.update_idletasks()
```

In the program, we are using similar methods for humidity and ambient light to update their labels respectively. As you can see in the following screenshot, the GUI now has the values for the temperature, humidity, and ambient light readings:

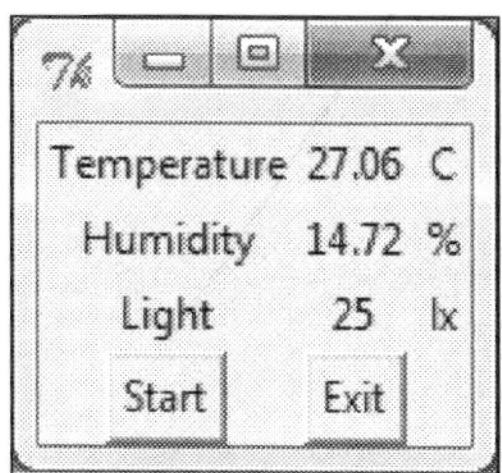

The **Start** and **Exit** buttons are programmed to call the `onStartButtonPress()` and `onExitButtonPress()` functions when they are clicked by the user. The `onStartButtonPress()` function executes the code necessary to create the user interface, while the `onExitButtonPress()` function closes all the opened windows, disconnects the thermostat sensor unit, and exits the code:

```
StartButton = Tkinter.Button(top,
                             text="Start",
                             command=onStartButtonPress)
StartButton.grid(column=1, row=4)
ExitButton = Tkinter.Button(top,
                            text="Exit",
                            command=onExitButtonPress)
ExitButton.grid(column=2, row=4)
```

You can play with the **Start** and **Exit** buttons to explore the Python code. To observe the changes in the sensor readings, try to blow air or place an obstacle over the thermostat sensor unit. If the program doesn't behave appropriately, check the terminal for error messages.

Plotting percentage humidity using matplotlib

We will use the `matplotlib` library to plot the relative humidity values in real time. We will plot the relative humidity values in this project, as the range of the data is fixed between 0 and 100 percent. Using a similar method, you can also plot temperature and ambient light sensor values. While developing the code to plot temperature and ambient light sensor data, make sure that you are using appropriate ranges to cover the sensor data in the same plot. Now, as we have specified in the `onStartButtonPress()` function, a window similar to the following screenshot will pop up once you press the push button for the plot:

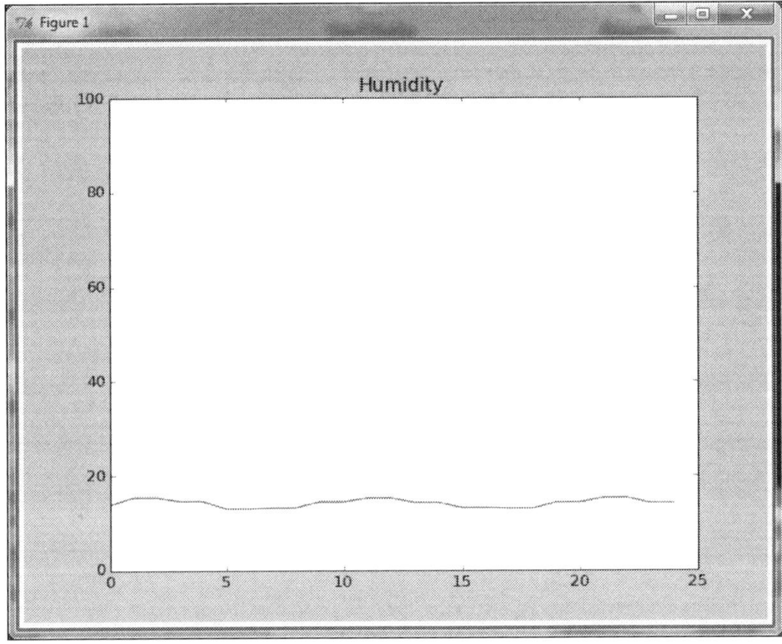

The following code snippet is responsible for plotting the line chart using the humidity sensor values. The values are limited between 0 and 100 on the *y* axis, where the *y* axis represents the relative humidity range. The plot is updated every time the program receives a new humidity value:

```
pyplot.figure()
pyplot.title('Humidity')
ax1 = pyplot.axes()
l1, = pyplot.plot(pData)
pyplot.ylim([0,100])
```

Using button interrupts to control the parameters

The push button interrupts are a critical part of the user experience, as the user can control the temperature unit and the plot using these interrupts. The Python features implemented using the push button interrupts are as follows.

Changing the temperature unit by pressing a button

The Arduino sketch contains the logic to handle interrupts from push buttons and use them to change the temperature unit. When an interrupt occurs, instead of printing the temperature in Fahrenheit, it sends the temperature in Celsius to the serial port. As you can see in the following screenshot, the Python code just prints the obtained numeric value of the temperature observation and the associated unit of measurement with it:

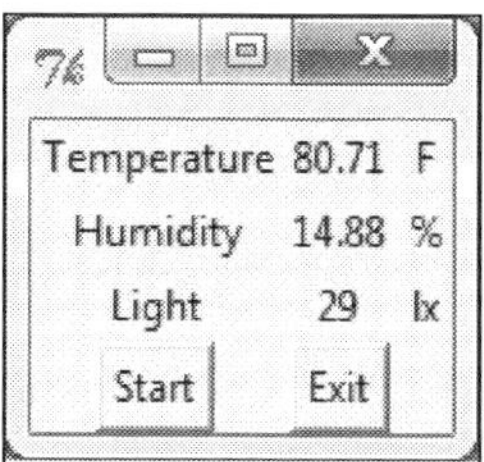

As you can see in the following code snippet, if the Python code receives the `Temperature(C)` string, it prints the temperature in `Celsius`, and if it receives the `Temperature(F)` string, it prints the temperature in `Fahrenheit`:

```
if (reading[0] == "Temperature(C)"):
    TempLabel.config(text=cleanText(reading[1]))
    TempUnitLabel.config(text="C")
    TempUnitLabel.update_idletasks()
if (reading[0] == "Temperature(F)"):
    TempLabel.config(text=cleanText(reading[1]))
    TempUnitLabel.config(text="F")
    TempUnitLabel.update_idletasks()
```

Swapping between the GUI and the plot by pressing a button

If the Python code receives the value of the flag from the serial port as `1` (HIGH), it creates a new plot and draws the humidity values as a line chart. However, it closes any open plots if it receives `0` (LOW) as the value of the flag. As you can see in the following code snippet, the program will always try to update the plot with the latest values for humidity readings. If the program can't find an opened plot to draw this value from, it will create a new plot:

```
if (reading[0] == "Flag"):
    print reading[1]
    if (int(reading[1]) == 1):
        try:
            l1.set_xdata(np.arange(len(pData)))
            l1.set_ydata(pData)  # update the data
            pyplot.ylim([0, 100])
            pyplot.draw()  # update the plot
        except:
            pyplot.figure()
            pyplot.title('Humidity')
            ax1 = pyplot.axes()
            l1, = pyplot.plot(pData)
            pyplot.ylim([0, 100])
    if (int(reading[1]) == 0):
        try:
            pyplot.close('all')
            l1 = None
        except:
```

By now, you should have a complete idea about the programs that are required by the thermostat sensor unit and the computation unit. Due to the complexity involved, you may face a few known problems during the execution of these programs. You can refer to the *Troubleshooting* section in case you run into any trouble.

Troubleshooting

Here are some of the errors that you may find, and their fixes:

- I2C sensor returns the error string:
    - Check the connections to the SDA and SCL pins.
    - Confirm that you are providing enough delay between the reading cycles of the sensor. Check the datasheet for the delay and message sequence.

- The plot window flickers instead of staying on when the button is pressed:
    - Don't try to press it multiple times. Hold and let go quickly. Make sure that your button is connected properly.
    - Adjust the delay in the Arduino sketch.

Stage 2 – using a Raspberry Pi for the deployable thermostat

We have now created a thermostat that exists as an Arduino prototype while the Python program runs from your computer. This prototype is still nowhere near a deployable or mobile state due to the connected computer, and the display monitor if you are using a desktop computer. A real-world thermostat device should have a small footprint, portable size, and miniature display to show limited information. The popular and practical way to achieve this goal is to use a small single-board computer that is capable of hosting an operating system and hence providing the essential Python programming interface. For this stage of the project, we will be utilizing a single-board computer—a Raspberry Pi—with a small LCD display.

> Note that this stage of the project is optional unless you want to extend the previous stage of the project to a device that can be used on a regular basis. If you are referring to the project to just learn Python programming, you can skip this entire section.

The following is an image of the Raspberry Pi Model B:

If you haven't worked with a single-board computer before, you may have a lot of unanswered questions, such as "What exactly does a Raspberry Pi consists of?", "What are the benefits of using a Raspberry Pi in our project?", and "Can't we just use Arduino for that?". These are legitimate questions and we will try to answer them in the following section.

What is a Raspberry Pi?

The Raspberry Pi is a small (almost the size of a credit card) single-board computer that was developed with the initial aim of helping students learn the basics of computer science. Today, the Raspberry Pi movement, guided by the Raspberry Pi Foundation, has turned into a DIY phenomenon and captured the attention of enthusiasts and developers around the world. The capabilities and features shipped with a Raspberry Pi at a nominal cost ($35) have boosted the popularity of the device.

The term single-board computer is used for devices that have all the necessary components to run an operating system on one board, such as a processor, RAM, graphics processor, storage device, and basic adaptors for expansion. This makes a single-board computer an appropriate candidate for portable applications, as they can be part of the portable hardware device that we are trying to create. Although there were a number of single-board computers in the market before the introduction of the Raspberry Pi, the open source nature of the hardware and the economical price are the main reasons behind the popularity and rapid adoption of the Raspberry Pi. The following figure shows the Raspberry Pi Model B with its major components:

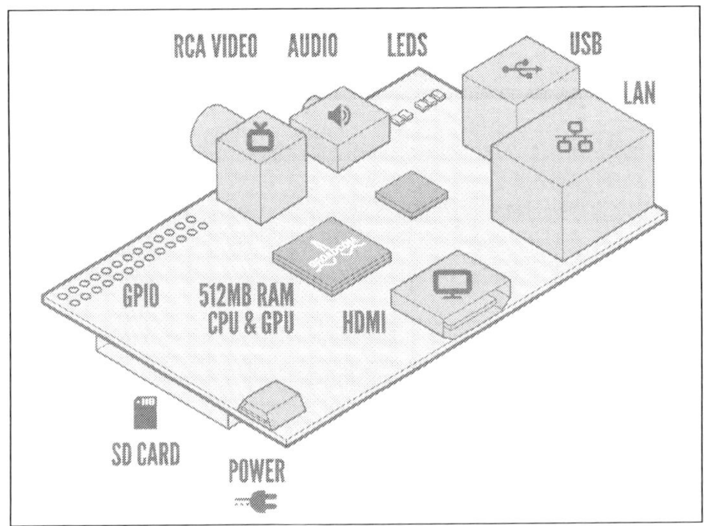

The computational capabilities of the Raspberry Pi are adequate for running a trimmed down version of Linux OS. Although people had tried to use many types of operating systems on a Raspberry Pi, we will be using the default and recommended operating system called **Raspbian**. Raspbian is a Debian distribution-based open source Linux OS, which is optimized for the Raspberry Pi. The Raspberry Pi uses an SD card as the storage device, which will be used to store your OS and program files. In Raspbian, you can avoid running the unnecessary OS components that are shipped with traditional OSes. These include the Internet browser, communication application, and in some cases even the graphical interface.

After its introduction, the Raspberry Pi has gone through a few major upgrades. The earlier version, called **Model A**, did not include the Ethernet port and only had a memory of 256 MB. In our project, we are using the Raspberry Pi's Model B that has a dedicated Ethernet port, 512 MB memory, and dual USB ports. The latest versions of Raspberry Pi, Model B+, can be also used as it is also equipped with an Ethernet port.

Installing the operating system and configuring the Raspberry Pi

Although the Raspberry Pi is a computer, it is different than traditional desktop computers when it comes to interfacing peripheral devices. Instead of supporting traditional VGA or DVI display ports, the Raspberry Pi provides a RCA video port for TVs and an HDMI port for the latest generation of monitors and TVs. In addition, the Raspberry Pi has only two USB ports that need to be utilized for connecting various peripheral devices such as the mouse, the keyboard, the USB wireless adapter, and the USB memory stick. Let's get started by collecting components and cables to start working with a Raspberry Pi.

What do you need to begin using the Raspberry Pi?

The hardware components required to get started with a Raspberry Pi are as follows:

- **A Raspberry Pi**: For this stage of the project, you will need a Raspberry Pi version Model B or latest. You can buy the Raspberry Pi from `http://www.raspberrypi.org/buy`.
- **A power cable**: The Raspberry Pi runs on 5V DC and requires at least 750 mA current. The power is applied through the micro USB port that is located on the board. In this project, you will need a micro USB power supply. Optionally, you can use a micro USB-based phone charger to supply power to the Raspberry Pi.

- **A display cable**: If you have an HDMI monitor or a TV, you can use an HDMI cable to connect it to your Raspberry Pi. If you want to use your VGA or DVI-based monitor, you will need a VGA to HDMI or DVI to HDMI adapter converter. You can buy these adapter converters from Amazon or Best Buy.
- **An SD card**: You are required to have at least an 8 GB SD card to get started. It is preferable to use an SD card that has a quality of class 4 or better. You can also buy an SD card with the preinstalled OS at `http://swag.raspberrypi.org/collections/frontpage/products/noobs-8gb-sd-card`.

The Raspberry Pi Model B+ requires a microSD card instead of a regular SD card.

- **A mouse and keyboard**: You will need a standard USB keyboard and a USB mouse to work with the Raspberry Pi.
- **A USB hub (optional)**: Since the Model B has just two USB ports, you will have to remove existing devices from the USB ports to make space for another device if you want to connect a Wi-Fi adapter or memory stick to it. A USB hub can be handy to attach multiple peripheral components to your Raspberry Pi. We recommend that you use a USB hub with external power supply, as the Raspberry Pi can drive a limited number of peripheral devices through the USB ports due to power limitations.

Preparing an SD card

To install and configure software components such as Python and the required libraries, first we need an operating system for the Raspberry Pi. A Raspberry Pi officially supports Linux-based open source operating systems that are preconfigured for custom Raspberry Pi hardware components. Various versions of these operating systems are available on Raspberry Pi's website (`http://www.raspberrypi.org/downloads`).

Raspberry Pi's website provides a variety of OSes for users who range from newbies to experts. It is difficult for a first-time user to identify the appropriate OS and its installation process. If this is your first attempt with a Raspberry Pi, we recommend that you use the **New Out Of Box Software (NOOBS)** package. Download the latest version of `NOOBS` from the previous link. The `NOOBS` package includes few different operating systems such as Raspbian, Pidora, Archlinux, and RaspBMC. `NOOBS` streamlines the entire installation process and helps you to install and configure your preferred version of the OS easily. It is important to note that `NOOBS` is just an installation package and you will be left with only the Raspbian OS once you complete the given installation steps.

Raspberry Pi uses the SD card to host the operating system and you need to prepare the SD card from your computer before placing it into the SD card slot of the Raspberry Pi. Insert your SD card into your computer and make sure that you have a backup of any important information that is on the SD card. During the installation process, you will lose all the data stored on the SD card. Let's start by preparing your SD card.

Follow these steps to prepare an SD card from Windows:

1. You will require a software tool to format and prepare the SD card for Windows. You can download the freely available formatting tool from `https://www.sdcard.org/downloads/formatter_4/eula_windows/`.
2. Download and install the formatting tool on your Windows computer.
3. Insert your SD card and start the formatting tool.
4. In the formatting tool, open the **Options** menu and set **FORMAT SIZE ADJUSTMENT** to **ON**.
5. Select the appropriate SD card and click on **Format**.
6. Then, wait for the formatting tool to finish formatting the SD card. Once this is done, extract the downloaded `NOOBS` ZIP file to the SD card. Make sure that you extract the content of the ZIP folder to the root location of the SD card.

Follow these directions to prepare SD card from Mac OS X:

1. You will require a software tool to format and prepare the SD card for Mac OS X. You can download the freely available formatting tool from `https://www.sdcard.org/downloads/formatter_4/eula_mac/`.
2. Download and install the formatting tool on your machine.
3. Insert your SD card and run the formatting tool.
4. In the formatting tool, select **Overwrite Format**.
5. Select the appropriate SD card and click on **Format**.
6. Then, wait for the formatting tool to finish formatting the SD card. Once this is done, extract the downloaded `NOOBS` ZIP file to the SD card. Make sure that you extract the content of the ZIP folder to the root location of the SD card.

Follow these steps to prepare the SD card from Ubuntu Linux:

1. To format the SD card on Ubuntu, you can use a formatting tool called `gparted`. Install `gparted` using the following command on the terminal:

   ```
   $ sudo apt-get install gparted
   ```

2. Insert your SD card and run `gparted`.
3. In the `gparted` window, select the entire SD card and format it using **FAT32**.
4. Once the format process is complete, extract the downloaded `NOOBS` ZIP file to the SD card. Make sure that you extract the content of the ZIP folder to the root location of the SD card.

If you have any trouble following these steps, you can refer to the official documentation for preparing the SD card for a Raspberry Pi at `http://www.raspberrypi.org/documentation/installation/installing-images/`.

The Raspberry Pi setup process

Once you have prepared your SD card with `NOOBS`, insert it into the SD card slot of the Raspberry Pi. Connect your monitor, mouse, and keyboard before connecting the micro USB cable for the power adapter. Once you connect the power adapter, the Raspberry Pi will turn on automatically and you will be able to see the installation process on the monitor. If you are not able to see any progress on the monitor after connecting the power adapter, refer to the troubleshooting section that is available later in this chapter.

Once the Raspberry Pi boots up, it will repartition the SD card and show you the following installation screen so that you can get started:

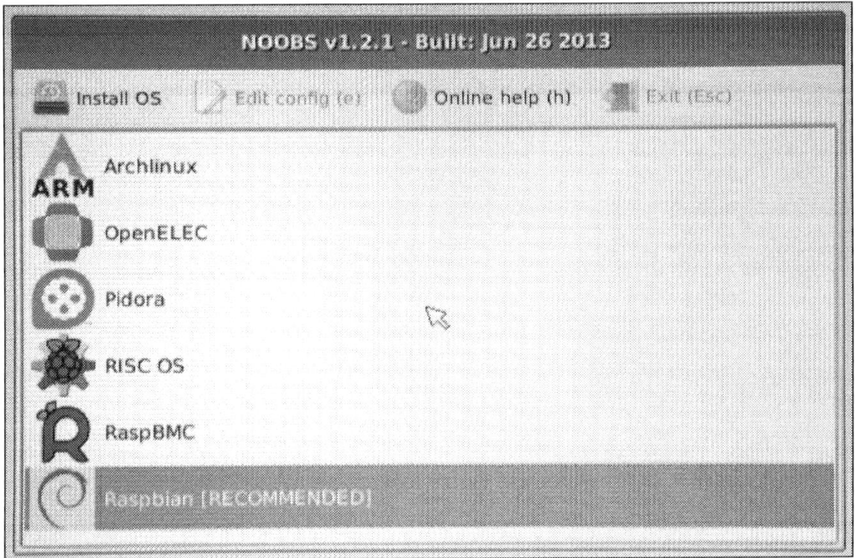

> The preceding screenshot is taken from `raspberry_pi_F01_02_5a.jpg` by Simon Monk and is licensed under Attribution Creative Commons license (`https://learn.adafruit.com/assets/11384`).

1. As a first-time user, select **Raspbian [RECOMMENDED]** as the recommended operating system and click on the **Install OS** button. Raspbian is a Debian-based OS that is optimized for the Raspberry Pi and it supports useful Linux commands that we have already learned in the previous chapters. The process will take about 10 to 20 minutes to complete.
2. On successful completion, you will be able to see a screen similar to the one displayed in the following screenshot. The screenshot displays the `raspi-config` tool that will let you set up the initial parameters. We will skip this process to complete the installation. Select **<Finish>** and press *Enter*:

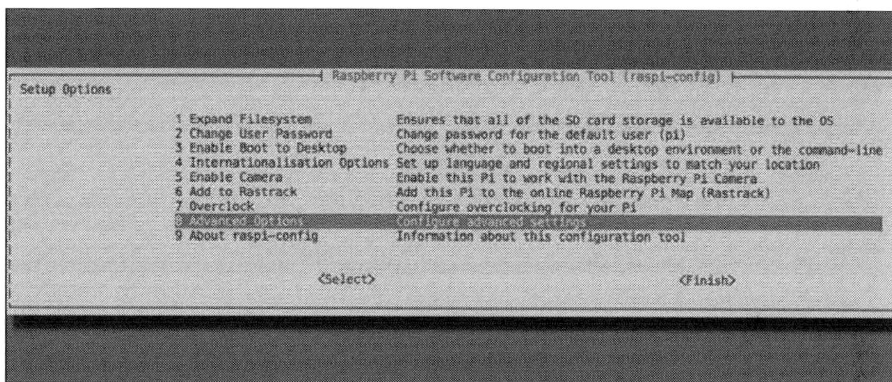

3. You can go back to this screen again, in case you want to change any parameter, by typing the following command in the terminal:

   ```
   $ sudo raspi-config
   ```

4. Raspberry Pi will now reboot and you will be prompted to the default login screen. Log in using the default username `pi` and password `raspberry`.
5. You can start the graphical desktop of the Raspberry Pi by typing the following command in the terminal:

   ```
   $ startx
   ```

6. To run the Python code that we developed in the first stage, you will need to set up required Python libraries on the Raspberry Pi. You will have to connect your Raspberry Pi to the Internet using the Ethernet cable to install the packages. Install the required Python packages on the Raspberry Pi terminal using the following command:

```
$ sudo apt-get install python-setuptools, python-matplotlib,
python-numpy
```

7. Install `pySerial` using Setuptools:

```
$ sudo easy_install pyserial
```

Now, your Raspberry Pi is ready with an operating system and the necessary components to support Python-Arduino programming.

Using a portable TFT LCD display with the Raspberry Pi

TFT LCD is a great way to expand the Raspberry Pi's functionalities and avoid the use of large display devices. These TFT LCD displays can be interfaced directly with GPIO pins. TFT LCD screens are available in various shapes and size, but for the Raspberry Pi we recommend that you use a screen with a size smaller than or equal to 3.2 inches due to interfacing convenience. Most of these small screens do not require additional power supply and can be directly powered using the GPIO pins. In a few cases, touch screen versions are also available to extend the functionality of the Raspberry Pi.

In this project, we are using a Tontec 2.4 inch TFT LCD screen that can be directly interfaced with the Raspberry Pi via GPIO. Although you can use any available TFT LCD screen, this book only cover the setup and configuration process for this particular screen. In most cases, manufacturers of these screens provide detailed configuration tutorials on their websites. Raspberry Pi forums and blogs are another good places to look for help if you are using a different type of the TFT LCD screen. The following image shows the back of the Tontec 2.4 inch TFT LCD screen with the location of the GPIO pins. Let's get started and use this screen with your Raspberry Pi:

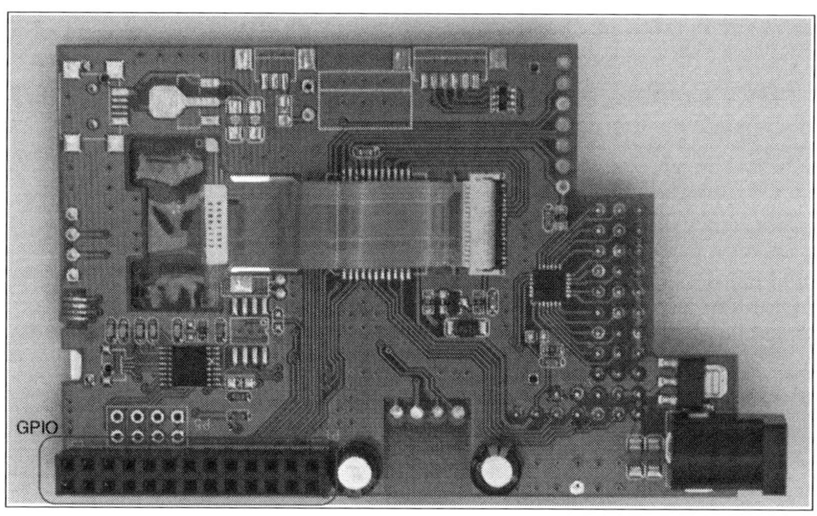

Connecting the TFT LCD using GPIO

Before we can use the screen, we will have to connect it to the Raspberry Pi. Let's disconnect the micro USB power adapter from the Raspberry Pi and locate the GPIO male pins near the RCA video port on the Raspberry Pi. Get your TFT screen and connect the GPIO pins as such you can see Raspberry Pi and the screen as displayed in the following image. In handful cases, the notations on the screen will be misleading, and therefore we suggest that you follow the guidelines from the manufacturer to make the connections:

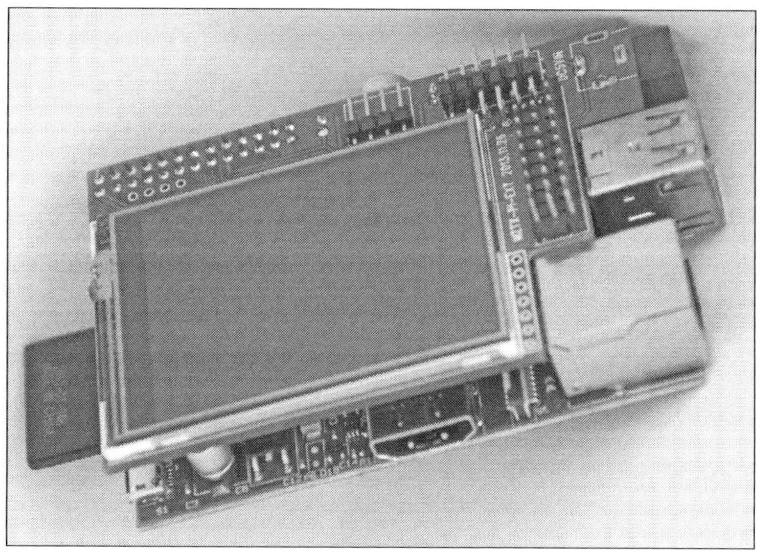

Once your screen is connected to the Raspberry Pi, power it up using the micro USB cable. Do not disconnect your HDMI cable yet, as your screen is still not ready. Before we go ahead with any of the configuration steps, let's first connect the Raspberry Pi to the Internet. Connect the Ethernet port of the Raspberry Pi to your home or office network using an Ethernet cable. Now, let's configure the TFT LCD screen in the Raspbian OS to make it work properly.

Configuring the TFT LCD with the Raspberry Pi OS

Once your Raspberry Pi is powered up, log in using your username and password. Complete the following steps to configure the screen with your Raspberry Pi:

1. Download the supporting files and manual using the following command on the terminal:

   ```
   $ wget https://s3.amazonaws.com/tontec/24usingmanual.zip
   ```

2. Unzip the file. The following command will extract the files into the same directory:

   ```
   $ unzip 24usingmanual.zip
   ```

3. Navigate to the `src` directory:

   ```
   $ cd cd mztx-ext-2.4/src/
   ```

4. Enter following command to compile the source files:

   ```
   $ make
   ```

5. Open the boot configuration files:

   ```
   $ sudo pico /boot/config.txt
   ```

6. In the `config.txt` file, locate and uncomment the following lines of code:

   ```
   framebuffer_width=320
   framebuffer_height=240
   ```

7. Save and exit the file.
8. Now, every time the Raspberry Pi restarts we need to execute a command to start the TFT LCD screen. To do this, open the `rc.local` file using the following command:

   ```
   $ sudo pico /etc/rc.local
   ```

9. Add the following line of code to the file that starts the screen:

   ```
   sudo /home/pi/mztx-ext-2.4/src/mztx06a &
   ```

10. Save and exit the file. Then, reboot the Raspberry Pi using the following command:

```
$ sudo reboot
```

You can remove your HDMI monitor now and start working with your TFT LCD screen. One thing that you will have to keep in mind is that the screen resolution is very small and it is not optimized for coding. We prefer to use the HDMI monitor to perform the major code modifications that are required in the next section. The utilization of the TFT LCD screen in this project is to accommodate the mobility and portability requirements of the thermostat.

Optimizing the GUI for the TFT LCD screen

The resolution of the TFT LCD screen that we configured in the previous section is only 320 x 240 pixels, but the windows that we created in first programming stage are quite large. Therefore, before we copy and run our Python code on the Raspberry Pi, we need to adjust a few parameters in the code.

In your regular computer where you have this chapter's folder from the book's source code, open the `Thermostat_Stage2.py` file. This file contains the details of the modification required to obtain the optimum size with minor cosmetic changes. You will be using this file, instead of the one that we used in the previous stage, on your Raspberry Pi. These adjustments in the code are explained in the following lines of code.

The first major alteration is in the port name. For the Raspberry Pi, you need to change the name of the Arduino port from that you were using in the first stage to `/dev/ttyACM0`, which is the address assigned to Arduino in the majority of the cases:

```
port = serial.Serial('/dev/ttyACM0',9600, timeout=1)
```

In this program file, the size of the `Tkinter` main window and the `matplotlib` figure are also adjusted to fit the screen size. If you are using a different-sized screen, change the following lines of code appropriately:

```
top.minsize(320,160)
pyplot.figure(figsize=(4,3))
```

Now, with the preceding changes, the GUI window should be able to fit within Raspberry Pi's screen. As the Raspberry Pi's screen will be used as the dedicated screen for the thermostat application, we need to adjust the text size on the screen to fit the window properly. Add the `font=("Helvetica", 20)` text in the declaration of the labels to increase the font size. The following line of code shows changes that are performed on the labels to contain the sensor names:

```
Tkinter.Label(top,
              text="Humidity",
              font=("Helvetica", 20)).grid(column=1, row=2)
```

Similarly, the `font` option is added to the observation labels:

```
HumdUnitLabel = Tkinter.Label(top,
                              text="%",
                              font=("Helvetica", 20))
```

The labels for the observation unit also carry similar modifications:

```
HumdLabel.config(text=cleanText(reading[1]),
                 font=("Helvetica", 20))
```

The `Thermostat_ Stage2.py` file already includes the preceding modifications and is ready to run on your Raspberry Pi. Before you run the file, first we need to copy the file to the Raspberry Pi. At this stage, the USB hub will be very handy to copy the files. If you don't have a USB hub, you can utilize two available USB ports simultaneously to attach the USB pen drive, mouse, and keyboard. With the use of the USB hub, connect the USB pen drive containing the Python files and copy them to the home folder. Attach the USB port of the Arduino board to one of the ends of the USB hub. From the start menu of the Raspberry Pi, open the **LXTerminal** program by navigating to **Accessories** | **LXterminal**. Run the Python code from the home folder and you will be able to see the optimized user interface window that opens on the Raspberry Pi's screen. If every step mentioned in the chapter is performed correctly, you will be able to see the sensor observation being printed when you click on the **Start** button:

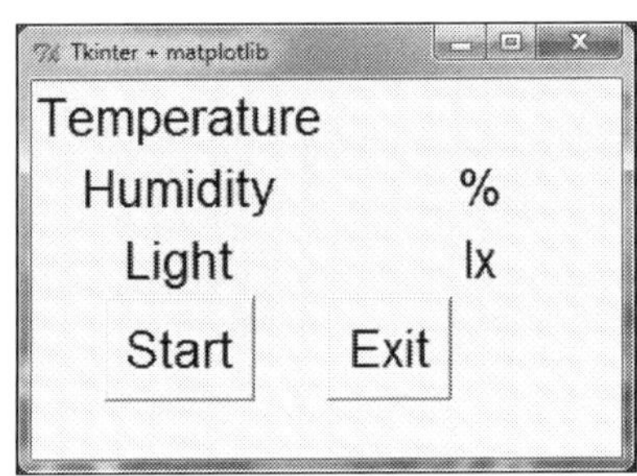

At the end of the chapter, you must be wondering what a mobile unit with sensors, Arduino, Raspberry Pi, and TFT screen might look like. The following image shows a sample thermostat that was developed using the instructions given in this chapter. We used an acrylic sheet to hold the Raspberry Pi and the Arduino board together and created a compact form factor:

Troubleshooting

There are a few known problems that you may face in this stage of the project. The following section describes these problems and their quick fixes:

- The Raspberry Pi is not booting up:
    - Make sure that the SD card is formatted properly with the specified tools. The Raspberry Pi won't boot if the SD card is not prepared properly.
    - Check the HDMI cable and the monitor to see whether they are working fine.
    - Make sure that the power adapter is compatible with the Raspberry Pi.
- The TFT LCD screen doesn't turn on:
    - Make sure that the screen is properly connected to the GPIO pins of the Raspberry Pi.

    - If you are using any other TFT LCD screen, make sure from its datasheet that your screen doesn't require additional power.
    - Check whether the screen is properly configured using the steps described in the *Optimizing the GUI for the TFT LCD screen* section.

- There is a slow refresh rate of the sensor data on the Raspberry Pi:
    - Try decreasing the delay between each serial message that is sent by Arduino.
    - Terminate any other application that is running in the background.

Summary

With this project, we successfully created a portable and deployable thermostat using Arduino, which monitors temperature, humidity, and ambient light. During this process, we assembled the thermostat sensor unit using the necessary components and developed custom Arduino program to support them. We also utilized Python programming methods including GUI development and plots using `Tkinter` and `matplotlib` libraries respectively. Later in the chapter, we utilized the Raspberry Pi to convert a mere project prototype into a practical application. Henceforth, you should be able to develop similar projects that require you to observe and visualize real-time sensor information.

Going forward, we will be expanding this project to accommodate upcoming topics such as Arduino networking, cloud communication, and remote monitoring. In the next level of the thermostat project, we will integrate these advanced features and make it a really resourceful DIY project that can be used in everyday life. In the next chapter, we are going to start the next stage of our journey from making simple Python-Arduino projects to Internet-connected and remotely accessible IoT projects.

8 Introduction to Arduino Networking

So far, we used a hardwired serial connection to interact with Arduino, a serial monitor to observe the Arduino serial data, and a Python serial library (`pySerial`) to transfer data between the Arduino and Python applications. During this entire exchange, the range of communication was limited due to the hardwired serial connection. As a solution, you can use a wireless protocol such as **ZigBee**, **Bluetooth**, or other RF channels to establish a communication channel for a remote serial interface. These wireless protocols are extensively used in remote hardware applications, and they use the serial interface to transfer data. Due to their use of serial communication, these protocols require very little to no additional programming changes on the Arduino or Python side. You may require additional hardware to enable these protocols, however. The major benefit of these protocols is that they are really easy to implement. However, they are restricted with only a small geographical coverage area and limited data bandwidth.

Besides serial communication methods, the other way to remotely access your Arduino device is to use a computer network. Today, computer networks are the most prolific way of communicating between computing units. In the next two chapters, we will explore various networking techniques using Arduino and Python, which range from establishing very basic Ethernet connectivity to developing complex, cloud-based web applications.

In this chapter, we will cover the following topics:

- The fundamentals of networking and hardware extensions that enable networking for Arduino
- Python frameworks used to develop **Hypertext Transfer Protocol** (**HTTP**) web servers on your computer
- Interfacing Arduino-based HTTP clients with the Python web server

- IoT messaging protocol MQTT (we will install a middleware tool called **Mosquitto** to enable MQTT on our computer)
- Utilizing the publisher/subscriber paradigm, used by MQTT, to develop Arduino-Python web applications

Arduino and the computer networking

Computer networking is a huge domain, and covering every aspect of networking is not the main objective of this book. We will, however, try to explain a few fundamentals of computer networking wherever this knowledge will need to be applied. Unlike the serial interface approach, where a point-to-point connection is required between devices, the network-based approach provides distributed access to resources. Specifically in hardware applications where a single hardware unit is required to be accessed by multiple endpoints (for example, in a personal computer, mobile phone, or remote server), the computer network stands superior.

In this section, we will cover the basics of networking and hardware components that enable networking in Arduino. Later in this chapter, we will use the Arduino library and a built-in example to demonstrate how remote access to Arduino using your local network works.

Networking fundamentals

Whenever you see a computer or mobile device, you are also looking at some type of computer network being used to connect those devices with other devices. In simple terms, a computer network is a group of interconnected computational devices (also called network nodes) that allow the exchange of data between these devices. These network nodes include various devices such as your personal computers, mobile phones, servers, tablets, routers, and other pieces of networking hardware.

A computer network can be classified into numerous types according to parameters such as geographical location, network topology, and organizational scope. In terms of geographical scale, a network can be categorized into **local area network** (**LAN**), **home area network** (**HAN**), **wide area network** (**WAN**), and so on. When you are utilizing your home router to connect to the Internet, you are using the LAN created by your router. With regards to the organization that handles the network, LAN can be configured as Intranet, Extranet, and Internet. The Internet is the largest example of any computer network, as it interconnects all types of networks deployed globally. In your implementation of various projects throughout this book, you will mostly be using your LAN and the Internet for the exchange of data between an Arduino, your computer, the Raspberry Pi, and the cloud services.

To standardize communication between network nodes, various governing bodies and organizations have created a set of rules called **protocols**. In the large list of standard protocols, there are a few protocols that your computer uses on a daily basis. The examples of those protocols associated with the local area network include Ethernet and Wi-Fi. In the IEEE 802 family of standards, the IEEE 802.3 standard describes different types of wired connectivity between nodes in a local area network, also called Ethernet. Similarly, Wireless LAN (also referred to as Wi-Fi), is part of the IEEE 802.11 standard, where a communication channel uses wireless frequency bands to exchange data.

Most network nodes deployed with IEEE 802 standards (that is, Ethernet, Wi-Fi, and so on) have a unique identifier assigned to the network interface hardware, called a **media access control** (**MAC**) address. This address is assigned by the manufacturer and is mostly fixed for each network interface. While using Arduino for network connectivity, we will need the MAC address to enable networking. A MAC address is a 48-bit address, and in human-friendly form it contains six groups of two hexadecimal digits. For example, 01:23:45:67:89:ab is the human-readable form of a 48-bit MAC address.

While the MAC address is associated with the hardware-level (that is, "physical") protocols, the **Internet Protocol (IP)** is a communication protocol that is widely used at the Internet level to enable internetworking between networked nodes. In the implementation of version 4 of the IP protocol suite (IPv4), each network node is assigned a 32-bit number called the **IP address** (for example, 192.168.0.1). When you connect a computer, phone, or any other device to your local home network, an IP address is assigned to that device by your router. One of the most popular IP addresses is 127.0.0.1, which is also called the **localhost** IP address. Apart from the IP address assigned to a computer by the network, each computer also has the localhost IP address associated with it. The localhost IP address is very useful when you want to internally access or call your computer from the same device. In the case of a remote-access application, you need to know the IP address assigned by the network.

Obtaining the IP address of your computer

Arduino is a resource-constrained device, and therefore it can only demonstrate a limited amount of network capability. While working with Arduino-based projects that include the utilization of a computer network, you will require a server or Gateway interface. These interfaces include, but are not limited to, a desktop computer, a laptop, the Raspberry Pi, and other remote computing instances. If you are using these interfaces as part of your hardware project, you will need their IP addresses. Ensure that they are under the same network as your Arduino. The following are the techniques to obtain IP addresses in major operating systems.

Windows

In most versions of the Windows OS, you can obtain the IP address from the **Network Connection** utility in **Control Panel**. Navigate to **Control Panel** | **Network and Internet** | **Network Connections** and open the **Local Area Connection Status** window. Click on the **Details** button to see the details of the **Network Connection Details** window. As you can see in this screenshot, the IP address of the network interface is listed as **IPv4 Address** in the opened window:

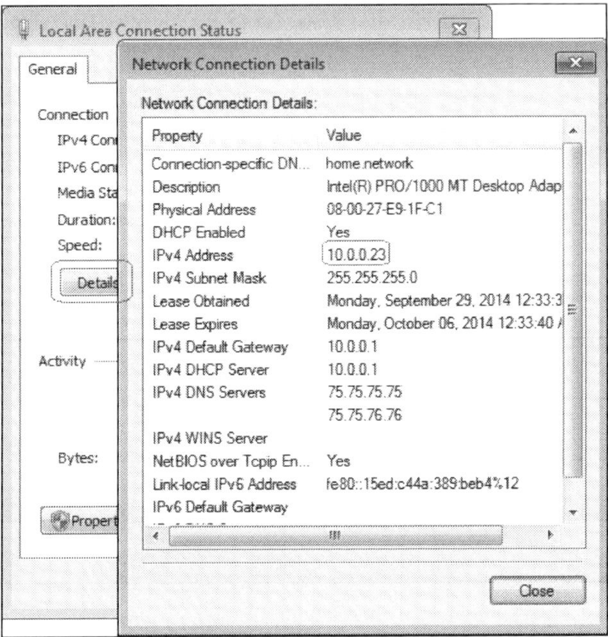

You can also obtain the IP address of your computer using the built-in `ipconfig` utility. Open the Command Prompt and enter the following command:

```
> ipconfig
```

As you can see in the following screenshot, the IP address of your computer is listed under the Ethernet adapter. If you are using a wireless connection to connect to your network, the Ethernet adapter will be replaced by the wireless Ethernet adapter.

```
C:\Windows\system32\cmd.exe
C:\Users\Test>ipconfig

Windows IP Configuration


Ethernet adapter Local Area Connection:

   Connection-specific DNS Suffix  . : home.network
   Link-local IPv6 Address . . . . . : fe80::15ed:c44a:389:beb4%12
   IPv4 Address. . . . . . . . . . . : 10.0.0.23
   Subnet Mask . . . . . . . . . . . : 255.255.255.0
   Default Gateway . . . . . . . . . : 10.0.0.1

Tunnel adapter isatap.home.network:

   Media State . . . . . . . . . . . : Media disconnected
   Connection-specific DNS Suffix  . : home.network

Tunnel adapter Local Area Connection* 9:

   Connection-specific DNS Suffix  . :
   IPv6 Address. . . . . . . . . . . : 2001:0:9d38:6abd:2438:1cfe:f5ff:ffe8
   Link-local IPv6 Address . . . . . : fe80::2438:1cfe:f5ff:ffe8%11
   Default Gateway . . . . . . . . . : ::
```

Mac OS X

If you are using Mac OS X, you can obtain the IP address from the network settings. Open **System Preferences** and click on the **Network** icon. You will see a window similar to what is shown in the next screenshot. In the left sidebar, click on the interface you are looking to obtain the IP address of.

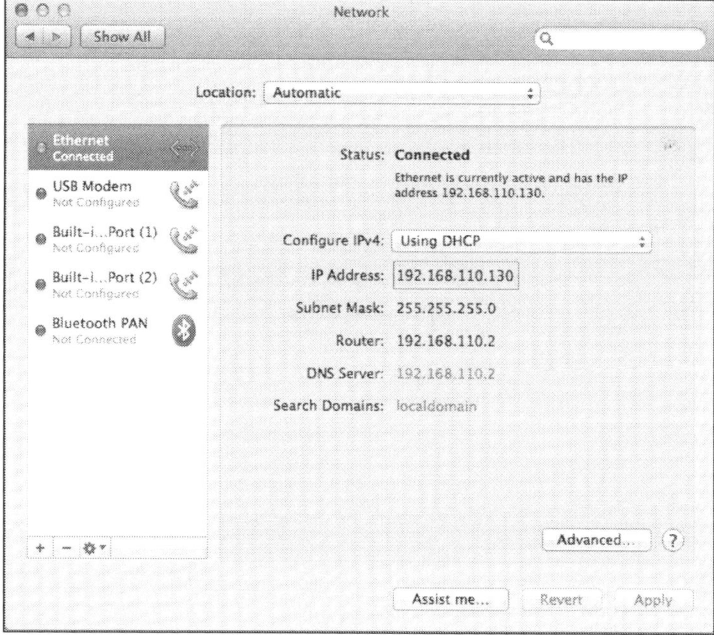

If you want to get the IP address using the terminal, you can use the following command. This command will require you to enter the system name of the interface, `en0`:

```
$ ipconfig getifaddr en0
```

If you are connected to multiple networks and are not aware of the network name, you can find the list of IP addresses associated with your computer, using the command shown here:

```
$ ifconfig | grep inet
```

As you can see in this screenshot, you will get all the network addresses associated with your Mac computer and other network parameters:

```
test — bash — 76×8
Tests-Mac:~ test$ ifconfig | grep inet
        inet6 ::1 prefixlen 128
        inet 127.0.0.1 netmask 0xff000000
        inet6 fe80::1%lo0 prefixlen 64 scopeid 0x1
        inet6 fe80::20c:29ff:fe14:2dc3%en0 prefixlen 64 scopeid 0x4
        inet 192.168.110.130 netmask 0xffffff00 broadcast 192.168.110.255
Tests-Mac:~ test$
```

Linux

On the Ubuntu OS, you can obtain the IP address of your computer from the **Network Settings** utility. To open it, navigate to **System Settings** | **Network** and click on the adapter through which the computer is connected to your home network. You can select an appropriate adapter to obtain the IP address, as displayed in the following screenshot:

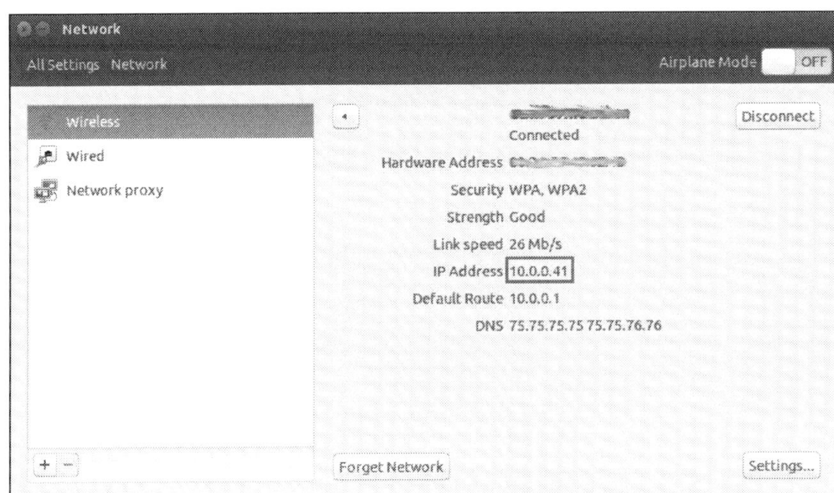

In a Linux-based system, there are multiple ways of obtaining the IP address from the command line. You can use the same command (`ifconfig`) that we used in Mac OS X in the Linux environment to obtain the IP address of your computer:

```
$ ifconfig
```

You can obtain the IP address from the `inet addr` field of the appropriate adapter, as displayed in this screenshot:

```
chheplo@chheplo-PPAF:~$ ifconfig
eth0      Link encap:Ethernet  HWaddr 08:00:27:fb:83:f6
          inet addr:10.0.0.15  Bcast:10.0.0.255  Mask:255.255.255.0
          inet6 addr: fe80::a00:27ff:fefb:83f6/64 Scope:Link
          UP BROADCAST RUNNING MULTICAST  MTU:1500  Metric:1
          RX packets:1549 errors:0 dropped:0 overruns:0 frame:0
          TX packets:802 errors:0 dropped:0 overruns:0 carrier:0
          collisions:0 txqueuelen:1000
          RX bytes:2262119 (2.2 MB)  TX bytes:61188 (61.1 KB)
```

If supported by your operating system, another command that can be utilized to obtain the IP address is `hostname`:

```
$ hostname -I
```

Be careful when using this utility to obtain the IP address, as you may end up getting the IP address of a different adapter if you are not familiar with the supported command options of the utility.

> If you are going to connect your Arduino to the same local area network as your computer, make sure you are choosing the proper IP address that is covered by the same domain as that of your computer. Also ensure that no other network device is using the same IP address that you have selected for your Arduino. This practice will help you avoid IP address conflicts within the network.

Networking extensions for Arduino

There are various hardware devices available in the Arduino community that enable networking for the Arduino platform. Among these devices, a few can be used as extensions for your existing Arduino board, while others exist as standalone Arduino modules with networking capabilities. The most popular extensions used to enable networking are the Arduino Ethernet Shield and Arduino WiFi Shield. Similarly, Arduino Yún is an example of a standalone Arduino platform that includes built-in networking capabilities. In this book, we are going to develop various networking applications around the Arduino Ethernet Shield. There are also a few other extensions (Arduino GSM Shield) and standalone Arduino platforms (Arduino Ethernet, Arduino Tre, and so on), but we are not going to cover them in detail. Let's get familiar with the following Arduino extensions and board.

Arduino Ethernet Shield

The Arduino Ethernet Shield is an officially supported and open source network extension designed to work with Arduino Uno. The Ethernet Shield is equipped with an RJ45 connector to enable Ethernet networking. The Ethernet Shield is designed to mount on top of Arduino Uno and it extends the layout of the pins from your Arduino Uno to the top of the board. The Ethernet Shield is also equipped with a microSD card slot to store important files over the network. Just like most of these shield extensions, the Ethernet Shield is powered by the Arduino board it is attached to.

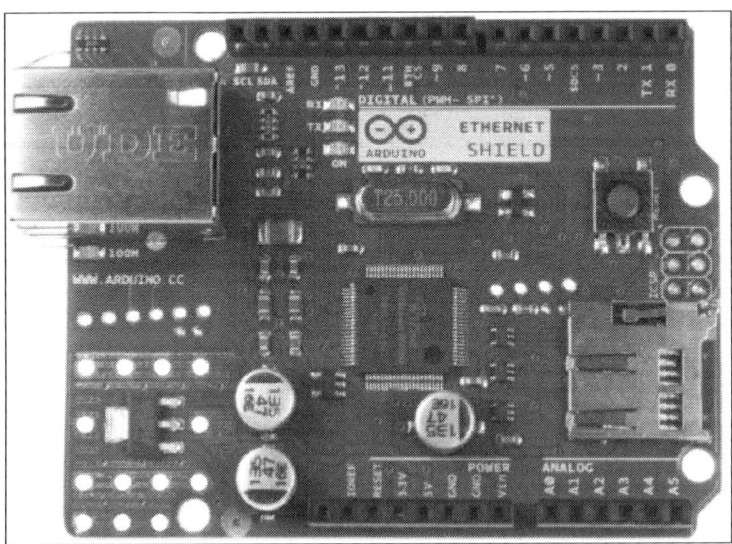

Source: `http://arduino.cc/en/uploads/Main/ArduinoEthernetShield_R3_Front.jpg`

Every Ethernet Shield board is equipped with a unique hardware (MAC) address. You can see it on the back of the board. You may want to note down this hardware address, as it will be required frequently in the upcoming exercises. Also make sure that you get familiar with mounting the Arduino Ethernet Shield for those exercises. Buy an Arduino Ethernet Shield module from SparkFun or Amazon before your start working on any exercises. You can obtain additional information about this Shield at `http://arduino.cc/en/Main/ArduinoEthernetShield`.

Arduino WiFi Shield

The Arduino WiFi Shield has a layout similar to that of the Arduino Ethernet Shield as far as mounting on top of the Arduino board is concerned. Instead of the Ethernet RJ45 connector, the WiFi Shield contains components to enable wireless networking. Using the WiFi Shield, you can connect to the IEEE 802.11 (Wi-Fi) wireless networks, which is one of the most popular ways of connecting computers to the home network nowadays.

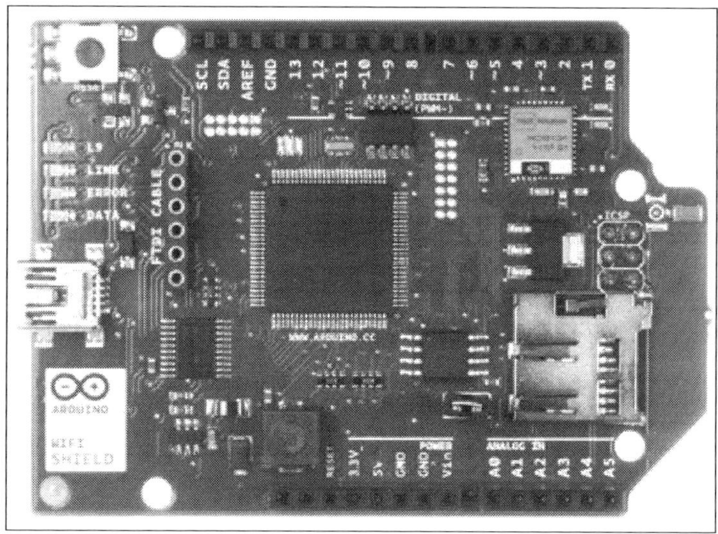

Source: `http://arduino.cc/en/uploads/Main/A000058_front.jpg`

The Arduino WiFi Shield requires additional power through a USB connector. It also contains a microSD slot to save files. Just like the Ethernet Shield, you can view the MAC address on the back of the board. More information about the Arduino WiFi Shield can be found at `http://arduino.cc/en/Main/ArduinoWi-FiShield`.

Arduino Yún

Unlike the Ethernet Shield and the WiFi Shield, the Arduino Yún is a standalone variant of the Arduino board. It includes both Ethernet- and Wi-Fi-based network connectivity, in addition to the basic Arduino component—the microcontroller. Yún is equipped with the latest and more powerful processing units compared to Uno. Instead of the traditional way of using Arduino code, Yún supports a lightweight version of the Linux operating system, providing functionality similar to a single-board computer such as the Raspberry Pi. You can use your Arduino IDE to program Yún even while running Unix shell scripts.

Source: `http://arduino.cc/en/uploads/Main/ArduinoYunFront_2.jpg`

You can find more information about Yún at the Arduino official website, at `http://arduino.cc/en/Main/ArduinoBoardYun`.

Arduino Ethernet library

The Arduino Ethernet library provides support for the Ethernet protocol, and hence provides support for Ethernet extensions of Arduino, such as the Ethernet Shield. This is a standard Arduino library and it gets deployed with the Arduino IDE.

The library is designed to accept incoming connection requests when deployed as a server and while making outgoing connections to other servers when being utilized as a client. The library concurrently supports up to four connections due to the limited computation capability of the Arduino board. To use the Ethernet library in your Arduino program, the first step you have to take is to import it in to your Arduino sketch:

```
#include <Ethernet.h>
```

The Ethernet library implements various functionalities through specific classes, which are described as follows.

We are going to describe only the important methods provided by these classes. You can obtain more information regarding this library and its classes from `http://arduino.cc/en/Reference/Ethernet`.

The Ethernet class

The `Ethernet` class is a core class of the Ethernet library, and it provides methods to initialize this library and the network settings. This is an essential class for any program that wants to use the Ethernet library to establish connections through the Ethernet Shield. The primary information required to establish this connection is the MAC address of the device. You'll need to create a variable that has the MAC address as an array of 6 bytes, as described here:

```
byte mac[] = { 0xDE, 0xAD, 0xBE, 0xEF, 0xFE, 0xED };
```

The Ethernet library supports the **Dynamic Host Control Protocol** (**DHCP**), which is responsible for dynamically assigning IP addresses to new network nodes. If your home network is configured to support DHCP, you can establish the Ethernet connection using the `begin(mac)` method from the `Ethernet` class:

```
Ethernet.begin(mac);
```

Keep in mind that when you are initializing an Ethernet connection using this class, you are only initializing the Ethernet connection and setting up the IP address. This means that you still need to configure Arduino as a server or a client in order to enable further communication.

The IPAddress class

In applications where you have to manually assign the IP address to your Arduino device, you will have to use the `IPAddress` class of the Ethernet library. This class provides methods to specify the IP address, which can be either local or remote depending upon the application:

```
IPAddress ip(192,168,1,177);
```

The IP address created using this method can be used in the initialization of the network connection that we performed in the previous section. If you want to assign a manual IP address to your Arduino, you can use the `begin(mac, ip)` method with the MAC and IP addresses:

```
Ethernet.begin(mac, ip);
```

The Server class

The `Server` class is designed to create a server using the Ethernet library on Arduino, which listens to incoming connection requests for a specific port. The `EthernetServer()` method, when specified with in integer value of the port number, initializes the server on Arduino:

```
EthernetServer server = EthernetServer(80);
```

By specifying port `80` in the previous line of code (which represents the HTTP protocol on the TCP/IP suite), we have specifically created a web server using the Ethernet library. To start listening to the incoming connection requests, you have to use the `begin()` method on the `server` object:

```
server.begin();
```

Once the connection is established, you can respond to a request using various methods supported by the server class, such as `write()`, `print()`, and `println()`.

The Client class

The `Client` class provides methods to create an Ethernet client to connect and communicate with servers. The `EthernetClient()` method initializes a client that can be connected to a specific server using its IP address and port number. The `connect(ip, port)` method on the `client` object will establish a connection with the server on the mentioned IP address:

```
EthernetClient client;
client.connect(server, 80);
```

The `Client` class also has the `connected()` method, which provides the status of the current connection in binary. This status can be `true` (connected) or `false` (disconnected). This method is useful for the periodic monitoring of the connection status:

```
client.connected()
```

Other important client methods include `read()` and `write()`. These methods help the Ethernet client to read the request from the server and to send messages to the server respectively.

Exercise 1 – a web server, your first Arduino network program

The best way to test the Arduino Ethernet library and the Ethernet Shield is by using the built-in examples that are deployed with the Arduino IDE. If you are using version 1.x of the Arduino IDE, you can find a bunch of Ethernet examples by navigating to **File** | **Examples** | **Ethernet**. By utilizing one of these examples, we are going to build a web server that delivers the sensor values when requested by a web browser. As Arduino will be connected to your home network through the Ethernet, you will be able to access it from any other computer connected to your network. The major goals for this exercise are listed here:

- Use the Arduino Ethernet library with the Arduino Ethernet Shield extension to create a web server
- Remotely access Arduino using your home computer network
- Utilize a default Arduino example to provide humidity and motion sensor values using a web server

To achieve these goals, the exercise is divided into the following stages:

- Design and build hardware for the exercise using your Arduino and the Ethernet Shield
- Run a default example from the Arduino IDE as the starting point of the exercise
- Modify the example to accommodate your hardware design and redeploy the code

The following is a Fritzing diagram of the circuit required for this exercise. The first thing you should do is mount the Ethernet Shield on top of your Arduino Uno. Ensure that all the pins of the Ethernet Shield are aligned with the corresponding pins of the Arduino Uno. Then you need to connect the previously used humidity sensor, HIH-4030, and the PIR motion sensor.

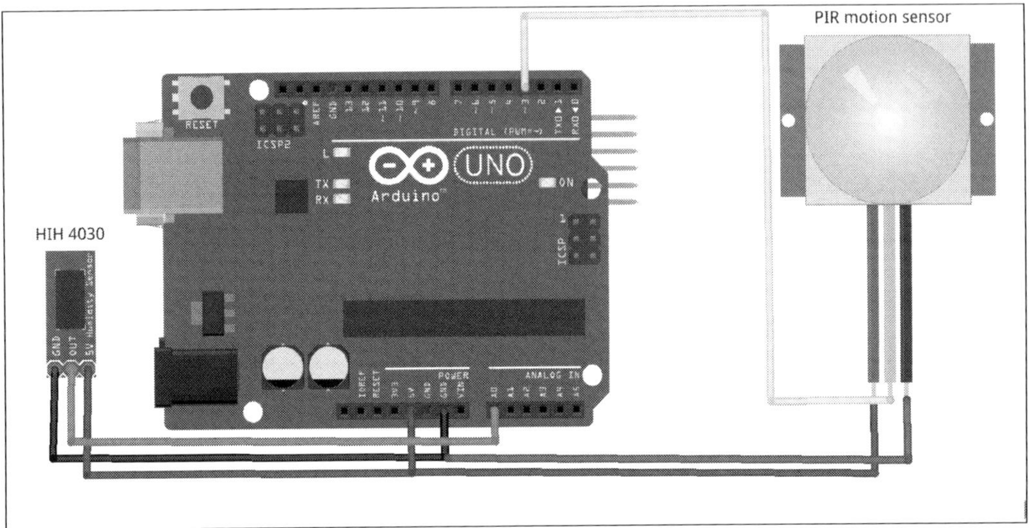

While deploying the Arduino hardware for remote connectivity without USB, you will have to provide external power for the board, as you no longer have a USB connection to power the board.

Now connect your Arduino Uno to a computer using a USB cable. You will also need to connect Arduino to your local home network using an Ethernet cable. To do that, use a straight CAT5 or CAT6 cable and connect one end of the cable to your home router. This router should be the same device that provides network access to the computer you are using. Connect the other end of the Ethernet cable to the Ethernet port of the Arduino Ethernet Shield board. If the physical-level connection has been established correctly, you should see a green light on the port.

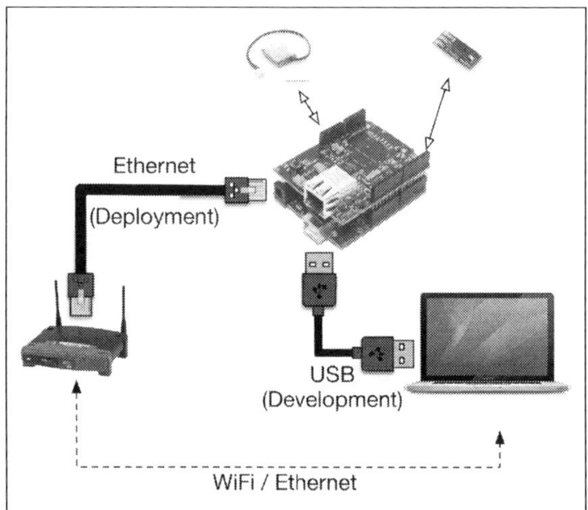

Now it's time to start coding your first Ethernet example. Open the **WebServer** example by navigating to **File | Examples | Ethernet | WebServer** in your Arduino IDE. As you can see, the Ethernet library is included with the other required libraries and the supported code. In the code, you will need to change the MAC and IP addresses to make it work for your configuration. While you can obtain the MAC address of the Ethernet Shield from the back of the board, you will have to select an IP address according to your home network configuration. As you have already obtained the IP address of the computer you are working with, select another address in the range. Ensure that no other network node is using this IP address. Use these MAC and IP addresses to update the following values in your code. You will need to repeat these steps for every exercise when you are dealing with Arduino Ethernet:

```
byte mac[] = {0x90, 0xA2, 0xDA, 0x0D, 0x3F, 0x62};
IPAddress ip(10,0,0,75);
```

In the IP network, the visible range of IP addresses for your network is a function of another address called **subnetwork** or **subnet**. The subnet of your LAN IP network can help you select the appropriate IP address for the Ethernet Shield in the range of the IP address of your computer. You can learn about the basics of the subnet at `http://en.wikipedia.org/wiki/Subnetwork`.

Before venturing further into the code, compile the code with these modifications and upload it to your Arduino. Once the uploading process is completed successfully, open a web browser and enter the IP address that you had specified in the Arduino sketch. If everything goes fine, you should see text displaying the values of the analog pins.

To better understand what happened here, let's go back to the code. As you can see, at the beginning of the code we initialize the Ethernet server library on port `80` using the `EthernetServer` method from the Ethernet library:

```
EthernetServer server(80);
```

During the execution of `setup()`, the program initializes the Ethernet connection through the Ethernet Shield using the `Ethernet.being()` method with the `mac` and `ip` variables that you defined earlier. The `server.begin()` method will start the server from here. Both of these steps are mandatory to start a server if you are using the Ethernet library for server code:

```
Ethernet.begin(mac, ip);
server.begin();
```

In the `loop()` function, we initialize a `client` object to listen to incoming client requests using the `EthernetClient` method. This object will respond to any request coming from connected clients that try to access the Ethernet server through port `80`:

```
EthernetClient client = server.available();
```

On receiving the request, the program will wait for the request payload to end. Then it will reply to the client with formatted HTML data using the `client.print()` method:

```
while (client.connected()) {
      if (client.available()) {
        char c = client.read();
        Serial.write(c);
       # Response code
}
```

If you try to access the Arduino server from the browser, you will see that the web server replies to the clients with the analog pin readings. Now, to obtain the proper values of the humidity and PIR sensors that we connected in the hardware design, you will have to perform the following modification to the code. You will notice here that we are replying to the clients with the calculated values of relative humidity, instead of raw readings from all the analog pins. We have also modified the text that will be printed in the web browser to match the proper sensor title:

```
if (c == '\n' && currentLineIsBlank) {
```

```
            // send a standard http response header
            client.println("HTTP/1.1 200 OK");
            client.println("Content-Type: text/html");
            client.println("Connection: close");
            client.println("Refresh: 5");
            client.println();
            client.println("<!DOCTYPE HTML>");
            client.println("<html>");
            float sensorReading = getHumidity(analogChannel,
temperature);
            client.print("Relative Humidity from HIH4030 is ");
            client.print(sensorReading);
            client.println(" % <br />");
            client.println("</html>");
            break;
          }
```

In this process, we also added an Arduino function, `getHumidity()`, that will calculate the relative humidity from the values observed from the analog pins. We have already used a similar function to calculate relative humidity in one of the previous projects:

```
float getHumidity(int analogChannel, float temperature){
  float supplyVolt = 5.0;
  int HIH4030_Value = analogRead(analogChannel);
  float analogReading = HIH4030_Value/1023.0 * supplyVolt;
  float sensorReading = 161.0 * analogReading / supplyVolt - 25.8;
  float humidityReading = sensorReading / (1.0546 - 0.0026 *
temperature);
  return humidityReading;
}
```

You can implement these changes to the **WebServer** Arduino example for the testing phase, or just open the `WebServer_Custom.ino` sketch from the `Exercise 1 - Web Server` folder of your code directory. As you can see in the opened sketch file, we have already modified the code to reflect the changes, but you will still have to change the MAC and IP addresses to the appropriate addresses. Once you are done with these minor changes, compile and upload the sketch to Arduino.

If everything goes as planned, you should be able to access the web server using your web browser. Open the IP address of your recently prepared Arduino in the web browser. You should be able to receive a similar response as displayed in the following screenshot. Although we are only displaying humidity values through this sketch, you can easily attach motion sensor values using additional `client.print()` methods.

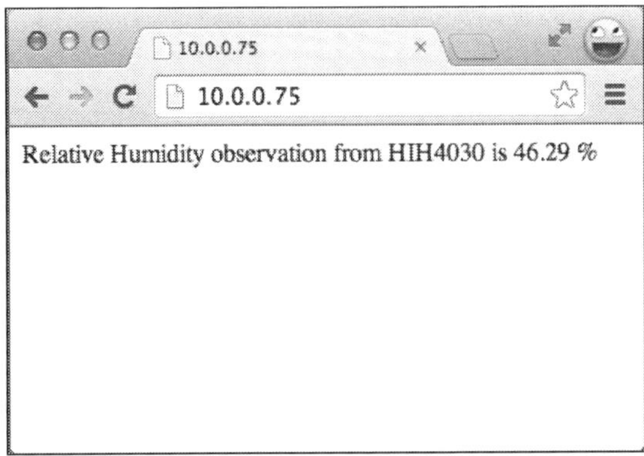

Just like the mechanism we implemented in this exercise, a web server responds to the request made by a web browser and delivers the web pages you are looking for. Although this method is very popular and universally used to deliver web pages, the payload contains a lot of additional metadata compared to the actual size of the sensor information. Also, the server implementation using the Ethernet server library occupies a lot of the Arduino's resources. Arduino, being a resource-constrained device, is not suitable for running a server application, as the Arduino's resources should be prioritized to handle the sensors rather than communication. Moreover, the web server created using the Ethernet library supports a very limited amount of connections at a time, making it unusable for large-scale applications and multiuser systems.

The best approach to overcome this problem is by using Arduino as a client device, or by using lightweight communication protocols that are designed to work with resource-constrained hardware devices. In the next few sections, you are going to learn and implement these approaches for Arduino communication on the Ethernet.

Developing web applications using Python

By implementing the previous program, you have enabled networking on Arduino. In the preceding example, we created an HTTP web server using methods available from the Ethernet library. By creating an Arduino web server, we made the Arduino resources available on the network. Similarly, Python also provides extensibility by way of various libraries to create web server interfaces. By running the Python-based web server on your computer or other devices such as the Raspberry Pi, you can avoid using Arduino to host the web server. Web applications created using high-level languages such as Python can also provide additional capabilities and extensibility compared to Arduino.

In this section, we will use the Python library, `web.py`, to create a Python web server. We will also use this library to create interactive web applications that will enable the transfer of data between an Arduino client and a web browser. After you have learned the basics of `web.py`, we will interface Arduino with `web.py` using serial ports to make Arduino accessible through the Python web server. Then we will upgrade the Arduino communication method from the serial interface to HTTP-based messaging.

Python web framework – web.py

A web server can be developed in Python using various web frameworks such as `Django`, `bottle`, `Pylon`, and `web.py`. We have selected `web.py` as the preferred web framework due to its simple yet powerful functionalities.

The `web.py` library was initially developed by the late Aaron Swartz with the goal of developing an easy and straightforward approach to create web applications using Python. This library provides two main methods, `GET` and `POST`, to support the HTTP **Representation State Transfer** (**REST**) architecture. This architecture is designed to support the HTTP protocol by sending and receiving data between clients and the server. Today, the REST architecture is implemented by a huge number of websites to transfer data over HTTP.

Installing web.py

To get started with `web.py`, you need to install the `web.py` library using Setuptools. We installed Setuptools for various operating systems in *Chapter 1, Getting Started with Python and Arduino*. On Linux and Mac OS X, execute either of these commands on the terminal to install `web.py`:

```
$ sudo easy_install web.py
$ sudo pip install web.py
```

On Windows, open the **Command Prompt** and execute the following command:

```
> easy_install.exe web.py
```

If Setuptools is set up correctly, you should be able to install the library without any difficulty. To verify the installation of the library, open the Python interactive prompt and run this command to see whether you have imported the library without any errors:

```
>>> import web
```

Your first Python web application

Implementing a web server using `web.py` is a very simple and straightforward process. The `web.py` library requires the declaration of a mandatory method, `GET`, to successfully start the web server. When a client tries to access the server using a web browser or another client, `web.py` receives a `GET` request and returns data as specified by the method. To create a simple web application using the `web.py` library, create a Python file using the following lines of code and execute the file using Python. You can also run the `webPyBasicExample.py` file from the code folder of this chapter:

```
import web
urls = (
    '/', 'index'
)
class index:
    def GET(self):
        return "Hello, world!"
if __name__ == "__main__":
    app = web.application(urls, globals())
    app.run()
```

On execution, you will see that the server is now running and accessible through the `http://0.0.0.0:8080` address. As the server program is running on the `0.0.0.0` IP address, you can access it using the same computer, localhost, or any other computer from the same network.

To check out the server, open a web browser and go to `http://0.0.0.0:8080`. When you are trying to access the server from the same computer, you can also use `http://127.0.0.1:8080` or `http://localhost:8080`. The `127.0.0.1` IP address actually stands for localhost, that is, the network address of the same computer on which the program is running. You will be able to see the response of the server displayed in the browser, as shown in the following screenshot:

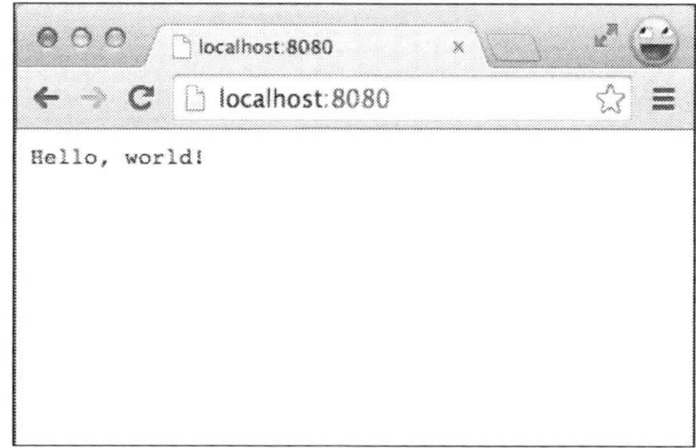

To understand how this simple code works, check out the `GET` method in the previous code snippet. As you can see, when the web browser requests the URL, the `GET` method returns the `Hello, world!` string to the browser. Meanwhile, you can also observe two other mandatory `web.py` components in your code: the `urls` and `web.application()` methods. The `web.py` library requires initialization of the response location in the declaration of the `urls` variable. Every `web.py`-based web application requires the `application(urls, global())` method to be called to initialize the web server. By default, the `web.py` applications run on port number `8080`, which can be changed to another port number by specifying it during execution. For example, if you want to run your `web.py` application on port `8888`, execute the following command:

```
$ python webPyBasicExample.py 8888
```

Although this only returns simple text, you have now successfully created your first web application using Python. We will take it forward from here and create more complex web applications in the upcoming chapters using the `web.py` library. To develop these complex applications, we will require more than just the `GET` method. Let's start exploring advance concepts to further enhance your familiarity with the `web.py` library.

Essential web.py concepts for developing complex web applications

The `web.py` library has been designed to provide convenient and simple methods to develop dynamic websites and web applications using Python. Using `web.py`, it is really easy to build complex websites by utilizing just a few additional Python concepts along with what you already know. Due to this limited learning curve and easy-to-implement methods, `web.py` is one of the quickest ways to create web applications in any programming language. Let's begin with understanding these `web.py` concepts in detail.

Handling URLs

You might have noticed that in our first `web.py` program, we defined a variable called `urls` that points to the root location (/) of the `Index` class:

```
urls = (
    '/', 'index'
)
```

In the preceding declaration, the first part, `'/'`, is a regular expression used to match the actual URL requests. You can use regular expressions to handle complex queries coming to your `web.py` server and point them to the appropriate class. In `web.py`, you can associate different landing page locations with appropriate classes. For example, if you want to redirect the `/data` location to the `data` class in addition to the `Index` class, you can change the `urls` variable as follows:

```
urls = (
    '/', 'index',
    '/data', 'data',
)
```

With this provision, when a client sends a request to access the `http://<ip-address>:8080/data` address, the request will be directed towards the `data` class and then the `GET` or `POST` method of that class.

The GET and POST methods

In exercise 1, where we created an Arduino-based web server running on port `80`, we used a web browser to access the web server. Web browsers are one of the most popular types of web clients used to access a web server; cURL, Wget, and web crawlers are the other types. A web browser uses HTTP to communicate with any web servers, including the Arduino web server that we used. `GET` and `POST` are two fundamental methods supported by the HTTP protocol to address server requests coming from a web browser.

Whenever you are trying to open a website in your browser or any other HTTP client, you are actually requesting the `GET` function from the web server; for example, when you open a website URL, `http://www.example.com/`, you are requesting that the web server that hosts this website serves you the `GET` request for the `'/'` location. In the *Handling URLs* section, you learned how to associate the `web.py` classes with URL landing locations. Using the `GET` method provided by the `web.py` library, you can associate the `GET` request with individual classes. Once you have captured the `GET` request, you need to return appropriate values as the response to the client. The following code snippet shows how the `GET()` function will be called when anyone makes a `GET` request to the `'/'` location:

```
def GET(self):
  f = self.submit_form()
  f.validates()
  t = 75
  return render.test(f,t);
```

The `POST` function of the HTTP protocol is mainly used to submit a form or any other data to the web server. In most cases, `POST` is embedded in a web page, and a request to the server is generated when a user submits the component carrying the `POST` function. The `web.py` library also provides the `POST()` function, which is called when a web client tries to contact the `web.py` server using the `POST` method. In most implementations of the `POST()` function, the request includes some kind of data submitted through forms. You can retrieve individual form elements using `f['Celsius'].value` which will give you a value associated with the form element called `Celsius`. Once the `POST()` function has performed the provided actions, you can return appropriate information to the client in response to the `POST` request:

```
def POST(self):
    f = self.submit_form()
    f.validates()
    c = f['Celsius'].value
    t = c*(9.0/5.0) + 32
    return render.test(f,t)
```

Templates

Now you know how to redirect an HTTP request to an appropriate URL, and also how to implement methods to respond to these HTTP requests (that is, `GET` and `POST`). But what about the web page that needs to be rendered once the request is received? To understand the rendering process, let's start with creating a folder called `templates` in the same directory where our `web.py` program is going to be placed. This folder will store the templates that will be used to render the web pages when requested. You have to specify the location of this template folder in the program using the `template.render()` function, as displayed in the following line of code:

```
render = web.template.render('templates')
```

Once you have instantiated the rendering folder, it is time to create template files for your program. According to the requirements of your program, you can create as many template files as you want. A language called **Templetor** is used to create these template files in `web.py`. You can learn more about it at `http://webpy.org/templetor`. Each template file created using Templetor needs to be stored in the HTML format with the `.html` extension.

Let's create a file called `test.html` in the `templates` folder using a text editor and paste the following code snippet in to the file:

```
$def with(form, i)
<form method="POST">
    $:form.render()
</form>
<p>Value is: $:i </p>
```

As you can see in the preceding code snippet, the template file begins with the `$def with()` expression, where you need to specify the input arguments as variables within the brackets. Once the template is rendered, these will be the only variables you can utilize for the web page; for example, in the previous code snippet, we passed two variables (`form` and `i`) as input variables. We utilized the `form` object using `$:form.render()` to render it inside the web page. When you need to render the `form` object, you can directly pass the other variable by simply declaring it (that is, `$:i`). Templetor will render the HTML code of the template file as it is, while utilizing the variables in the instances where they are being used.

Now you have a template file, `test.html`, ready to be used in your `web.py` program. Whenever a `GET()` or `POST()` function is executed, you are required to return a value to the requesting client. Although you can return any variable for these requests, including `None`, you will have to render a template file where the response is associated with loading a web page. You can return the template file using the `render()` function, followed by the filename of the template file and input arguments:

```
return render.test(f, i);
```

As you can see in the preceding line of code, we are returning the rendered `test.html` page by specifying the `render.test()` function, where `test()` is just the filename without the `.html` extension. The function also includes a form object, `f`, and variable, `i`, that will be passed as input arguments.

Forms

The `web.py` library provides simple ways of creating form elements using the `Form` module. This module includes the capability to create HTML form elements, obtain inputs from users, and validate these inputs before utilizing them in the Python program. In the following code snippet, we are creating two form elements, `Textbox` and `Button`, using the `Form` library:

```
submit_form = form.Form(
  form.Textbox('Celsius', description = 'Celsius'),
  form.Button('submit', type="submit", description='submit')
)
```

Besides `Textbox` (which obtains text input from users) and `Button` (which submits the form), the `Form` module also provides a few other form elements, such as `Password` to obtain hidden text input, `Dropbox` to obtain a mutually exclusive input from a drop-down list, `Radio` to obtain mutually exclusive inputs from multiple options, and `Checkbox` to select a binary input from the given options. While all of these elements are very easy to implement, you should select form elements only according to your program requirements.

In the `web.py` implementation of `Form`, the web page needs to execute the `POST` method every time the form is submitted. As you can in see in the following implementation of the form in the template file, we are explicitly declaring the form submission method as `POST`:

```
$def with(form, i)
<form method="POST">
    $:form.render()
</form>
```

Exercise 2 – playing with web.py concepts using the Arduino serial interface

Now you have a general idea of the basic `web.py` concepts used to build a web application. In this exercise, we will utilize the concepts you learned to create an application to provide the Arduino with sensor information. As the goal of this exercise is to demonstrate the `web.py` server for Arduino data, we are not going to utilize the Ethernet Shield for communication. Instead, we will capture the Arduino data using the serial interface, while using the `web.py` server to respond to the requests coming from different clients.

As you can see in the following diagram, we are using the same hardware that you designed for exercise 1, but without utilizing the Ethernet connection to our home router. Your computer running the web.py server, which is also a part of your home network, will serve the client requests.

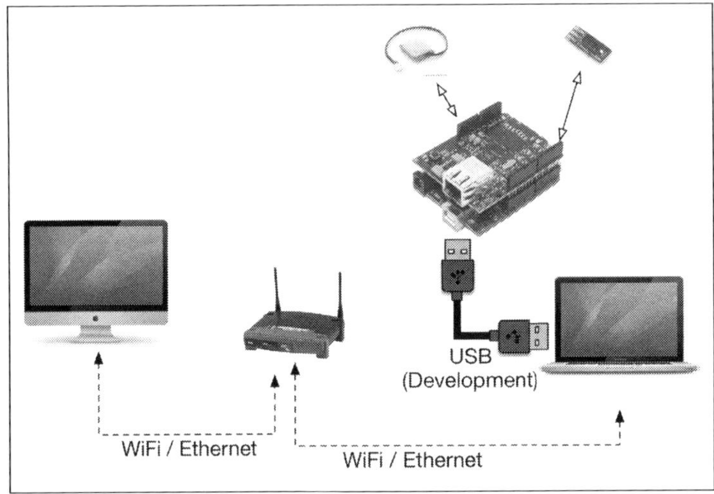

In the first step, we are going to code Arduino to periodically send the humidity sensor value to the serial interface. For the Arduino code, open the WebPySerialExample_Arduino.ino sketch from the Exercise 2 folder of your code directory. As you can see in the following code snippet of the Arduino sketch, we are sending raw values from the analog port to the serial interface. Now compile and upload the sketch to your Arduino board. Open the **Serial Monitor** window from the Arduino IDE to confirm that you are receiving the raw humidity observations. Once you have confirmed it, close the **Serial Monitor** window. You won't be able to run the Python code if the **Serial Monitor** window is using the port:

```
void loop() {
  int analogChannel = 0;
  int HIH4030_Value = analogRead(analogChannel);
  Serial.println(HIH4030_Value);
  delay(200);
}
```

Once the Arduino code is running properly, it is time to execute the Python program, which contains the web.py server. The Python program for this exercise is located in the WebPySerialExample_Python directory. Open the webPySerialExample.py file in your code editor. The Python program is organized in two sections: capturing sensor data from the serial interface using the pySerial library, and using the web.py server-based server to respond to the requests from the clients.

In the first stage of the code, we are interfacing the serial port using the `Serial()` method from the `pySerial` library. Don't forget to change the serial port name as it may be different for your computer, depending on the operating system and physical port that you are using:

```
import serial
port = serial.Serial('/dev/tty.usbmodemfa1331', 9600, timeout=1)
```

Once the `port` object for the serial port is created, the program starts reading the text coming from the physical port, using the `readline()` method. Using the `relativeHumidity()` function, we convert the raw humidity data to appropriate relative humidity observations:

```
line = port.readline()
if line:
  data = float(line)
  humidity = relativeHumidity(line, 25)
```

On the web server side, we will be using all the major `web.py` components you learned in the previous section to complete this goal. As part of it, we are implementing an input form for the temperature value. We will capture this user input and utilize it with the raw sensor data to calculate relative humidity. Therefore, we need to define the `render` object to use the `template` directory. In this exercise, we are only using the default landing page location (`'/'`) for the web server, which is directed towards the `Index` class:

```
render = web.template.render('templates')
```

As you can see in the `WebPySerialExample_Python` folder, we have a directory called `templates`. This directory contains a template with the `base.html` filename. As this is an HTML file, it is likely that if you just click on the file, it opens in a web browser. Make sure that you open the file in a text editor. In the opened file, you'll see that we are initializing the template file with `$def with(form, humidity)`. In this initialization, `form` and `humidity` are input variables that are required by the template during the rendering process. The template declares the actual `<form>` element with the `$:form.render()` method, while displaying the humidity value using the `$humidity` variable:

```
<form method="POST">
    $:form.render()
</form>
<h3>Relative Humidity is:</h3>
<p name="temp">$humidity </p>
```

Although the template file renders the `form` variable, we have to define this variable in the Python program first. As you can see in the following code snippet, we have declared a variable called `submit_form` using the `form.Form()` method of the `web.py` library. The `submit_form` variable includes a `Textbox` element to capture the temperature value and a `Button` element to enable the submit action:

```
submit_form = form.Form(
  form.Textbox('Temperature', description = 'Temperature'),
  form.Button('submit', type="submit", description='submit')
  )
```

When you want to access the current submitted values of the `submit_form` variable, you will have to validate the form using the `validates()` method:

```
f = self.submit_form()
f.validates()
```

Now we have the user-facing web page and input components designed for the exercise. It is time to define the two main methods, `GET` and `POST`, to respond to the request coming from the web page. When you launch or refresh the web page, the `web.py` server generates the `GET` request, which is then handled by the `GET` function of the `Index` class. So during the execution of the `GET` method, the program obtains the latest raw humidity value from the serial port and calculates the relative humidity using the `relativeHumidity()` method.

In the process of dealing with the `GET` request, we are not submitting any form with the user input. For this reason, in the `GET` method, we will use the default value of temperature (`25`) for the `relativeHumidity()` method.

Once the humidity value is derived, the program will render the `base` template using the `render.base()` function, as displayed in the following code snippet, where `base()` refers to the base template:

```
def GET(self):
  f = self.submit_form()
  f.validates()
  line = port.readline()
  if line:
    data = float(line)
    humidity = relativeHumidity(line, 25)
    return render.base(f,humidity);
  else:
    return render.base(f, "Not valid data");
```

Contrary to the `GET` method, the `POST` method is invoked when the form is submitted to the web page. The submitted form includes the temperature value provided by the user, which will be used to obtain the value of the relative humidity. Like the `GET()` function, the `POST()` function also renders the `base` template with the recent humidity value once the humidity is calculated:

```
def POST(self):
  f = self.submit_form()
  f.validates()
  temperature = f['Temperature'].value
  line = port.readline()
  if line:
    data = float(line)
    humidity = relativeHumidity(line, float(temperature))
    return render.base(f, humidity);
  else:
    return render.base(f, "Not valid data");
```

Now it is time to run the `web.py`-based web server. In the Python program, make the necessary changes to accommodate the serial port name and any other appropriate values. If everything is configured correctly, you will be able to execute the program from the terminal without any errors. You can access the web server, which is running on port `8080`, from a web browser on the same computer, that is, `http://localhost:8080`. Now the goal of the exercise is to demonstrate the remote accessibility of the web server from your home network, and you can do this by opening the website from another computer in your network, that is, `http://<ip-address>:8080`, where `<ip-address>` refers to the IP address of the computer that is running the `web.py` service.

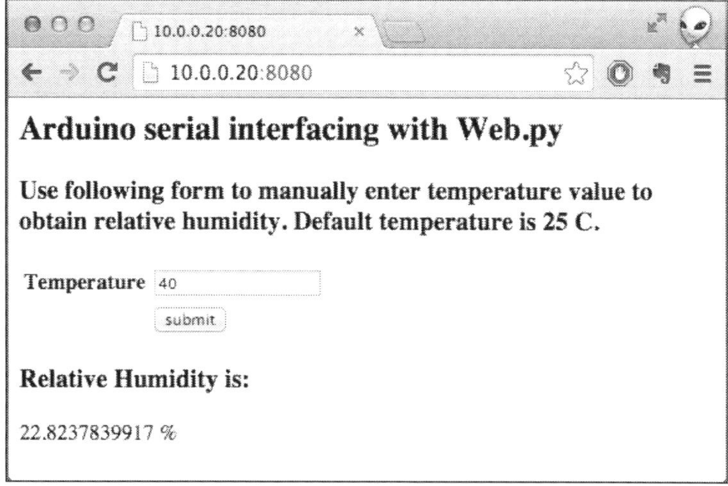

The preceding screenshot shows how the web application will look when opened in a web browser. When you load the website, you will be able to see a relative humidity value obtained using the `GET` method. Now you can enter an appropriate temperature value and press the **submit** button to invoke the `POST` method. On successful execution, you will be able to see the latest relative humidity value, which is calculated based on the temperature value that you submitted.

RESTful web applications with Arduino and Python

In the previous exercise, we implemented the `GET` and `POST` requests using the `web.py` library. These requests are actually part of the most popular communication architecture of the **World Wide Web** (**WWW**) called REST. The REST architecture implements a client-server paradigm using the HTTP protocol for operations such as `POST`, `READ`, and `DELETE`. The `GET()` and `POST()` functions, implemented using `web.py`, are functional subsets of these standard HTTP REST operations, that is, `GET`, `POST`, `UPDATE`, and `DELETE`. The REST architecture is designed for network applications, websites, and web services to establish communication through HTTP-based calls. Rather than being just a set of standard rules, the REST architecture utilizes existing web technologies and protocols, making it a core component of the majority of the websites we use today. Due to this reason, the WWW can be considered to be the largest implementation of REST-based architecture.

Designing REST-based Arduino applications

The REST architecture uses a client-server model, where the server acts as a centralized node in the network. It responds to the requests made by the distributed network nodes (called **clients**) that query it. In this paradigm, the client initiates a request for the state directed towards the server, while the server responds to the state request without storing the client context. This communication is always one-directional and always initiated from the client side.

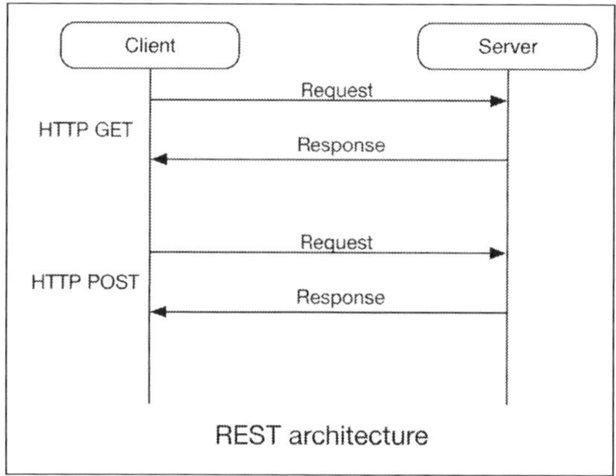

To further explain the state transfer for the `GET` and `POST` requests, check out the previous diagram. When a client sends a `GET` request to a server using a URL, the server responds with raw data as the HTTP response. Similarly, in the `POST` request, the client sends data as payload to the server, while the server responds with simply a "received confirmation" message.

REST methods are relatively simple to implement and develop using simple HTTP calls. We are going to start developing Arduino networking applications using REST-based requests, as they are easy to implement and understand and are directly available through examples. We will begin by individually implementing REST-based Arduino clients for HTTP-based `GET` and `POST` methods. Later in this chapter, we will go through an exercise to combine the `GET` and `POST` methods through the same Arduino REST client, while developing the HTTP server using `web.py`.

Working with the GET request from Arduino

In this exercise, we will implement the HTTP `GET` client on Arduino, while using an HTTP server that was developed using `web.py`. The premise of this programming exercise is to use the Ethernet Shield extension and the Ethernet library to develop a physical Arduino HTTP client that supports the `GET` request.

The Arduino code to generate the GET request

The Arduino IDE ships with a few basic examples that utilize the Ethernet library. One of these examples is **WebClient**, which can be found by navigating to **File** | **Examples** | **Ethernet** | **WebClient**. It is designed to demonstrate the `GET` request by implementing the HTTP client on Arduino. Open this sketch in the Arduino IDE, as we are going to use this sketch and modify it to accommodate the Arduino hardware we created.

The first thing you need to change in the opened sketch is the IP address and the MAC address of your Arduino Ethernet Shield. Replace the following variables with the variables appropriate for your system. The following code snippet shows the IP address and the MAC address for our hardware, and you need to change it to accommodate yours:

```
byte mac[] = { 0x90, 0xA2, 0xDA, 0x00, 0x47, 0x28 };
IPAddress ip(10,0,0,75);
```

As you can see, the example uses Google as a server to get a response. You need to change this address to reflect the IP address of your computer, which will host the `web.py` server:

```
char server[] = "10.0.0.20";
```

In the `setup()` function, you will have to change the server IP address again. Also change the default HTTP port (`80`) to the port used by `web.py` (`8080`):

```
if (client.connect(server, 8080)) {
  Serial.println("connected");
  // Make a HTTP request:
  client.println("GET /data HTTP/1.1");
  client.println("Host: 10.0.0.20");
  client.println("Connection: close");
  client.println();
}
```

Once you have made all of these changes, go to the `Arduino_GET_Webpy\ArduinoGET` folder and open the `ArduinoGET.ino` sketch. Compare your modified sketch with this sketch and perform the appropriate changes. Now you can save your sketch and compile your code for any errors.

At this stage, we are assuming that you have the Arduino Ethernet Shield mounted on your Arduino Uno. Connect the Ethernet Shield to your local network using an Ethernet cable, and connect Uno with your computer using a USB cable. Upload the sketch to the Arduino board and open the **Serial Monitor** window to check the activity. At this stage, Arduino would not be able to connect to the server because your `web.py` server is still not running. You can close the serial monitor for now.

The HTTP server using web.py to handle the GET request

In your first `web.py` application, you developed a server that returned `Hello, world!` when requested from a web browser. Despite all the additional tasks it can perform, your web browser is an HTTP client at its core. This means that if your first `web.py` server code was able to respond to the `GET` request made by the web browser, it should also be able to respond to the Arduino web client. To check this out, open your first `web.py` program, `webPyBasicExample.py`, and change the return string from `Hello World!` to `test`. We are performing this string change to differentiate it from the other instances of this program. Execute the Python program from the terminal and open the **Serial Monitor** window in the Arduino IDE again. This time, you will be able to see that your Arduino client is receiving a response for the `GET` request it sent to the `web.py` server. As you can see in the following screenshot, you will be able to see the `test` string printed in the **Serial Monitor** window, which is returned by the `web.py` server for the `GET` request:

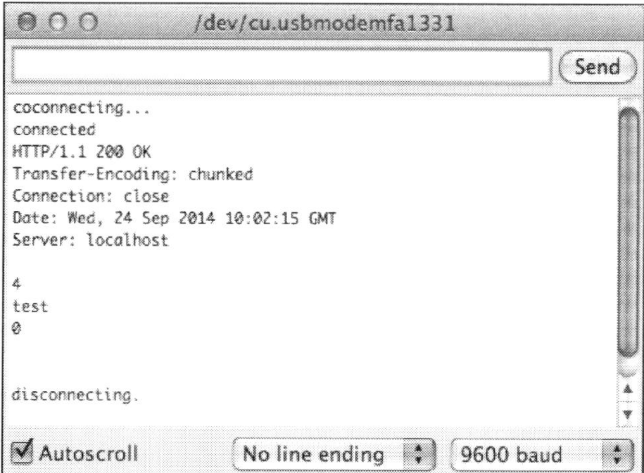

Although in this example we are returning a simple string for the `GET` request, you can extend this method to obtain different user-specified parameters from the web server. This `GET` implementation can be used in a large number of applications where Arduino requires repeated input from the user or other programs. But what if the web server requires input from the Arduino? In that case, we will have to use the `POST` request. Let's develop an Arduino program to accommodate the HTTP `POST` request.

Working with the POST request from Arduino

Since we have now implemented the `GET` request, we can use a similar approach to exercise the `POST` request. Instead of asking the server to provide a response for a state request, we will send sensor data as payload from Arduino in the implementation of the `POST` request. Similarly, on the server side, we will utilize `web.py` to accept the `POST` request and display it through a web browser.

The Arduino code to generate the POST request

Open the Arduino sketch `ArduinoPOST.ino` from the `Arduino_POST_Webpy\ArduinoPOST` folder of the code repository. As in the previous exercise, you will first have to provide the IP address and the MAC address of your Arduino.

Once you have completed these basic changes, observe the following code snippet for the implementation of the `POST` request. You might notice that we are creating payload for the `POST` request as the variable data from the values obtained from analog pin 0:

```
String data;
data+="";
data+="Humidity ";
data+=analogRead(analogChannel);
```

In the following Arduino code, we'll first create a `client` object using the Ethernet library. In the recurring `loop()` function, we'll use this `client` object to connect to the `web.py` server running on our computer. You will have to replace the IP address in the `connect()` method with the IP address of your `web.py` server. Once connected, we'll create a custom `POST` message with the payload data we calculated previously. The Arduino `loop()` function will periodically send the updated sensor value generated by this code sample to the `web.py` server:

```
if (client.connect("10.0.0.20",8080)) {
  Serial.println("connected");
  client.println("POST /data HTTP/1.1");
  client.println("Host: 10.0.0.20");
  client.println("Content-Type: application/x-www-form-urlencoded");
  client.println("Connection: close");
  client.print("Content-Length: ");
  client.println(data.length());
  client.println();
  client.print(data);
  client.println();
  Serial.println("Data sent.");
}
```

Once you have performed the changes, compile and upload this sketch to the Arduino board. As the `web.py` server is yet not implemented, the `POST` request that originated from Arduino will not be able to reach its destination successfully, so let's create the `web.py` server to accept `POST` requests.

The HTTP server using web.py to handle the POST request

In this implementation of the `POST` method, we require two `web.py` classes, `index` and `data`, to individually serve requests from the web browser and Arduino respectively. As we are going to use two separate classes to update common sensor values (that is, `humidity` and `temperature`), we are going to declare them as global variables:

```
global temperature, humidity
temperature = 25
```

As you may have noticed in the Arduino code (`client.println("POST /data HTTP/1.1")`), we were sending the `POST` request to the URL located at `/data`. Similarly, we will use the default root location, `'/'`, to land any request coming from the web browser. These requests for the root location will be handled by the `index` class, just as we covered in exercise 2:

```
urls = (
    '/', 'index',
    '/data','data',
)
```

The `data` class takes care of any `POST` request originating from the `/data` location. In this case, these `POST` requests contain payload that has sensor information attached by the Arduino `POST` client. On receiving the message, the method splits the payload string into sensor-type and value, updating the global value of the `humidity` variable in this process:

```
class data:
    def POST(self):
        global humidity
        i = web.input()
        data = web.data()
        data = data.split()[1]
        humidity = relativeHumidity(data,temperature)
        return humidity
```

Each POST request received from Arduino updates the raw humidity value, which is represented by the data variable. We are using the same code from exercise 2 to obtain manual temperature values from the user. The relative humidity value, humidity, is updated according to the temperature value you updated using the web browser and the raw humidity value is obtained from your Arduino.

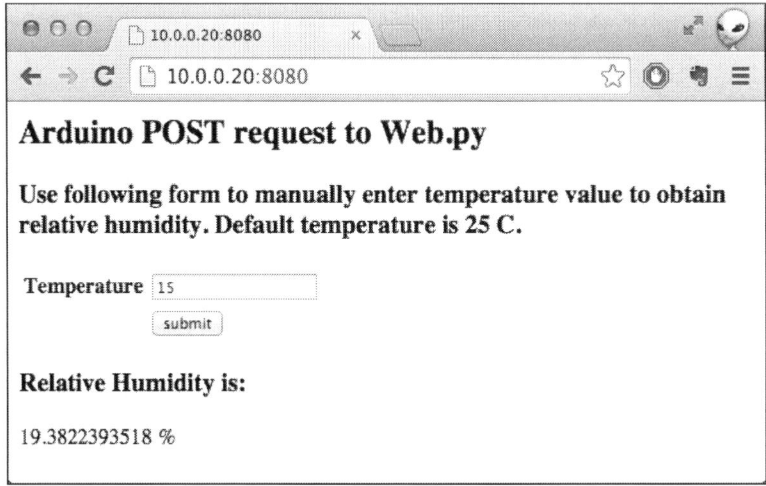

To check out the Python code, open the WebPyEthernetPOST.py file from the code repository. After making the appropriate changes, execute the code from the terminal. If you don't start getting any updates from the Arduino on the terminal, you should restart Arduino to reestablish the connection with the web.py server. Once you start seeing periodic updates from the Arduino POST requests at the terminal, open the location of the web application in your browser. You will be able to see something similar to the preceding screenshot. Here, you can submit the manual temperature value using the form, while the browser will reload with the updated relative humidity according to the temperature value entered.

Exercise 3 – a RESTful Arduino web application

The goal of this exercise is to simply combine the GET and POST methods you learned in the previous two sections in order to create a complete REST experience using Arduino and Python. The architecture for this exercise can be described as follows:

- The Arduino client periodically uses the GET request to obtain the sensor type from the server. It uses this sensor type to select a sensor for observation. In our case, it is either a humidity or motion sensor.

- The web server responds to the GET request by returning the current sensor type of the sensor selected by the user. The user provides this selection through a web application.
- After receiving the sensor type, the Arduino client utilizes POST to send sensor observation to the server.
- The web server receives the POST data and updates the sensor observation for that particular sensor type.
- On the user side, the web server obtains the current sensor type through the web browser.
- When the **submit** button in the browser is pressed, the server updates the sensor value in the browser with the latest value.

The Arduino sketch for the exercise

Using the same Arduino hardware we built, open the Arduino sketch named `WebPyEthernetArduinoGETPOST.ino` from the `Exercise 3 - RESTful application Arduino and webpy` code folder. As we described in the exercise's architecture earlier, the Arduino client should periodically send GET requests to the server and get the corresponding value of the sensor type in the response. After comparing the sensor type, the Arduino client fetches the current sensor observation from the Arduino pins and sends that observation back to the server using POST:

```
if (client.connected()) {
      if (client.find("Humidity")){
           # Fetch humidity sensor value
           if (client.connect("10.0.0.20",8080)) {
           # Post humidity values
          }
      }
      else{
           # Fetch motion sensor value
           if (client.connect("10.0.0.20",8080)) {
           # Post motion values
          }
      }
     # Add delay
}
```

After changing the appropriate server's IP address in the code, compile and upload it to the Arduino. Open the **Serial Monitor** window, where you will find unsuccessful connection attempts, as your `web.py` server is not yet running. Close any other instance or program of the `web.py` server running on your computer.

The web.py application to support REST requests

Open the `WebPyEthernetGETPOST.py` file from the `Exercise 3 - RESTful application Arduino and webpy` code folder. As you can see, the `web.py` based web server implements two separate classes, `index` and `data`, to support the REST architecture for the web browser and the Arduino client, respectively. We are introducing a new concept for the `Form` element, called `Dropdown()`. Using this `Form` method, you can implement the drop-down selection menu and ask the user to select one option from the list of options:

```
form.Dropdown('dropdown',
          [('Humidity','Humidity'),('Motion','Motion')]),
form.Button('submit',
         type="submit", description='submit'))
```

In the previous `web.py` program, we implemented the `GET` and `POST` methods for the `index` class and only the `POST` method for the `data` class. Moving forward in this exercise, we'll also add the `GET` method to the `data` class. This method returns the value of the `sensorType` variable when the `GET` request is made for the `/data` location. From the user side, the value of the `sensorType` variable is updated when the form gets submitted with an option. This action sends a selected value to the `POST` method of the `index` class, ultimately updating the `sensorType` value:

```
class data:
    def GET(self):
        return sensorType
    def POST(self):
        global humidity, motion
        i = web.input()
        data = web.data()
        data = data.split()[1]
        if sensorType == "Humidity":
            humidity = relativeHumidity(data,temperature)
            return humidity
        else:
            motion = data
            return motion
```

Before you run this Python program, make sure you have checked every component of the code and updated the values where needed. Then execute the code from the terminal. Your web server will now run on your local computer on the port number `8080`. Power-cycle your Arduino device in case the connection attempt from Arduino fails. To test your system, open the web application from your web browser. You will see a web page open in your browser, as displayed in the following screenshot:

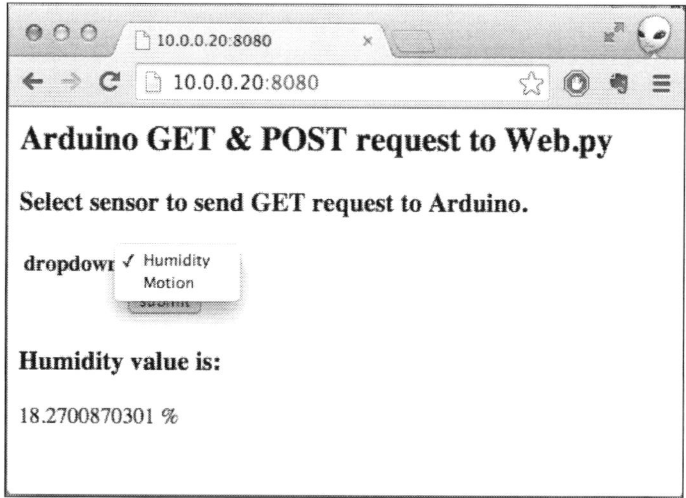

You can choose the sensor type from the **dropdown** menu (**Humidity** or **Motion**) before pressing the **Submit** button. On submission, you will be able to see the page updated with the appropriate sensor type and its current value.

Why do we need a resource-constrained messaging protocol?

In the previous section, you learned how to use the HTTP `REST` architecture to send and receive data between your Arduino and the host server. The HTTP protocol was originally designed to serve textual data through web pages on the Internet. The data delivery mechanism used by HTTP requires a comparatively large amount of computation and network resources, which may be sufficient for a computer system but not for resource-constrained hardware platforms such as Arduino. As we discussed earlier, the client-server paradigm implemented by the HTTP REST architecture creates a tightly coupled system. In this paradigm, both sides (the client and the server) need to be constantly active, or live, to respond. Also, the REST architecture only allows unidirectional communication from client to server, where requests are always initialized by the client and the server responds to the client. This request-response-based architecture is not suitable for constrained hardware devices because of (but not limited to) the following reasons:

- These devices should avoid active communication mode to save power
- The communication should have less data overhaul to save network resources

- They usually do not have enough computational resources to enable bidirectional REST communication, that is, implementing both client and server mechanisms on each side
- The code should have a smaller footprint due to storage constraints

[The REST-based architecture can still be useful when the application specifically requires a request-response architecture, but most sensor-based hardware applications are limited due to the preceding points.]

Among other data delivery paradigms that solve the preceding problems, the architecture based on **publisher/subscriber** (**pub/sub**) stands tall. The pub/sub architecture enables bidirectional communication capabilities between the node that generates the data (**Publisher**) and the node that consumes the data (**Subscriber**). We are going to use MQTT as the protocol that uses the pub/sub model of message transportation. Let's begin by covering the pub/sub architecture and MQTT in detail.

MQTT – A lightweight messaging protocol

Just like REST, pub/sub is one of the most popular messaging patterns, mostly deployed to transfer short messages between nodes. Instead of deploying client-server-based architecture, the pub/sub paradigm implements messaging middleware called a **broker** to receive, queue, and relay messages between the subscriber and publisher clients:

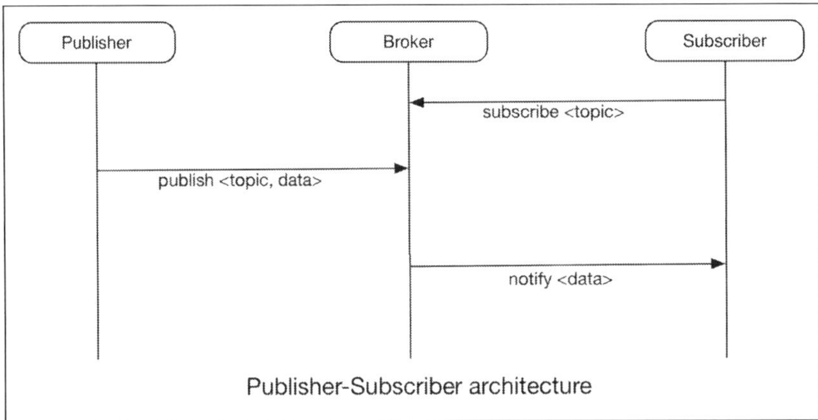

Publisher-Subscriber architecture

The pub/sub architecture utilizes a topic-based system to select and process messages, where each message is labeled with a specific topic name. Instead of sending a message directly to the subscriber, the publisher sends it first to the broker with a topic name. In a totally independent process, the subscriber registers its subscription for particular topics with the broker. In the event of receiving a message from the publisher, the broker performs topic-based filtering on that message before forwarding it to the subscribers registered for that topic. As publishers are loosely coupled to subscribers in this architecture, the publishers do not need to know the whereabouts of the subscribers and can work uninterrupted without worrying about their status.

While discussing the limitations of the REST architecture, we noticed that it requires the implementation of both the HTTP client and server on the Arduino end to enable bidirectional communication with Arduino. With the broker-based architecture demonstrated by pub/sub, you only need to implement lightweight code for the publisher or subscriber client on Arduino, while the broker can be implemented on a device with more computation resources. Henceforth, you will have bidirectional communication enabled on Arduino without using significant resources.

Introduction to MQTT

Message Queue Telemetry Transport (**MQTT**) is a very simple, easy, and open implementation of the pub/sub paradigm. IBM has been working on standardizing and supporting the MQTT protocol. The documentation for the latest specification of the MQTT protocol, v3.1, can be obtained from the official MQTT website at `http://www.mqtt.org`.

As a standard for machine messaging, MQTT is designed to be extremely lightweight and with a smaller footprint for code, while also using a lower network bandwidth for communication. MQTT is very specifically designed to work on embedded systems—like hardware platforms such as Arduino and other appliances—that carry limited processor and memory resources. While MQTT is a transport layer messaging protocol, it uses TCP/IP for network-level connectivity. As MQTT is designed to support the pub/sub messaging paradigm, the implementation of MQTT on your hardware application provides support for one-to-many distributed messaging, eliminating the limitation of unidirectional communication demonstrated by HTTP REST. As MQTT is agnostic of the content of the payload, there is no restriction on the type of message you can pass using this protocol.

Due to all the benefits associated with the pub/sub paradigm and its implementation in the MQTT protocol, we will be using the MQTT protocol for the rest of the exercises to have messages communicated between Arduino and its networked computer. To achieve this, we will be using the MQTT broker to provide the ground work for message communication and host topics, while deploying the MQTT publisher and subscriber clients at the Arduino and Python ends.

Mosquitto – an open source MQTT broker

As we described, MQTT is just a protocol standard, and it still requires software tools so that it can be implemented in actual applications. **Mosquitto** is an open source implementation of the message broker, which supports the latest version of the MQTT protocol standard. The Mosquitto broker enables the pub/sub paradigm implemented by the MQTT protocol, while providing a lightweight mechanism to enable messaging between machines. Development of Mosquitto is supported through community efforts. Mosquitto is one of the most popular MQTT implementations, freely available and widely supported on the Internet. You can obtain further information regarding the actual tool and community from its website, at `http://www.mosquitto.org`.

Setting up Mosquitto

The installation and configuration of Mosquitto are very straightforward processes. At the time of writing this book, the latest version of Mosquitto is 1.3.4. You can also obtain the latest updates and installation information regarding Mosquitto at `http://www.mosquitto.org/download/`.

On Windows, you can simply download the latest version of the installation files for Windows, which is made for Win32 or Win64 systems. Download and run the executable file to install the Mosquitto broker. To run Mosquitto from the command prompt, you will have to add the Mosquitto directory to the `PATH` variables in the environment variables of the system properties. In *Chapter 1, Getting Started with Python and Arduino*, we comprehensively described the process of adding a `PATH` variable to install Python. Using the same method, add the path of the Mosquitto installation directory at the end of the `PATH` value. If you are using a 64-bit operating system, you should use `C:\Program Files (x86)\mosquitto`. For a 32-bit operating system, you should use `C:\Program Files\mosquitto` as the path. Once you are done with adding this value at the end of the `PATH` value, close any existing command prompt windows and open a new Command Prompt window. You can validate the installation by typing the following command in the newly opened window. If everything is installed and configured correctly, the following command should execute without any errors:

```
C:\> mosquitto
```

For Mac OS X, the best way to install Mosquitto is to use the Homebrew tool. We already went through the process of installing and configuring Homebrew in *Chapter 1, Getting Started with Python and Arduino*. Install the Mosquitto broker by simply executing the following script on the terminal. This script will install Mosquitto with the Mosquitto utilities and also configure them to run from the terminal as commands:

```
$ brew install mosquitto
```

On Ubuntu, the default repository already has the installation package for Mosquitto. Depending on the version of Ubuntu you are using, this Mosquitto version could be older than the current version. In that case, you must add this repository first:

```
$ sudo apt-add-repository ppa:mosquitto-dev/mosquitto-ppa
$ sudo apt-get update
```

Now you can install the Mosquitto packages by simply running the following command:

```
$ sudo apt-get install mosquitto mosquitto-clients
```

Getting familiar with Mosquitto

Due to the multiple installation methods involved for different operating systems, the initialization of Mosquitto may be different for your instance. In some cases, Mosquitto might already be running on your computer. For a Unix-based operating system, you can check whether Mosquitto is running or not with this command:

```
$ ps aux | grep mosquitto
```

Unless you find a running instance of the broker, you can start Mosquitto by executing the following command in the terminal. After executing it, you should be able to see the broker running while printing the initialization parameters and other requests coming to it:

```
$ mosquitto
```

When you installed the Mosquitto broker, the installation process would also have installed a few Mosquitto utilities, which include the MQTT clients for the publisher and the subscriber. These client utilities can be used to communicate with any Mosquitto broker.

To use the subscriber client utility, `mosquitto_sub`, use the following command at the terminal with the IP address of the Mosquitto broker. As we are communicating to the Mosquitto broker running on the same computer, you can avoid the `-h <Broker-IP>` option. The subscriber utility uses the `-t` option to specify the name of the topic that you are planning to subscribe. As you can see, we are subscribing to the `test` topic:

```
$ mosquitto_sub -h <Broker-IP> -t test
```

Similar to the subscriber client, the publisher client (`mosquitto_pub`) can be used to publish a message to the broker for a specific topic. As described in the following command, you are required to use the `-m` option followed by a message to successfully publish it. In this command, we are publishing a `Hello` message for the `test` topic:

```
$ mosquitto_pub -h <Broker-IP> -t test -m Hello
```

Other important Mosquitto utilities include `mosquitto_password` and `mosquitto.conf`, which can be used to manage the Mosquitto password files and the setup broker configuration, respectively.

Getting started with MQTT on Arduino and Python

Now that you have the Mosquitto broker installed on your computer, it means that you have a working broker that implements the MQTT protocol. Our next goal is to develop the MQTT clients in Arduino and also in Python so that they will work as publishers and subscribers. After implementing the MQTT clients, we will have a fully-functional MQTT system, where these clients communicate through the Mosquitto broker. Let's begin with deploying MQTT on the Arduino platform.

MQTT on Arduino using the PubSubClient library

As MQTT is a network-based messaging protocol, you will always need an Ethernet Shield to communicate with your network. For the following exercise, we will continue using the same hardware that we have been using throughout this chapter.

Installing the PubSubClient library

To use Arduino for pub/sub and enable simple MQTT messaging, you need the Arduino client library for MQTT, also known as the `PubSubClient` library. The `PubSubClient` library helps you develop Arduino as an MQTT client, which can then communicate with the MQTT server (Mosquitto broker in our case) running on your computer. As the library provides methods to create only an MQTT client and not a broker, the footprint of the Arduino code is quite small compared to other messaging paradigms. The `PubSubClient` library extensively utilizes the default Arduino Ethernet library and implements the MQTT client as a subclass of the Ethernet client.

To get started with the `PubSubClient` library, you'll first need to import the library to your Arduino IDE. Download the latest version of the `PubSubClient` Arduino library from `https://github.com/knolleary/pubsubclient/`. Once you have the file downloaded, import it to your Arduino IDE.

We will be using one of the examples installed with the `PubSubClient` library to get started. The goal of the exercise is to utilize a basic example to create an Arduino MQTT client, while performing minor modifications to accommodate the local network parameters. We will then use the Mosquitto commands you learned in the previous section to test the Arduino MQTT client. Meanwhile, ensure that your Mosquitto broker is running in the background.

Developing the Arduino MQTT client

Let's start with opening the `mqtt_basic` example by navigating to **File | Examples | PubSubClient** in our Arduino IDE menu. In the opened program, change the MAC and IP address values for Arduino by updating the `mac[]` and `ip[]` variables, respectively. In the previous section, you successfully installed and tested the Mosquitto broker. Use the IP address of the computer running Mosquitto to update the `server[]` variable:

```
byte mac[]    = {  0x90, 0xA2, 0xDA, 0x0D, 0x3F, 0x62 };
byte server[] = { 10, 0, 0, 20 };
byte ip[]     = { 10, 0, 0, 75 };
```

As you can see in the code, we are initializing the client using the IP address of the server, Mosquitto port number, and Ethernet client. Before using any other method for the `PubSubClient` library, you will always have to initialize the MQTT client using a similar method:

```
EthernetClient ethClient;
PubSubClient client(server, 1883, callback, ethClient);
```

Further on in the code, we are using the `publish()` and `subscribe()` methods on the `client` class to publish a message for the `outTopic` topic and subscribe to the `inTopic` topic. You can specify the name of the client using the `client.connect()` method. As you can see in the following code snippet, we are declaring `arduinoClient` as the name for this client:

```
Ethernet.begin(mac, ip);
if (client.connect("arduinoClient")) {
  client.publish("outTopic","hello world");
  client.subscribe("inTopic");
}
```

As we are using this code in the `setup()` function, the client will only publish the `hello world` message once—during the initialization of the code—while the `subscribe` method will keep looking for new messages for `inTopic` due to the use of the `client.loop()` method in the Arduino `loop()` function:

```
client.loop();
```

Now, while running Mosquitto in the background, open another terminal window. In this terminal window, run the following command. This command will use a computer-based Mosquitto client to subscribe to the `outTopic` topic:

```
$ mosquitto_sub -t "outTopic"
```

Compile your Arduino sketch and upload it. As soon as the upload process is complete, you will be able to see the `hello world` string printed. Basically, as soon as the Arduino code starts running, the Arduino MQTT client will publish the `hello world` string to the Mosquitto broker for the `outTopic` topic. On the other side, that is, on the side of the Mosquitto client, you've started using the `mosquitto_sub` utility and will receive this message, as it is subscribed to `outTopic`.

Although you ran the modified Arduino example, `mqtt_basic`, you can also find the code for this exercise from this chapter's code folder. In this exercise, the Arduino client is also subscribed to `inTopic` to receive any message that originates for this topic. Unfortunately, the program doesn't display or deal with messages it obtains as a subscriber. To test the subscriber functionalities of the Arduino MQTT client, let's open the `mqtt_advance` Arduino sketch from this chapter's code folder.

As you can see in the following code snippet, we have added code to display the received message in the `callback()` method. The `callback()` method will be called when the client receives any message from the subscribed topics. Therefore, you can implement all types of functionality on the received message from the `callback()` method:

```
void callback(char* topic, byte* payload, unsigned int length) {
  // handle message arrived
```

```
    Serial.print(topic);
    Serial.print(':');
    Serial.write(payload,length);
    Serial.println();
  }
```

In this mqtt_advance Arduino sketch, we have also moved the publishing statement of outTopic from setup() to the loop() function. This action will help us to periodically publish the value for outTopic. In future, we will expand this method to use sensor information as messages so that the other devices can obtain those sensor values by subscribing to these sensor topics:

```
void loop()
{
  client.publish("outTopic","From Arduino");
  delay(1000);
  client.loop();
}
```

After updating the mqtt_advance sketch with the appropriate network addresses, compile and upload the sketch to your Arduino hardware. To test the Arduino client, use the same mosquitto_sub command to subscribe to outTopic. This time, you will periodically get updates for outTopic on the terminal. To check out the subscriber functionality of your Arduino client, open your **Serial Monitor** window in your Arduino IDE. Once the **Serial Monitor** window begins running, execute the following command in the terminal:

```
$ mosquitto_pub - t "inTopic" -m "Test"
```

You can see in the **Serial Monitor** window that the Test text is printed with the topic name as inTopic. Henceforth, your Arduino will serve as both an MQTT publisher and an MQTT subscriber. Now let's develop a Python program to implement the MQTT clients.

MQTT on Python using paho-mqtt

In the previous exercise, we tested the Arduino MQTT client using command-line utilities. Unless the published and subscribed messages are captured in Python, we cannot utilize them to develop all the other applications we've built so far. To transfer messages between the Mosquitto broker and the Python interpreter, we use a Python library called paho-mqtt. This library used to be called mosquitto-python before it was donated to the Paho project. Identical to the Arduino MQTT client library, the paho-mqtt library provides similar methods to develop the MQTT pub/sub client using Python.

Installing paho-mqtt

Like all other Python libraries we used, `paho-mqtt` can also be installed using Setuptools. To install the library, run this command in the terminal:

```
$ sudo pip install paho-mqtt
```

For the Windows operating system, use `easy_install.exe` to install the library. Once it is installed, you can check the successful installation of the library using the following command in the Python interactive terminal:

```
>>> import paho.mqtt.client
```

Using the paho-mqtt Python library

The `paho-mqtt` Python library provides very simple methods to connect to your Mosquitto broker. Let's open the `mqttPython.py` file from this chapter's code folder. As you can see, we have initialized the code by importing the `paho.mqtt.client` library method:

```
import paho.mqtt.client as mq
```

Just like the Arduino MQTT library, the `paho-mqtt` library also provides methods to connect to the Mosquitto broker. As you can see, we have named our client `mosquittoPython` by simply using the `Client()` method. The library also provides methods for activities, for example, when the client receives a message, `on_message`, and publishes a message, `on_publish`. Once you have initialized these methods, you can connect your client to the Mosquitto server by specifying the server IP address and the port number.

To subscribe to or publish for a topic, you simply need to implement the `subscribe()` and `publish()` methods on the client, respectively, as displayed in the following code snippet. In this exercise, we are using the `loop_forever()` method for the client to periodically check the broker for any new messages. As you can see in the code, we are executing the `publishTest()` function before the control enters the loop:

```
cli = mq.Client('mosquittoPython')
cli.on_message = onMessage
cli.on_publish = onPublish
cli.connect("10.0.0.20", 1883, 15)
cli.subscribe("outTopic", 0)
publishTest()
cli.loop_forever()
```

It is very important to run all the required functions or pieces of code before you enter the loop, as the program will enter the loop with the Mosquitto server once `loop_forever()` is executed. During this period, the client will only execute the `on_publish` and `on_message` methods for any update on the subscribed or published topics.

To overcome this situation, we are implementing the multithreading paradigm of the Python programming language. Although we are not going to dive deep into multithreading, the following example will teach you enough to implement basic programming logic. To understand more about the Python threading library and supported methods, visit `https://docs.python.org/2/library/threading.html`.

To better understand our implementation of the threading method, check out the following code snippet. As you can see in the code, we are implementing recursion for the `publishTest()` function every 5 seconds, using the `Timer()` threading method. Using this method, the program will start a new thread that is separate from the main program thread that contains the loop for Mosquitto. Every 5 seconds, the `publishTest()` function will be executed, recursively running the `publish()` method, and ultimately publishing a message for `inTopic`:

```
import threading
def publishTest():
    cli.publish("inTopic","From Python")
    threading.Timer(5, publishTest).start()
```

Now, in the main thread, when the client gets a new message from the subscribed topics, the thread invokes the `onMessage()` function. In the current implementation of this function, we are just printing the topic and message for demonstration purposes. In real applications, this function can be used to implement any kind of operation on the received message, for example, writing a message to a database, running an Arduino command, selecting an input, calling other functions, and so on. In short, this function is the entry point of any input you receive through the Mosquitto broker from your subscribed topics:

```
def onMessage(mosq, obj, msg):
    print msg.topic+":"+msg.payload
```

Similarly, every time you publish a message from the second thread, the `onPublish()` function is executed by the program. Just like the previous function, you can implement various operations within this function, while the function behaves as the exit point of any message published using this Python MQTT client. In the current implementation of `onPublish()`, we are not performing any operations:

```
def onPublish(mosq, obj, mid):
    pass
```

In the opened Python file, `mqttPython.py`, you will only need to change the IP address of the server running the Mosquitto broker. If you are running the Mosquitto broker on the same computer, you can use `127.0.0.1` as the IP address of the localhost. Before you execute this Python file, ensure that your Arduino is running with the MQTT client we created in the previous exercise. Once you run this code, you can start seeing the messages being sent from your Arduino in the Python terminal, as displayed in the following screenshot. Whenever a new message is received, the Python program prints the **outTopic** topic name followed by the **From Arduino** message. This confirms that the Python client is receiving messages for `outTopic`, to which it is subscribed. If you look back at the Arduino code, you will notice that it is the same message that we were publishing from the Arduino client.

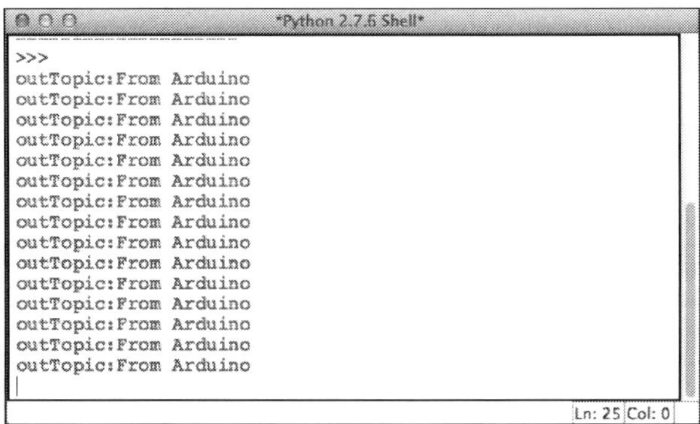

Now, to confirm the publishing operation of the Python MQTT client, let's open the **Serial Monitor** window from your Arduino IDE. As you can see in the **Serial Monitor** window, text that contains the **inTopic** topic name and the **From Python** message is being printed every 5 seconds. This validates the Python publisher, as we are publishing the same message for the same topic every 5 seconds through the `publishTest()` function.

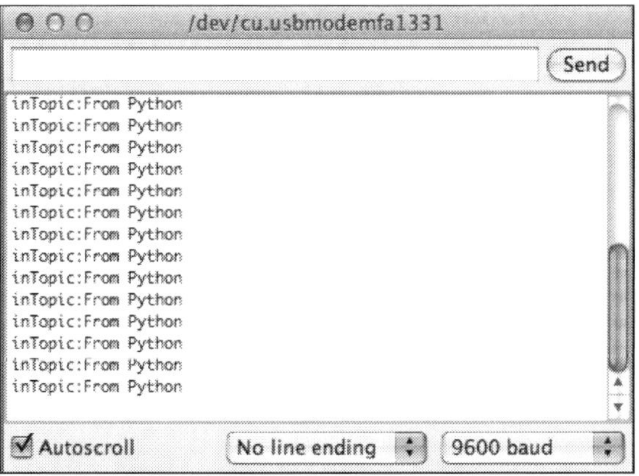

Exercise 4 – MQTT Gateway for Arduino

In exercise 3, we used the REST architecture to transfer motion and humidity sensor data between our Arduino and the web browser. In this exercise, we will develop an MQTT Gateway using the Mosquitto broker and the MQTT clients to transfer sensor information from our Arduino to the web browser. The goal of the exercise is to replicate the same components that we implemented in the REST exercise, but with the MQTT protocol.

As you can see in the architectural sketch of the system, we have Arduino with the Ethernet Shield connected to our home network, while the computer is running the Mosquitto broker and the Python applications on the same network. We are using the same sensors (that is, a motion sensor and a humidity sensor) and the same hardware design that we used in the previous exercises in this chapter.

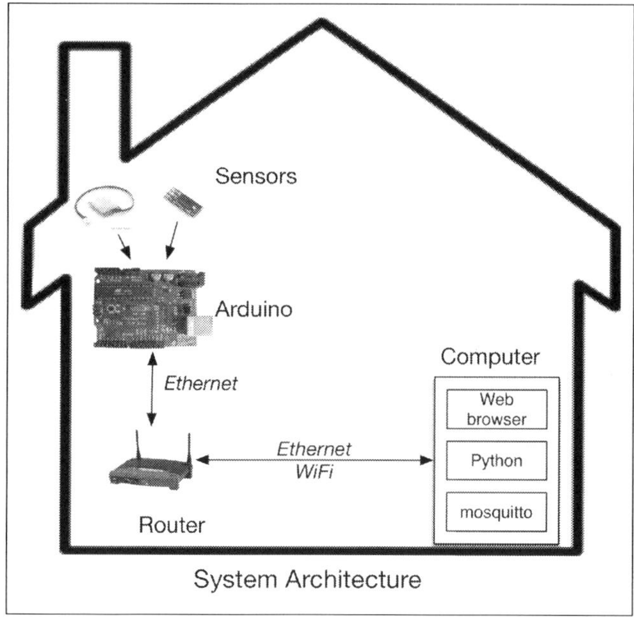

System Architecture

In the software architecture, we have the Arduino code that interfaces with the humidity and motion sensors using analog pin 0 and digital pin 3, respectively. Using the `PubSubClient` library, the Arduino publishes sensor information to the Mosquitto broker. On the MQTT Gateway, we have two different Python programs running on the computer. The first program uses the `paho-mqtt` library to subscribe and retrieve sensor information from the Mosquitto broker and then `post` it to the web application. The second Python program, which is based on `web.py`, implements the web applications while obtaining sensor values from the first Python program. This program provides a user interface front for the MQTT Gateway.

Although both of the preceding Python programs can be part of a single application, we are delegating the tasks of communicating with Mosquitto and serving information using the web application to separate applications for the following reasons:

- We want to demonstrate the functions of both libraries, `paho-mqtt` and `web.py`, in separate applications
- If you want to run routines based on `paho-mqtt` and `web.py` in the same application, you will have to implement multithreading, as both of these routines need to be run independently
- We also want to demonstrate the transfer of information between the two Python programs using Python-based REST methods with the help of the `httplib` library

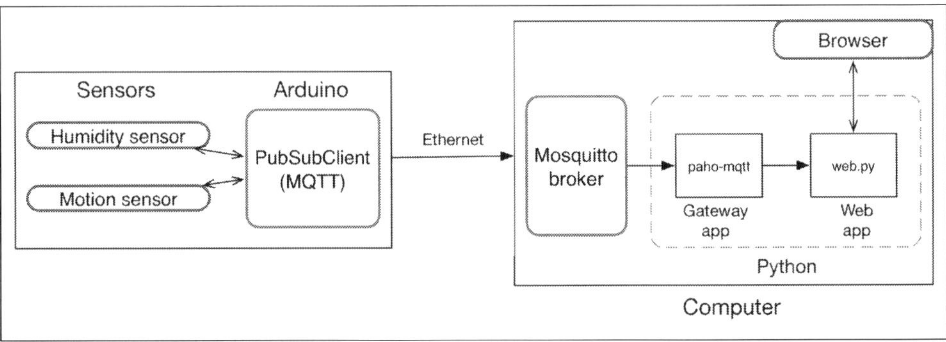

In this exercise, we are labeling humidity and motion sensor information with the topic labels `Arduino/humidity` and `Arduino/motion`, respectively. The Arduino-based MQTT publisher and the Python-based MQTT subscriber will be utilizing these topic names if they want to transfer information through the Mosquitto broker. Before we begin with implementing the MQTT client on our Arduino, let's start the Mosquitto broker on our computer.

Developing Arduino as the MQTT client

The goal of the Arduino MQTT client is to periodically publish the humidity and motion data to the Mosquitto broker running on your computer. Open the `Step1_Arduino.ino` sketch from the `Exercise 4 - MQTT gateway` folder in your code repository. Like all the other exercises, you first need to change the MAC address and the server address value, and assign an IP address for your Arduino client. Once you are done with these modifications, you can see the `setup()` function that we are publishing as a one-time connection message to the Mosquitto broker to check the connection. You can implement a similar function on a periodic basis if you have a problem with keeping your Mosquitto connection alive:

```
if (client.connect("Arduino")) {
    client.publish("Arduino/connection","Connected.");
  }
```

In the `loop()` method, we are executing the `publishData()` function every 5 seconds. It contains the code to publish sensor information. The `client.loop()` method also helps us keep the Mosquitto connection alive and avoids the connection timeout from the Mosquitto broker.

```
void loop()
{
  publishData();
  delay(5000);
  client.loop();
}
```

As you can see in the following code snippet, the `publishData()` function obtains the sensor values and publishes them using the appropriate topic labels. You might have noticed that we are using the `dtostrf()` function in this function to change the data format before publishing. The `dtostrf()` function is a function provided by the default Arduino library that converts a double value into an ASCII string representation. We are also adding a delay of another 5 seconds between the successive publishing of sensor data to avoid any data buffering issues:

```
void publishData()
{
  float humidity = getHumidity(22.0);
  humidityC = dtostrf(humidity, 5, 2, message_buff2);
  client.publish("Arduino/humidity", humidityC);
  delay(5000);
  int motion = digitalRead(MotionPin);
  motionC = dtostrf(motion, 5, 2, message_buff2);
  client.publish("Arduino/motion", motionC);
}
```

Complete any other modification you want to implement, and then compile your code. If your code is compiled successfully, you can upload it to your Arduino board. If your Mosquitto is running, you will be able see that a new client is connected as Arduino, which is the client name you specified in the preceding Arduino code.

Developing the MQTT Gateway using Mosquitto

You can have the Mosquitto broker running on the same computer as the Mosquitto Gateway, or on any other node in your local network. For this exercise, let's run it on the same computer. Open the program file named `mosquittoGateway.py` for this stage from the `Step2_Gateway_mosquitto` folder, which is inside the `Exercise 4 - MQTT gateway` folder. The first stage of the Gateway application includes the `paho-mqtt` based Python program, which subscribes to the Mosquitto broker for the `Arduino/humidity` and `Arduino/motion` topics:

```
cli.subscribe("Arduino/humidity", 0)
cli.subscribe("Arduino/motion", 0)
```

When this MQTT subscriber program receives a message from the broker, it calls the `onMessage()` function, as we've already described in the previous coding exercise. This method then identifies the appropriate sensor type and sends the data to the `web.py` program using the `POST` method. We are using the default Python library, `httplib`, to implement the `POST` method in this program. While using the `httplib` library, you have to use the `HTTPConnection()` method to connect to the web application running on port number `8080`.

> Although this program requires that your web application (second stage) must run in parallel, we are going to implement this web application in the upcoming section. Make sure that you first run the web application from the next section before executing this program; otherwise you will end up with errors.

The implementation of this library requires that you first import the library into your program. Being a built-in library, `httplib` does not require an additional setup process:

```
import httplib
```

Once the connection is established with the web application, you have to prepare the data that needs to be sent in the `POST` method. The `httplib` method uses the `request()` method on the opened connection to post the data. You can also use the same method in other applications to implement the `GET` function. Once you are done with sending the data, you can close the connection using the `close()` method. In the current implementation of the `httplib` library, we are creating and closing the connection on each message. You can also declare the connection outside the `onMessage()` function and close it when you terminate the program:

```
def onMessage(mosq, obj, msg):
    print msg.topic
    connection = httplib.HTTPConnection('10.0.0.20:8080')
```

```
    if msg.topic == "Arduino/motion":
        data = "motion:" + msg.payload
        connection.request('POST', '/data', data)
        postResult = connection.getresponse()
        print postResult
    elif msg.topic == "Arduino/humidity":
        data = "humidity:" + msg.payload
        connection.request('POST', '/data', data)
        postResult = connection.getresponse()
        print postResult
    else:
        pass
    connection.close()
```

Once you have performed the appropriate modifications, such as changing the IP address of the Mosquitto broker and the `web.py` application, go to the next exercise before running the code.

Extending the MQTT Gateway using web.py

The MQTT Gateway code provides the user interface with the sensor information using the `web.py` based web application. The code is quite similar to what you implemented in exercise 3. The program file is named `GatewayWebApplication.py` and located in your `Exercise 4 - MQTT gateway` code folder. In this application, we have removed the sensor selection process by simply implementing a button, displayed as **Refresh**. This application waits for the `POST` message from the previous program, which will be received on the `http://<ip-address>:8080/data` URL, ultimately triggering the `data` class. The `POST` method in this class will split the received string to identify and update the value of the `humidity` and `motion` global sensor variables:

```
class data:
    def POST(self):
        global motion, humidity
        i = web.input()
        data = web.data()
        data = data.split(":")
        if data[0] == "humidity":
            humidity = data[1]
        elif data[0] == "motion":
            motion = data[1]
        else:
            pass
        return "Ok"
```

The default URL, `http://<ip-address>:8080/`, displays the `base` template with the **Refresh** button, populated using the `Form()` method. As displayed in the following code snippet, the default `index` class renders the template with the updated (current) `humidity` and `motion` values when it receives the `GET` or `POST` request:

```
class index:
    submit_form = form.Form(
        form.Button('Refresh',
                    type="submit",
                    description='refresh')
    )
    # GET function
    def GET(self):
        f = self.submit_form()
        return render.base(f, humidity, motion)

    # POST function
    def POST(self):
        f = self.submit_form()
        return render.base(f, humidity, motion)
```

Run the program from the command line. Make sure that you are running both programs from separate terminal windows.

Testing your Mosquitto Gateway

You have to follow these steps in the specified order to successfully execute and test all the components of this exercise:

1. Run the Mosquitto broker.
2. Run the Arduino client. If it is running already, restart the program by powering off the Arduino client and powering it on again.
3. Execute the web application in your terminal or from the Command Prompt.
4. Run the `paho-mqtt` Gateway program.

If you follow this sequence, all of your programs will start without any errors. If you get any errors while executing, make sure that you follow all the instructions correctly, while also confirming the IP addresses in your programs. To check out your Arduino MQTT client, open the **Serial Monitor** window in your Arduino IDE. You will be able to see the periodic publication of the sensor information, as displayed in this screenshot:

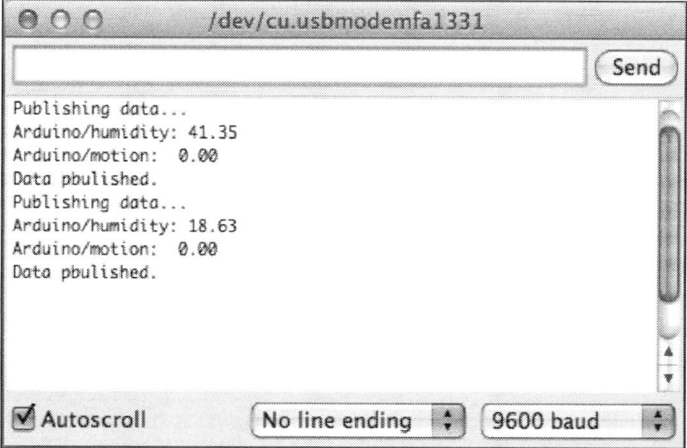

Now open a web browser on your computer and go to the URL of your web application. You should be able to see a window that looks like what is shown in the following screenshot. You can click on the **Refresh** button to check out the updated sensor values.

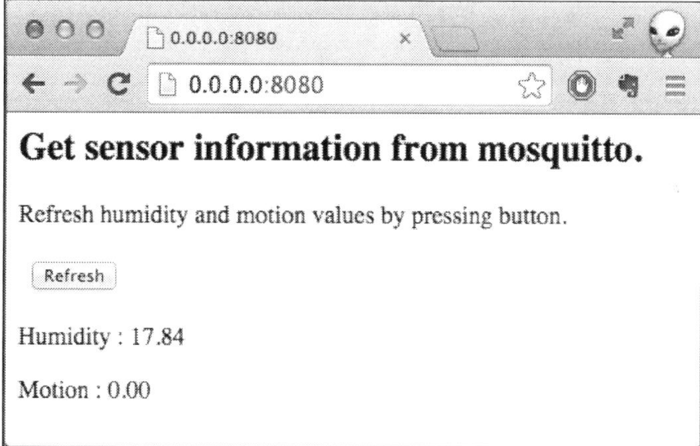

We have set a delay of 5 seconds between successive sensor updates. Henceforth, you won't be able to see the updated values if you rapidly press the **Refresh** button.

On the Gateway program terminal, you will be able to see the label of the topic every time the program receives a new message from Mosquitto. If the delay between successive sensor updates is not sufficient and `httplib` doesn't have enough time to get the response back from the `web.py` application, the program will generate an error message with the `httplib` function. Although we require an additional delay for `httplib` to successively send the data and receive the response, we will be able to avoid this delay when we implement the core Python code with threading, avoiding the entire notion of `POST` in between the programs:

```
*Python 2.7.6 Shell*
Python 2.7.6 (default, Apr 28 2014, 02:15:56)
[GCC 4.2.1 Compatible Apple LLVM 5.1 (clang-503.0.40)] on darwin
Type "copyright", "credits" or "license()" for more information.
>>> ================================ RESTART ================================
>>>
Arduino/humidity
<httplib.HTTPResponse instance at 0x10d5387a0>
Arduino/motion
<httplib.HTTPResponse instance at 0x10d5387a0>
Arduino/humidity
<httplib.HTTPResponse instance at 0x10d5387a0>
Arduino/motion
<httplib.HTTPResponse instance at 0x10d5387a0>
|
                                                              Ln: 12 Col: 0
```

With this exercise, you have implemented two different types of messaging architecture to transfer data between your Arduino and your computer or web applications using your home network. Although we recommend the use of hardware-centric and lightweight MQTT messaging paradigms over REST architecture, you can use either of these communication methods according to the application's requirements.

Summary

Connectivity to computer networks can really open up limitless possibilities for future application development using Arduino. We started the chapter by explaining important computer network fundamentals, while also covering hardware extensions that enable computer networking for Arduino. Regarding the various methods of enabling networking, we began the chapter by establishing a web server for Arduino. We concluded that the web server on Arduino is not the best way for network communication due to the limited number of connections offered by the web server. Then we demonstrated the use of Arduino as a web client to enable HTTP-based `GET` and `POST` requests. Although this method is useful for request-based communication and requires fewer resources compared to a web server, it is still not the best way for sensor communication due to the additional data overhead. In the later part of the chapter, we described a lightweight messaging protocol, MQTT, designed specifically for sensor communication. We demonstrated its superiority to HTTP-based protocols using a few exercises.

With the help of each method of Arduino Ethernet communication, you learned about compatible Python libraries used to support these communication methods. We used the `web.py` library to develop a web server using Python, and demonstrated the use of the library with multiple examples. To support the MQTT protocol, we explored an MQTT broker, Mosquitto, and employed the Python library, `paho_mqtt`, to serve the MQTT requests.

Overall, we covered every major aspect of Arduino and Python communication methods throughout this chapter, and demonstrated them with simple exercises. In the upcoming chapters, we will build upon the basics you learned in this chapter, in order to develop advanced Arduino-Python projects that will enable remote access to our Arduino hardware through the Internet.

9
Arduino and the Internet of Things

In the previous chapter, we learned how to access Arduino using Ethernet from a remote location. The main objective was to get you started with developing Arduino-based network applications using Python. We were able to accomplish this using various tools such as the `web.py` Python library, Mosquitto MQTT broker, and the Arduino Ethernet library. Remote access to sensor data via a Python-like extensible language can open up limitless possibilities for sensor-based web applications. In recent years, the rapid growth of these applications has enabled the development of a domain called the **Internet of Things** (**IoT**).

In the last chapter, we worked on Arduino networking. However, it was limited to LAN and the premise of the exercises was limited to your home or office. We didn't even involve the Internet to enable global access in our exercises. Traditional IoT applications require Arduino to be accessed remotely from any part of the world via the Internet. In this chapter, we will extend the Arduino networking concepts by interfacing Arduino with cloud-based platforms. We will also develop web applications to access the sensor data from these cloud platforms. Later in the chapter, we will go through the process of setting up your cloud-based messaging platform to serve sensor data. At the end of this chapter, you should be able to design and develop full-stack IoT applications, using Arduino, Python, and the cloud.

Getting started with the IoT

Long before the Internet, sensor- and actuator-based electronic control systems existed in high-tech automation systems. In those systems, sensors were interfaced to the microcontroller via hard-wired connections. Due to extensibility limitations, the coverage area of these systems was geographically restricted. Examples of these high-tech systems included factory automation, satellite systems, weapon systems, and so on. In most cases, the sensors used in these systems were huge and the microcontrollers were also limited by their low computational capabilities.

With recent advancements in technology, especially in the semiconductor industry, the physical size of sensors and microcontrollers has significantly reduced. It has also been made possible to manufacture low-cost and highly efficient electronic components, hence today it is relatively inexpensive to develop small and efficient sensor-based hardware products. Arduino and Raspberry Pi are great examples of these achievements. These sensor-and actuator-based hardware systems interface with the physical world that we live in. The sensors measure various elements from the physical environment, while the actuators manipulate the physical environment. These types of hardware-based electronic systems are also known as **physical systems**.

On the other front, advancements in the semiconductor industry also enabled the development of highly efficient computation units, empowering personal computer and networking industries. This movement led to the worldwide network of connected computers called CyberWorld or the Internet. Every day, petabytes of data get generated and transferred across the Internet.

The domain of IoT stands at the crossroads of these progresses in physical and cyber systems, where ancient hardwired sensor-based systems are ready to get upgraded to more powerful and efficient systems that are also highly connected through the Internet. Due to the large number of sensors involved, these systems generate and send an avalanche of data. The data generated by these sensors has already eclipsed the data generated by humans.

The IoT has started to become a significant domain in recent years after a large number of consumer IoT products have started entering the market. These products include applications in home automation, health care, activity tracking, smart energy, and so on. One of the major reasons behind the rapid growth of the IoT domain is the introduction of these visible solutions. In a large number of cases, this was made possible due to fast and inexpensive prototyping that was enabled by Arduino and other open source hardware platforms.

Up to this point in the book, we have learned various methods of interfacing sensors and then developing applications using these connected sensors. In this chapter, we will learn the last step in the development of a full-stack IoT application—enabling access for your Python-Arduino application through the Internet. Now, let's try to first understand the architecture of the IoT.

Architecture of IoT web applications

In this book, we have covered three major concepts in the first eight chapters:

- **Physical layer**: We used various sensors and actuators with the Arduino board to deal with the physical environment. The sensors such as the temperature sensor, humidity sensor, and motion sensor were used measured the physical phenomenon, while the actuators such as LEDs were utilized to alter or produce physical elements.
- **Computation layer**: We used Arduino sketches and Python programs to convert these physical elements into numerical data. We also utilized these high-level languages to perform various computations such as calculating relative humidity, developing user interfaces, plotting data, and providing web interfaces.
- **Interfacing layer**: Throughout the material that we covered, we also utilized various interfacing methods to establish communication between Arduino and Python. For interfacing part of the interfacing layer between the physical and computation layers, we used serial port libraries, established network-based communication using the REST and MQTT protocol, and developed web applications.

As you can see, we have developed applications with tightly-coupled physical, computation, and interfacing layers. In the research domain, these types of applications are also known as cyber-physical systems. One of the widely used and popular terms for the domain of cyber-physical system is the IoT. Although the cyber-physical domain is thoroughly defined compared to the IoT, the IoT has recently gained more popularity due to the large number of subdomains—industrial Internet, wearable devices, connected devices, smart grid, and so on—that are covered under this umbrella term. In simple terms, an application can qualify as an IoT application if it consists of hardware devices that deal with the physical world and have sufficient computational capabilities with Internet connectivity. Let's try to understand the architecture of the IoT from the material that we have already covered.

On the physical side, the following figure shows the hardware components that we utilized to deal with the physical environment. The sensors and actuators that interface with the actual physical world can be connected to Arduino using multiple low-level protocols. These components can be connected using GPIO pins and using the I2C or SPI protocols. The data acquired from these components gets processed on the Arduino board using the code that is uploaded by the user. Although the Arduino code can be made self-reliant to execute tasks without any external inputs, these inputs from users or other applications are required in advanced applications.

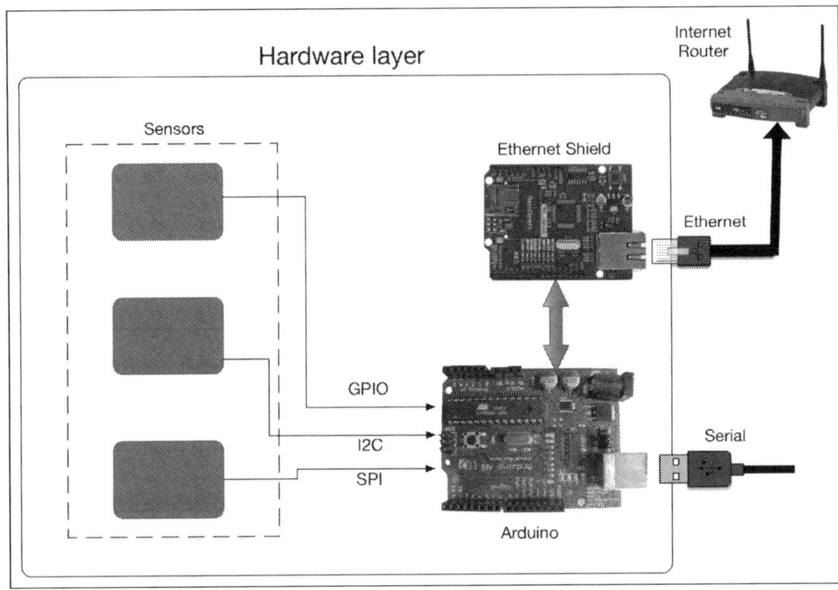

As part of the communication layer, Arduino can be connected locally to other computers using USB. One can extend the coverage range by utilizing Ethernet, Wi-Fi, or any other radio communication method.

As illustrated in the following figure, the sensor data is collected using computation units for advance processing. These computation units are powerful enough to host operating systems and programming platforms. In this book, we utilized Python to develop various features at the computation layer. At this level, we performed high-level computation tasks such as developing graphical user interfaces using the `Tkinter` library, plotting charts using the `matplotlib` library, and developing web applications using the `web.py` library.

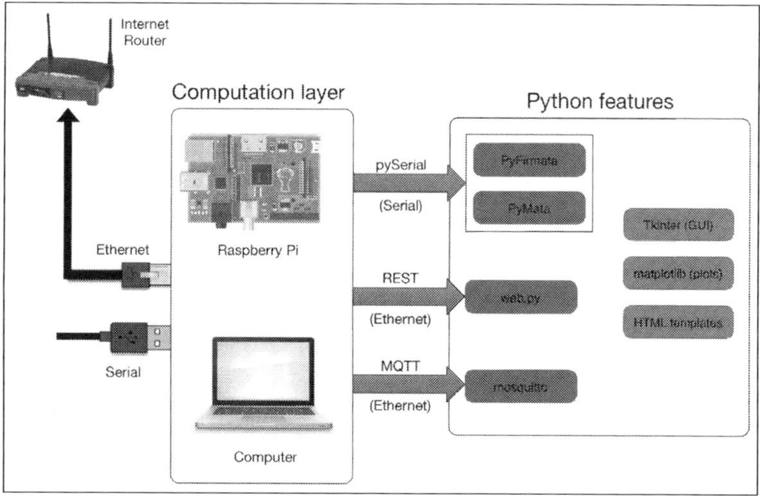

In all the coding exercises that we performed previously, the physical coverage areas of the projects were limited because of hardwired serial interfaces or local Ethernet network, as displayed in the following figure:

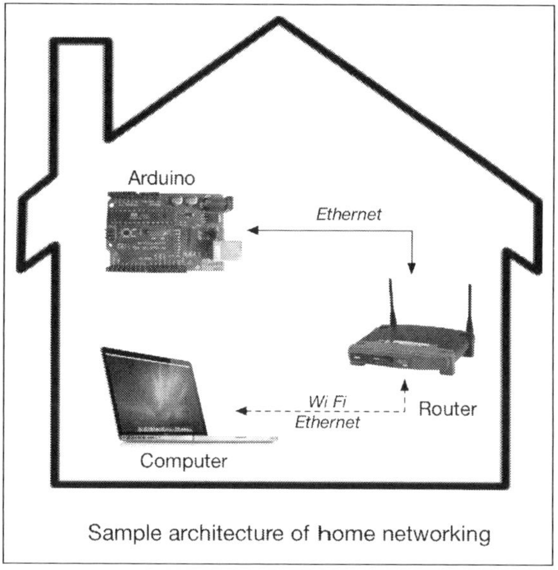

Sample architecture of home networking

To develop full-stack IoT applications, we need to remotely access Arduino or host the computation layer on the Internet. In this chapter, we are going to work on this missing link and develop various applications to provide Internet connectivity to the exercises. To perform this operation, we are going to utilize a commercial cloud platform in the first section and develop our customized platform in the later section.

As the focus of this chapter is going to be on cloud connectivity, we are not going to develop a hardware circuit for each exercise. We will go through the hardware design exercise only once and keep using the same hardware for all the programming exercises. Similarly, we will also reuse the `web.py` programs that we developed in the previous chapter to focus on code snippets that are associated with Python libraries to develop cloud applications.

Hardware design

Let's begin by developing standard hardware for all the upcoming exercises. We will need the Arduino board that is attached to the Ethernet Shield to use the Ethernet protocol for network connectivity. In terms of components, you will be using simple sensors and actuators that you already used in the previous coding exercises. We will use the PIR motion sensor and the HIH-4030 humidity sensor to provide digital and analog outputs, respectively. We will also have an LED as part of the hardware design and this will be used in coding exercises as an actuator. For more information regarding the properties and detailed explanations of these sensors, you can refer to previous chapters.

To begin assembly of the hardware components, first attach the Ethernet Shield on top of the Arduino board. Connect the sensors and actuators to the appropriate pins, as displayed in the following figure. Once you have the hardware assembled, you can connect the Ethernet Shield to your home router using the Ethernet cable. You will need to power the board using the USB cable to upload the Arduino code from your computer. In case you want to deploy the Arduino board to a remote location, you will need an external 5V supply to power Arduino.

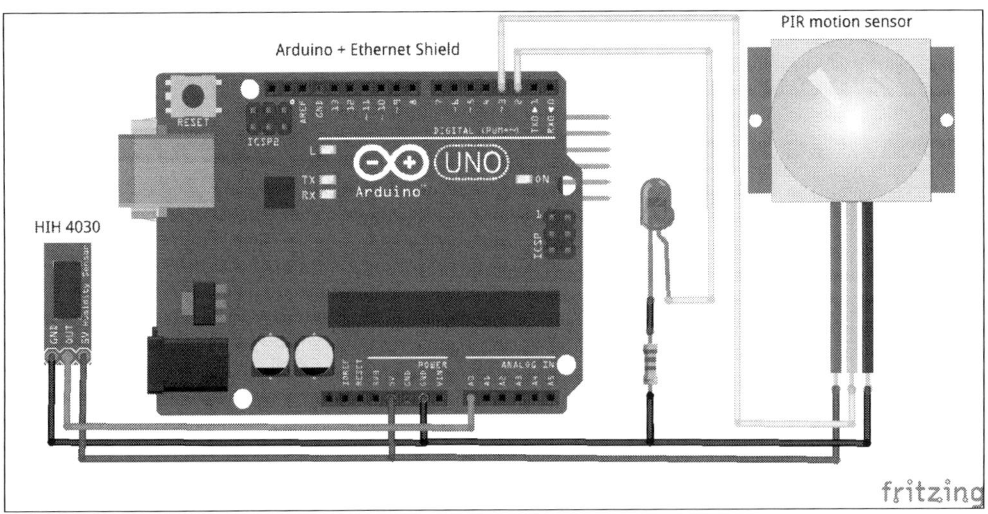

The IoT cloud platforms

The term **IoT cloud platform** is used for the cloud platforms that provide very specific services, protocol support, and web-based tools for IoT applications. In more informal terms, these cloud IoT platforms can be used to upload your sensor data and access them from anywhere using the Internet. With these basic features, they also provide tools to access, visualize, and process your sensor data on various platforms such as computers and smartphones. Examples of similar IoT cloud platforms include Xively (`http://www.xively.com`), 2lemetry (`http://www.2lemetry.com`), Carriots (`http://www.carriots.com`), ThingSpeak (`http://thingspeak.com`), and so on.

The following figure shows the architecture of an IoT system with an Arduino-based sensor system that is sending data to a cloud platform, while a computation unit is accessing the data remotely from the cloud:

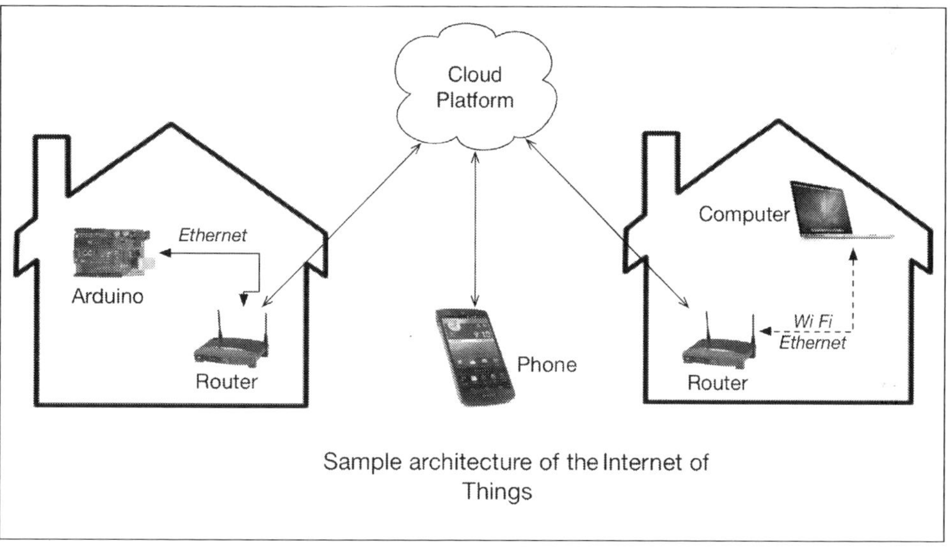

Sample architecture of the Internet of Things

Xively, being the oldest and most popular IoT platform, has a large amount of community-based online help that is available for beginners. This is one of the major reasons why we have chosen Xively as our platform of choice for the upcoming exercises. Recently, Xively has changed their policy of creating free developer accounts and a user has to request access to this free account instead of obtaining one freely. In case you want to use another platform other than Xively, we have briefly covered a few similar platforms at the end of this section.

Xively – a cloud platform for the IoT

Xively is one of the very first IoT-specific cloud platforms that was founded in 2007 as Pachube. It went through multiple name changes, as it was called Cosm, but it is currently known as Xively. Xively provides an IoT cloud platform with tools and services to develop connected devices, products, and solutions. As mentioned on its website, Xively is the public cloud that is specifically built for the IoT.

Setting up an account on Xively

Now, we can go ahead and set up a new user account for the Xively platform. To set up an account, you need to execute following steps in the given order:

1. To begin the sign up process on `Xively.com`, open `https://xively.com/signup` in a web browser.
2. On the sign up page, you will be prompted to select the username and the password, as displayed in the following screenshot:

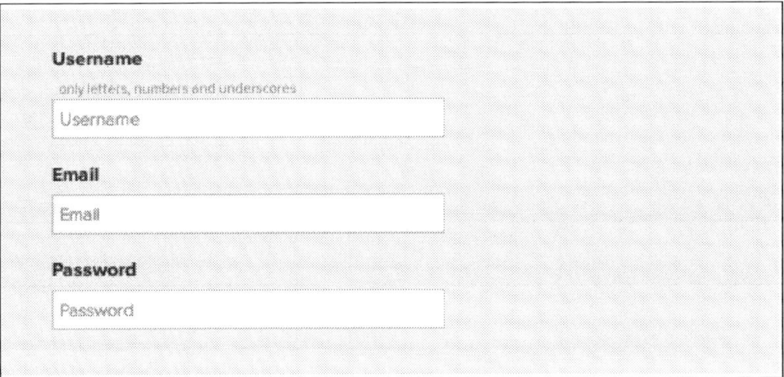

3. On the next page, you will be asked to enter some additional information that includes your full name, organization's name, country, zip code, time zone, and so on. Fill out the form appropriately and click on the **Sign Up** button:

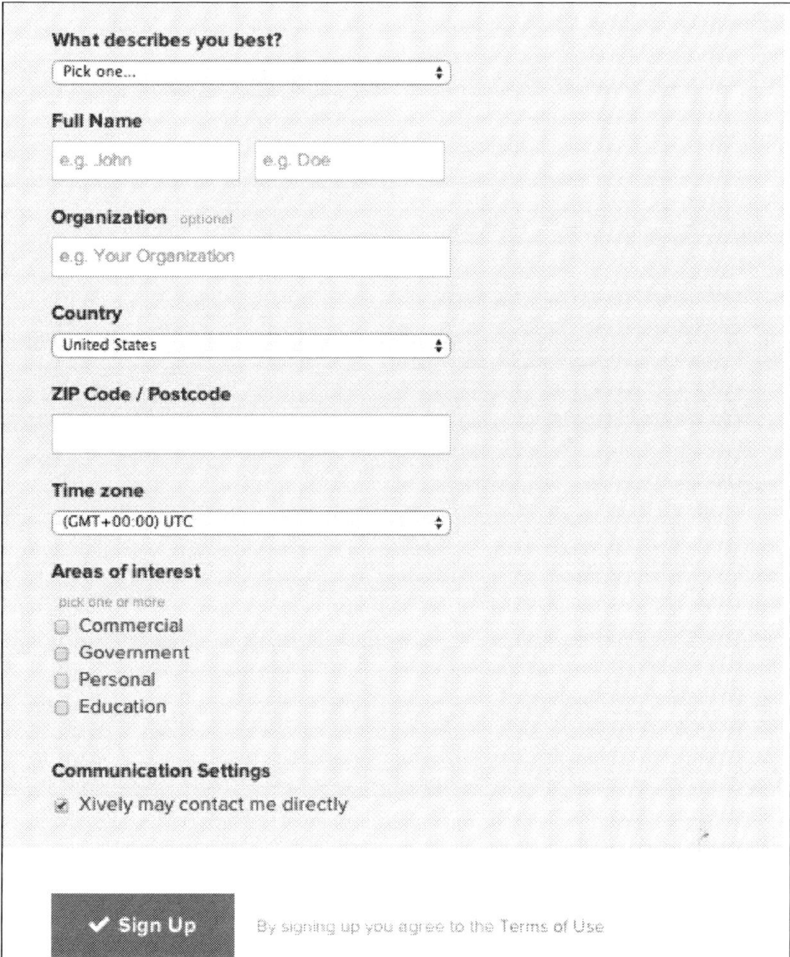

4. Xively will send an activation e-mail to the e-mail account that you specified in the form. Open the e-mail and click on the activation link. Check your spam folder if you don't see the e-mail in your inbox.
5. Once you click on the activation link, you will be redirected to the welcome page on Xively's website. We advise you to go through the tutorials provided on the welcome page, as it will help you to get familiar with the Xively platform.
6. After completing the tutorials, you can come back to the main user screen from the page using the `https://xively.com/login` link.

   If you are not already logged in, you will require your e-mail address as the username and an appropriate password to log into the Xively platform.

Working with Xively

The Xively platform lets you create cloud device instances that can be connected to the actual hardware device, app, or service. Perform the following steps in order to work with Xively:

1. To begin working with the Xively platform, add a device from the main page, as displayed in the following screenshot:

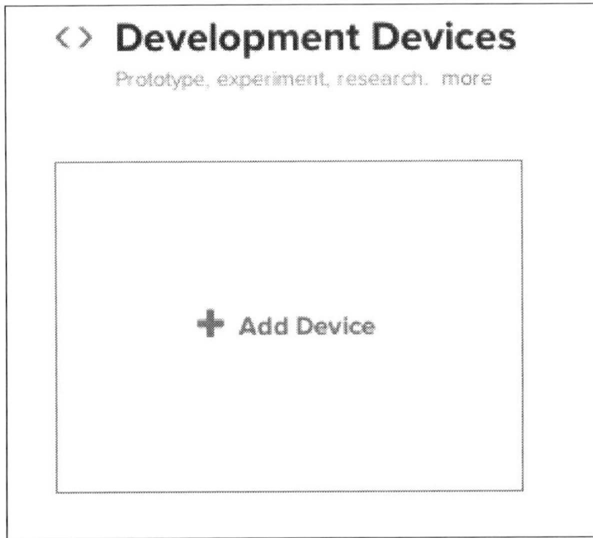

2. Once you click on the **Add Device** button, it will prompt you to the following window where you will be asked to provide the device name, description, and privacy status of the device that you are going to assign. In the form, select a device name that you want your development device to be called, provide a brief description, and select **Private Device** as the privacy status:

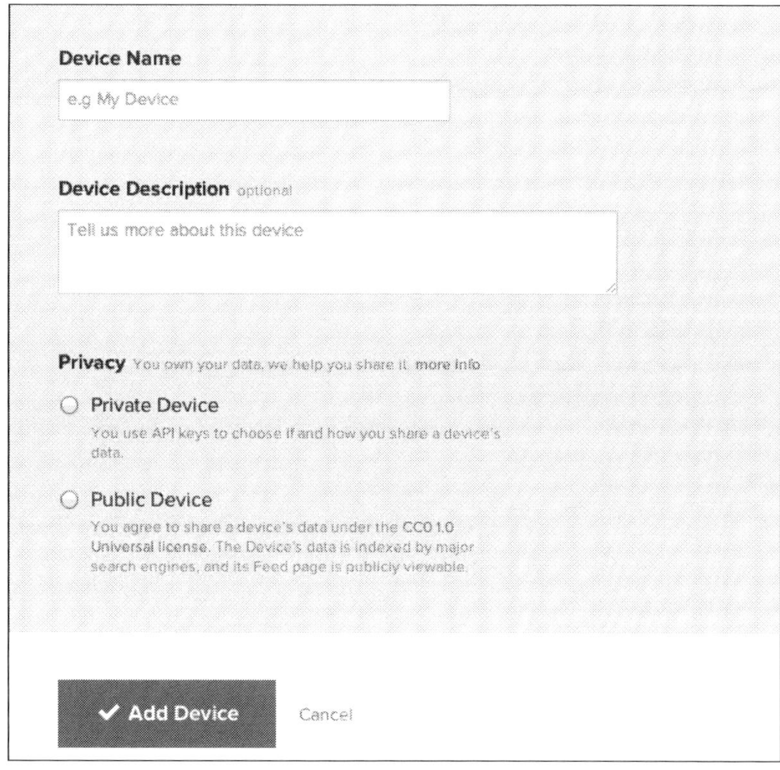

3. Once you click the **Add Device** button, Xively will create a device instance with automatically-generated parameters and prompt you to the development workbench environment. On the page of the device that you just added, you can see various identification and security parameters such as **Product ID**, **Serial Number**, **Feed ID**, **Feed URL**, and **API Endpoint**. From among these parameters, you will frequently need the **Feed ID** information for the upcoming exercises:

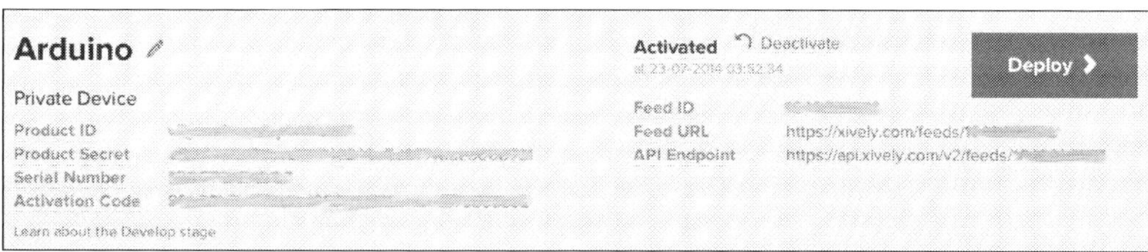

4. A unique and secure API key of the newly created device is also located in the right-hand side bar of the page. This API key is very important and needs to be secured just like your password, as anyone with the API key can access the device.

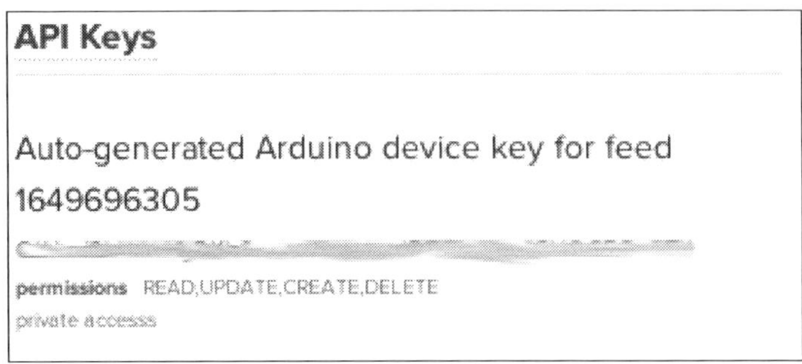

5. Now, to remotely access this device, open the terminal and use the cURL command to send data to it. In the following command, change the `<Your_Feed_ID>` and `<Your_API_key>` values with the ones available for your device:

```
$ curl --request PUT --data "0,10" --header "X-ApiKey: <Your_API_key" https://api.xively.com/v2/feeds/<Your_Feed_ID>.csv
```

6. As you can see, the previous command sent the value of 10 on channel 0 of your device on Xively. After executing the previous command, you will notice that the Xively workbench is updated with the information that you just sent using cURL:

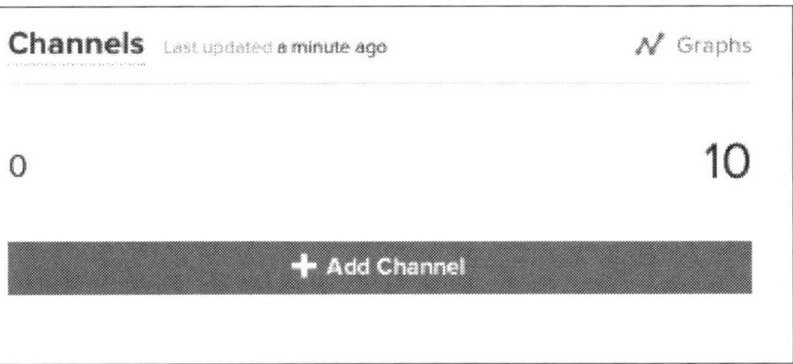

7. Try sending multiple values on channel 0 using the previous command. On the Xively workbench, you will be able to see a plot being generated by these values in real time. Access the plot by clicking on channel 0 in the workbench:

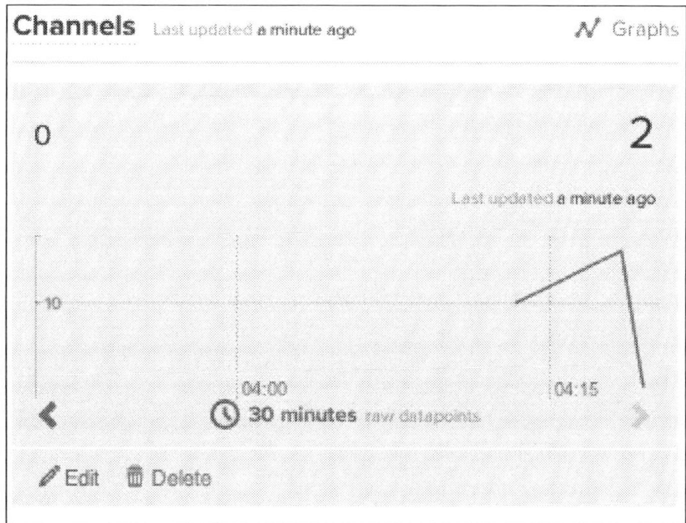

Using the method that we used in this example, we can also configure Arduino to send sensor values automatically to the Xively platform. This will enable the storage and visualization of Arduino data on Xively.

Alternative IoT platforms

In this section, we have provided important links for the ThingSpeak and Carriots platforms. As we are not covering these platforms in detail, these links will help you to find similar examples to interface Arduino and Python with ThingSpeak and Carriots.

ThingSpeak

The tutorials in the following links will help you to get familiar with the ThingSpeak platform if you chose to use it instead of Xively:

- **The official website**: `https://thingspeak.com/`
- **Using Arduino and Ethernet to update a ThingSpeak channel**: `http://community.thingspeak.com/tutorials/arduino/using-an-arduino-ethernet-shield-to-update-a-thingspeak-channel/`
- **Arduino examples for ThingSpeak**: `https://github.com/iobridge/ThingSpeak-Arduino-Examples`
- **Communicating with ThingSpeak using Python**: `http://www.australianrobotics.com.au/news/how-to-talk-to-thingspeak-with-python-a-memory-cpu-monitor`

- **Using Arduino and Python to talk to a ThingSpeak channel**: `http://vimeo.com/19064691`
- **Series of ThingSpeak tutorials**: `http://community.thingspeak.com/tutorials/`

ThingSpeak is an open source platform and you can create your own customized version of ThingSpeak using the files provided. You can obtain these files and the associated guideline from `https://github.com/iobridge/ThingSpeak`.

Carriots

Carriots also provides a free, basic account for developers. If you want to use Carriots as an alternative to Xively, use the tutorials in the following links to get started:

- **The official website**: `https://www.carriots.com/`
- **Setting up an account on Carriots**: `https://learn.adafruit.com/wireless-gardening-arduino-cc3000-wifi-modules/setting-up-your-carriots-account`
- **The Carriots library for Arduino**: `https://github.com/carriots/arduino_library`
- **A Carriots example for Arduino**: `https://github.com/carriots/arduino_examples`
- **Connect Carriots to the Python web application**: `http://www.instructables.com/id/Connect-your-Carriots-Device-to-Panics-Status-Boa/`

Developing cloud applications using Python and Xively

Now, you have a basic idea about the available commercial IoT platforms and you can select one according to your comfort level and requirements. It will be very difficult to comprehensively explain every cloud platform with practical examples, as the objective of this chapter is to make you familiar with integrating the cloud platform with Python and Arduino. For this reason, we are going to use Xively as the de facto IoT cloud platform for the rest of the integration exercises.

Now that you know how to create an account on Xively and work with the Xively platform, it is time to start interfacing real hardware with the Xively platform. In this section, we will go through methods to upload and download data from Xively. We will combine the Arduino hardware that we built with the Python programs to show you basic methods of communicating with Xively.

Interfacing Arduino with Xively

The first stage to establish communication with Xively includes interfacing the Arduino board with the Xively platform via standalone Arduino code. We have already built the necessary hardware using the Arduino Uno, Ethernet Shield, and a few sensors. Let's connect it to your computer using the USB port. You also need to connect the Ethernet Shield to your home router using the Ethernet cable.

Uploading Arduino data to Xively

The Arduino IDE has a built-in example that can be used to communicate with the Xively service. This is known as **PachubeClient** (Pachube was Xively's previous name).

> It is important to note that the reason behind using this default example is to give you a jump-start in the interfacing exercises. This particular sketch is rather old and may get dropped as a default exercise in the upcoming releases of the Arduino IDE. In that case, you can directly jump to the next exercise or develop your custom sketch to perform the same exercise.

Perform the following steps to upload Arduino data to Xively:

1. Open the Arduino IDE and then open the **PachubeClient** example by navigating to **File | Examples | Ethernet | PachubeClient**.
2. To establish communication with Xively, you will need the feed ID and the API key of your Xively device, which you obtained in the last section.
3. In the opened Arduino sketch, perform the following changes using the obtained feed ID and API key. You can specify any project name for the `USERAGENT` parameter:

```
#define APIKEY          "<Your-API-key>"
#define FEEDID           <Your-feed-ID>
#define USERAGENT        "<Your-project-name>"
```

4. In the Arduino sketch, you will also have to change the MAC address and the IP address of your Ethernet Shield. You should be familiar with obtaining these addresses from the exercise that you performed in the previous chapter. Use these values and modify the following lines of code appropriately:

```
byte mac[] = {0x90, 0xA2, 0xDA, 0x0D, 0x3F, 0x62};
IPAddress ip(10,0,0,75);
```

5. As the opened Arduino example was created for the Pachube, you need to update the server address to `api.xively.com` as specified in the following code snippet. Comment the IP address line as we will not need it anymore and add the `server[]` parameter:

   ```
   //IPAddress server(216,52,233,122);
   char server[] = "api.xively.com";
   ```

6. In the `sendData()` function, change the channel name to `HumidityRaw` as we have our HIH-4030 humidity sensor connected to the analog port. We are not performing any relative humidity calculations at this stage and are going to upload just the raw data from the sensor:

   ```
   // here's the actual content of the PUT request:
   client.print("HumidityRaw,");
   client.println(thisData);
   ```

7. Once you have performed these changes, open the `XivelyClientBasic.ino` file from the folder containing codes for this chapter. Compare them with your current sketch and compile/upload the sketch to the Arduino board if everything seems satisfactory. Once you have uploaded the code, open the **Serial Monitor** window in the Arduino IDE to observe the following output:

8. If you see an output in the **Serial Monitor** window that is similar to the one displayed in the previous screenshot, your Arduino is successfully connected to Xively and is uploading data on the HumidityRaw channel.

9. Open your device in Xively's website and you will be able to see an output that is similar to the following screenshot on the web page. This confirms that you have successfully uploaded data to an IoT cloud platform using your remotely-located Arduino:

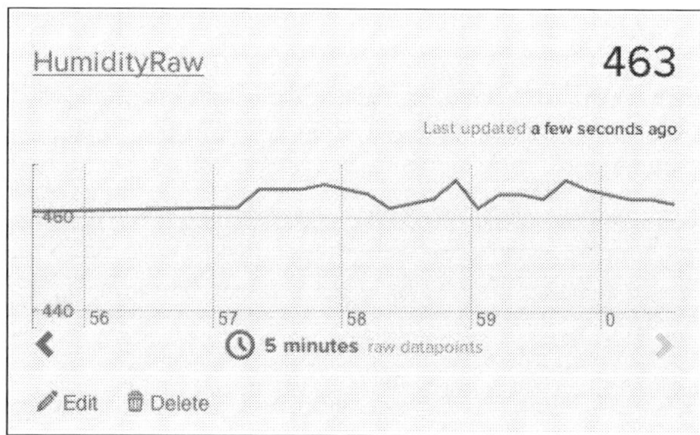

Downloading data to Arduino from Xively

In the previous coding exercise, we used a default Arduino example to communicate with Xively. However, Xively also provides a very efficient Arduino library with built-in functions for rapid programming. In the next exercise, we will use an alternative method to communicate with the Xively platform using the `Xively-Arduino` library. Although you can use either of these methods, we recommend that you use the `Xively-Arduino` library as it is officially maintained by Xively.

In this exercise, we will download digital values from a channel called LED. Later, we will use these digital values, 0 and 1, to switch an LED that is connected to our Arduino board. As an input to this channel, we will alter the current value of the channel on the Xively platform's website while letting the Arduino download that value and perform the appropriate task.

Let's begin by importing the `Xively-Arduino` library and its dependencies. As you already know how to import libraries in the Arduino IDE, visit `https://github.com/amcewen/HttpClient` to download and import the `HttpClient` library. This is a dependency that is required by the `Xively-Arduino` library to function.

Once you have imported the `HttpClient` library, download the `Xively-Arduino` library from `https://github.com/xively/xively_arduino` and repeat the import process.

The `Xively-Arduino` library ships with few examples so that you can get started. We will use their example as base code for downloading data for our exercise.

1. In the Arduino IDE, navigate to **File | Examples | Xively_arduino | DatastreamDownload** and open the **DatastreamDownload** example. Change the default API key to your own API key that was obtained from the device that you created. As displayed in the following code snippet, you need to also identify your channel name, which is LED in this case:

   ```
   char xivelyKey[] = "<Your-API-key>";
   char ledId[] = "LED";
   ```

2. The `Xively-Arduino` library requires you to define the `XivelyDatastream` variable as an array. You can also specify multiple data streams according to your application:

   ```
   XivelyDatastream datastreams[] = {
     XivelyDatastream(ledId, strlen(ledId), DATASTREAM_FLOAT),
   };
   ```

3. You also need to declare a variable called `feed` using the `XivelyFeed` function. As displayed in the following line of code, replace the default feed ID with the appropriate one. In the initialization of the `feed` variable, the value `1` represents the number of `datastreams` in the `XivelyDatastream` array:

   ```
   XivelyFeed feed(<Your-feed-ID>, datastreams, 1);
   ```

4. In our exercise, we want to periodically retrieve the value of the LED channel and turn the actual LED on or off accordingly. In the following code snippet, we obtain the float value from `feed[0]`, where `0` specifies the data stream located at the `0` position in the `datastreams` array:

   ```
   Serial.print("LED value is: ");
   Serial.println(feed[0].getFloat());

   if (feed[0].getFloat() >= 1){
      digitalWrite(ledPin, HIGH);
   }
      else{
      digitalWrite(ledPin, LOW);
   }
   ```

5. As you now know that the parameters need to be changed for this exercise, open the `XivelyLibBasicRetrieveData.ino` Arduino sketch from the code folder. This sketch contains the exact code that you need to use for the exercise. Although this sketch includes the necessary modifications, you will still have to change the values for account-specific parameters, that is, the API key, feed ID, and so on. Before you go ahead and upload this sketch, go to the Xively platform and create a channel called `LED` with **Current Value** as `1`, as displayed in the following screenshot:

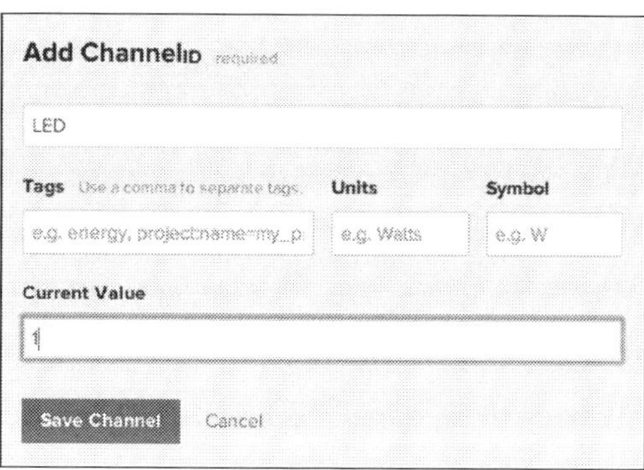

6. Now, compile and upload the code to your Arduino.
7. Once you have uploaded the compiled code to your Arduino, open the **Serial Monitor** window and wait for an output that is similar to the one displayed in following screenshot. You will notice that the LED on the Arduino hardware is turned on:

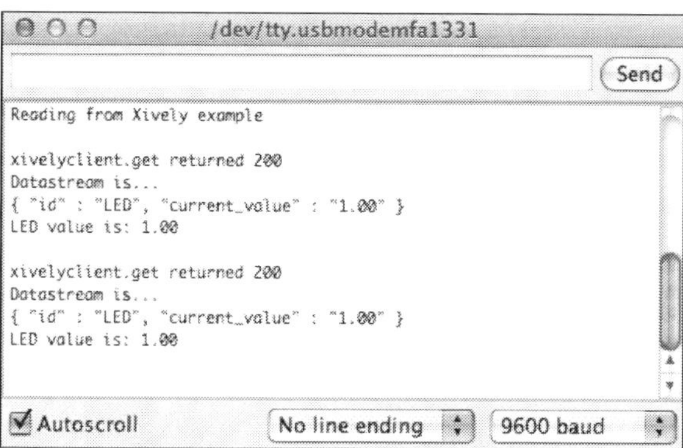

8. You can go back to the Xively LED channel and change the **Current Value** field to `0`. Within a few seconds, you will notice that the LED on the Arduino hardware is turned off. With this exercise, you have successfully established two-way communication between Arduino and the Xively platform.

Advanced code to upload and download data using Arduino

In the previous two Arduino exercises, we individually performed the uploading and downloading tasks. In this exercise, we want to create an Arduino program where we can upload data from the connected sensors (the PIR motion sensor and the HIH-4030 humidity sensor) while retrieving the value to control the LED. Open the Arduino sketch, `XivelyLibAdvance.ino`, which contains the code that demonstrates both the functionalities. As you can see in the following code snippet, we have defined three separate channels for each component while having independent `XivelyDatastream` objects for upload (`datastreaU[]`) and download (`datastreamD[]`). Similarly, we have also created two different feeds, `feedU` and `feedD`. The main reason behind delegating the upload and download tasks to different objects is to independently update the value of the LED channel while uploading the data stream for channels, `HumidityRaw` and `MotionRaw`:

```
char ledId[] = "LED";
char humidityId[] = "HumidityRaw";
char pirId[] = "MotionRaw";

int ledPin = 2;
int pirPin = 3;

XivelyDatastream datastreamU[] = {
  XivelyDatastream(humidityId, strlen(humidityId), DATASTREAM_FLOAT),
  XivelyDatastream(pirId, strlen(pirId), DATASTREAM_FLOAT),
};

XivelyDatastream datastreamD[] = {
  XivelyDatastream(ledId, strlen(ledId), DATASTREAM_FLOAT),
};

XivelyFeed feedU(<Your-feed-ID>, datastreamU, 2);
XivelyFeed feedD(<Your-feed-ID>, datastreamD, 1);
```

In the `loop()` function of the Arduino code, we periodically fetch the current value of the LED channel from `feedD` and then perform the LED action:

```
int retD = xivelyclient.get(feedD, xivelyKey);
Serial.print("xivelyclient.get returned ");
```

In the second stage of the periodic function, we obtain the raw sensor values from the analog and digital pins of the Arduino board and then upload those values using `feedU`:

```
int humidityValue = analogRead(A0);
datastreamU[0].setFloat(humidityValue);
int pirValue = digitalRead(pirPin);
datastreamU[1].setFloat(pirValue);

int retU = xivelyclient.put(feedU, xivelyKey);
Serial.print("xivelyclient.put returned ");
```

Make the appropriate changes in the code to accommodate feed ID and API key and then upload the sketch to the Arduino board. Once you upload this Arduino sketch to your platform, you should be able to see the following output on the **Serial Monitor** window. You can now disconnect your Arduino from the USB port and connect the external power supply. Now that you have connected your Arduino assembly to your local network using an Ethernet cable, you can place the Arduino assembly at any location in your workplace.

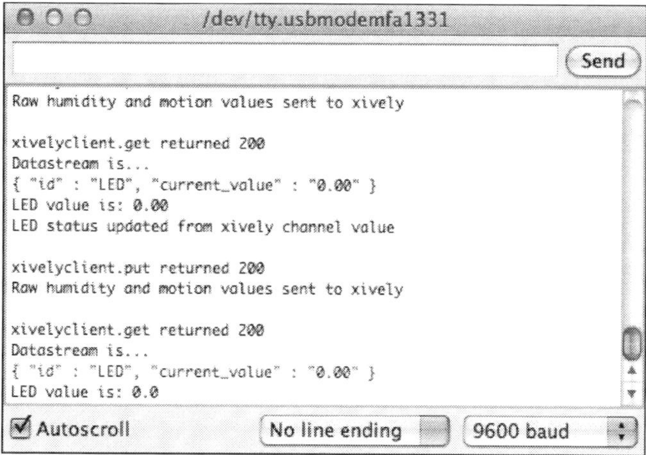

Python – uploading data to Xively

Similar to how we interfaced Arduino to Xively, we will now explore methods to connect the Xively platform via Python and thus complete the loop. In this section, we will focus on different ways of uploading data to Xively using Python. We will start with a basic method of communicating with Xively and extend it further with `web.py` to implement the interface using a web application.

To begin with, let's first install Xively's Python library, `xively-python`, on your computer using the following command:

```
$ sudo pip install xively-python
```

The basic method for sending data

Once again, you will need the API key and feed ID of your virtual device that you created on the Xively platform. Python, assisted by the `xively-python` library, provides very simple methods to establish a communication channel with the Xively platform. From your code folder, open the `uploadBasicXively.py` file. As specified in the code, replace the `FEED_ID` and `API_KEY` variables with the appropriate feed ID and API key:

```
FEED_ID = "<Your-feed-ID>"
API_KEY = "<Your-API-key>"
```

Using the `XivelyAPIClient` method, create an `api` instance and create the `feed` variable by using the `api.feeds.get()` method:

```
api = xively.XivelyAPIClient(API_KEY)
feed = api.feeds.get(FEED_ID)
```

Just as we did in the Arduino exercises, you will need to create data streams for each channel from the feeds. As specified in the following code snippet, try to get the specified channel from the feed or create one if it is not present on the Xively virtual device. You can also specify tags and other variables while creating a new channel:

```
try:
  datastream = feed.datastreams.get("Random")
except HTTPError as e:
  print "HTTPError({0}): {1}".format(e.errno, e.strerror)
  datastream = feed.datastreams.create("Random", tags="python")
  print "Creating 'Random' datastream"
```

Once you have opened the data stream for a channel, you can specify the current value using the `datastream.cuurent_value` method and update the value, which will upload this value to the specified channel:

```
datastream.current_value = randomValue
datastream.at = datetime.datetime.utcnow()
datastream.update()
```

Once you have performed the specified modifications to the `uploadBasicXively.py` file, execute it using the following command:

```
$ python uploadBasicXively.py
```

Open your virtual device on the Xively website to find the `Random` channel populated with the data that you uploaded. It will look similar to the following screenshot:

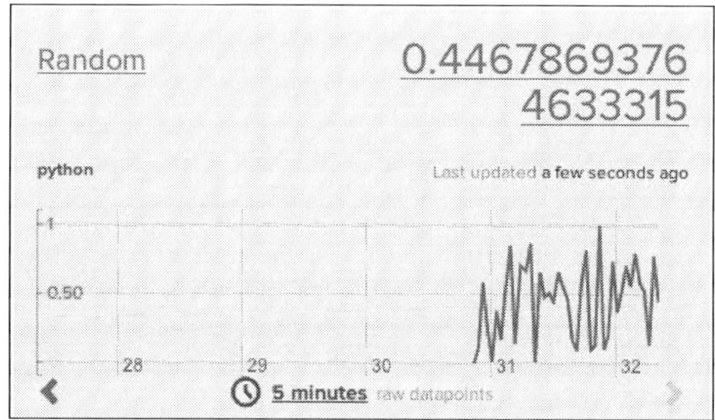

Uploading data using a web interface based on web.py

In the previous chapter, we worked with the `web.py` library while developing templates and web applications. In this exercise, we will utilize one of the programs in which we created the `web.py` forms with the Xively code that we developed in the previous exercise. The goal of this exercise is to send data to the LED channel using a web application while observing the LED's behavior on the Arduino hardware.

You can find the Python program for this exercise in this chapter's folder with the name `uploadWebpyXively.py`. As you can see in the code, we are using the `web.py` forms to obtain two inputs, `Channel` and `Value`. We will use these inputs to modify the current value of the LED channel:

```
submit_form = form.Form(
        form.Textbox('Channel', description = 'Channel'),
        form.Textbox('Value', description = 'Value'),
        form.Button('submit', type="submit", description='submit')
        )
```

The template file, `base.html`, is also modified to accommodate minor changes that are required by this exercise. As you can see in the opened Python file, we are using the same code that we used to interface with Xively in the previous exercise. The only major modification is done to the `datastream.update()` method, which is now placed in the `POST()` function. This method will be executed when you submit the form. Once you change the API key and feed ID in this file, execute the Python code and open `http://localhost:8080` in your web browser. You can see the web application running, as displayed in the following screenshot. Enter the value as displayed in the figure to turn on the LED on the Arduino board. You can change the **Value** parameter to `0` to turn off the LED.

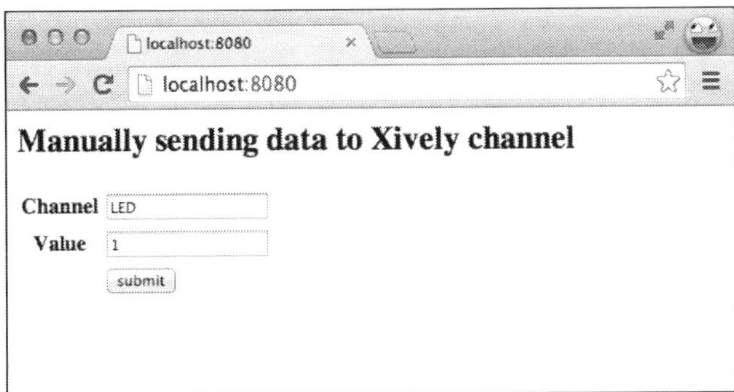

Python – downloading data from Xively

The process of downloading data from Xively includes requesting the **Current Value** parameter for the specified channel. In the next exercise, we will develop a reference code that will be used in the next downloading exercise. In that exercise, we will develop an advanced web application to retrieve data from a specific Xively channel.

As we are using functions based on the REST protocol to communicate with Xively, Xively will not simply notify you about any new, available update, instead you will have to request it. At this point, it is important to note that we will have to periodically request data from Xively. However, Xively provides an alternative method called **triggers** to overcome this problem, which is explained later in this section.

The basic method for retrieving data from Xively

Just like the uploading exercises, the downloading exercises also require a similar code to instantiate the `XivelyAPIClient()` and `api.feeds.get()` methods. As we are retrieving the data instead of sending it, we will only use the `feed.datastreams.get()` method and avoid the `feed.datastreams.create()` method. The download process requires the channel to be already present and this is the main reason why we only have to use the `get()` method:

```
try:
  datastream = feed.datastreams.get("Random")
except HTTPError as e:
  print "HTTPError({0}): {1}".format(e.errno, e.strerror)
  print "Requested channel doesn't exist"
```

Once the `datastream` object is initialized, the latest available value from the channel can be obtained using the `datastream.current_value` method:

```
latestValue = datastream.current_value
```

To enable the complete code to perform this exercise, open the `downloadXivelyBasic.py` code and change the values for the feed ID and API key to the appropriate ones. In this exercise, we are working with the `Random` channel that we created in the uploading exercise. Before you execute this Python code, you need to execute the `uploadXivelyBasic.py` file that will continuously provide random data to the `Random` channel. Now, you can execute the `downloadXivelyBasic.py` file that will fetch the current value of the `Random` channel periodically (with a delay specified by the `sleep()` function). As you can see in the following screenshot, we are getting a new value for the `Random` channel every 10 seconds:

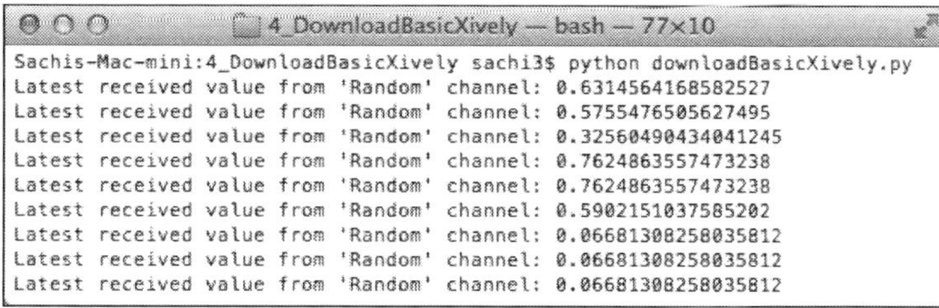

Retrieving data from the web.py web interface

This is an advanced exercise where we will upload data to one Xively channel after fetching data from another Xively channel, and process it by using the data entered via the web form. As you know, the analog pin on which the HIH-4030 sensor is connected provides you with raw sensor value, whereas the relative humidity depends upon the value of the current temperature. In this exercise, we will develop a web application so that the user can manually enter the temperature value and we will use this to calculate relative humidity from the raw sensor data.

Before we begin with the details of the code, let's first open the `uploadWebpyXively.py` file, change the appropriate parameters, and execute the file. Now, in a web browser, open the `http://localhost:8080` location. You will be able to see following web application, asking you to provide it with the current temperature value. Meanwhile, upload the `XivelyLibAdvance.ino` sketch to the Arduino board after making the appropriate changes. With this program, Arduino will start sending raw motion and humidity values to the `MotionRaw` and `HumidityRaw` channels. In the web application that is running, submit the form with the custom temperature value and you will be able to see the web application load the current relative humidity in percentage units. Internally, when you submitted the form, the web application retrieved the current raw humidity value from the `HumidityRaw` channel, executed the `relativeHumidity(data, temperature)` function, uploaded the calculated humidity value to a new channel called `Humidity`, and then displayed that value in the web application.

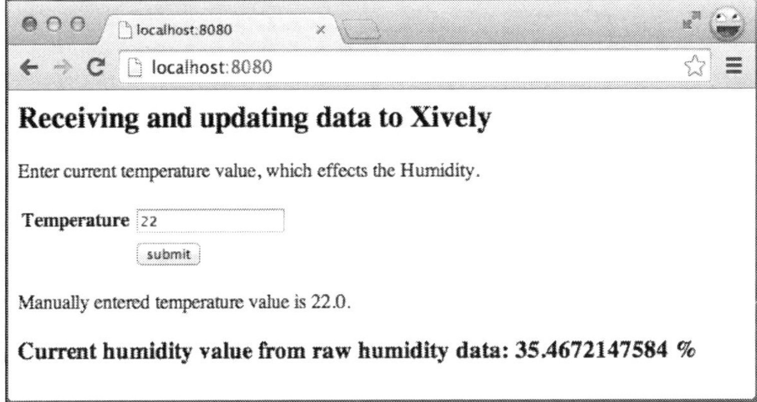

If you open your Xively platform page on a web browser, you will be able to see a newly created `Humidity` channel with the current value for relative humidity. You can submit multiple values for temperature in the web application to see the results reflected on the graph of the `Humidity` channel, as displayed in the following screenshot. Although this exercise demonstrates a single use case, this web application can be extended in multiple ways to create complex applications.

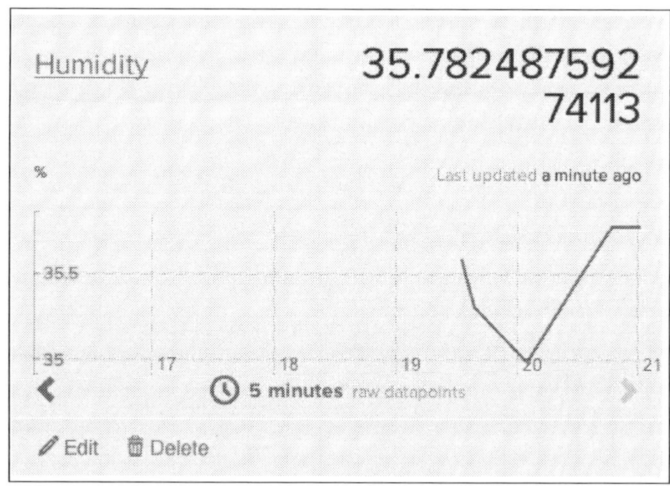

Triggers – custom notifications from Xively

The Xively platform primarily deploys services based on the REST protocol, which doesn't have a provision to automatically publish data when it is updated with a new value. In order to overcome this limitation, Xively implements the concept of triggers, which provide additional functionality beyond just publishing data when it is changed. Through this, you can basically create a trigger for any channel to perform the `POST` operation on the specified location when conditions that are set for that trigger get satisfied by the incoming data. For example, you can set a trigger on the `Humidity` channel to send you a notification when the value of humidity changes, that is, increases above or decrease below a given threshold. You can create a trigger in your Xively platform account by just clicking on the **Add Trigger** button, as displayed in the following screenshot:

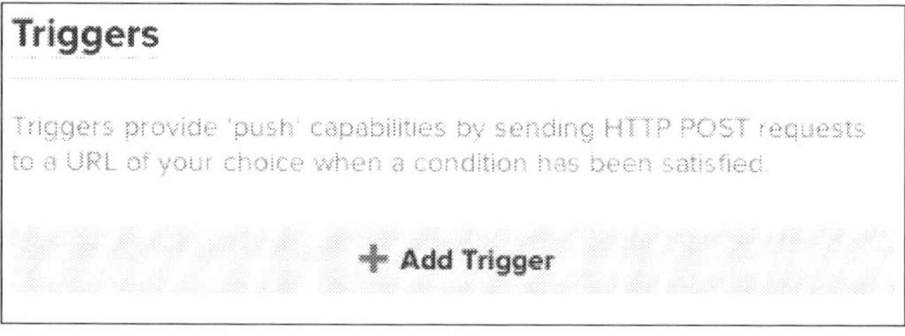

While creating a trigger, you can specify the channel you want to monitor and the condition to trigger a notification on the specified HTTP `POST` URL. As shown in the following screenshot, complete the information for **Channel**, **Condition**, and **HTTP POST URL** before saving the trigger. The major drawback with this approach is that Xively requires an actual URL to send the `POST` notification. If your current computer doesn't have a static IP address or a DNS address, the trigger won't be able to send you the notification:

Your own cloud platform for the IoT

In the previous section, we worked with a commercial IoT platform that also provides restricted, free access to basic functionalities. We also learned various ways to communicate with Xively that is based on the REST protocol. For any small projects or prototypes, Xively and other similar IoT platforms provide a sufficient solution and are therefore recommended by us. However, the limited free service provided by Xively may not satisfy all of your requirements to develop a full-stack IoT product. The following are a few cases where you may want to configure or develop your own IoT platform:

- Develop your own commercial IoT platform
- Develop custom features that are exclusive to your product
- Add more control features and communication protocols while also securing your data
- Require an inexpensive solution for large-scale projects

This section will guide you through the step-by-step process of creating an elementary small-level IoT cloud platform. The goal of the section is to make you familiar with the requirements and the process of creating an IoT platform. To develop a large-scale, diverse, and feature-rich platform such as Xively, you will need a significant amount of knowledge and experience in the domains of cloud and distributed computing. Unfortunately, cloud and distributed computing are out of scope of this book and we will stick with the implementation of the basic features.

To develop a cloud platform that is accessible through the Internet, you will at least require a computational unit with Internet connection and a static IP or DNS address. Today, the majority of consumer-oriented **Internet Service Providers** (**ISPs**) do not provide static IPs with their Internet service, making it difficult to host a server at home. However, various companies such as Amazon, Google, and Microsoft, provide free or cost-effective cloud computing services, which make it easier to host your cloud on their platforms. These services are highly scalable and they are equipped with a large amount of features to satisfy the majority of consumer requirements. In the following section, you will be creating your first cloud computing instance on **Amazon Web Services** (**AWS**). Later in this chapter, we will install and configure the appropriate software tools such as Python, Mosquitto broker, and so on, to utilize this Amazon instance as an IoT cloud platform.

The major reason behind developing or configuring a personal cloud platform is to have access to your IoT hardware through the Internet. Due to the lack of a static IP address for your home network, you may not be able to access you prototypes or projects from a remote location. A cloud platform can be used as the de facto computation unit for your network-based projects.

Getting familiar with the Amazon AWS platform

AWS is a collection of various cloud services offered by Amazon, which together make up a cloud computing platform. One of the original and most popular services offered by AWS is its **Elastic Computer Cloud** (**EC2**) service. The EC2 service lets a user create instances of a virtual machine with different combinations of computation power and operating systems from their large cloud infrastructure. It is also really easy to change the computational properties of these virtual instances at any time, making them highly scalable. When you are trying to create your own IoT platform using EC2, this scalability feature greatly helps you as you can expand or compress the size of your instances according to demand. If you are not familiar with the concept of cloud computing or AWS as a particular product, you can learn more about them from `http://aws.amazon.com`.

The EC2 cloud platform is different from Xively as it provides general-purpose cloud instances, virtual machines, with computation power and storage that can be converted to any feature-specific platform by installing and configuring platform-specific software. It is important to note that you really do not have to be an expert in cloud computing to further advance in this chapter. The upcoming sections provide an intuitive guide to perform basic tasks, such as setting up an account, creating and configuring your virtual machines, and installing software tools to create IoT platforms.

Setting up an account on AWS

Amazon provides one year of free access to the basic instance of the cloud-based virtual machine. This instance includes 750 hours of free usage time per month and this is greater than the number of hours in any month, thereby making it free for the entire month. The data storage capacity and bandwidth of the AWS account are sufficient for basic IoT or Arudino projects. To create a free account for a year on Amazon's AWS cloud platform, perform the following steps:

1. Open `http://aws.amazon.com` and click on the button that asks you to try AWS for free or some other similar text.
2. This action will lead you to a **Sign In or Create an AWS Account** page as displayed in the following screenshot. Enter the e-mail address that you want to use for this account when you select the **I am a new user.** option and click on the **Sign in using our secure server** button. If you already have an AWS account and you know how to create an account on Amazon AWS, you can use those credentials and skip to the next section:

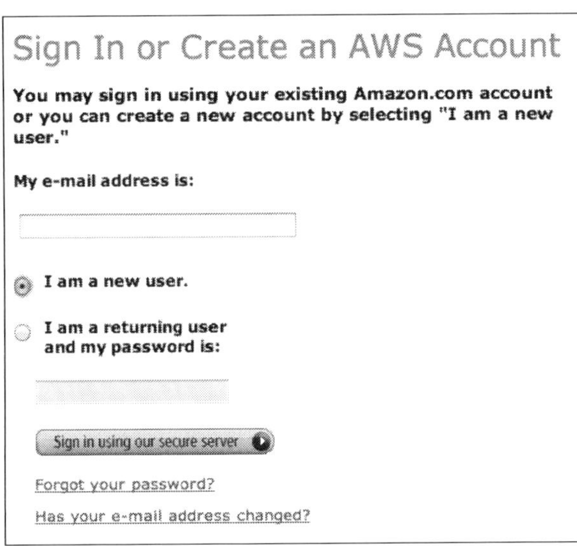

Amazon only allows one free instance for each account. If you are an existing AWS user and your free instance is already occupied with another application, you can use the same instance to accommodate the MQTT broker or buy another instance.

3. On the next page, you will be prompted to enter your name, e-mail address, and a password, as displayed in the following screenshot. Fill in the information to continue with the sign up process:

4. You will be asked to enter your credit card information during the sign up process. However, you won't be charged for using the services included in the free account. Your credit card will be only used if you exceed any limitations or buy any additional services.
5. The next stage includes the verification of your account using your phone number. Follow the instructions that are displayed in the following screenshot to complete the identity verification process:

6. Once you have verified your identity, you will be redirected to the page that lists the available Amazon AWS plans. Select the appropriate plan that you want to subscribe to and continue. If you are not sure, you can select the **Basic (Free)** plan option, which we recommend for our purpose. The **Amazon Management Console** page will let you select other plans if you want to upgrade the current one.
7. Launch the Amazon management console.

As you have an Amazon AWS account now, let's create your virtual instance on it.

Creating a virtual instance on the AWS EC2 service

In order to create a virtual instance on Amazon's EC2 platform, first log in to AWS using your credentials and open the management console. Next, click on the **EC2** tab and execute the following instructions step by step:

1. On the **EC2 Console** page, go to **Create Instance** and click on the **Launch Instance** button. This will open a wizard to create an instance that will guide you through the setup process:

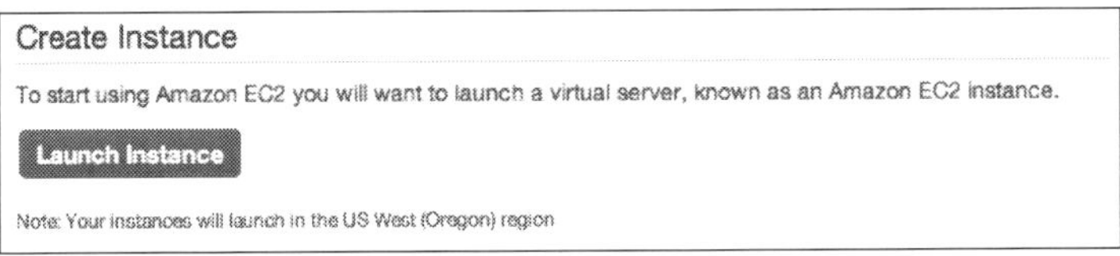

2. On the first page of the wizard, you will be prompted to select an operating system for your virtual instance. Select **Ubuntu Server 14.04 LTS** as displayed in the next screenshot, which is eligible for the free tier. To avoid any charges for using an advanced instance, make sure that the option you select is eligible for the free tier:

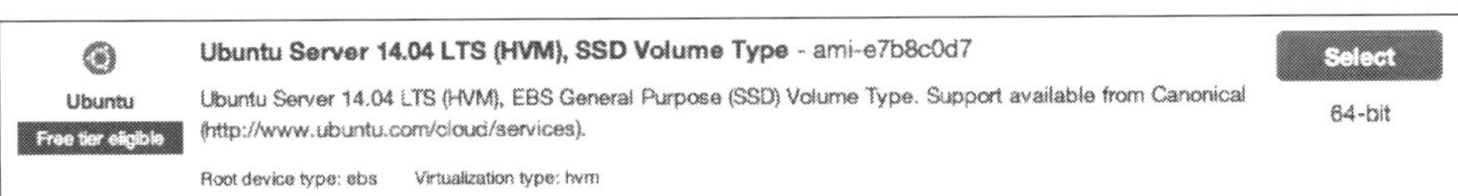

3. In next window, you will be prompted with a list of options that have different configurations of computational capacity. From the **General purpose** family, select the **t2.micro** type, which is eligible for the free tier. The computational capabilities provided by the **t2.micro** tier are sufficient for the exercises that we are going to perform in the book and for most of the DIY projects. Make sure that you do not select any other tier unless you are confident of your selection.

	Family	Type	vCPUs	Memory (GiB)	Instance Storage (GB)	EBS-Optimized Available	Network Performance
■	General purpose	t2.micro Free tier eligible	1	1	EBS only	-	Low to Moderate
	General purpose	t2.small	1	2	EBS only	-	Low to Moderate
	General purpose	t2.medium	2	4	EBS only	-	Low to Moderate
	General purpose	m3.medium	1	3.75	1 x 4 (SSD)	-	Moderate
	General purpose	m3.large	2	7.5	1 x 32 (SSD)	-	Moderate

4. Once you have selected the specified tier, click on the **Review and Launch** button to review the final configuration of the instance.
5. Review the configuration and make sure that you have selected the appropriate options, as mentioned earlier. You can now click on the **Launch** button to proceed further.
6. This will open a pop-up window that will prompt you to create a new key pair that will be used for authentication in the upcoming steps:

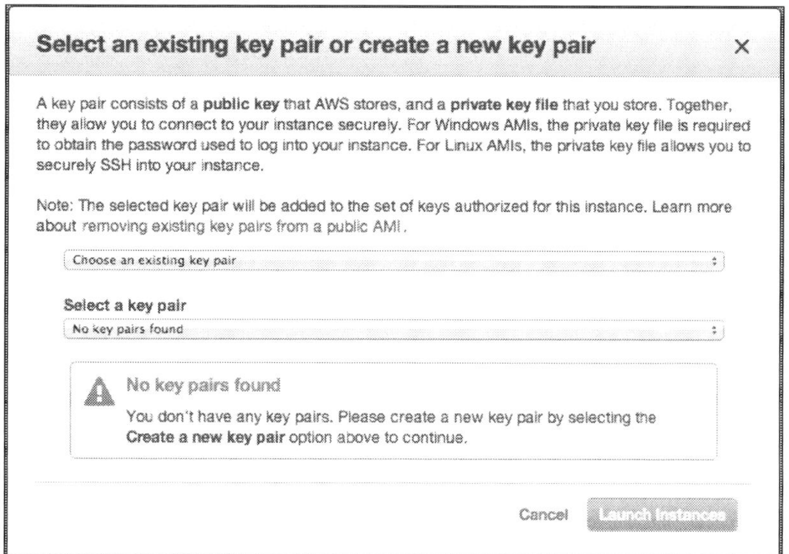

7. As shown in the previous screenshot, select **Create a new key pair** from the first drop-down menu while providing a name for the key pair. Click on the **Download Key Pair** button to download the key. The downloaded key will have the name that you provided in the previous option with the `.pem` extension. If you already have an existing key, you can select the appropriate options from the first drop-down menu. You will need this key every time you want to log in to this instance. Save this key in a safe place.

8. Once again, click on the **Launch Instances** button to finally start the instance. Your virtual instance is launched on AWS now and it is running in the EC2.
9. Now, click on the **View Instance** button that will take you back to the EC2 console window. You will be able to see your recently created `t2.micro` instance in the list.
10. To find out more details about your virtual instance, select it from the list. As soon as you select your instance, you will be able to see additional information in the bottom tab. This information includes the public DNS, private DNS, public IP address, and so on.

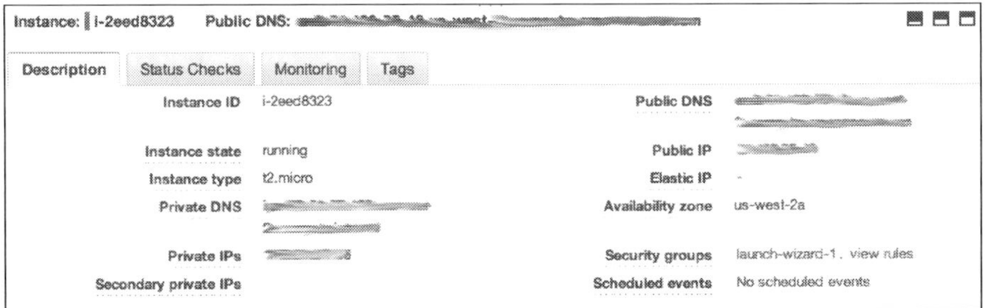

11. Save this information, as you will need it to log in to your instance.

Now, you have successfully created and turned on a virtual cloud instance using Amazon AWS. However, this instance is running in the Amazon EC2 and you will have to remotely authenticate into this instance to access its resources.

Logging into your virtual instance

In reality, your virtual instance is a virtual computer on a cloud with computation resources that are similar to your regular computer. You now need to log in to the running virtual instance to access files, run scripts, and install additional packages. To establish a secure authentication and access procedure, you need to use the **Secure Shell** (**SSH**) protocol and there are multiple ways to use SSH from your computer. If you are using Mac OS X or Ubuntu, an SSH client program already exists within your operating system. For Windows, you can download the PuTTY SSH client from `http://www.putty.org/`.

From the EC2 management window, retrieve the public IP address of your instance. To use the default SSH client in the Linux or Mac environment, open the terminal and navigate to the folder where you have saved your key file with the `.pem` extension. In the terminal window, execute the following command to make your key accessible:

```
$ chmod 400 test.pem
```

Once you have changed permission for your key file, run the following command to log in to the virtual instance. In the command, you will have to replace `<key-name>` with the file name of your key and `<public-IP>` with the public IP that you retrieved from the management console:

```
$ ssh -i <key-name>.pem ubuntu@<public-IP>
```

Once you execute this command, you will be asked to continue with the connection process if you are authenticating the instance for the very first time. At the prompt, write `yes` and press *Enter* to continue. On successful authentication, you will be able to see the command prompt of your virtual instance in the same terminal window.

In case you are using the Windows operating system and are not sure about the status of your SSH client, select your instance in the EC2 window and click on the **Connect** button in the top navigation bar, which is displayed in the following screenshot:

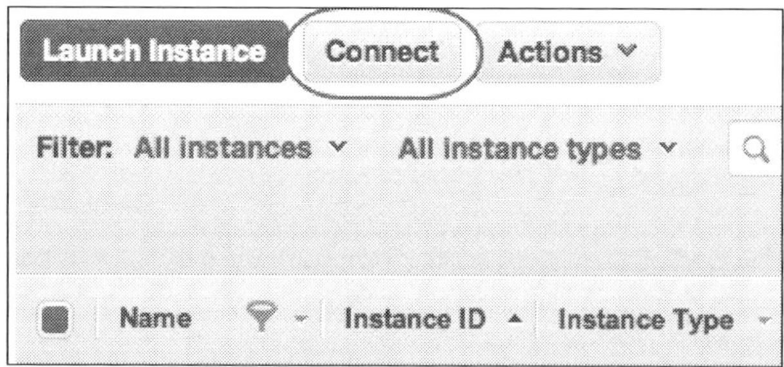

This action will open a pop-up window with a short tutorial that explains the connection process. This tutorial is also linked to the step-by-step authentication guide for PuTTY.

Creating an IoT platform on the EC2 instance

As you have successfully set up an Amazon EC2 instance, you have a virtual computer that is running in the cloud and has a static IP address to enable remote access. However, this instance cannot be categorized as an IoT platform, as it only contains a plain operating system (Ubuntu Linux in our case) and lacks the necessary software packages and configurations.

There are two distinct ways of setting up a custom IoT cloud platform on your virtual instance:

- Setting up an open source IoT platform such as ThingSpeak
- Separately installing and configuring the required software tools

Keep the following points in mind when setting up an open source IoT platform:

- ThingSpeak is one of the open source IoT platforms that provides supporting files to create and host your own replica of the ThingSpeak platform.
- Setting up this platform on your AWS instance is quite simple and you can obtain the necessary files and guidelines to install it via `https://github.com/iobridge/ThingSpeak`.
- Although this personalized version of the ThingSpeak platform will provide sufficient tools to start developing IoT applications, the functionalities of the platform will be confined to the supplied feature set. To have complete control over customization, you may have to use the next option.

If you want to separately install and configure the necessary software tools, here's what you need to remember:

- This option includes furnishing project-specific software tools such as Python and the Mosquitto broker with the required Python libraries such as `web.py` and `paho_mqtt`.
- We have already worked with exercises that implemented applications which were based on the Mosquitto broker and `web.py`. This version of the custom IoT cloud platform can reduce the complexity of installing additional open source platform tools and still provide the necessary support to host applications.
- The Arduino program can directly communicate with this custom platform using REST or MQTT protocols. It can also behave as the remote computation unit to communicate with Xively or other third-party IoT cloud platforms.

In the next section, we will begin the platform deployment process by installing the Mosquitto broker and the necessary packages on your virtual instance. This will be followed by the configuration of the virtual instance to support the MQTT protocol. Once your IoT cloud platform is up and running, you can just run the Python-based Mosquitto code from the last chapter from the instance with minor or no modifications. In future, this IoT platform that contains the Mosquitto broker and the Python project can be extended to accommodate additional features, protocols, and extra security.

Installing the necessary packages on AWS

Using the SSH protocol and the key pair, log into your virtual instance. Once you are at the Command Prompt, the first task that you need to perform is to update all the outdated packages in Ubuntu, the operating system of your virtual instance. Successively execute the following commands:

```
$ sudo apt-get update
$ sudo apt-get upgrade
```

Ubuntu already comes with the latest version of Python. However, you will still need to install Setuptools to install the additional Python packages:

```
$ sudo apt-get install python-setuptools
```

Ubuntu's package repository also hosts Mosquitto and it can be directly installed using the following command. With this command, we will install the Mosquitto broker, Mosquitto client, and all other dependencies together. During the installation, you will be asked to confirm the installation of additional packages. Enter `Yes` at the terminal and proceed with the installation:

```
$ sudo apt-get install mosquitto*
```

Now you have installed the Mosquitto broker on your virtual instance and you can run it by executing the Mosquitto command. To develop Python-based Mosquitto applications, we need the Python Mosquitto library on our instance. Let's install the library using Setuptools, through the following commands:

```
$ sudo easy_install pip
$ sudo pip install paho_mqtt
```

In the previous chapter, we developed a web application based on `web.py` that utilizes the `paho_mqtt` library to support the MQTT protocol. As with the first project, we are going to deploy the same web application on the EC2-based virtual instance to demonstrate your custom IoT cloud platform. As a dependency of this project, you first need the `web.py` Python library, which you can install using the following command:

```
$ sudo pip install web.py
```

Now you have all the necessary software packages to run the IoT application. To make your web application accessible via the Internet, you need to configure the security of you virtual instance.

Configuring the security of the virtual instance

First, we will configure the virtual instance to securely host the Mosquitto broker. Later, we will go through the methods to set up basic security to prevent the abuse of your Mosquitto server by automated bots or spamming attempts.

To change any parameters on your virtual instance, you will have to use the **Security Groups** tools from the **Network & Security** section of your **AWS Management Console** page. Open the **Security Groups** section, as displayed in the following screenshot:

Each virtual instance has a default security group that is generated automatically to allow access to your instance through the SSH port 22. This security configuration is responsible for letting you access your virtual instance through the SSH client from your computer. The Mosquitto broker uses the TCP port number `1883` to establish communication with publishers and subscriber clients. To allow incoming access from this Mosquitto port, you will have to edit the current inbound rules and add an entry for port `1883`:

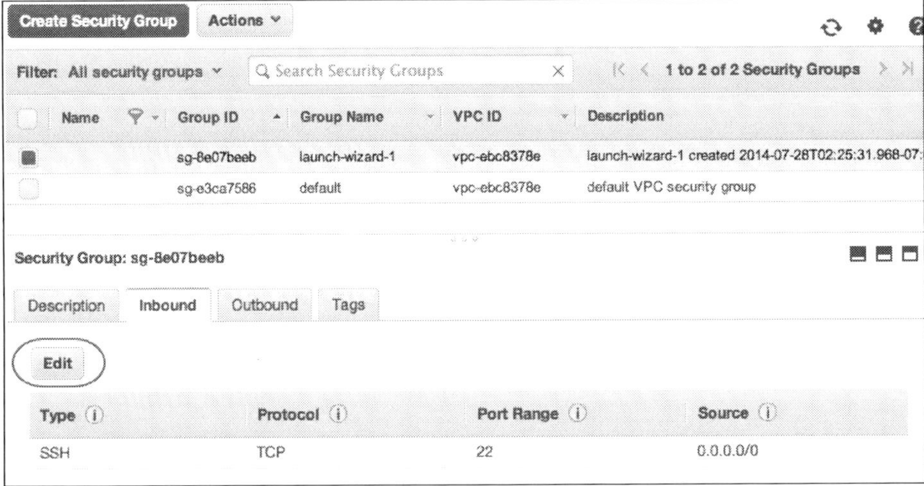

Once you click on the **Edit** button, the website will open a pop-up window to add new rules and edit the existing rules. Click on the **Add Rule** button to create an additional rule to accommodate the Mosquitto broker:

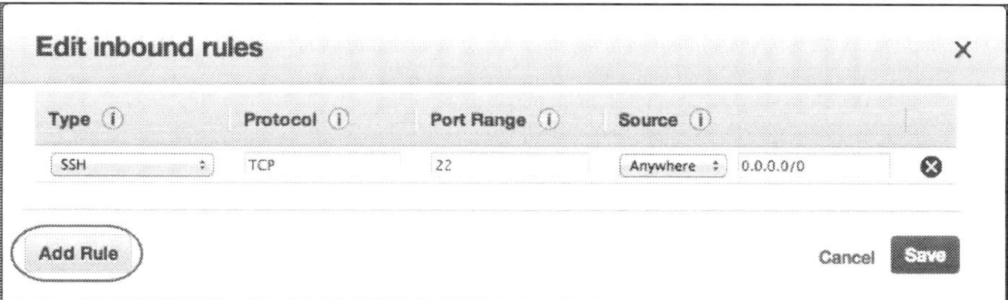

As displayed in the following screenshot, enter the TCP port's number as `1883` and complete the other information in the form. Once you have completed the form with the given values, save the rules and exit the window:

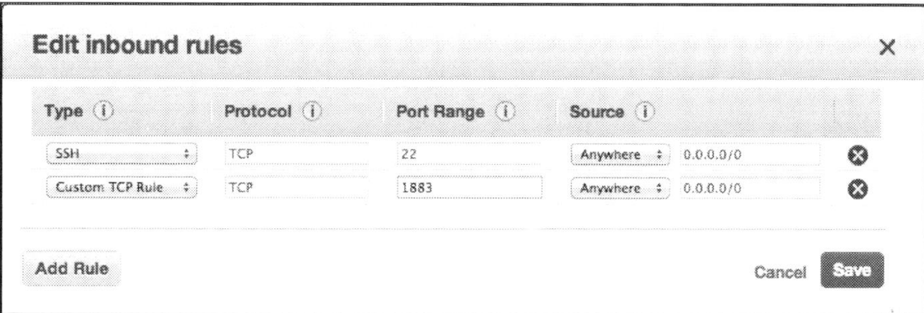

Now, with this configuration, port `1883` is accessible by other devices and enables remote communication with the Mosquitto broker. You can use the same method to add a rule for port `8080` to allow access to Python's web applications that were developed using `web.py`. In future, you can add any additional ports to allow access to various services. Although it is very easy to change the security rules on your virtual instance, make sure that you refrain from opening excessive ports to avoid any security risk.

Testing your cloud platform

In this testing section, we will first perform checks for the Mosquitto broker from your computer and then set up authentication parameters for the Mosquitto broker. Later, we will upload files and folders containing the Python code to our virtual instance using the SSH file transfer protocol.

Testing the Mosquitto service

The first thing that we are going to check on our IoT platform is the accessibility of the Mosquitto broker. Open the terminal on your computer and execute the following command, after replacing `<Public-IP>` with the public IP or public DNS address of your virtual instance:

```
$ mosquitto_pub -h <Public-IP> -t test -m 3
```

This command will publish the message value `3` for the `test` topic for the Mosquitto broker that is specified at the given IP address; in our case, this is the virtual instance. Now, open a separate terminal window and execute the following command to subscribe to the `test` topic on our broker:

```
$ mosquitto_sub -h <Public-IP> -t test
```

On the execution of this command, you will be able to see the latest value that is published for this topic. Use the `mosquitto_pub` command to post multiple messages and you can see the output of these messages in the other terminal window that is running the `mosquitto_sub` command.

Configuring and testing basic security

As you saw in the previous example, the publishing and subscribing commands just used the IP address to send and receive data without using any authentication parameters. This is a major security loophole, as anyone on the Internet can send data to your Mosquitto broker. To avoid unauthorized access to your broker, you have to establish authentication credentials. You can specify these parameters by following these steps in the given order:

1. If you have not already logged into your instance through SSH, open a terminal window and log in using SSH. Once you are logged in, navigate to the Mosquitto directory and create a new file called `passwd` using the following set of commands. We will use this file to store the usernames and passwords:

   ```
   $ cd /etc/mosquitto
   $ sudo nano passwd
   ```

2. In the file, enter the username and password information separated by using the colon operator (`:`). For testing purposes, we will use the following credentials, which can be changed any time once you are more familiar with the Mosquitto configuration:

   ```
   user:password
   ```

3. Press *Ctrl* + *X* to save and exit the file from the nano editor. When you are prompted to confirm the save operation, select **Y** and press *Enter*.
4. In the same folder, open the Mosquitto configuration file using the nano editor:

   ```
   $ sudo nano mosquitto.conf
   ```

5. In the opened file, scroll down the text content until you reach the security section. In this section, find the `#allow_anonymous true` line of the code and replace it with `allow_anonymous false`. Make sure that you have removed the # symbol. With this operation, we have disabled the anonymous access to the Moquitto broker and only those clients with proper credentials can access it.
6. After performing the previous changes, scroll further down in the file, uncomment the line `#password_file`, and replace it with this:

   ```
   password_file /etc/mosquitto/passwd
   ```

7. Now that you have configured the basic security parameters for your broker, you must restart the Mosquitto service for the changes to take effect. In Ubuntu, Mosquitto is installed as part of the background service and you can restart it using the following command:

   ```
   $ sudo service mosquitto restart
   ```

8. To test these authentication configurations, open another terminal window in your computer and execute the following command with the public IP address of your instance. If you are able to successfully publish your message without any errors, your Mosquitto broker now has a security configuration:

   ```
   $ mosquitto_pub -u user -P password -h <Public-Ip> -t test -m 3
   ```

9. Also, check your Mosquitto subscriber using the following command:

   ```
   $ mosquitto_sub -u user -P password -h <Public-Ip> -t test
   ```

Uploading and testing a project on the instance

As we discussed in the previous chapters, you can always use your computer for development purposes. Once you are ready for deployment, you can utilize this newly configured virtual instance as the deployment unit. You can copy your files from your local computer to the virtual instance using a utility called PuTTY (`https://docs.aws.amazon.com/AWSEC2/latest/UserGuide/putty.html`) or using the SCP (SSH copy) command.

Now it is time to upload the project files from the final coding exercise of the previous chapter, which implemented the MQTT protocol using Python and the Mosquitto library. As a reminder, the final exercise is located in the folder named `Exercise 4 - MQTT gateway` of the previous chapter's code repository. We will be using the SCP utility to upload these files to your virtual instance. Before we use this utility, let's first create a directory on your virtual instance. Log in to your virtual instance and go to the user directory of the virtual instance by using the following command:

```
$ ssh -i <key-name>.pem ubuntu@<public-ip>
$ cd ~
```

Using the character tilde (~) with the `cd` command will change the current directory to the home directory, unless you are planning to use any other location on your virtual instance. At this location, create a new empty directory named `project` by using following command:

```
$ mkdir project
```

Now, on the computer you are working on (Mac OS X or Linux), open another terminal window and use the following command to copy the entire directory to the remote instance:

```
$ scp -v -i test.pem -r <project-folder-path> ubuntu@<your-ec2-static-ip>:~/project
```

Once you have successfully copied the files to this location, you can go back to the terminal that is logged in to your virtual instance and change the directory to `project`:

```
$ cd project
```

Before running any commands, make sure that you have changed the appropriate IP addresses in the Arduino sketch and the Python programs. You will have to replace the previous IP address with the one of your virtual instance. Now that you have made these changes, you can execute the Python code containing the Mosquitto Gateway and web application to start the program. Open your web browser from the `http://<Public-Ip>:8080` location to see you web application running on the custom IoT platform. From now on, you should be able to access this application from any remote location through the Internet.

> Do not forget to change the IP address of the Mosquitto broker in the Arduino sketch and upload the sketch to the Arduino board again. You may not be able to obtain the sensor data if the appropriate IP address changes are not applied.

Summary

At the end of this chapter, and hence the end of the contextual part of the book, you should be able to develop your own Internet of Things projects. In this chapter, we used a commercial IoT cloud platform to handle your sensor data. We also deployed a cloud instance to host open source IoT tools and created our own version of the customized IoT cloud platform. Certainly, the content that you learned is not sufficient to develop scalable and fully-stacked commercial products, but it is really helpful to get you started with them. In a large number of cases, this material is sufficient to develop DIY projects and product prototypes that will ultimately lead you to the final product. In the next two chapters, we will put the material that we learned to the test and develop two complete IoT hardware projects. We are also going to learn a project development methodology that is specific to hardware-based IoT products, which can be applied to convert your prototypes into real products.

10

The Final Project – a Remote Home Monitoring System

It is now time to combine every topic that we learned in the previous chapters into a project that combines Arduino programming, Python GUI development, MQTT messaging protocol, and a Python-based cloud application. As you might have already figured out from the chapter title, we are going to develop a remote home monitoring system using these components.

The first section of the chapter covers the project design process, including goals, requirements, architecture, and UX. Once we are done with the design process, we will jump into the actual development of the project, which is divided into three separate stages. Next, we will cover common troubleshooting topics that are usually faced while working with large projects. In our efforts to develop utilizable DIY projects, the later section covers tips and features to extend the project. As this is quite a large project compared to other projects in the book, we are not going to jump straight into the actual development process without having any strategy. Let's start by getting ourselves familiar with the standard design methodology for hardware projects.

The design methodology for IoT projects

The process of developing a complex product that tightly couples hardware devices with high-level software services requires an additional level of planning. For this project, we will exercise a proper product development approach to help you get familiar with the process of creating real-world hardware projects. This method can then be used to plan your own projects and take them to the next level. The following diagram describes a typical prototype development process, which always begins by defining the major goals that you want to achieve with your product:

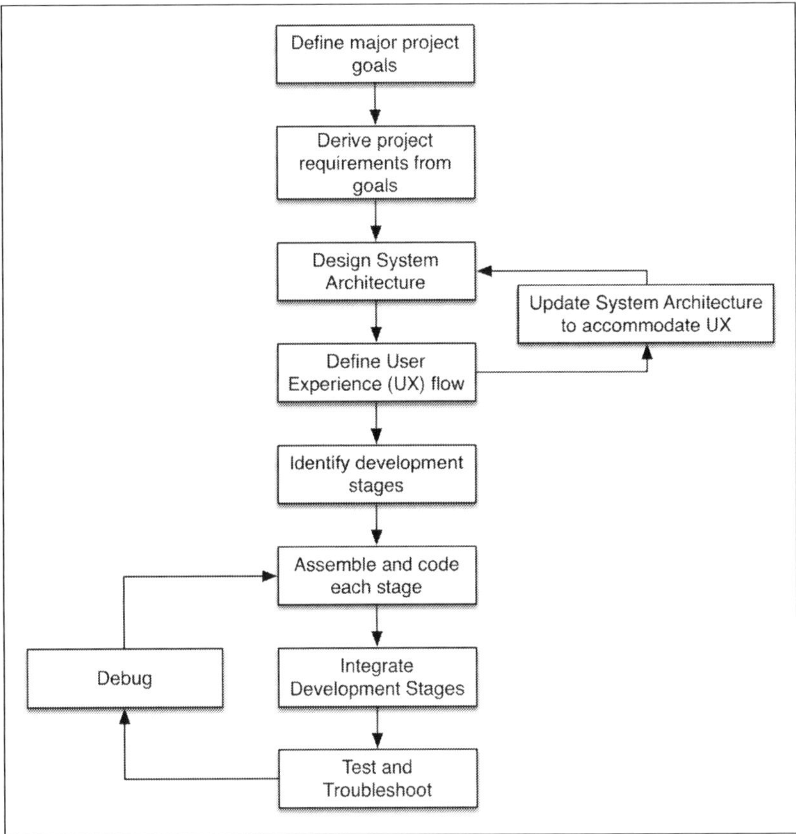

Once you have defined the set of major goals, you need to break them down into project requirements that include every detail of the tasks that your prototype should execute to achieve these goals. Using the project requirements, you need to sketch out the overall architecture of the system. The next step includes the process of defining the UX flow that will help you to lay out the user interaction points for your system. At this stage, you will be able to identify any changes that are required in the system architecture and the hardware and software components to start the development.

As you have defined the interaction points, now you need to distribute the entire project development process into multiple stages and delegate the tasks between these stages. Once you have completed the development of these stages, you will have to interface these stages with each other according to your architecture and debug the components if it is needed. At the end, you will have to test your project as a whole system and troubleshoot minor problems. In hardware projects, it is very difficult to work on your electric circuits again after the completion of complex development processes, as the changes can have recurring effects on all other components. This process will help you to minimize any hardware rework and subsequent software modifications.

Now that you have learned about the methodology, let's begin with the actual development process for our remote home monitoring system.

Project overview

The smart home is one of the most well-defined and popular subdomains of the IoT. The most important feature of any smart home is its capability to monitor the physical environment. Fortunately, the exercises and projects that we covered in the previous chapters include components and features that can be used for the same purpose. In this chapter, we are going to define a project that will utilize these existing components and programming exercises. In the midterm project of *Chapter 7, The Midterm Project – a Portable DIY Thermostat*, we created a deployable thermostat with the ability to measure temperature, humidity, and ambient light. If we want to utilize this midterm project, the nearest IoT project that we can build on top of it is the remote home monitoring system. The project will have Arduino as the main point of interaction between the physical environment and the software-based services. We will have a Python program as the middle layer, which will bridge the sensor information coming from Arduino with the user-facing graphical interface. Let's start by defining the goals that we want to achieve and the project requirements to satisfy these goals.

The project goals

The Nest thermostat provides an idea of the type of features that a properly designed remote monitoring system with professional features should have. Achieving this level of system capabilities requires a lot of development effort from a large team. Although it will be difficult to include each of the features that are supported by a commercial system in our project, we will still try to implement the common features that can be incorporated by a prototype project.

The top-level features that we are planning to incorporate in this project can be described by the following goals.

- Observe the physical environment and make it accessible remotely
- Provide basic level controls to the user to interact with the system
- Demonstrate a primitive level of built-in situational awareness

The project requirements

Now that we have defined the major goals, let's convert them into detailed system requirements. On the completion of the project, the system should be able to satisfy the following requirements:

- It must be able to observe physical phenomenon such as temperature, humidity, motion, and ambient light.
- It should provide local access to sensor information and control over actuators such as a buzzer, a button switch, and an LED.
- The monitoring should be done by a unit that is developed using the open source hardware platform, Arduino.
- The monitoring unit should be limited to collect sensor information and communicate it to the control unit.
- The control unit should not comprise of a desktop computer or laptop. Instead, it should be made deployable using a platform such as a Raspberry Pi.
- The control unit should demonstrate a primitive level of situation awareness capability by utilizing the collected sensor information.
- The control unit should have a graphical interface to provide the sensor's observation and the current state of the system.
- The system must be accessible via the Internet using cloud-based services.
- The web application that provides remote access should have the capability to display the sensor's observations through a web browser.
- The system should also provide basic control of the actuators to complete the remote access experience by using the web application.
- As the monitoring unit can be constrained by computation resources, the system should use hardware-oriented messaging protocols to transfer information.

Although there are many other minor requirements that can be part of our project, they have been skipped in this book. If you have any additional plans for your remote home monitoring system, this is the time that you must define these requirements before you jump into designing the architecture. Any future changes to the requirements can significantly affect the development stage and make hardware and software modification difficult. In the last section of the chapter, we have laid down a number of additional features that you may want to consider implementing for your future projects.

Designing system architecture

Continuing from project goals, first, you need to sketch out a high-level architecture of the system. This architectural sketch should include major components that enable the system to pass on information between the sensors and the remote users. The following figure shows an architectural sketch for our project:

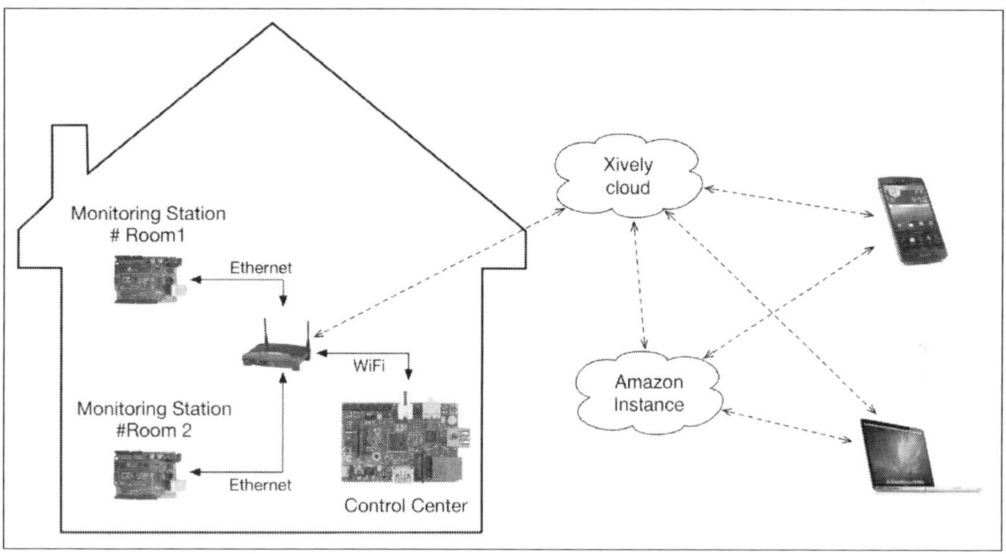

According to the goals, the user should be able to access the system using the Internet; this means that we need cloud components in the architecture. The system also needs to monitor the physical environment using a resource-constrained device, and this can be executed using Arduino. The middle layer, which connects the cloud service and the sensor system, can be built using a Raspberry Pi. In the last project, we connected Arduino and the Raspberry Pi using a serial connection, but we want to move away from serial connections and start using our home's Ethernet network to make the system deployable. Hence, the Arduino-based unit is connected to the network using Ethernet while the Raspberry Pi uses Wi-Fi to connect to the same network.

In order to lay out the overall system architecture, let's utilize the sketch that we designed, which can be seen in the preceding figure. As you can see in the next figure, we have converted the overall system into three main architectural units:

- Monitoring station
- Control center
- Cloud service

In this figure, we have addressed each and every major component that we are going to utilize in the project along with their association to each other. In the following sections, we are going to define these three main units briefly. The comprehensive description and implementation steps for these units are provided later in the chapter under separate sections.

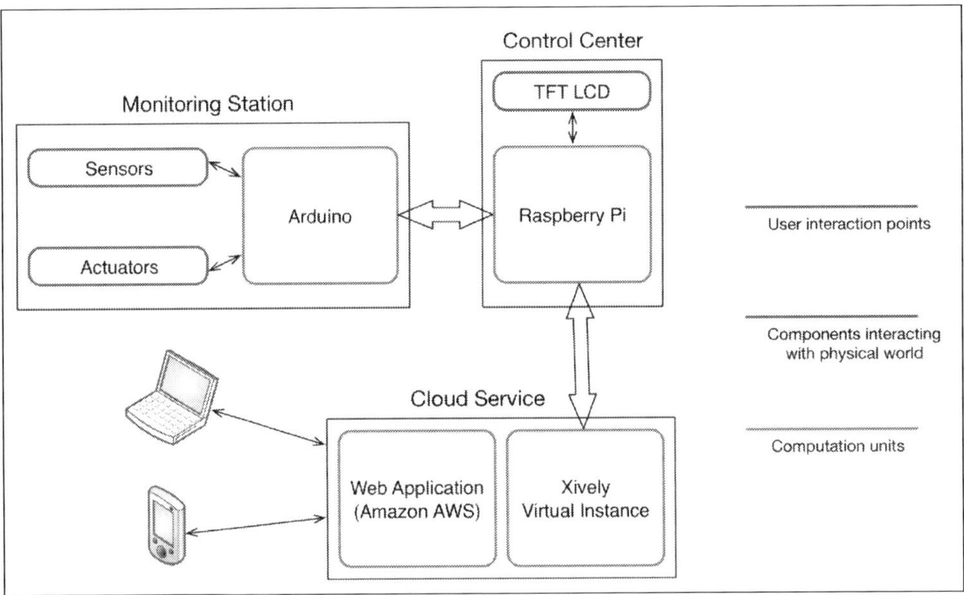

The monitoring station

We need a resource-constrained and robust unit that will communicate with the physical environment periodically. This monitoring unit can be built using Arduino since low-level microcontroller programming can provide uninterrupted stream of sensor data. The usage of Arduino at this stage will also help us to avoid the direct interfacing of basic low-level sensors with computers that are running on complex operating systems. The sensors and the actuators are connected to Arduino using digital, analog, PWM, and I2C interfaces.

The control center

The control center behaves as the main user interaction point between the sensor information and the user. It is also responsible for conveying the sensor information from the monitoring station to the cloud services. The control center can be developed using your regular computer or a single-board computer such as a Raspberry Pi. We are going to utilize a Raspberry Pi since it can be easily deployed as a hardware unit and it is also capable enough at hosting Python programs. We will replace a computer screen with a small TFT LCD screen for the Raspberry Pi to display the GUI.

The cloud services

The main purpose of the cloud services is to provide an Internet-based interface for the control center so that the user can access it remotely. Before we host a web application to perform this operation, we will need an intermediate data relay. This sensor data relay works as a host between the cloud-based web application and the control center. In this project, we will be using Xively as the platform to collect this sensor data. The web application can be hosted on an Internet server; in our case, we are going to use Amazon AWS due to our familiarity with it.

Defining UX flow

Now, although we know what the architecture of the overall system looks like, we haven't defined how the user is going to interact with it. This process of designing user interaction for our system will also help us to figure out data flow between major components.

Let's begin with the components that are operating locally at your house, that is, the monitoring station and the control center. As you can see from the following figure, we have our first user interaction point at the control center. The user can observe the information or act upon it if the system's status is an alert. The user action to dismiss the alert prompts multiple operations to take place at the control center and the monitoring station. We recommend you thoroughly examine the figure to better understand the flow of the system.

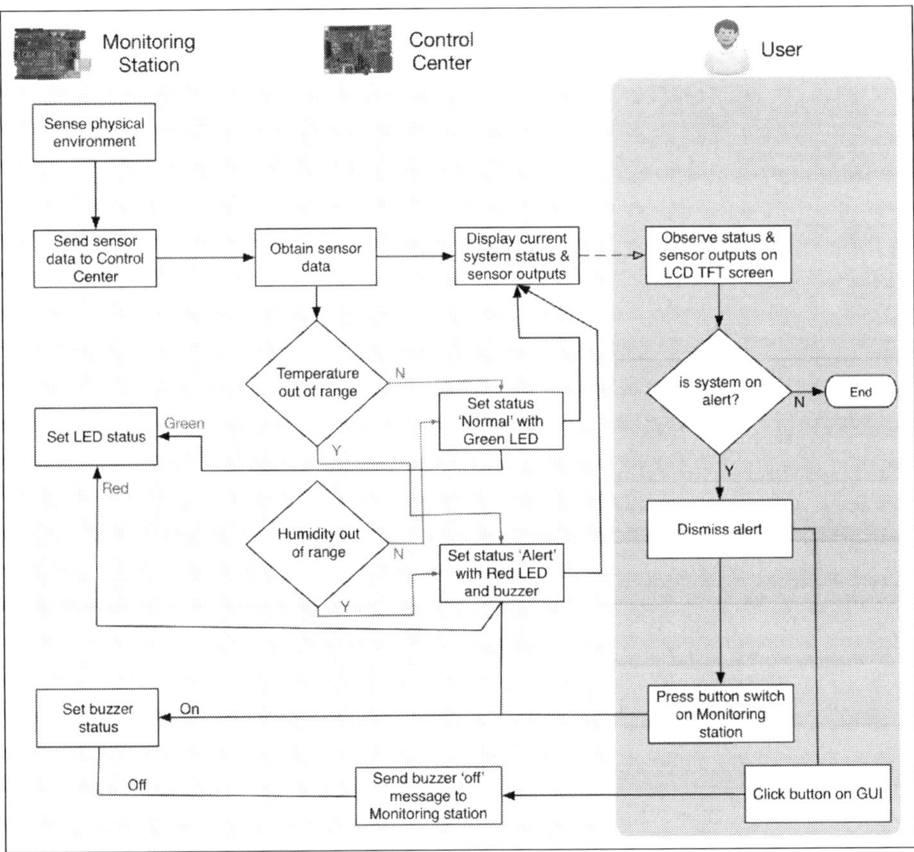

Similarly, the second user interaction point is located at the web application. The web application displays the observations and system's status that we calculated at the control center and provides an interface to dismiss the alert. In this scenario, the dismiss action will travel through Xively to the control center where the appropriate actions for the control center will remain the same as in the previous scenario. However, in the web application, the user has to load the web browser every time to request the data, which was happening automatically at the control center. Take a look at the following figure to understand the UX flow for the web application:

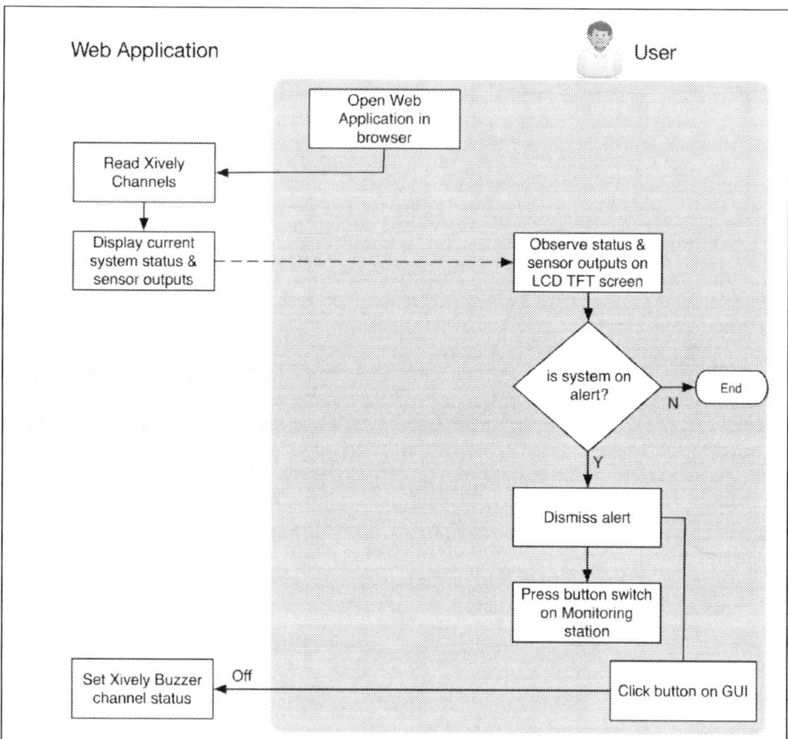

The list of required components

The necessary components for the project are derived using three main criteria:

- Ease of availability
- Compatibility with the Arduino board
- Familiarity with the components due to previous utilization in this book

This is the list of the components that you will need to start working on the project. If you have completed the previous exercises and projects, you should already have most of the components. If you don't want to disassemble the projects, you can obtain them from the websites of SparkFun, Adafruit, or Amazon, whose links are provide in the next table.

The hardware components for the monitoring station are as follows:

Component (first stage)	Quantity	Link
Arduino Uno	1	https://www.sparkfun.com/products/11021
Arduino Ethernet Shield	1	https://www.sparkfun.com/products/9026
Breadboard	1	https://www.sparkfun.com/products/9567
TMP102 temperature sensor	1	https://www.sparkfun.com/products/11931
HIH-4030 humidity sensor	1	https://www.sparkfun.com/products/9569
Mini photocell	1	https://www.sparkfun.com/products/9088
PIR motion sensor	1	https://www.sparkfun.com/products/8630
Super-flux RGB LED, common anode	1	http://www.adafruit.com/product/314
Buzzer	1	http://www.adafruit.com/products/160
Push button switch	1	https://www.sparkfun.com/products/97
USB cable for Arduino (for development stage)	1	https://www.sparkfun.com/products/512
Arduino power supply (for deployment stage)	1	http://www.amazon.com/Arduino-9V-1A-Power-Adapter/dp/B00CP1QLSC/
Resistors	As required	220 ohm, 1 kilo-ohm, and 10 kilo-ohm
Connection wires	As required	

The hardware components for the control center are as follows:

Component (first stage)	Quantity	Link
Raspberry Pi	1	https://www.sparkfun.com/products/11546
TFT LCD screen	1	http://www.amazon.com/gp/product/B00GASHVDU/
SD card (8 GB)	1	https://www.sparkfun.com/products/12998
Wi-Fi dongle	1	http://www.amazon.com/Edimax-EW-7811Un-150Mbps-Raspberry-Supports/dp/B003MTTJOY

Component (first stage)	Quantity	Link
Raspberry Pi power supply	1	`http://www.amazon.com/CanaKit-Raspberry-Supply-Adapter-Charger/dp/B00GF9T3I0`
Keyboard, mouse, USB hub, and monitor	As required	Requried for development and debugging stages

Defining the project development stages

As per the system architecture, we have three main units that collaboratively create the remote home monitoring project. The overall hardware and software development process is also aligned with these three units and can be distributed as follows:

- Monitoring station development stage
- Control center development stage
- Web application development stage

The software development for the monitoring station stage includes developing the Arduino code to monitor sensors and perform actuator actions on one side, while publishing this information to the control center on the other side. The middle layer of the development stage, that is, the Raspberry Pi-based control center, hosts the Mosquitto broker. This stage also contains the Python program that contains the GUI, situation awareness logic, and subroutines to communicate with the Xively cloud service. The last stage, the cloud services, includes two distinct components, sensor data relay and a web application. We will be using the Xively platform as our sensor data relay and the web application will be developed in Python on the Amazon AWS cloud instance. Now, let's jump into the actual development process and our first stop will be the Arduino-based monitoring station.

Stage 1 – a monitoring station using Arduino

As we discussed, the main tasks of the monitoring systems are to interface sensor components and communicate the information generated by these sensors to the observers. You will be using Arduino Uno as the central microcontroller component to integrate these sensors and actuators. We also need a means of communication between the Arduino Uno and the control center and we will be utilizing the Arduino Ethernet Shield for this purpose. Let's discuss the hardware architecture of the monitoring station and its components.

Designing the monitoring station

We already designed units based on Arduino and the Ethernet Shield in various exercises in *Chapter 8, Introduction to Arduino Networking*, and *Chapter 9, Arduino and the Internet of Things*. Therefore, we have assumed that you are familiar with interfacing the Ethernet Shield with the Arduino board. We will connect various sensors and actuators with the Arduino board, as displayed in the following diagram. As you can see in this diagram, the sensors will provide the data to the Arduino board while the actuators will seek the data from the Arduino board. Although we are automatically collecting environment data for these sensors, the data from the button will be collected from manual user inputs.

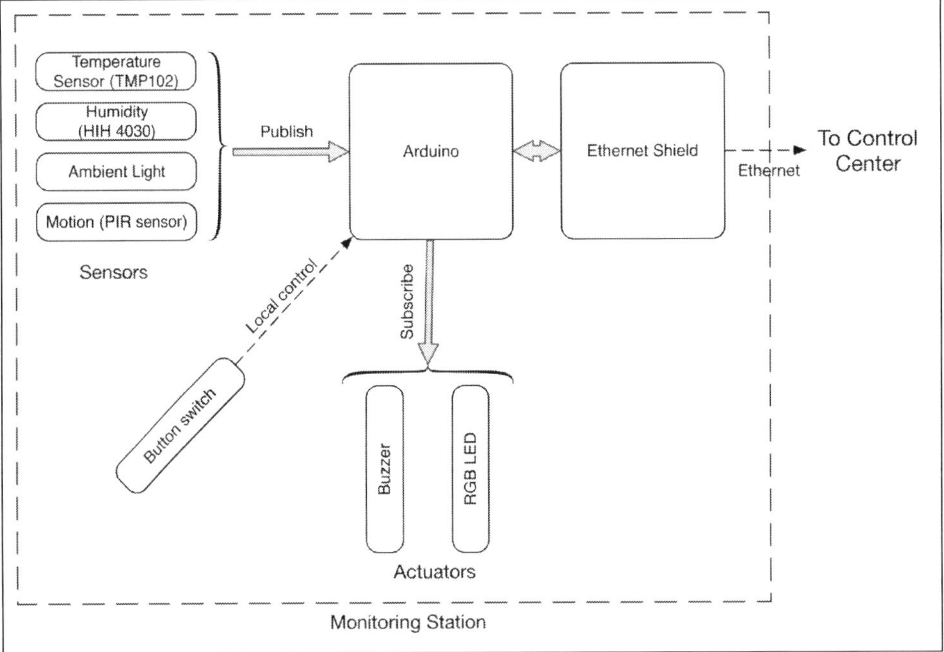

Check out the following Fritzing diagram for the detailed connections in the monitoring station. As you can see in our hardware design, the temperature sensor TMP102 is connected through the I2C interface, which means that we will need the SDA and SCL lines. We will be using analog pins 5 and 6 of the Arduino board to interface SDA and SCL respectively. The humidity (HIH-4030) and ambient light sensors also provide analog output and are connected to the analog pins of the Arduino board. Meanwhile, the buzzer, the button switch, and the PIR motion sensor are connected through the digital I/O pins. The super-flux RGB LED is a common anode LED; this means that it is always powered using the common anode pins and the R, G, and B pins are controlled by using the PWM pins.

Make sure that you properly connect all the components to the pins that are specified in the following diagram:

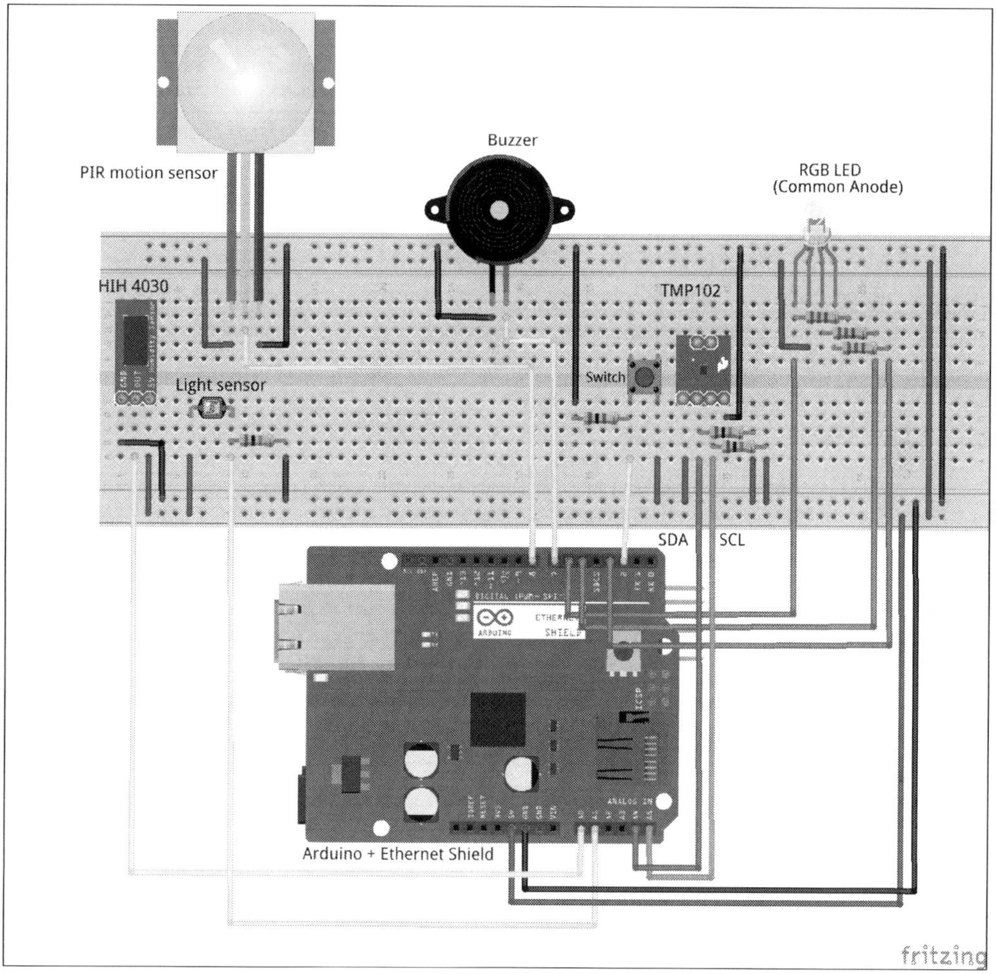

You can learn more about the interfacing of RGB LED with Arduino from the tutorial at `https://learn.adafruit.com/all-about-leds`.

If you are using an Arduino board other than Arduino Uno, you will have to adjust the appropriate pin numbers in the Arduino code. In addition, make sure that this Arduino board is compatible with the Ethernet Shield.

In terms of circuit connections, you can use a breadboard as shown in the previous diagram, or if you are comfortable, you can use a PCB prototype board and solder the components. In our setup, we first tested the components on the breadboard and once they were tested, we soldered the components, as shown in the following figure. If you venture to solder the PCB board, make sure that you have the necessary components for the job. The PCB prototype will yield a robust performance compared to the breadboard, but it will also make it difficult for you to debug and change the components afterwards.

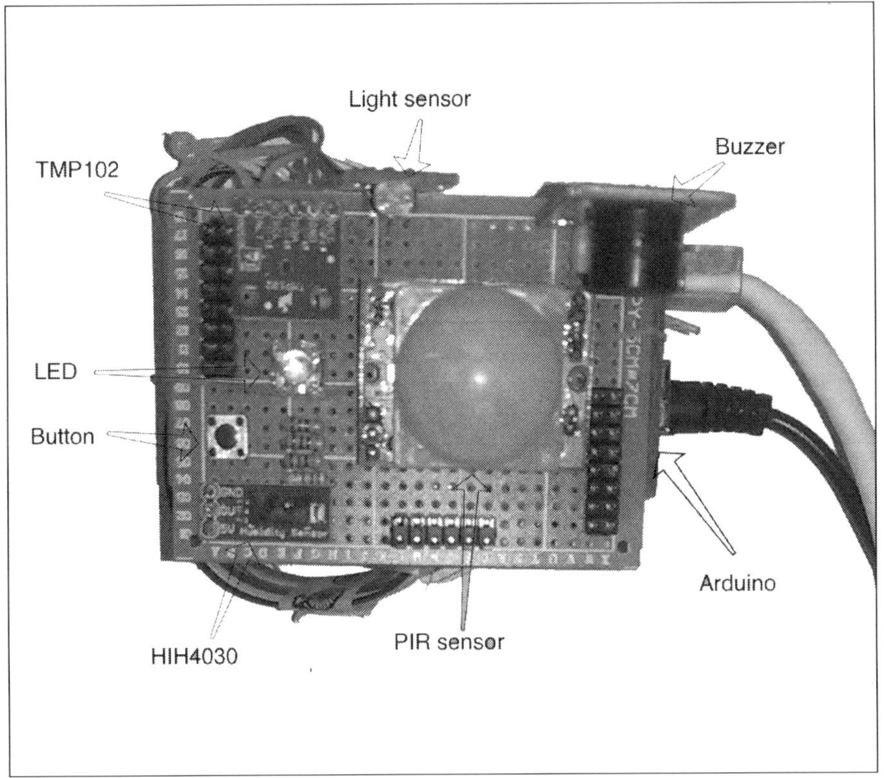

If you are ready with your circuit connection, connect your Arduino to your computer using the USB cable. Also, connect the Ethernet Shield to your home router using an Ethernet cable.

The Arduino sketch for the monitoring station

Before jumping into the coding stage, make sure that you have collected the prebuilt Arduino code for the project. You can find it in the code folder of this chapter with the filename `Arduino_monitoring_station.ino`. The code implements the necessary logic to support the overall UX flow at the monitoring station, which we discussed in the previous section. In the following sections, we will go through the major areas of the program so that you can better understand these code snippets. Now, open this sketch in the Arduino IDE. You are already familiar with setting up the IP address for Arduino. You also learned how to use the Arduino MQTT library `PubSubClient` in the previous chapter, which means that your Arduino IDE should already have the `PubSubClient` library installed on it. At the beginning of the code, we have also declared few constants, such as the IP addresses of the MQTT server and Arduino and the pin numbers of various sensor and actuators.

You will have to change the IP address of the monitoring station and the control center according to your network setup. Make sure that you perform these modifications before uploading the Arduino code.

In the code structure, we have two mandatory Arduino functions, `setup()` and `loop()`. In the `setup()` function, we will set up the Arduino pin types and the MQTT subscriber channels. In the same function, we will also attach an interrupt for the press of the button while setting up the timer for the `publishData()` function.

Publishing sensor information

The `publishData()` function reads the sensor inputs and publishes this data to the Mosquitto broker that is located on the control center. As you can see in the following code snippet, we are measuring sensors values one by one and publishing them to the broker using the `client.publish()` method:

```
void publishData (){
    Wire.requestFrom(partAddress,2);
    byte MSB = Wire.read();
    byte LSB = Wire.read();

    int TemperatureData = ((MSB << 8) | LSB) >> 4;

    float celsius = TemperatureData*0.0625;
    temperatureC = dtostrf(celsius, 5, 2, message_buff2);
    client.publish("MonitoringStation/temperature", temperatureC);
```

```
    float humidity = getHumidity(celsius);
    humidityC = dtostrf(humidity, 5, 2, message_buff2);
    client.publish("MonitoringStation/humidity", humidityC);

    int motion = digitalRead(MotionPin);
    motionC = dtostrf(motion, 5, 2, message_buff2);
    client.publish("MonitoringStation/motion", motionC);

    int light = analogRead(LightPin);
    lightC = dtostrf(light, 5, 2, message_buff2);
    client.publish("MonitoringStation/light", lightC);
}
```

If you check out the `setup()` function, you will notice that we have used a library called `SimpleTimer` to set up a `timer` method for this function. This method executes the `publishData()` function periodically without interrupting and blocking the actual flow of the Arduino execution cycle. In the following code snippet, the number `300000` represents the time delay in milliseconds, that is, 5 minutes:

```
timer.setInterval(300000, publishData);
```

You will need to download and import the `SimpleTimer` library to compile and run the code successfully. You can download the library from `https://github.com/infomaniac50/SimpleTimer`.

Subscribing to actuator actions

You can see in the `setup()` function that we are initializing the code by subscribing to the `MonitoringStation/led` and `MonitoringStation/buzzer` channels. The `client.subscribe()` method will make sure that whenever the Mosquitto broker gets any updates for these channels, the Arduino-based monitoring system gets notified:

```
if (client.connect("MonitoringStation")) {
    client.subscribe("MonitoringStation/led");
    client.subscribe("MonitoringStation/buzzer");
  }
```

Programming an interrupt to handle the press of a button

We have taken care of the publishing and subscribing functions of the monitoring station. Now, we will need to integrate the button switch that is controlled by inputs from the user. In the Arduino programming routines, we run a periodic loop to check the status of the pins. However, this may not be useful if the button is pressed since it requires immediate action. This action of pressing the button is handled using the Arduino interrupts, as shown in the following line of code:

```
attachInterrupt(0, buttonPress, RISING);
```

The preceding line of code associates an interrupt at pin 0 (digital pin 2) with the `buttonPress()` function. This function sets off the buzzers whenever the state of the interrupt is changed. In other words, when the button is pressed by the user, the buzzer will be instantaneously turned off irrespective of the current status of the buzzer:

```
void buttonPress(){
    digitalWrite(BUZZER, LOW);
    Serial.println("Set buzzer off");
}
```

Testing

The current Arduino code communicates with the control center for publishing and subscribing the data, but we haven't yet set up the Mosquitto broker to handle these requests. You can still go ahead and upload the Arduino sketch to your monitoring station using the USB cable. This will not result in any fruitful actions from the monitoring station and you will only be able to use the `Serial.prinln()` command to print various sensor measurements. Therefore, we will develop the control center next so that we can start addressing communication requests from the monitoring station.

Stage 2 – a control center using Python and the Raspberry Pi

In order to deliver the status of the system and other sensor observations to the user, the control center needs to perform various operations that include obtaining raw sensor data from the monitoring station, calculating the status of the system, reporting this data to the cloud services, and displaying observation using GUI. While the control center includes two major hardware components (the Raspberry Pi and TFT LCD screen), it is also comprised of two major software components (the Mosquitto broker and Python code) to handle the control center logic.

We are using a Raspberry Pi instead of a regular computer as we want the control center to be a deployable and portable unit that can be mounted on a wall.

You can still use your own computer to edit and test the Python code for development purposes instead of using a Raspberry Pi directly. However, we recommend that you switch back to the Raspberry Pi once you are ready for deployment.

The control center architecture

The Raspberry Pi is the main computation unit of the control center and works as the brain of the entire system. Since the Raspberry Pi is used as a replacement for a regular computer, the architecture of the control center can interchangeably use a computer in place of the Raspberry Pi. As you can see in the following diagram, the control center is connected to the home network using Wi-Fi and this will make it accessible to the monitoring station. The control center includes the Mosquitto broker; this is used as the communication point between the monitoring station and the Python program for the control center. The Python program utilizes the `Tkinter` library for GUI and the `paho_mqtt` library to communicate with the Mosquitto broker. By utilizing these two libraries, we can convey sensor information from the monitoring station to the user. However, we will need a separate arrangement to establish communication between the control center and cloud services. In our overall system architecture, the control center is designed to communicate with the intermediate data relay, Xively. The Python code uses the `xively-python` library to enable this communication.

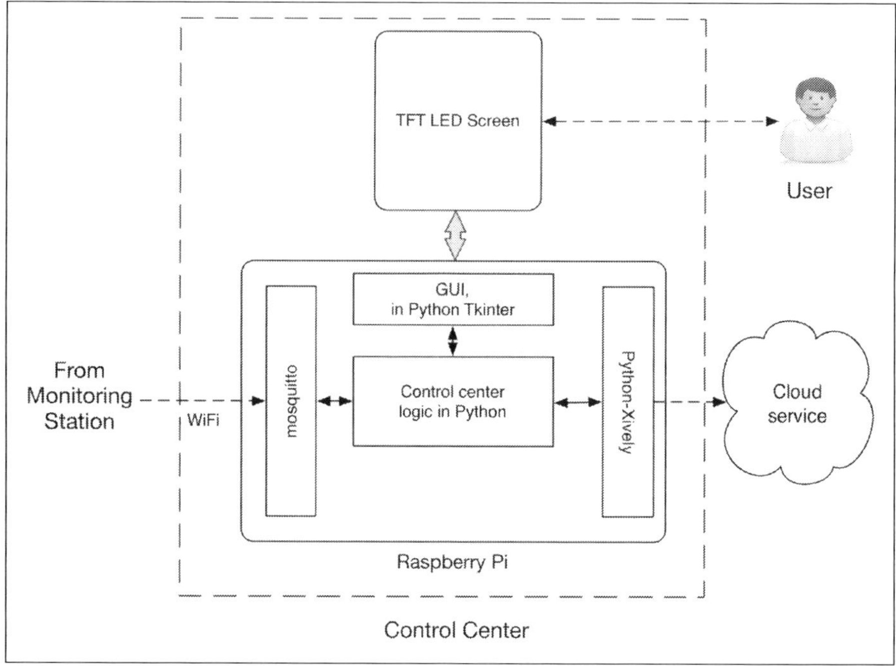

In *Chapter 8, Introduction to Arduino Networking*, we already provided you with methods to install the Mosquitto broker, the `Python-mosquitto` library, and the `xively-python` library. We also learned the process of setting up the TFT LCD screen with the Raspberry Pi in *Chapter 7, The Midterm Project – a Portable DIY Thermostat*. Please refer to those tutorials in case you haven't completed those exercises yet. Assuming that you have configured the Mosquitto broker and the required Python libraries, you can move on to the next section, which includes the actual Python programming.

The Python code for the control center

Before you start interfacing these libraries in the Python code, start your Mosquitto broker first from the command line using this simple command:

```
$ mosquitto
```

Make sure that you restart your monitoring station every time you start or restart the Mosquitto broker. This action will make sure that your monitoring station is connected to the Mosquitto broker, since the process of establishing the connection only gets executed once in our Arduino code, that is, at the beginning of the setup process.

The Python code for the current project is located in the code folder of this chapter with the name `controlCenter.py`. Open this file using your Python IDE and modify the values of the appropriate parameters before executing it. These parameters include the IP address of the Mosquitto broker along with the feed ID and the API key of the Xively virtual device. You should already have the feed ID and the API key of your Xively virtual device from the previous chapter:

```
cli.connect("10.0.0.18", 1883, 15)
FEED_ID = "<feed-id>"
API_KEY = "<api-key"
```

If you are using a local instance of the Mosquitto broker, you can replace the IP address with `127.0.0.1`. Otherwise, replace the `10.0.0.18` address with the appropriate IP address of the computer that is hosting the Mosquitto broker. Let's try to understand the code now.

> Sometimes on Mac OS X, you won't be able to run `Tkinter` window and Python threads in parallel due to an unknown bug. You should be able to execute the program successfully in Windows and Linux environments. This program has been tested with the Raspberry Pi, which means you won't encounter the same bug while deploying the control center.

Creating the GUI using Tkinter

In the previous exercises, we always used a single Python thread to run the program. This practice will not help us to perform multiple tasks in parallel such as obtaining sensor observation from the monitoring station and simultaneously updating the GUI with that information. As a solution, we have introduced multithreading in this exercise. As we need two separate loops, one each for `Tkinter` and `paho-mqtt`, we will be running them independently in separate threads. The main thread will run methods that are related to Mosquitto and the cloud services, while the second thread will handle the `Tkinter` GUI. In the following code snippet, you can see that we have initialized the `controlCenterWindow()` class with the `threading.thread` parameter. Therefore, when we execute `window = controlCenterWindow()` in the main program, it will create another thread for this class. Basically, this class creates the GUI window while populating labels and other GUI components. The labels need to be updated when new sensor observations arrive, are declared as class variables, and are accessible from the class instant. As you can see in the following code snippet, we have declared the labels for temperature, humidity, light, and motion as class variables:

```
class controlCenterWindow(threading.Thread):
    def __init__(self):
```

```
        # Tkinter canvas
        threading.Thread.__init__(self)
        self.start()
    def callback(self):
        self.top.quit()
    def run(self):
        self.top = Tkinter.Tk()
        self.top.protocol("WM_DELETE_WINDOW", self.callback)
        self.top.title("Control Center")
        self.statusValue = Tkinter.StringVar()
        self.statusValue.set("Normal")
        self.tempValue = Tkinter.StringVar()
        self.tempValue.set('-')
        self.humdValue = Tkinter.StringVar()
        self.humdValue.set('-')
        self.lightValue = Tkinter.StringVar()
        self.lightValue.set('-')
        self.motionValue = Tkinter.StringVar()
        self.motionValue.set('No')

        # Begin code subsection
        # Declares Tkinter components
        # Included in the code sample of the chapter
        # End code subsection

        self.top.mainloop()
```

The previous code snippet doesn't contain the portion where we declared the `Tkinter` components, as it is similar to what we coded in the midterm project. If you have questions regarding Tkinter-related issues, please refer to *Chapter 6, Storing and Plotting Arduino Data*, and *Chapter 7, The Midterm Project – a Portable DIY Thermostat*.

Communicating with the Mosquitto broker

At the control center level, we subscribe to topics that are published from the monitoring station, that is, `MonitoringStation/temperature`, `MonitoringStation/humidity`, and so on. If you have performed any modification to the Arduino code to change the MQTT topics, you need to reflect those changes in this section. If the topics published by the monitoring station do not match the topics in the control center's code, you will not get any updates. As you can see in the Python code, we are associating the `on_message` and `on_publish` methods with very important function. Whenever a message arrives from the subscriber, the client will call the functions associated with the `on_message` method. However, every time a message gets published from the Python code, the `onPublish()` function will get called:

```
cli = mq.Client('ControlCenter')
cli.on_message = onMessage
```

```
cli.on_publish = onPublish

cli.connect("10.0.0.18", 1883, 15)

cli.subscribe("MonitoringStation/temperature", 0)
cli.subscribe("MonitoringStation/humidity", 0)
cli.subscribe("MonitoringStation/motion", 0)
cli.subscribe("MonitoringStation/light", 0)
cli.subscribe("MonitoringStation/buzzer", 0)
cli.subscribe("MonitoringStation/led", 0)
```

Calculating the system's status and situation awareness

The control center is assigned with the task of calculating the status of the overall system. The control center calculates the status of the system as `Alert`, `Caution`, or `Normal` using the current values of temperature and humidity. To calculate the status, the control center executes the `calculateStatus()` function every time it gets an update for the temperature or humidity from the monitoring station. According to the current situation awareness logic, if the temperature is measured above 45 degree Celsius or below 5 degree Celsius, we call the system's status as `Alert`. Similarly, you can identify the range of temperature and humidity values for `Caution` and `Normal` statuses from the following code snippet:

```
def calculateStatus():
    if (tempG > 45):
        if (humdG > 80):
            status = "High Temperature, High Humidity"
        elif (humdG < 20):
            status = "High Temperature, Low Humidity"
        else:
            status = "High Temperature"
        setAlert(status)

    elif (tempG < 5):
        if (humdG > 80):
            status = "Low Temperature, High Humidity"
        elif (humdG < 20):
            status = "Low Temperature, Low Humidity"
        else:
            status = "Low Temperature"
        setAlert(status)
    else:
```

```
        if (humdG > 80):
            status = "High Humidity"
            setCaution(status)
        elif (humdG < 20):
            status = "Low Humidity"
            setCaution(status)
        else:
            status = "Normal"
            setNormal(status)
```

Communicating with Xively

The control center is also required to communicate with Xively when it receives a message from the subscribed topics. We are already familiar with the process of setting up virtual devices and data streams on Xively. Open your Xively account and create a virtual device called `ControlCenter`. Note down the feed ID and API key for this device and replace them in the current code. Once you have these values, create the `Temperature`, `Humidity`, `Light`, `Motion`, `Buzzer`, and `Status` channels in this virtual device.

Looking at the Python code, you can see that we have declared the individual data stream for each topic and associated them with the appropriate Xively channel. The following code snippet shows the data stream for just the temperature observation, but the code also contains a similar configuration for all the other sensor observations:

```
try:
  datastreamTemp = feed.datastreams.get("Temperature")
except HTTPError as e:
  print "HTTPError({0}): {1}".format(e.errno, e.strerror)
  datastreamTemp = feed.datastreams.create("Temperature", tags="C")
  print "Creating new channel 'Temperature'"
```

Once the control center receives a message from the monitoring station, it updates the data stream with the latest values and pushes these changes to Xively. At the same time, we will also update the appropriate label in the `Tkinter` GUI using the `onMessage()` function. We will use the same code snippet for all the subscribed channels:

```
if msg.topic == "MonitoringStation/temperature":
  tempG = float(msg.payload)
  window.tempValue.set(tempG)
  datastreamTemp.current_value = tempG
  try:
    datastreamTemp.update()
```

```
    except HTTPError as e:
      print "HTTPError({0}): {1}".format(e.errno, e.strerror)
```

The control center also implements the function to set the system's status across the system, once it is calculated using the `calculateStatus()` function. There are three different functions to perform this task using a method that is similar to what we described in the previous code snippet. These functions include `setAlert()`, `setCaution()`, and `setNormal()` and these are associated with `Alert`, `Caution`, and `Normal` respectively. While updating the system's status, these functions also perform buzzer and LED actions by publishing the LED and buzzer values to the Mosquitto broker:

```
def setAlert(status):
    window.statusValue.set(status)
    datastreamStatus.current_value = "Alert"
    try:
        datastreamStatus.update()
    except HTTPError as e:
        print "HTTPError({0}): {1}".format(e.errno, e.strerror)
    cli.publish("MonitoringStation/led", 'red')
    cli.publish("MonitoringStation/buzzer", 'ON')
```

Checking and updating the buzzer's status

In the control center, we set the buzzer's status to `ON` if the system's status is determined as `Alert`. If you look back at the UX flow, you will notice that we also want to include a feature for the user to manually turn off the buzzer. The `checkBuzzerFromXively()` function keeps track of the buzzer's status from Xively and if the user manually turns off the buzzer using the web application, this function sets off the buzzer.

To continue this process independently from the GUI and situation awareness threads, we will need to create another thread for this function. The timer on this thread will automatically execute the function every 30 seconds:

```
def checkBuzzerFromXively():
  try:
    datastreamBuzzer = feed.datastreams.get("Buzzer")
    buzzerValue = datastreamBuzzer.current_value
    buzzerValue = str(buzzerValue)
    cli.publish("MonitoringStation/buzzer", buzzerValue)
  except HTTPError as e:
    print "HTTPError({0}): {1}".format(e.errno, e.strerror)
    print "Requested channel doesn't exist"
  threading.Timer(30, checkBuzzerFromXively).start()
```

With this function running in a separate thread every 30 seconds, the control center will check the status of the Xively channel and stop the buzzer if the status is set to `OFF`. We will explain how the user can update the Xively channel for the buzzer in the next section.

Testing the control center with the monitoring station

Assuming your Mosquitto broker is running, execute the `controlCenter.py` code with the changed parameters. Then, start the monitoring station. After a few moments, you will see on the terminal that the control center has already started getting messages from the publishers that are initialized on the monitoring station. The update interval for the messages from the publisher at the control center depends upon the configured publishing interval at the monitoring station.

The Arduino code executes the process of connecting to the Mosquitto broker only once after powering on. If you start your Mosquitto broker after that, it won't be able to communicate with the broker. So, you need to make sure that you start the Mosquitto broker before powering on the monitoring station.

If you need to restart the Mosquitto broker for any reason, remove and restart the monitoring station first.

```
pi@raspberrypi: ~/Deskt
File Edit Tabs Help
MonitoringStation/temperature 0 27.31
MonitoringStation/humidity 0 48.49
MonitoringStation/motion 0  0.00
MonitoringStation/light 0 831.00
MonitoringStation/led 0 off
MonitoringStation/buzzer 0 OFF
MonitoringStation/buzzer 0 OFF
MonitoringStation/buzzer 0 OFF
MonitoringStation/buzzer 0 OFF
MonitoringStation/buzzer 0 OFF
MonitoringStation/buzzer 0 OFF
MonitoringStation/buzzer 0 OFF
MonitoringStation/buzzer 0 OFF
MonitoringStation/buzzer 0 OFF
MonitoringStation/buzzer 0 OFF
MonitoringStation/temperature 0 27.31
MonitoringStation/humidity 0 48.65
MonitoringStation/motion 0  0.00
MonitoringStation/light 0 831.00
MonitoringStation/led 0 off
MonitoringStation/buzzer 0 OFF
MonitoringStation/buzzer 0 OFF
MonitoringStation/buzzer 0 OFF
```

On execution of the program, you will be able to see a small GUI window, as shown in the following screenshot. This window displays the sensor's values for temperature, humidity, ambient light, and motion. Along with these values, the GUI also displays the status of the system, which is **Normal** in this screenshot. You can also observe that every time the control center gets updates from the monitoring station, the system's status and sensor observations change in real time:

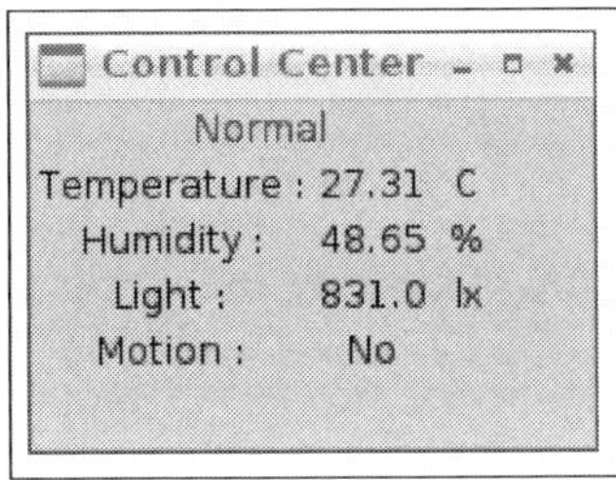

If this setup is working correctly on your computer, let's move on to deploy the control center on the Raspberry Pi.

Setting up the control center on the Raspberry Pi

The process of installing the Raspbian operating system is explained in *Chapter 7, The Midterm Project – a Portable DIY Thermostat*. You can use the same module that you used in the Midterm project or set up a new one. Once you have installed Raspbian and configured the TFT screen, connect the Wi-Fi dongle through a USB port. At this stage, we assume that your Raspberry Pi is connected with a monitor, a keyboard, and a mouse to perform the basic changes. Although we won't recommend it, you can also use the TFT screen for the following operations, if you are comfortable with it:

1. Start your Raspberry Pi and log in. At the command prompt, execute the following command to enter the visual desktop mode:

   ```
   $ startx
   ```

2. Once your graphical desktop starts, you will be able to see the icon of the **WiFi config** utility. Double-click on this icon and open the **WiFi config** utility. Scan for wireless networks and connect to the Wi-Fi network that has the monitoring station. When asked, enter the password of your network in the form window called **PSK**, and connect to your network.

3. Now, your Raspberry Pi is connected to the local home network and to the Internet through it. It's time to update the existing packages and install the required ones. To update the Raspberry Pi's existing system, execute the following commands in the terminal:

```
$ sudo apt-get update
$ sudo apt-get upgrade
```

4. Once your system is updated with the latest version, it's time to install the Mosquitto broker on your Raspberry Pi. The Raspbian OS has Mosquitto in the default repository, but it doesn't have the current version that we need. To install the latest version of Mosquitto, execute following commands in the terminal:

```
$ curl -O http://repo.mosquitto.org/debian/mosquitto-repo.gpg.key
$ sudo apt-key add mosquitto-repo.gpg.key
$ rm mosquitto-repo.gpg.key
$ cd /etc/apt/sources.list.d/
$ sudo curl -O http://repo.mosquitto.org/debian/mosquitto-repo.
list
$ sudo apt-get update
$ sudo apt-get install mosquitto, mosquitto-clients
```

5. To install other Python dependencies, let's first install the Setuptools package using `apt-get`:

```
$ sudo apt-get install python-setuptools
```

6. Using Setuptools, we can now install all the required Python libraries such as `paho_mqtt`, `xively-python`, and `web.py`:

```
$ sudo easy_install pip
$ sudo pip install xively-python web.py paho_mqtt
```

Now that we have installed all the necessary software tools that are required to run our control center on the Raspberry Pi, it is time to configure the Raspberry Pi so that it can provide uninterrupted operation for a critical system such as a remote home monitoring system:

1. In the current configuration of the Raspberry Pi, the screen of the Raspberry Pi will go to sleep after some time and the Wi-Fi connection will be terminated when this happens. To avoid this problem and force the screen to remain active, you will need to perform the following changes. Open the `lightdm.conf` file using the following command:

```
$ sudo nano /etc/lightdm/lightdm.conf
```

2. In the file, navigate to the `SetDefaults` section and edit the following line:

```
xserver-command-X -s 0 dpms
```

3. Now that your Raspberry Pi is set up, it is time to copy the program file from your computer to the Raspberry Pi. You can use SCP, PuTTY, or just a USB drive to transfer the necessary file to the Raspberry Pi.

If you install and configure everything as specified, your program should run without any errors. You can run the Python program constantly in the background using the following command:

```
$ nohup python controlCenter.py &
```

The last thing that we want to set up on the Raspberry Pi is the TFT LCD screen. The installation and configuration processes of the TFT LCD screen are described in *Chapter 7, The Midterm Project – a Portable DIY Thermostat*. Please follow the steps in the given order to set up the screen. The control center module along with the Raspberry Pi and the TFT screen can now be deployed in any part of your house.

Stage 3 – a web application using Xively, Python, and Amazon cloud service

The cloud services module of the overall system enables remote access to your monitoring station through the Internet. The unit interacts with the user via a web application as an extended version of the control center. With the use of this web application, the user can observe the sensor information from the monitoring station and the system's status calculated by the control center while having remote control to turn off the buzzer. So, what does the architecture of the cloud services look like?

Architecture of the cloud services

The architecture of the cloud services module with its associated components is displayed in the following diagram. In the cloud services architecture, we are using Xively as the intermediate data relay between the web application and the control center. The control center pushes the observations obtained from the monitoring station to the Xively channels. Xively stores and relays the data to the web application that is hosted on the Amazon AWS. The server instance on the Amazon AWS is used to make the web application accessible through the Internet. The server instance runs the Ubuntu operating system and the web application that is developed using the `web.py` library in Python.

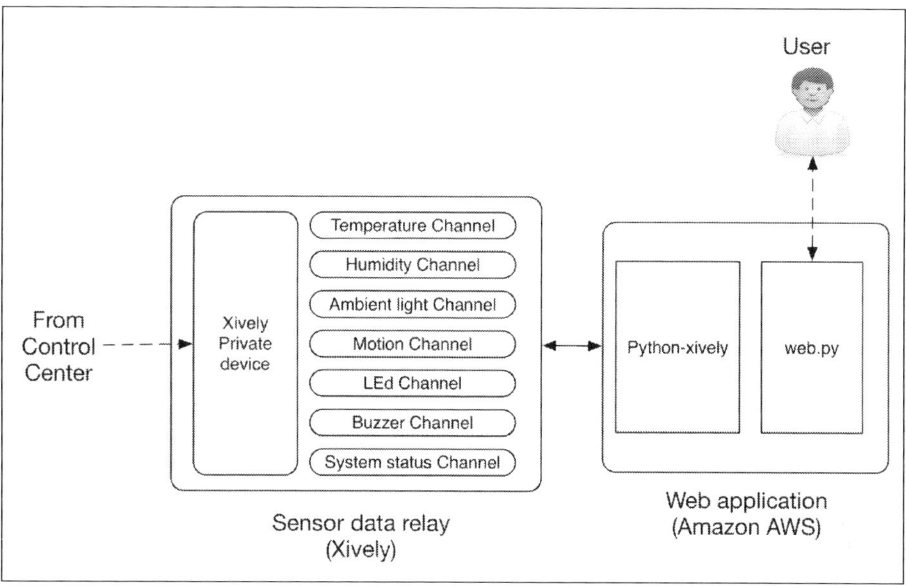

In the previous stage, we already covered the process of setting up Xively and the channels to accommodate sensor data. In the control center code, we also explained how we can push the updated observations to the appropriate Xively channels. Therefore, we really do not have any ground to cover for the Xively platform at this stage and we can move on to the web application.

Python web application hosted on Amazon AWS

In the previous chapter, we set up an Amazon AWS cloud instance to host a web application. You can use the same instance to host the web application for the remote home monitoring system too. However, make sure that you have installed the `web.py` library on your server.

1. In your computer, open the `Web_Application` folder and then the `RemoteMonitoringApplication.py` file in your editor.
2. In the code, you will be able to see that we just expand the web application program that we created in *Chapter 9, Arduino and the Internet of Things*. We use the templates based on `web.py` and the `GET()` and `POST()` functions to enable the web application.

3. In the application, we fetch information from each Xively channel and process it via a separate function. For example, the `fetchTempXively()` function obtains the temperature information from Xively. Every time the `POST()` function is executed, the `fetchTempXively()` function fetches the latest value of temperature reading from Xively. This also means that the web application does not populate and refresh the latest information automatically and waits for `POST()` to execute the appropriate functions:

```
def fetchTempXively():
  try:
    datastreamTemp = feed.datastreams.get("Temperature")
  except HTTPError as e:
    print "HTTPError({0}): {1}".format(e.errno, e.strerror)
    print "Requested channel doesn't exist"
  return datastreamTemp.current_value
```

4. The web application also provides access to control the buzzer from the user interface. The following code snippet adds the **Buzzer Off** button with other `Form` components. When the form is submitted after this button is pressed, the web application executes the `setBuzzer()` function:

```
inputData = web.input()
if inputData.btn == "buzzerOff":
    setBuzzer("OFF")
```

5. The `setBuzzer()` function access the Xively channel, `Buzzer`, and sends the off value if the **Buzzer Off** button is pressed. The current web application doesn't include the **Buzzer On** button, but you can easily implement this functionality by reusing the code that we developed for the **Buzzer Off** button. This function provides the reference code for other control points, which you can reuse with minor modifications:

```
def setBuzzer(statusTemp):
  try:
    datastream = feed.datastreams.get("Buzzer")
  except HTTPError as e:
    print "HTTPError({0}): {1}".format(e.errno, e.strerror)
    datastream = feed.datastreams.create("Buzzer",
                                          tags="buzzer")
    print "Creating new Channel 'Buzzer"
  datastream.current_value = statusTemp
  try:
    datastream.update()
  except HTTPError as e:
    print "HTTPError({0}): {1}".format(e.errno, e.strerror)
```

6. In the code, you will also have to modify the Xively feed ID and the API key and replace them with the values that your obtained from your virtual device. Once you have performed this modification, run the following command. If everything goes as planned, you will be able to open the web application in your web browser.

   ```
   $ python RemoteMonitoringApplication.py
   ```

If you are running the Python code on your computer, you can open `http://127.0.0.1:8080` to access the application. If you are running the application on the cloud server, you need to enter the IP address or domain name of your server to access the web application, `http://<AWS-IP-address>:8080`. If the web application is running from the cloud, it can be accessed from anywhere using the Internet, which was one of the original project requirements. With this last step, you have successfully completed the development of the remote home monitoring system that is based on Arduino and Python.

Testing the web application

When you open the web application in a browser, you will be able to see a similar output as shown in the following screenshot. As you can see, the web application displays the temperature, humidity, light, and motion values. The **Refresh** button fetches the sensor data from Xively again and loads the application once more. The **Buzzer Off** button sets the value of the Xively's `Buzzer` channel to `OFF`, which then get picked up by the control center, and it turns off the buzzer at the monitoring station subsequently:

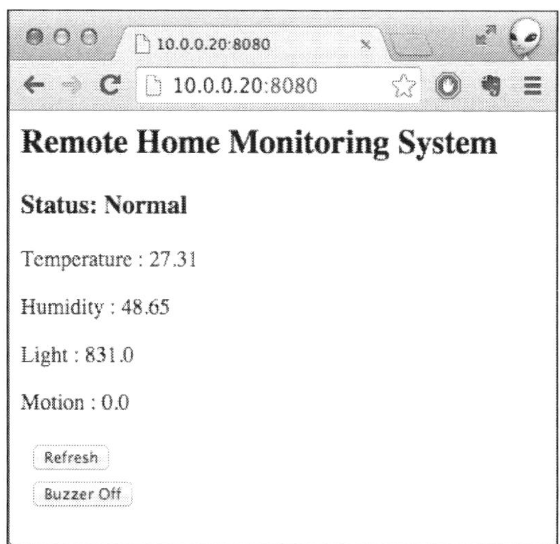

Testing and troubleshooting

Due to the number of components involved and complex programming associated with them, the overall project is a complex system to test and debug. Before you jump into troubleshooting, make sure that you have properly followed the steps that were described in the previous sections in order. The following are a few solutions to possible problems that can occur during the execution of the project:

- Troubleshoot individual sensor performance:
    - If your sensor measurements are way off the expected values, the first thing that you want to evaluate is the connection of the sensor pins to the Arduino board. Make sure that you have connected the digital, analog, and PWM pins correctly.
    - Check whether your Ethernet Shield board is properly connected to Arduino Uno.
    - Evaluate the connections of the 5V power supply and ground for each component.
- Avoid Xively's update limit
    - Xively imposes a limit on the maximum number of transactions that you can perform in a limited amount of time. While running your control center code, if you encounter an error for exceeding the limit, wait for 5 minutes before your access limit gets lifted.
    - Increase the delay between consecutive Xively updates at the control center level:

      ```
      threading.Timer(120, checkBuzzerFromXively).start()
      ```

    - Reduce the frequency of published messages at the monitoring station:

      ```
      timer.setInterval(600000, publishData);
      ```

    - You can also combine various Xively channels by formatting data into JSON or XML.
- Working with the maximum current draw limitation of Arudino:
    - The +5V power pin and digital pin of Arduino can provide a maximum current of 200 mA and 40 mA respectively. When running sensors directly from the Arduino board, make sure that you do not exceed these limits.
    - Make sure the combined current requirement of all the sensors is less than 200 mA. Otherwise, the components won't be able to get enough power to run and this will translate into faulty sensor information.

- You can provide external power to the components that require large amounts of current and control this power mechanism via Arduino itself. You will need a transistor that is acting as a switch that can then be controlled using the digital pins of Arduino. The tutorial at `https://learn.adafruit.com/adafruit-arduino-lesson-13-dc-motors/transistors` shows a similar example for a DC motor.

- Solve network problems:
    - In some scenarios, your monitoring station won't be able to communicate with the control center due to network problems.
    - This problem can be solved by using manual IP addresses for both, Arduino and the Raspberry Pi. In our project, we use a manual IP address for the Arduino, but the Raspberry Pi is connected using the Wi-Fi network. In most cases, when you are using your home Wi-Fi network, Wi-Fi routers are set up to provide dynamic IP addresses to the device every time they reconnect to the router.
    - You can solve this by configuring your Wi-Fi router to a fixed IP address for the Raspberry Pi. As the type and model of the Wi-Fi router is different for every scenario, you will have to use its user manual or online help forums for setting it up.
- Working with buzzer-related issues:
    - Sometimes the buzzer sound can be too loud or too quiet, depending upon the sensor that you are using. You can use PWM to configure the intensity of the buzzer. In our project, we used the Arduino digital pin 9 to connect the buzzer. This pin also supports PWM. In your Arduino code, modify the line to reflect changes for the PWM pin. Replace the `digitalWrite(BUZZER, HIGH);` line with `analogWrite(BUZZER, 127);`.
    - This routine will reduce the intensity of the buzzer by half from the original level. You can also change the PWM value from 0 to 255 and set the intensity of the buzzer sound from lowest to highest.
- Control center GUI calibration:
    - Depending upon the size of the TFT LCD screen that you are using, you will have to adjust the size of the main window of `Tkinter`.
    - First, run the current code on your Raspberry Pi and if you see that the GUI window does not match the screen, add the following line of code after initializing the main window:

      ```
      top.minsize(320,200)
      ```

  - This code will fix the problem with the size for a 2.8 inch TFT LCD screen. In the previous code snippet, `320` and `200` represent the pixel sizes for width and length respectively. For other screen sizes, change the pixel size accordingly.

- Test the LED:
  - In current code configuration, the LED is turned on only when the system changes to `Alert` or `Caution`. That means you won't be able to test the LEDs unless these situations occur. To check whether they are working correctly, execute the following command at the control center:

    ```
    $ mosquitto_pub -t "MonitoringStation/led" -m "red"
    ```

  - This command will light up the LED in red. To turn off the LED, just use `off` instead of `red` in the previous code.
  - If nothing lights up, you should check the connection wires of the LEDs. In addition, check for network-related issues as the Mosquitto itself might not be working.
  - If you see any color other than red, this means that you haven't connected the LED correctly and you need to interchange the pin configuration of your LED. If you are using an LED different than super-flux RGB, you should check out the pin layout in the datasheet and reorganize the connections.

Extending your remote home monitoring system

To successfully create commercial products from DIY project prototypes, you will need an additional layer of features on top of basic functionalities. These features actually make things convenient for a user when they interact with the system. The other distinguishable feature is the tangibility of the system, which makes large-scale production and support possible. Although there are plenty of features that you can implement, we recommend the following major improvements to elevate the level of the current project.

Utilizing multiple monitoring stations

In this project, we developed a monitoring station as a prototype with a range of functionality that is demonstrated by a remote home monitoring system. A remote monitoring system can have multiple numbers of monitoring stations to cover various geographical locations, such as different rooms inside a house, or different office cubicles. Basically, a large number of monitoring stations can cover an extended area and provide efficient surveillance of the domain that you are trying to monitor. If you want to extend the current project with an array of monitoring stations, you will require some of the following modifications:

- Each monitoring station can have its own control center or a centralized control center for all of them, depending upon the application requirements.
- You will have to update the Python code for the control center to accommodate the changes. Examples of these changes include modifying topic titles for MQTT, coordinating between these monitoring stations, updating data models for Xively updates, and so on.
- The free Xively account may not be able to handle the large amounts of data coming from the monitoring stations. In this case, you can either optimize the update rate and/or payload size or upgrade your Xively account to comply with the requirements. You can also resort to other free services such as ThingSpeak, Dweet.io, and Carriots, but you will have to make substantial modifications to the existing code structure.
- You can also update the web application to provide you with a selection menu for the monitoring stations or display all of them at once. You will also have to change the code to yield the modified data models.

Extending sensory capabilities

In term of sensors, we are only interfacing temperature, humidity, ambient light, and motion sensors. However, the actuation is limited to the buzzer and LED. You can implement the following changes to improve the sensory capabilities of the project.

- In a real scenario, a remote home monitoring system should be able to interface with other existing sensors such as the security system, monitoring cameras, refrigerator sensors, door sensors, and garage sensors throughout a home.
- You can also interface this project with other appliances such as the air conditioner, heater, and security alarm, which can help you to control the environment that you are already monitoring. As a trial, these components can be interfaced using a set of relays and switches.

- You can upgrade the current sensors at the monitoring station with more powerful, efficient, and accurate sensors. However, the monitoring station with the upgraded sensors may require a more powerful version of Arduino with more I/O pins and computation capabilities.
- You can also use additional sensors other than those used in this project at the monitoring station. There are large amount of heterogeneous, Arduino-supported DIY sensors that you can buy off the shelf. Examples of these sensors include the Alcohol Gas Sensor (MQ-3), LPG Gas Sensor (MQ-6), Carbon Monoxide Sensor (MQ-7), Methane Gas Sensor (MQ-4), and so on. These sensors can be simply interfaced with the Arduino just like the other sensors that we connected earlier.
- To accommodate these changes, you will be required to change the control center logic and algorithms. If you are interfacing a third-party component, you may also have to revisit the system architecture and adjust it.
- Similarly, you will also have to run frequent updates to Xively for the additional number of sensors, making the free version inadequate. To resolve this, you can pay for the commercial version of a Xively account or use a limited number of requests using a JSON file format similar to the one displayed in the following code snippet:

```
{
    "version": "1.0.0",
    "datastreams": [
        {
            "id": "example",
            "current_value": "333"
        },
        {
            "id": "key",
            "current_value": "value"
        },
        {
            "id": "datastream",
            "current_value": "1337"
        }
    ]
}
```

Improving UX

When we designed the user experience for this project, our goal was to demonstrate the usefulness of a UX design in developing the software flow. In the current UX design, the control center and the web application have limited control and features for a user. The following are a few changes that you need to implement to improve the UX of the project:

- Add tooltips and proper naming conventions for the various descriptions. Implement a proper layout to differentiate between the various information categories.
- Add buttons for the buzzer and the LED control on the control center GUI.
- In the web application, use a JavaScript and Ajax-based interface to automatically refresh the changes in sensor values.
- Provide a UI mechanism so that the user can change the update interval at the control center and the web application. Once these changes are made, propagate them through each program so that the monitoring station can start publishing messages at the new interval.

Expanding cloud-based features

In the current setup, we are using two stages to provide cloud-based capabilities and enable remote monitoring. We have Xively as a data relay and Amazon AWS to host the web application. If you are working on a commercial-grade product and want to reduce the complexity of the architecture, you can implement the following changes:

- You can develop your own data relay on your cloud instance using open source tools such as ThingSpeak. Your control center will then communicate directly to your server and eliminate dependency on third-party IoT services.
- If Xively is your platform, you can also use additional features, such as graphs on your smart phone, which are provided by Xively. Once your phone is paired with Xively, you can access this feature directly.
- Alternatively, you can use other cloud services such as Microsoft Azure and Google App engine instead of Amazon AWS. You can also set up your own cloud server, depending upon your familiarity with cloud computing. Although having your own cloud will give you complete control of the server, third-party services such as Amazon can be more cost effective and require less maintenance compared to self-hosted servers.

- If you are planning to develop a large-scale system that is based on the current architecture, you can increase the computing capability of your existing cloud instance. You can also implement a distributed server system to accommodate the large number of remote monitoring systems that can be accessed by an even greater number of users.

Improving intelligence for situation awareness

In this project, we have used four different sensors to monitor the physical environment—each sensor obtains user inputs with two types of actuators for notification. Although we are using a good amount of information sources, our situation awareness algorithm is limited to identifying out-of-range temperature and humidity values. You can implement a few extended features to make your system more versatile and useful:

- Implement different logic for day and night scenarios, which can help you to avoid unwarranted false alarms at night.
- Implement an intruder detection algorithm using the motion sensor for when you are not at home.
- Utilize a combination of ambient light sensor values with motion sensors to identify energy wastage. For example, a scenario in which more light is recorded during the night when the motions are significantly low explains that you may have forgotten to turn off the lights during the night.

Creating an enclosure for hardware components

Just like software-based features, the hardware components also require a major revamp if you develop a commercial-grade product. Nowadays, 3D printers have become viable and it is really easy to design and print plastic 3D components. You can also use professional 3D printing services such as Shapeways (`http://www.shapeways.com`), Sculpteo (`http://www.sculpteo.com`), or makexyz (`http://www.makexyz.com`) for your enclosures. You can even use a laser cutter or other means of model making to create the hardware enclosures. These are a few hardware improvements that you can implement:

- The sensor and actuators that are assembled on a prototype board can be organized on a PCB and permanently fixed for stable and robust operation.

- A hardware enclosure for the monitoring station can make it portable and easily deployable in any environment. When designing this enclosure, you should also consider the proper placement of the motion sensor and the ambient light sensor, along with a button to make them accessible to the user.
- The Raspberry Pi and TFT LCD screen, which make up the control center hardware, can also be enclosed in a mountable package.
- Adding touch screen capabilities to the TFT LCD screen can enable additional control over the system, expanding the UX use cases.

Summary

In this chapter, we developed a working prototype of a remote home monitoring system and also learned the process of hardware product development simultaneously. In the project, we utilized most of the hardware components and software tools that we used throughout the book. We began by designing the system architecture so that we could coordinate the utilization of these tools. Later, we ventured into the actual development stages, which included designing the hardware units and developing programs to run these units. In the end, we provided a list of improvements to make this prototype into a real commercial product. You are welcome to use this methodology to develop your future projects and products, as you now have experience working with this one.

In the last chapter, we are going to utilize the same project development methodology to create an interesting project that utilizes your messages from a social network website to give you control over your hardware.

11
Tweet-a-PowerStrip

Smart power management units or strips are part of some of the most popular IoT subdomains, smart homes and smart grids. Nowadays, smart power strips are commercially available and provide a large number of features, such as remote access, smart power usage, and power management. In this project, we are going to create a smart DIY power strip that can be controlled remotely using status messages posted on Twitter, the popular social media website (`http://www.twitter.com`). These messages are also known as **tweets**. Basically, just like you can control sensors remotely using a web browser, you can control them by sending a tweet. We've already worked with low-power sensors in the previous project, so let's work with AC appliances in this project. We will be implementing the same project development methods that we utilized in the previous project. This chapter avoids additional explanations about the process and sticks only to the details associated with the project.

Project overview

This project requires the development of a smart power strip using Arduino and Python, while the control inputs to the strips are tweets. Although we are only enabling remote access to the power strip, there are a large number of additional features that can be implemented in future to elevate this DIY project to a commercial product.

The major goals we want to achieve in this project are as follows:

- The user should be able to turn the individual power ports on and off using customized tweets
- The user should be able to check the status of the power ports using Twitter

Project requirements

Here are the initial project requirements, derived from the goals:

- The system should have 110V (or 220V) AC power ports interfaced with relays.
- An Arduino-based unit should be able to control these relays, ultimately controlling the appliance connected through the power ports.
- The system should be able to decode the tweets sent by the user and convert them into appropriate control messages for Arduino.
- The Python-based program that processes the tweets should then publish these messages so that Arduino can complete those actions using the relays.
- To sum up, the relays should be controlled in a near real-time manner using the tweets sent by the user.
- The system should also understand keywords to check the status of the relays and automatically tweet the status. The system should process a tweet only once and should be able to remember the last tweet processed.

110V versus 220V AC power

Depending on the country, your AC power supply may have voltage ratings of 110/120V or 220/240V. Although the circuit diagram used by this project mentions a 110V AC power supply, the same circuit should also work for a 220V power supply. If you are using a 220V supply, check out the following notes before moving forward:

- Ensure that the appliances you are trying to operate, such as fans, lights, and so on, are rated for similar AC power
- You have to ensure that the relays used by the project are compatible with your AC power supply
- Arduino works on a DC power supply, and it is not affected by any variation in AC power

System architecture

From the preceding requirements, let's sketch the architecture of the Tweet-a-PowerStrip system. The system architecture tries to utilize the hardware components and software tools you learned in the previous chapters, while having a relay component as the only exceptional component. As you can see in the architecture in the following diagram, we are employing the relay to control various home appliances. These appliances are usually powered by a common 110V AC power supply available in each home. Instead of controlling a single appliance, we are implementing a four-channel relay to control at least four appliances, such as a lamp, a fan, a toaster, and a coffee machine.

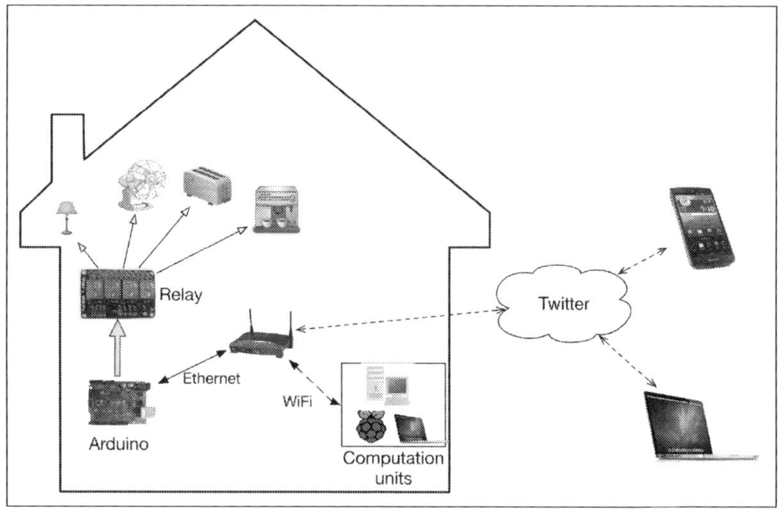

The relay is controlled using the digital pins of the Arduino Uno board, which utilizes the Ethernet Shield to connect to your home network. A computation unit that may consist of a computer, a Raspberry Pi, or a server, uses Python and its supporting libraries to access tweets. The computation unit also deploys a Mosquitto broker. This broker handles the topics from the Python program and Arduino to control the relays. The user can post tweets containing keywords from any platform, such as a phone or a browser, and the tweets are ultimately captured by the computation unit.

Required hardware components

This project will require the following hardware components throughout the development and the deployment stages:

Component	Amount	Website/note
Arduino Uno	1	`https://www.sparkfun.com/products/11021`
Arduino Ethernet Shield	1	`https://www.sparkfun.com/products/9026`
Relay (four-channel, Arduino-compatible)	1	`http://www.amazon.com/JBtek-Channel-Module-Arduino-Raspberry/dp/B00KTEN3TM/`
PowerSwitch Tail	4	`http://www.powerswitchtail.com/` Alternative to relay

Component	Amount	Website/note
Power strip	Optional	
Breadboard	1	For development stage
USB cable for Arduino	1	For development stage
Arduino power supply	1	For deployment stage
Electric tape	As per requirements	
Connection wires	As per requirements	

Relays

As you can see in the following image, we are introducing a new hardware component that was not utilized in any of the previous chapters—a relay:

This is an electromagnetic device that uses electricity to be operated as a switch. A typical relay contains three contacts on the high-power side, **normally connected** (**NC**), **common** (C), and **normally open** (**NO**). The other side (the control side) of the relay requires an activation voltage to toggle the connection from common-NC to common-NO. This action demonstrates the switch functionalities for the connection on the high-power side. We'll use Arduino-compatible relays from manufacturers such as Keyes or SainSmart. These relays are available in single-, two- or four-channel configurations. On the high-power side, the relays support up to 250V, 10A AC power or 30V, 10A DC power. The relays are controlled using 5V DC on the low-power side, which is provided using the digital I/O pins of the Arduino board.

PowerSwitch Tail

Working with AC power can be hazardous if you haven't dealt with it previously or if you are not familiar with the necessary precautions and measurements. If you are not comfortable with working with open relays or connecting AC power to them, there is another device that you can use to replace the relay—the PowerSwitch Tail, a safely enclosed box that contains optically isolated solid-state relays and provides a convenient way to interface your AC appliance with the Arduino board. The following is an image of the PowerSwitch Tail, which can be obtained from its official website (`http://www.powerswitchtail.com/`):

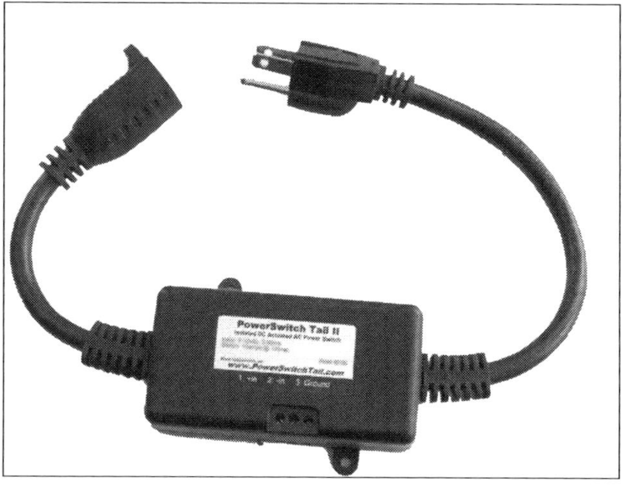

> If you are dealing with a 220V/240V power supply, the PowerSwitch Tail website also provides an assembly kit for 200V to 240V power supply, at `http://www.powerswitchtail.com/Pages/PowerSwitchTail240vackit.aspx`.
>
> It is really easy to assemble the kit from the guidelines provided at `http://www.powerswitchtail.com/Documents/PSSRTK%20Instructions.pdf`.

For this project, you will need four of these devices to replace the four-channel relay that we are going to use. As you can see in the following diagram, one end of the Tail goes into the regular power port, while you need to connect your appliance to the other port. Meanwhile, you can use the three control inputs to control the relay. We are using one of the digital I/O pins of the Arduino board to send the control signal to the Tail. When going ahead with the Tails instead of the relays, make sure that you make necessary amendments to the upcoming hardware design.

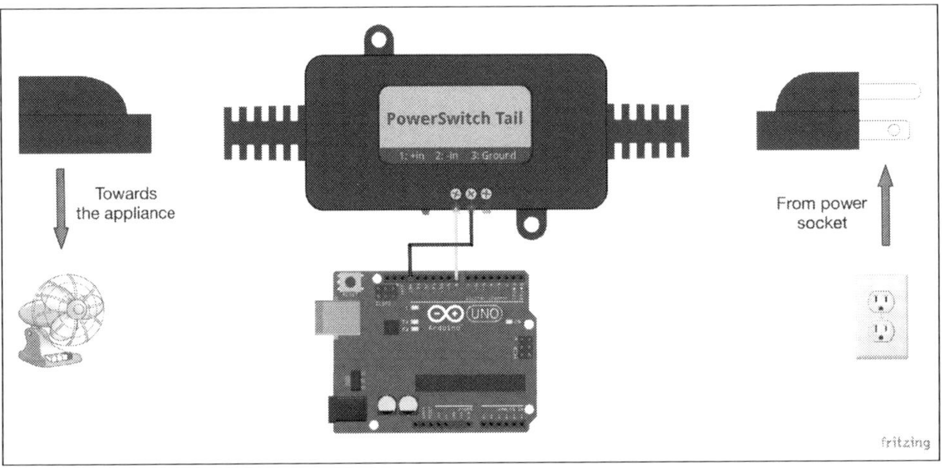

User experience flow

From the system architecture we have created, what should the **user experience** (**UX**) flow while working with the Tweet-a-PowerStrip be? We have divided the UX into two separate sections: controlling the power to the appliances, and checking the status of the power strip.

In the first UX flow design, as displayed in the following diagram, the user begins by sending a tweet containing the name of the appliance (#fan, #lamp, #toaster, or #coffee) and the control command (#on or #off). The system should be able to handle the tweet from the point of parsing until the appliance has behaved as asked for. The system should also provide a hassle-free experience for the user, where the user doesn't have to perform any further actions than simply sending tweets.

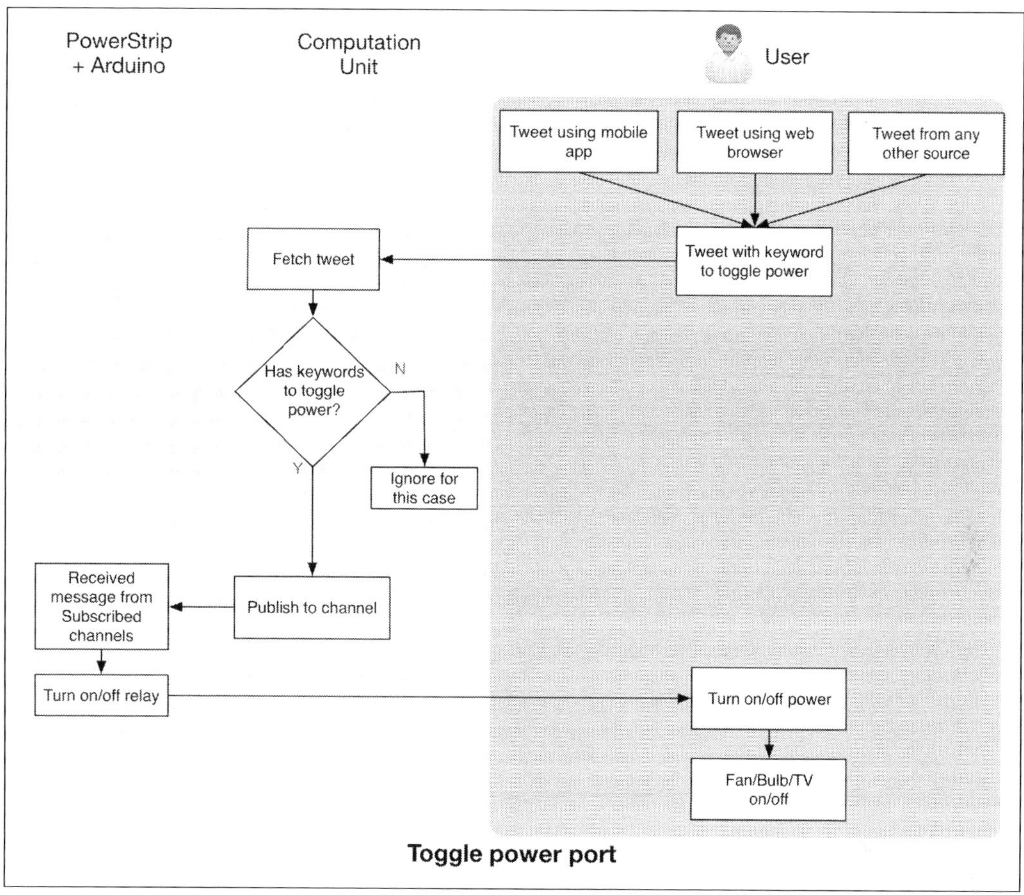

Toggle power port

Similarly, the user should be able to post **#status #check** tweets and simply obtain the status report posted back by the system. The system should handle checking the status of the power ports, publishing it to the computation unit, and posting a tweet with the message without any additional input from the user.

The following diagram shows the UX flow for checking the system status:

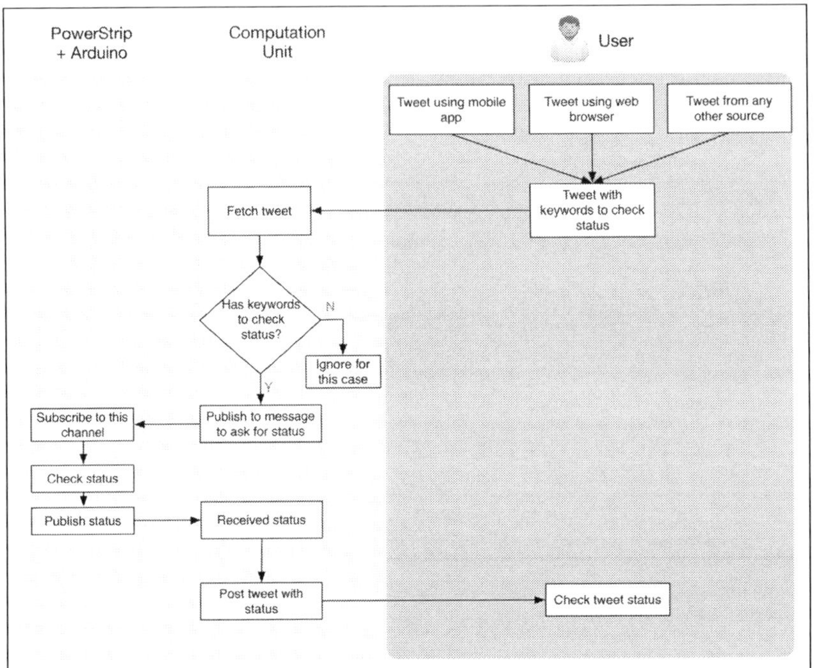

Development and deployment stages

According to the architecture, we require two main development stages to complete the project. The first stage, which interacts with the appliance through the relays, is developed using Arduino. This unit subscribes to the topics associated with the appliances, and once it receives an appropriate message, it executes the action on the relay level. In the second stage, we deal with the individual tweets, where we parse the tweets from the Twitter account, check for duplicates, decode actions from the messages, and also post tweets with status reports. During these development stages, we are going to use a breadboard and jumper wires to test the Arduino and Python programs. At this stage, the project is still not ready to deploy as a portable unit for daily usage.

The deployment stage contains tasks of creating a PCB for the breadboard connections and insulating wires to avoid any electric hazard. You can also buy or create an enclosure box to isolate the open hardware from physical contact. As the development stage contains everything that is required to convert the project into its working state, we are not going to dive deep into the deployment stage. You can perform addition deployment tasks according to your personal requirements.

Let's start from the hardware design stage and develop the physical section of the smart power strip using Arduino.

Stage 1 – a smart power strip with Arduino and relays

The hardware of Tweet-a-PowerStrip contains Arduino as the main controller unit that interfaces with the relays and the Ethernet Shield to communicate with the computation unit. The Arduino code implements the MQTT client, using the `PubSubClient` library to publish and subscribe to the topics. Although we are using some example appliances to control the use of the relay, you can select any other appliance you own. You can also use a commercial power strip instead of an individual power plug.

Hardware design

While assembling the hardware components, as displayed in the following diagram, make sure you are precise in connecting the appliances with the AC power plugs. One wire of the AC plug is directly connected to the appliance, while the other is connected between the C and NO ports of the relay. We have connected the control side of the relay to the digital pin of our Arduino. As we are using a four-channel relay, we will have to utilize four digital IO pins from the Arduino board. Complete the remaining connections as shown here:

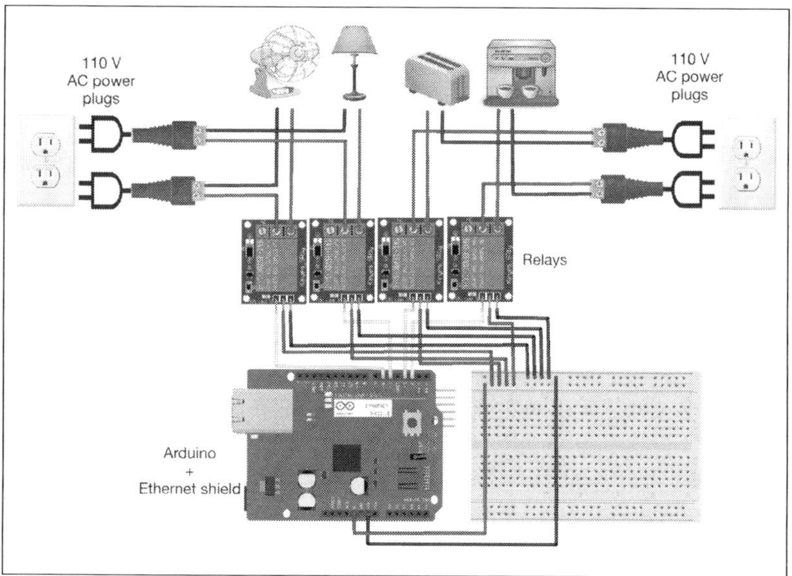

Connecting the hardware unit is fairly simple, but requires a lot of precision because it involves high-power AC connections.

You should cover the open 110V AC power cords going to the relay and the appliance with electric tape to avoid any type of electrical hazard. Keeping these live wires open can be really dangerous due to the large amount of current being carried by them. In the deployment stage, a plastic cover or a box around the relay unit can also be helpful in covering the live power wires.

Once you are ready with the connections, connect the Arduino board to your computer using a USB port, as shown in the following image:

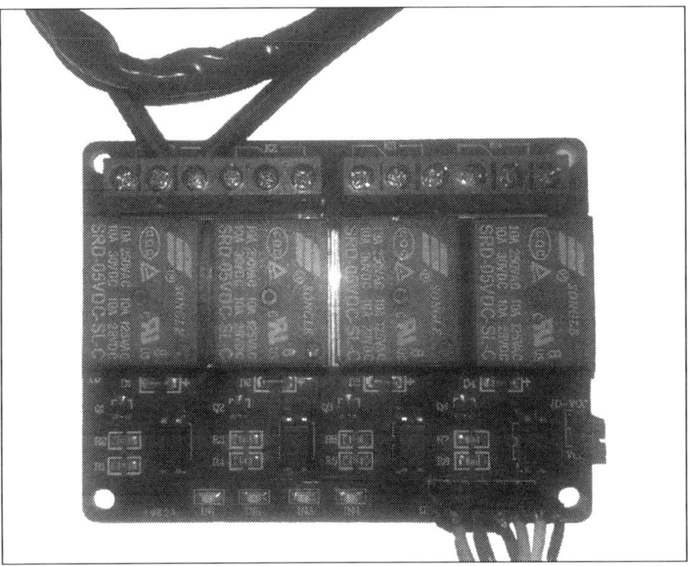

The Arduino code

The Arduino sketch for this section is located in the folder containing the chapter code with the `Arduino_powerstrip.ino` filename. You can open the file in the Arduino IDE to explore the code. As usual, you will have to change the IP addresses of the device and the Mosquitto server to the appropriate IP addresses, while also changing the MAC address of the Ethernet Shield. The following code snippet shows the declaration of the Arduino pins and their roles in the main function, `setup()`. Make sure that you are using the same pin numbers that you have used to connect the relay. Alternatively, you can change the appliance name to that of the appliance you are using. Also, make sure whatever changes you make in the variable names should be reflected in the entire code to avoid any compilation errors:

```
pinMode(FAN, OUTPUT);
pinMode(LAMP, OUTPUT);
pinMode(TOASTER, OUTPUT);
pinMode(COFFEEMAKER, OUTPUT);
fanStatus = false;
lampStatus = false;
toasterStatus = false;
coffeemakerStatus = false;
digitalWrite(FAN, LOW);
digitalWrite(LAMP,LOW);
digitalWrite(TOASTER, LOW);
digitalWrite(COFFEEMAKER, LOW);
```

In the `setup()` function, the code also subscribes to the appropriate MQTT channels so that it can receive messages from the Mosquitto broker as soon as they are available. As you can see, we are also subscribing to the `PowerStrip/statuscheck` channel to deal with the status report:

```
if (client.connect("PowerStrip")) {
  client.subscribe("PowerStrip/fan");
  client.subscribe("PowerStrip/lamp");
  client.subscribe("PowerStrip/toaster");
  client.subscribe("PowerStrip/coffeemaker");
  client.subscribe("PowerStrip/statuscheck");
}
```

In the `callback()` function, we use the `if` statement to match the topic with the appropriate `digitalWrite()` action. As you can see, we are setting up `HIGH` and `LOW` statuses for the digital pin when the program receives `on` and `off` messages, respectively (for that appliance). With this action, we are also changing the state of the Boolean variable associated with the appliance, which will be helpful in retrieving the status of the port. The same process is then repeated for all appliances:

```
if(topicS == "PowerStrip/fan"){
  if (payloadS.equalsIgnoreCase("on")) {
    digitalWrite(FAN, HIGH);
    fanStatus = true;
  }
  if (payloadS.equalsIgnoreCase("off")){
    digitalWrite(FAN, LOW);
    fanStatus = false;
  }
}
```

When the system receives a `get` message that is associated with the status check, the program creates a message using the Boolean variables that we toggled earlier. The program then publishes the status to the `PowerStrip/statusreport` channel:

```
if(topicS.equals("PowerStrip/statuscheck")){
    if (payloadS.equalsIgnoreCase("get")) {
        String report = "";
        if (fanStatus) report += "Fan:on,";
        else report += "Fan:off,";

        if (lampStatus) report += "Lamp:on,";
        else report += "Lamp:off,";

        if (toasterStatus) report += "Toaster:on,";
        else report += "Toaster:off,";

        if (coffeemakerStatus) report += "Coffeemaker:on";
        else report += "Coffeemaker:off";

        report.toCharArray(reportChar, 100);
        client.publish("PowerStrip/statusreport", reportChar);
    }
}
```

Just as we did in the previous project, you can set up the code to periodically send `keep alive` messages to avoid the termination of the connection with the Mosquitto broker. Once you are ready with the code, connect the Ethernet cable, compile the code, and then upload it to your Arduino. Your Arduino should be in receiving mode now, and it will wait for the message from the subscribed channels. As we discussed in the previous the project, you need to ensure that your Mosquitto broker is running on the server IP address you specified in the Arduino code.

Stage 2 – the Python code to process tweets

As the user is interacting with the system at the level of the Twitter application, we do not require a deployable computation or control unit for this project. Due to this, we can just use any computer capable of hosting Python and Mosquitto as the computation unit. You still need to ensure that the unit is always on and connected to the Internet, otherwise the system will not work as expected. For simplicity, you can deploy the system on the Raspberry-Pi-based control center that you developed in the previous project, or even on the Amazon AWS server. For the development stage, let's start with the regular computer that you have been using all along. We are assuming that this computer has the Mosquitto broker installed and running. Note down the IP address of this unit, as you will need it in the Arduino code that you developed in the previous section.

Python software flow

The Python code deals with two services during execution, the Twitter API to get or post tweets and the Mosquitto broker to relay messages to the hardware unit. The program begins by parsing the latest tweet from the user account and checking whether it has been utilized in the previous action or not. This avoids any command duplication, as the frequency of new tweets is significantly lower than the frequency of the program loop. Once the code finds a new tweet with the appropriate keywords to perform operations on the appliance (or appliances), it publishes the message to the Mosquitto broker. If the tweet contains a message to check the status, the code requests the status from your Arduino and posts a new tweet with the status after receiving it.

The following diagram shows the detailed program flow of the computation unit:

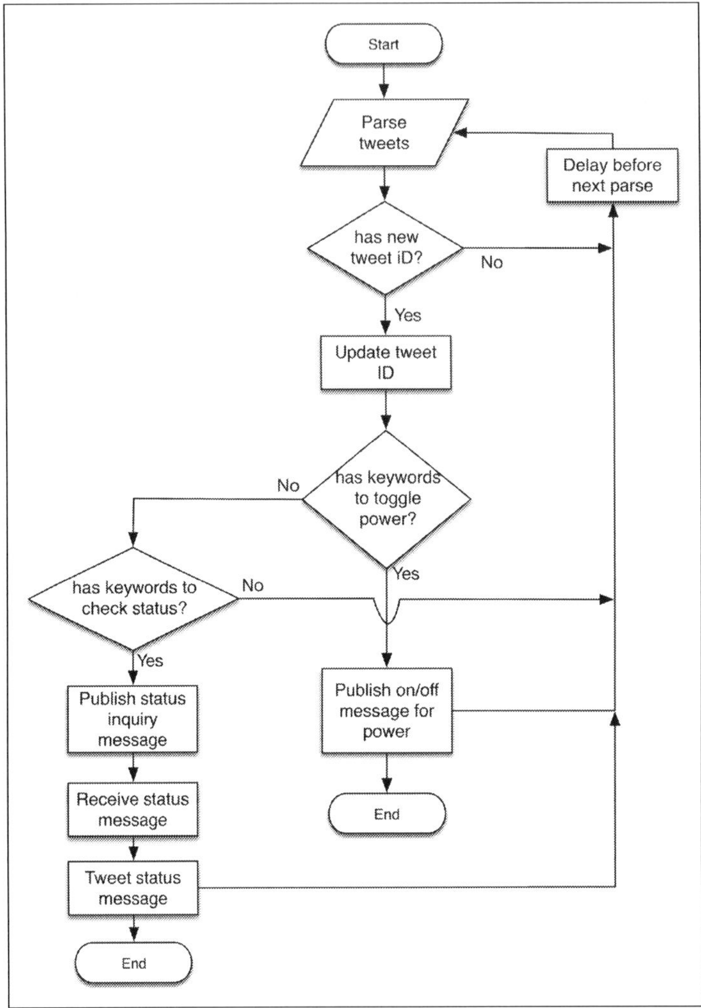

You can change the program flow to accommodate any other feature you want to add at the Python level. The logic behind identifying and toggling the appliance can be improvised to accommodate more complex tweet text.

Setting up the Twitter application

We are assuming that you have a Twitter account by now. If you don't, you can create a new account just for this project to avoid changes to your own profile. With the introduction of the latest APIs, Twitter requires you to authenticate using OAuth before accessing any information from your account. To do that, you will have to create a Twitter app using your account. Execute the following steps in order to create a new Twitter app for this project:

1. Log in to your Twitter account and open the `https://apps.twitter.com` address in your web browser.
2. Click on the **Create New App** icon on the page, and you will be directed to a page asking for your application details, as displayed in the following screenshot:

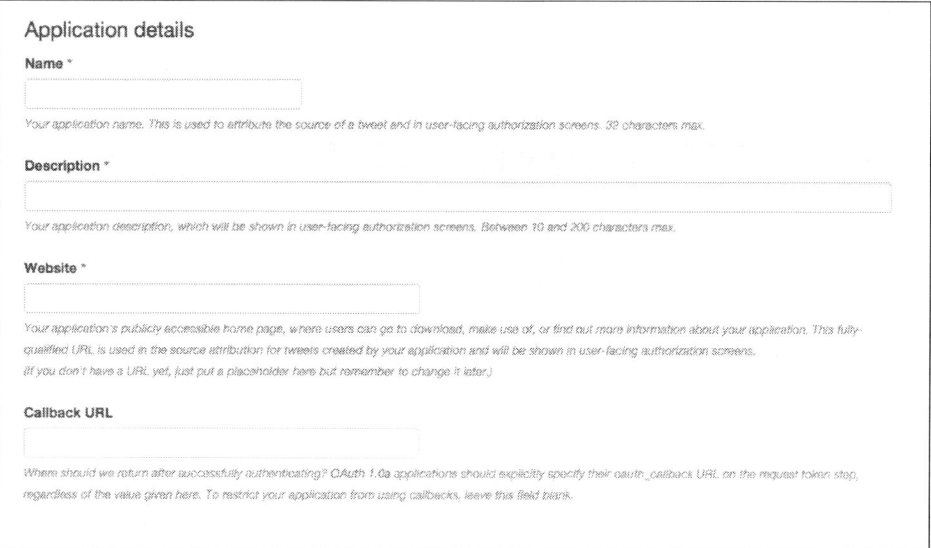

3. Fill in all the required details (marked with red asterisks) and continue to the next page. Ensure that your application name is unique, as Twitter asks for a unique application name.

4. Once your application is created, you can click on the **API Keys** tab and find the consumer key (**API key**) and consumer secret (**API secret**) for your app. Save this information in a safe place, as you will need them to authenticate with the Twitter API.

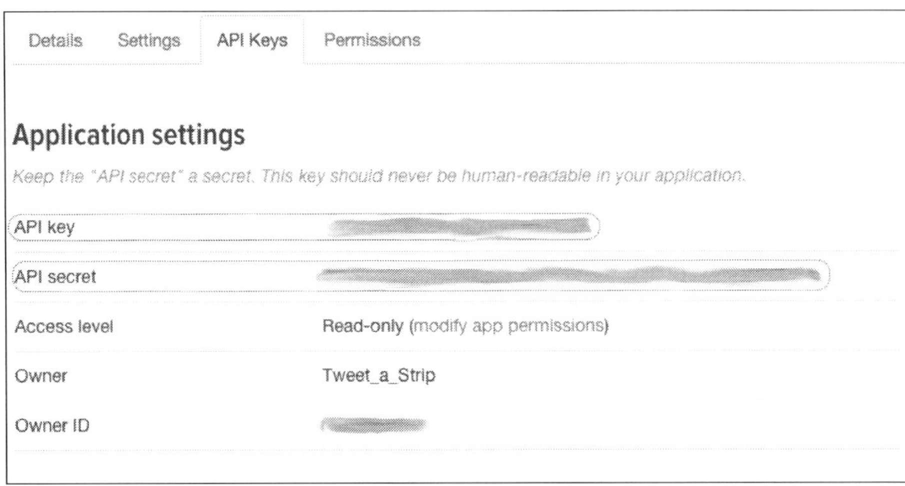

5. As the UX of the Tweet-a-PowerStrip project requires the system to automatically send the system status, we need read-and-write access to our application. Go to the **Permissions** tab, select the **Read and Write** option, and save it for the changes to take effect.

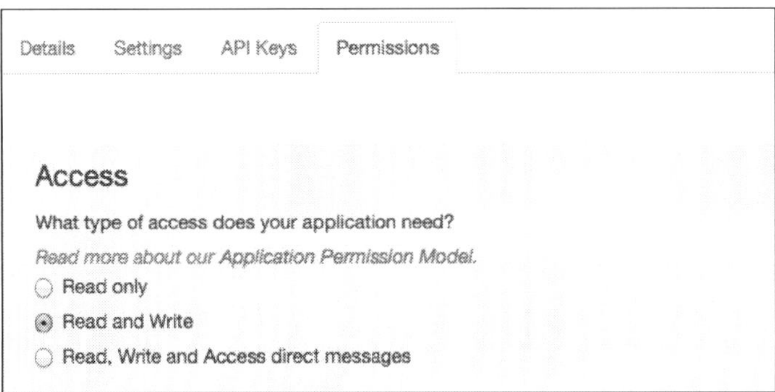

6. Once you are done with setting up the permissions for the application, go back to the API keys tab and click on the **Create Access Token** icon to generate a new access token for this application. After a while, you should be able to see the access token on the same page, as displayed in this screenshot:

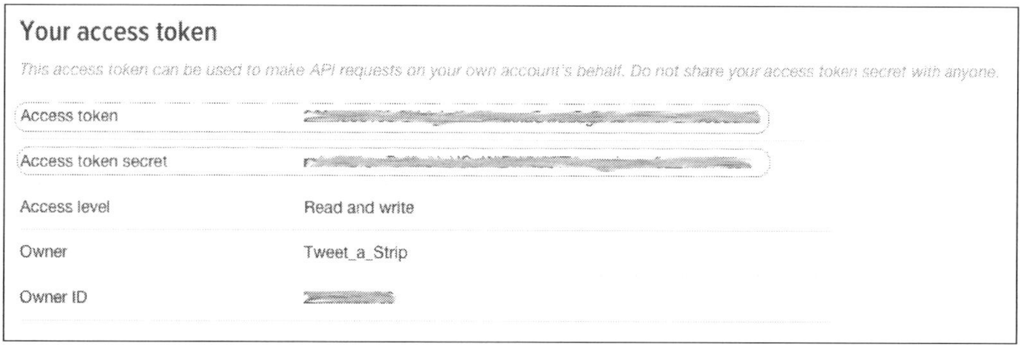

Your access token

This access token can be used to make API requests on your own account's behalf. Do not share your access token secret with anyone.

Access token	[illegible]
Access token secret	[illegible]
Access level	Read and write
Owner	Tweet_a_Strip
Owner ID	[illegible]

7. Save the **Access token** and **Access token secret** information. Your application is now ready for use and can help you to authenticate with the Twitter API.

Now let's move on to the Python code.

The Python code

Before you jump into the code, you are required to install the Twitter library for Python. Use the Setuptools or `pip` to install the library using the following command. We are assuming that you already have the latest `paho_mqtt` library installed on your computer:

```
$ sudo pip install python-twitter
```

The Python code for this section is located in the code folder with the `PythonTweetAPowerStrip.py` filename. Open the code in your IDE and start exploring it. The code contains two parallel threads to handle the tweets and the Mosquitto library separately.

As you can see in the following code snippet, we are using the `Api` class from the `python-twitter` library to establish a connection with the Twitter API. We are using the `consumer key`, `consumer secret`, `access token key`, and `access token secret` values for this authentication. Once the authentication is established, the `Api` class can be used to get the latest status from the timeline using the `GetHomeTimeline()` function call, and to post the new status using the `PostUpdate()` function call. The `GetHomeTimeline()` function gives an array of statuses from the user; we need the latest status, which can be fetched using `statuses[0]` (the first element of the array):

```
api = twitter.Api(consumer_key='<consumer-key>',
                  consumer_secret='<consumer-secret>',
                  access_token_key='<access-token-key>',
                  access_token_secret='access-token-secret>')
```

Once we have retrieved the latest tweet, we need to make sure that we haven't used that tweet already. So we save the latest tweet ID in a global variable, as well as in a file in case we need to run the code again:

```
with open('lastTweetID.txt', 'w+') as fh:
  lastTweetId = fh.readline()
  print "Initializing with ID: " + lastTweetId
```

We retrieve the ID of the previous tweet from the `lastTweetID.txt` file to match with the latest ID. If it doesn't match, we update the `lastTweetID.txt` file with the latest ID for the next loop:

```
if lastTweetId != str(currentStatus.id):
  lastTweetId = str(currentStatus.id)
  print "Updated file with ID: " + lastTweetId
  with open('lastTweetID.txt', 'w+') as fh:
    fh.write(lastTweetId)
    currentStatusText = currentStatus.text
    print currentStatusText
```

Once we have identified the latest unique tweet, we use the Python string operation to decode the keywords for the appliance and power commands. As you can see in the following code snippet, the keyword we are looking for in the tweeted text to access the fan is `#fan`. Once we have identified that the message is directed to the fan, we check for action keywords such as `#on` and `#off`, and then take the associated action of publishing the message to the Mosquitto broker. We repeat this action for all the appliances connected to the system. Your Arduino takes an action using the published message, and completes the UX flow for the controlled appliances:

```
if "#fan" in currentStatusText.lower():
  if "#on" in currentStatusText.lower():
    cli.publish("PowerStrip/fan", "on")
  if "#off" in currentStatusText.lower():
    cli.publish("PowerStrip/fan", "off")
```

Similarly, when the code receives an update from the `PowerStrip/statusreport` topic, it obtains the status from the message payload and posts it as a new tweet to the user timeline of that Twitter account. This completes the UX flow for the status check using Twitter:

```
def onMessage(mosq, obj, msg):
    if msg.topic == "PowerStrip/statusreport":
        print msg.payload
        api.PostUpdate(msg.payload)
```

Testing and troubleshooting

Testing can simply be performed by posting the `#fan #on` status to the Twitter account used in this project. You should be able to see the fan turning on by using the command shown here:

Similarly, send the `#fan #off` status to turn off the fan. You may find some lagging, as the loop used to retrieve the tweets is set with a delay of a minute.

To access the status of the system, post the `#status #get` status to the account, and you will be able to see the system status automatically posted by the computation unit.

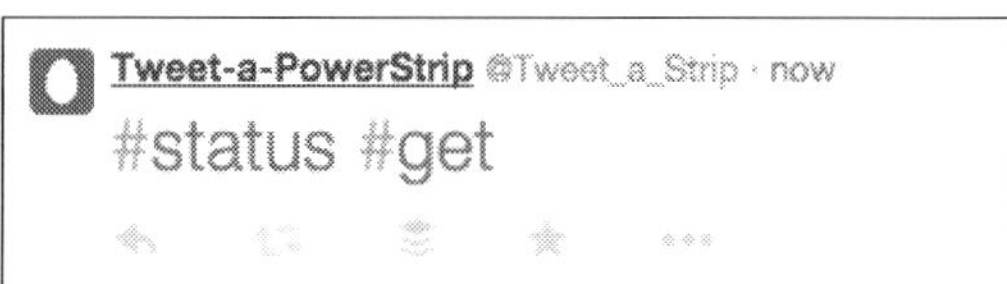

The tweet shown in the following screenshot is generated using the Tweet-a-PowerStrip unit. It displays the status of all the connected appliances.

While working with the system, you will want to either avoid the following scenarios or troubleshoot them:

- `'Twitter rate limit exceed' error`: Twitter imposes a limit on the number of requests you can make to their public API. If you are requesting the API too often (this often occurs when you reduce the sleep time between consecutive queries), your application will exit with an exception. To avoid this, set a longer sleep time in the Python program loop before requesting the API again. There is a trade-off between the frequency of requests and the response time of your appliances. You can learn about this limitation at `http://dev.twitter.com/rest/public/rate-limiting` and adjust your request interval accordingly. Once you have received this error, you will have to wait for some time (approximately 10 to 15 minutes) before making requests to the Twitter API again.
- `'Read-only application cannot post' error`: This error will only occur if you forgot to change the permissions on your application to **Read and Write** from **Read only**. Make sure that you have performed this change. Also, Twitter takes some time for the changes to take effect.

Extending the project with additional features

The current system can be expanded to include multiple features:

- You can start saving the time duration in which a particular appliance was on or off, and then provide a detailed analysis to the user. You can also use this information to calculate the energy being expended by these appliances.
- You can utilize the current measurement sensors to calculate the power load at each port. Combining it with the time the device was on, you can calculate very comprehensive power usage to further improve power management.
- You can use the system clock with the motion sensor to intelligently turn off the appliance during nights and periods of no activity.
- The Tweet-a-PowerStrip project can be interfaced with the remote home monitoring system that we developed in the previous project, in order to obtain useful information from other sensors being used in the same house.

- One of the modifications you can easily implement is to utilize Twitter's private messages instead of its tweets to control the appliances. This will extend the access permissions of your system to other trusted Twitter accounts. For security reasons, you should tighten the access level and only let approved people post such messages to your account.

Summary

You have now successfully completed two different IoT projects using just two base technologies, Arduino and Python. With the current project, it is obvious that it is very easy to interface any other technology, tool, or API with Arduino and Python. The project development methodology we used in these two projects will also help you with your DIY projects and other future products. Happy prototyping! And happy coding!

Index

A

B

C

D

E

F

G

H

I

L

M

N

O

P

R

S

T

U

V

W

Z

Thank you for buying
Python Programming for Arduino

About Packt Publishing

Packt, pronounced 'packed', published its first book, *Mastering phpMyAdmin for Effective MySQL Management*, in April 2004, and subsequently continued to specialize in publishing highly focused books on specific technologies and solutions.

Our books and publications share the experiences of your fellow IT professionals in adapting and customizing today's systems, applications, and frameworks. Our solution-based books give you the knowledge and power to customize the software and technologies you're using to get the job done. Packt books are more specific and less general than the IT books you have seen in the past. Our unique business model allows us to bring you more focused information, giving you more of what you need to know, and less of what you don't.

Packt is a modern yet unique publishing company that focuses on producing quality, cutting-edge books for communities of developers, administrators, and newbies alike. For more information, please visit our website at `www.packtpub.com`.

About Packt Open Source

In 2010, Packt launched two new brands, Packt Open Source and Packt Enterprise, in order to continue its focus on specialization. This book is part of the Packt Open Source brand, home to books published on software built around open source licenses, and offering information to anybody from advanced developers to budding web designers. The Open Source brand also runs Packt's Open Source Royalty Scheme, by which Packt gives a royalty to each open source project about whose software a book is sold.

Writing for Packt

We welcome all inquiries from people who are interested in authoring. Book proposals should be sent to `author@packtpub.com`. If your book idea is still at an early stage and you would like to discuss it first before writing a formal book proposal, then please contact us; one of our commissioning editors will get in touch with you.

We're not just looking for published authors; if you have strong technical skills but no writing experience, our experienced editors can help you develop a writing career, or simply get some additional reward for your expertise.

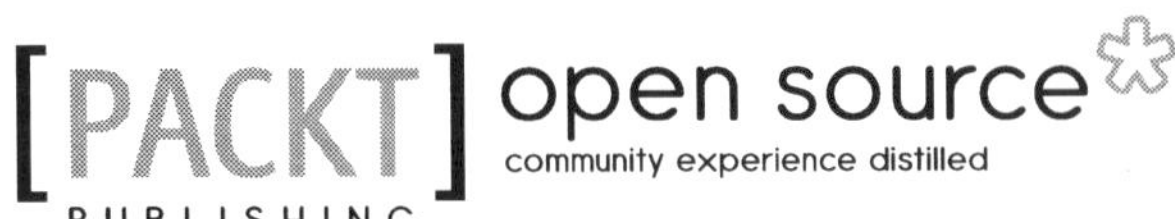

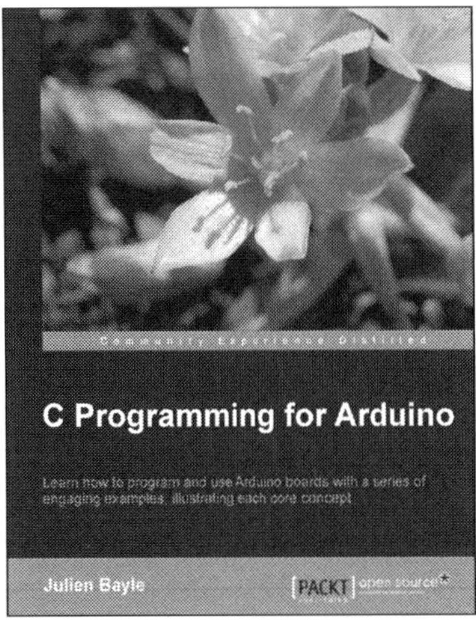

C Programming for Arduino

ISBN: 978-1-84951-758-4 Paperback: 512 pages

Learn how to program and use Arduino boards with a series of engaging examples, illustrating each core concept

1. Use Arduino boards in your own electronic hardware and software projects.
2. Sense the world by using several sensory components with your Arduino boards.
3. Create tangible and reactive interfaces with your computer.

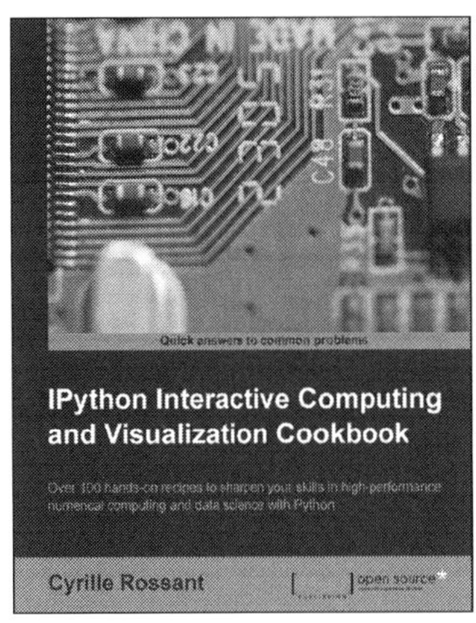

IPython Interactive Computing and Visualization Cookbook

ISBN: 978-1-78328-481-8 Paperback: 512 pages

Over 100 hands-on recipes to sharpen your skills in high-performance numerical computing and data science with Python

1. Leverage the new features of the IPython Notebook for interactive web-based big data analysis and visualization.
2. Become an expert in high-performance computing and visualization for data analysis and scientific modeling.
3. A comprehensive coverage of scientific computing through many hands-on, example-driven recipes with detailed, step-by-step explanations.

Please check **www.PacktPub.com** for information on our titles

Raspberry Pi Home Automation with Arduino

ISBN: 978-1-84969-586-2 Paperback: 176 pages

Automate your home with a set of exciting projects for the Raspberry Pi

1. Learn how to dynamically adjust your living environment with detailed step-by-step examples.
2. Discover how you can utilize the combined power of the Raspberry Pi and Arduino for your own projects.
3. Revolutionize the way you interact with your home on a daily basis.

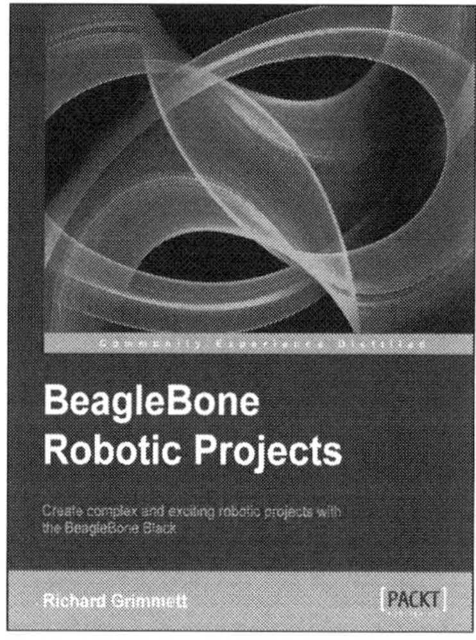

BeagleBone Robotic Projects

ISBN: 978-1-78355-932-9 Paperback: 244 pages

Create complex and exciting robotic projects with the BeagleBone Black

1. Get to grips with robotic systems.
2. Communicate with your robot and teach it to detect and respond to its environment.
3. Develop walking, rolling, swimming, and flying robots.

Made in the USA
Lexington, KY
29 July 2016